Schooling and Society
Myths of Mass Education

This new book is a wide-ranging, contemporary and accessible analysis of familiar and recurring myths about mass education in the United Kingdom. Looking at a variety of important issues and problems, each chapter begins by dispelling myths and assumptions about the classroom, going beyond class, race and gender, to offer analysis of topics such as discipline, youth cultures, information technology and globalisation. Utilising an interdisciplinary lens, this book offers knowledge from disciplines as diverse as sociology, philosophy, jurisprudence and cultural studies. Gordon Tait examines the strengths and weaknesses of different theoretical approaches to education, from critical theory to postmodernism, and Foucaultian governance to post-colonialism. Analysing the many assumptions about education taken for granted in British public discourse, important conclusions are drawn about which of these assumptions are fair and reasonable, and which we should challenge. This book is an essential resource for advanced undergraduate and postgraduate courses on the sociology of education, culture and education, and the philosophy of education.

Gordon Tait is a Professor in the Faculty of Education at Queensland University of Technology. An award-winning teacher, he has taught Sociology and Philosophy for over 30 years, and has published books on education, sociology, cultural studies, philosophy and criminology.

Schooling and Society
Myths of Mass Education

GORDON TAIT
Queensland University of Technology

CAMBRIDGE
UNIVERSITY PRESS

CAMBRIDGE
UNIVERSITY PRESS

University Printing House, Cambridge CB2 8BS, United Kingdom

One Liberty Plaza, 20th Floor, New York, NY 10006, USA

477 Williamstown Road, Port Melbourne, VIC 3207, Australia

4843/24, 2nd Floor, Ansari Road, Daryaganj, Delhi – 110002, India

79 Anson Road, #06–04/06, Singapore 079906

Cambridge University Press is part of the University of Cambridge.

It furthers the University's mission by disseminating knowledge in the pursuit of education, learning, and research at the highest international levels of excellence.

www.cambridge.org
Information on this title: www.cambridge.org/9781107158009
10.1017/9781316662533

© Gordon Tait 2017

First published 2017

Printed in the United Kingdom by Clays, St Ives plc

A catalogue record for this publication is available from the British Library.

ISBN 978-1-107-15800-9 Hardback
ISBN 978-1-316-61054-1 Paperback

For Steve, Mike, Nigel and Kev: my much-loved mates from school – most of whose social, political and philosophical opinions I do not share.

Thanks for nearly 200 years of collective friendship.

And before you all start complaining about having a book like this dedicated to you, you might just try reading it first (or any book, for that matter…).

CONTENTS

ACKNOWLEDGEMENTS

I would like to thank everyone at Cambridge University Press for giving me the opportunity to write this book – most appreciated. I'd also like to thank the Faculty of Education at QUT for giving me the space to get it finished, and my brilliant colleagues for contributing over the years to many of the ideas herein, and probably more importantly, to a very happy work environment. Finally, I would like to thank my wonderful family – Belinda, Ella and Buddy – because they made it crystal clear they'd be annoyed if I didn't.

INTRODUCTION

Everyone has opinions about mass education. Not only did we all go to school – so we know what it's like from the inside – but also we hear about educational issues and concerns in the news every day. These might include questions such as, should we go back to basics when teaching literacy? Should we reduce funding to state schools that do poorly on standardised testing? Should we teach more about the environment? Our opinions on these specific matters, assuming we have any, tend to be shaped by our more general beliefs about education – schools aren't educating our children properly; our education system seems pretty fair; the modern curriculum is full of trendy rubbish. The problem here is that many of these things we think we know about our system of mass education don't stand up to any kind of close scrutiny; they are often myths, and this book will address the most important of these myths.

This demythologising approach is unusual, but by no means unheard of, within social analysis. One of the greatest of all writers in the field, Peter Berger, suggests in his seminal text *Invitation to Sociology* (1963, 51) that 'debunking' is one of the most crucial elements of the discipline, and that there is 'a logical imperative to unmask the pretentions and the propaganda' by which people cloak their actions with each other. To put it another way, he proposes that our social world is full of stories we tell ourselves, and it is a sociologist's job to see which ones hold (at least some) water, and which ones don't.

However, not only is debunking/demythologising one of the central responsibilities of the social analyst, it is also an excellent pedagogic approach to the discipline. LeMoyne and Davis (2011) contend that the most effective way of coming to grips with complex social problems is to begin by examining important taken-for-granted cultural beliefs, and from there these beliefs can be systematically questioned – by illustrating the ways in which those beliefs evolved, by unpacking their theoretical domain assumptions, by providing concrete evidence that speaks to these beliefs, and by providing a vocabulary of other ways of seeing the same issues.

This final element is of particular importance. The intention of this approach is not to simply point at a particular social myth and state: '*This is wrong; the following is correct*'. As will be discussed in this book, truth doesn't work that way. Instead, the intention is simply to point out the flaws, biases and shortcomings in some of our dominant ways of understanding familiar educational issues, and then to propose a range of alternatives that might be a little more convincing, and a little less vulnerable to easy criticism. To paraphrase the logic of the philosopher Karl Popper (1963), *there's no such thing as being absolutely and unequivocally right, but there's a million ways to be completely wrong.*

Making Sense of Mass Education

One of the many exasperating things about our education system is that it keeps changing: how we think it works, what we think it seeks to accomplish, and what we think its consequences are. It certainly isn't like the study of human anatomy, where a book from the 1920s will still give a pretty accurate account of how the human body works, and what goes where. A book on education from the same era is unlikely to make any mention of many of the issues we now consider to be of importance. Take, for example, *Education and the General Welfare* by Sechrist (1920). With chapters on 'School Attendance' and 'Why Children are Dull', the focus was firmly on the pragmatics of how to make a school function effectively.

By the 1950s, however, new ways of thinking about schools had emerged. Concerns did not necessarily begin and end with educational efficiency, but also sought to address the relationship between schools and society. The influential theorist Parsons, in his book *The Social System* (Parsons 1965), regarded education as a vital component within a complex machine, and this was a machine that needed 'dull children' to do dull work. This wasn't seen as a problem; this was part of the design. Society was a finely tuned instrument, and education helped its cogs turn.

The average book on education soon changed its focus again. *Understanding Schooling* by Henry *et al.* (1988) was far more interested in the relationship between education and social power – as in the myth of our 'meritocratic' education system, and in the way class, gender and race directly correlated with schooling success – than it was on society as a 'finely tuned instrument'. Finely tuned for whom? There was nothing in this book about 'why children are dull', rather the emphasis was on why our system seems to confuse 'dull' with 'disadvantaged'.

What about today? Do any of these approaches to education still have currency? After all, some children probably *are* dull; society *is* complex; and the notion of a genuine 'meritocracy' *is* rather dubious. What kind of approach ought we to take, and what issues should be covered? In the second decade of the twenty-first century, what should a general book on education look like? Hopefully, it should look rather like this one.

Changing Contexts of Education

The world serviced by our contemporary education system is very different from the one written about by Sechrist (1920); consequently, the anxieties we now have, about how our schools work – and who gets to benefit – are also very different. Certainly, we are no longer as concerned about education for racial or national efficiency, or for the glory of the British Empire, as we were a hundred years ago. We now have a variety of other concerns, as evidenced by a series of debates about the state and direction of our education system. There are now debates over the conversion of many schools to 'Academies', over levels of funding for public education, and the ongoing flight of the middle classes into the private school system. There are concerns over standardisation, and the relentless imperative to collect data and rank schools. Some newspapers continually tell us that our schools have lost their way, and that we should return to traditional educational techniques and philosophies, ones based upon tried and trusted truths of yesterday. There are also worries about the levels of difference – physical, intellectual and even cultural – that schools should be required to accommodate. Should we return to the logic of the special school?

These debates raise a number of questions, but one is particularly important: how do we approach such dilemmas conceptually? Or to put it another way: is there a single theoretical model that can help us make sense of these problems, or do we have to address them on an issue-by-issue, case-by-case basis? This question has wider implications, not just about understanding specific changes and tensions within the institutions of mass schooling, such as the ones outlined above, but also about how to make sense of contemporary education in the broadest of ways.

Arguably, almost every general work dealing with the sociology and philosophy of education has attempted to answer this question, and this book will add to that tradition. However, this is not intended as just an updated repetition of previous approaches, which have tended to take one of three forms: first, some have taken a single approach, for example Critical Theory as in the book by Henry *et al.* (1988). This is fine if that approach is stated explicitly, right upfront (which it was). Otherwise, the book is in danger of passing off a particular perspective as the singular, unequivocal and uncontested truth of the matter – which isn't very honest. Second, some books have appeared to take no specific approach at all, in which case they are either kidding themselves, or their readers. All sociological analyses – and for that matter, all histories and all philosophies, in fact, probably all forms of knowledge – come from a particular perspective; the trick is to know what it is, and again, to be honest about it. Finally, others still employ a mishmash of theories, either because they don't realise it, because they hope no one will notice it, or because they are trying to be all things for everyone.

This book adopts none of these forms, instead presenting a number of different approaches, which are placed in relation to each other, and which are shown to offer specific kinds of advantages (and disadvantages), to answer questions in particular kinds of ways, and to be useful in addressing given kinds of problems. As such, the intention has not been simply to produce an updated version of previous books on education, it has been to offer something new altogether, and hopefully, to keep moving the analysis onwards.

Some Problems With Modernist Sociologies

But what exactly is *onwards*? One of the wonderful things about modernism was that we used to be able to answer that question without hesitation; now it's nowhere near as straightforward. If anyone needs reminding, modernity is generally regarded as beginning in the final years of the eighteenth century, at the end of the Enlightenment. Lasting some two hundred years, this was to be an era characterised by the underpinning belief that through the use of reason, it would be possible to solve humanity's problems. With its mantra of truth, objectivity and progress, and under the banner of its greatest exemplar – science – society now was to be free of the superstitions and dogmas that had previously decided our fates; humanity had come of age.

Unfortunately, towards the end of the twentieth century an increasing number of voices pointed to some significant problems with this optimistic narrative. It was suggested that the modernist project had failed, and that we had entered a new era, the era after modernity: that of postmodernity. By rejecting the grand narratives of modernism, postmodernists such as Lyotard (1984b) and Baudrillard (1993) sought to describe a world characterised not by truth and progress, but by many different truths, and by the belief that history is not synonymous with progress, such that all we could really make claim to was 'change'. Other writers, most notably Giddens (1990, 1991), while reluctant to call time on modernity altogether, argued instead that we have simply entered a period of late modernity (an era still largely modernist, but now characterised by continual crisis, and a greater scepticism towards the power of reason). These writers still seek to question the belief that we are making 'progress' in any manageable way.

And therein lies part of the problem with the notion of onwards. Though we aren't necessarily convinced that we are making theoretical progress, in any real sense, certainly approaches to education have largely mirrored the broader move from modernism to postmodernism. Therefore, if 'moving the analysis onwards' means anything, in the context of this book, it means precisely that.

Most books on education revolve around explanatory features characteristic of modernist sociologies – most notably class, gender and race. The idea here is that these three elements represent objective 'facts' about how our society is structured, and its populations ranked and organised. This logic suggests that when we understand how these three social axes work, we will be able to account for their effects and solve the problem. This book will take a somewhat different approach.

Beyond Modernist Sociologies of Education

This book will begin by addressing these three familiar conceptual axes, but then extend the analysis into a more postmodern interpretation of each of the same generalised notions. For example, when discussing issues of the relationship between schooling and gender, modernist accounts have stressed the role played by patriarchy – the global system of male domination – in the ongoing educational subordination of women. Such second-wave feminist accounts have now been largely replaced by more nuanced, less deterministic explanations of the same generalised area, and those will be discussed here.

This is not the only way of altering the focus on education, of moving the analysis onwards. There is an alternative tradition of analysis that largely avoids the modern/postmodern dichotomy, one based around Foucault's work on governance. Rather than concentrating on issues of power and inequality, this paradigm focuses instead upon the techniques and practices by which we are shaped as particular types of individual, and by which we have our conduct regulated. From the early nineteenth century onwards, the school has had a central role to play in producing a disciplined and docile population, in producing the categories of difference necessary to permit effective, targeted social management, and latterly, even providing the primary site for the governance of students' subjective experience.

This book will not only address the broadest issues within education, it will also attempt to understand education's place within a complex and changing society, and supply the conceptual tools for providing non-reductionist accounts of a number of contemporary cultural forms. Whether addressing the effects of the news media, or of popular culture, or how digital technologies are reshaping both the classroom and the capacities of the people in them, arguably many previous attempts to describe the relationship between these issues and our education system have relied upon modernist binaries to provide their foundation. This book will not do so.

The overall intention here is to provide the best possible tools for understanding contemporary schooling; however, the tools available within sociology and cultural studies are not the only ones on offer. If we are to understand the ideas that have animated education over the past 2500 years – or, more importantly, if we are to recognise which of these ideas still have currency within contemporary mass education, and how those ideas are operationalised – then the discipline of philosophy is required. Arguably, philosophy's utility also extends beyond these issues, into assessments of schooling, ethics and inclusive education, as well as understanding epistemology and the educational legacy of the United Kingdom's role as a former colonial power.

The Structure of the Book

This book is organised in a somewhat unusual way, both in the way the chapters are located within four distinct parts (each with a different focus and theoretical alignment), and in terms of the structure of the chapters. All fourteen chapters of the book are organised in the same way: they are based around a number of familiar myths common to popular discourses on the topic in question. For example, Chapter 1 on Social Class is based around three myths: '*The UK is no longer a country characterised by social inequality*', '*Schooling success is only about individual ability*', and '*Social class is all about money*'. In the process of debunking these statements, it is also possible to ascertain what each different approach to understanding mass education can offer us.

Part I is entitled *Re-Assessing the Three Pillars: Modern and Postmodern Sociologies of Education*. This sets out the dominant framework for the study of mass education. The familiar axes of class, race and gender, and the resulting forms of disadvantage that emerge from them, are assessed and, in many ways, found wanting in the light of the broader changes associated with contemporary educational thought. The challenge then becomes to determine how these categories and concerns can now best be utilised.

Chapter 1 – *Social Class* – will address the logic of meritocracy, and examine the viability of oppositional conceptions of social class. It will be concluded that the way forward within educational research lies with more nuanced understandings of social distinctions, based around the notion of habitus, and the specifics of language use. Chapter 2 – *Gender* – will assess the contributions made to educational debates by first- second- and third-wave feminist logics. Remaining inequities within the schooling system will be analysed, as will the role played by education in the formation of gendered identities. This latter concept will be used as a device for reworking the notion of 'hegemonic masculinity', and illustrating the complex ways in which schools shape 'acceptable' boys and girls, both culturally and sexually. Finally, having debunked long-standing, yet persistent, biological arguments concerning race, Chapter 3 – *Race/Ethnicity* – will examine the cultural construction of racial difference, address a number of contemporary perspectives on educational issues, and unpack 'white privilege' theory. The central goal of the chapter is to assess what remains – at a practical level – of a concept that appears to have lost almost all of its intellectual purchase. This chapter will also address the central logic of discrimination, focusing on the notion of 'othering', as well as the rise of cultural discrimination.

Part II is called *The Foundations of an Alternative Approach: Education and Governance*. This part outlines the possibility of an alternative approach to the social analysis of education – based around the work of writers such as Foucault, Hunter and Rose – which can augment, or arguably replace, even the more sophisticated application of modernist sociology outlined in Part I.

Chapter 4 – *Governance* – details the historical circumstances that gave rise to the phenomenon of mass schooling. Working as a history of the present, the intention here is to explain not only how the familiar, central features of modern educational institutions came about – timetables, record-keeping, surveillance – but also how these came to constitute fundamental foundations of our broader society. This chapter will also address the importance of various forms of liberalism in shaping the logic of the modern school. Chapter 5 – *Subjectivity* – will extend the analysis beyond the 'objective' regulation of schools described in Chapter 4, to the governance of the 'subjective' experiences of students. It will be argued here that the rise of psychology in schools has resulted in the steady pathologisation of student behaviour, and that rather than simply uncovering and explaining student differences, the discipline of psychology is now instrumental in their production and distribution. That is, using examples such as the rise of ADHD, it can be shown that students are increasingly regulated via 'categories of abnormality'. Chapter 6 – *Pre-Adulthood* – examines the rise of the persona of the child, and its most recent variant, youth. As a rebuttal to naturalist understandings of children, this chapter will seek to explain constructs such as the child and youth, not as simple stages of life, but rather as the products of various forms of governance, constructed in a range of different sites, and by a multiplicity of practices of self-making. Chapter 7 – *Big Data* – explores the effects of the giant data sets now available to businesses, social planners and educators. It is argued that this 'tsunami of printed numbers' will have significant effects upon a number of areas within our education system, not least within the context of standardised testing, such as the SATs.

Part III is called *Cultural Contexts of Contemporary Education*. Theoretical foundations and interpretations of education aside, it is important to locate modern mass schooling within some important cultural, political and technical contexts. This part will raise questions about the relationship between school knowledge and popular culture, the effects of public discourse on educational debates, the rise and rise of digital technologies within the classroom, and the effects of globalisation on British education.

Chapter 8 – *The Media* – examines the way in which educational debates, perceptions, and policies are shaped by public discourse. While arguing against simplistic understandings of the hegemonic power of the mass media, the focus will fall upon a nuanced account of the frequent moral panics associated with issues such as 'asylum seekers' and the teaching of literacy, as well as the recurrent scapegoating of teachers for their 'failure' in various aspects of broader social governance. Chapter 9 – *Popular Culture* – attempts to go beyond the neo-Leavisite view that popular culture has nothing of value to offer the modern classroom, while at the same time recognising that organising content around the simple maintenance of student interest is an insufficient rationale for a valid education. At which point, the question becomes a philosophical one: what constitutes a valid education? Chapter 10 – *Technology* – attempts to avoid the speculation and crystal-ball gazing common to writing on the subject. It will be argued here that the issue is not whether digital technologies constitute a bright new dawn of virtually limitless educational possibility, nor whether they simply represent new possibilities of student disadvantage and professional redundancy. Rather, the central issue should be more about the role teachers will have to play in articulating the distinction between information and knowledge. Chapter 11 – *Globalisation* – examines the different ways this concept can be understood, and the types of knowledge that seek to explain it. It also addresses the various ways in which the different practices and processes of globalisation have reshaped our education system. Finally, this chapter examines the link between globalisation and our environment.

Part IV – *Philosophy and Mass Education* – examines some of the many ways that philosophy can help us better understand our schooling system. That is, philosophy is not just some abstract university knowledge system doomed to fail the most basic tests of utility. The mass school is a site of great ethical and epistemological complexity, and philosophy can help us make sense of it in ways that other disciplines can't.

Chapter 12 – *Philosophy* – argues the importance of philosophy as a subject in the school curriculum, not just in terms of clarity of thought, but also for improving student sensitivity to social and ethical issues. In addition, it allows us to better understand why our education system has taken its current form, and it provides a vocabulary of ways for teachers to organise their own professional practice. Chapter 13 – *Ethics, Disability and the Law* – sets out to unpack the relationship between ethics, education and school exclusion. The chapter addresses the three great normative systems of Virtue Ethics, Consequentialism and Kantian Ethics, and in particular the institutional pressures to adopt Consequentialist ethical decision-making practices, particularly when deciding who belongs, and who does not belong, within a mainstream classroom. Chapter 14 – *Truth and Postcolonialism* – will examine the ways in which particular sets of truth become prioritised within the curriculum, and how different forces shape not only what counts as knowledge, but also how that knowledge is approached, organised and deployed. It will also address the issue of our past as a colonial power, and the effect this still has, not only on our own curriculum, but also on other countries around the globe.

In summary, and in keeping with all good social analysis, this book will attempt to address the central myths and domain assumptions surrounding the institutions of mass education. After all, the meritocratic belief that schooling is a fair race – there to be won by the best and brightest – is as prevalent now as it was at the beginning of the last century. This book will also provide a contemporary assessment of some of the ideas that have traditionally dominated education research, asking: to what extent do notions such as 'social class', 'childhood' and 'hegemonic masculinity' still have purchase within current debates, and do any viable conceptual alternatives exist? Finally, this book will seek to blur some of the disciplinary boundaries within the field of education. It will draw not only upon traditional sociology, but also cultural studies, history, philosophy, ethics and jurisprudence – and hopefully, the resulting analyses will be the stronger, more comprehensive and more convincing as a result.

PART I

RE-ASSESSING THE THREE PILLARS: MODERN AND POSTMODERN SOCIOLOGIES OF EDUCATION

Open any book on sociology, whether it is about education or not, and you can almost guarantee that there will be chapters on social class, gender and race. There are also likely to be other common themes – the family, ageing, deviance, and so on – but none of them is regarded as quite as foundational as the three familiar pillars of social structure. That is, not everyone has a family, or is old, or deviant, but everyone is deemed to have a social class, a gender and a race/ethnicity, and, more often than not, where you stand in relation to these categories correlates fairly directly with access to power, resources. . . and education. This part of the book will examine these three social axes and draw some conclusions about how they structure our society, and how they affect the probability of success within our schools.

Though these conclusions may still be interesting and informative, sociological analysis has moved on somewhat from the belief that there are three straightforward categories that shape the structure of our society, categories that have an objective reality that we can come to know – i.e. the singular 'truth' of social class, gender and race/ethnicity. While this modernist understanding has had some interesting things to tell us, it has largely been superseded by more postmodern approaches to the same issues. These approaches attempt to avoid the sweeping generalisations, and the either/or logic, of previous work in the area. As such – while staying on the same terrain as social class, gender and race/ethnicity – this section will also examine how these three solidly nineteenth and twentieth-century concepts can be best understood in the more nuanced sociological environment of the twenty-first century.

Chapter 1 – *Social Class* – examines the relationship between the first of the three pillars and our education system. It begins by questioning the common assertion that the United Kingdom is no longer a particularly unequal society; it also questions the belief that how well we do in school is determined by our intellect, and not our social backgrounds; finally, it challenges the assumption that social class is determined solely by how rich you are.

Chapter 2 – *Gender* – investigates the second of the three pillars and its relationship to mass education. It questions the common view that gender is simply a function of sex; that while gender differences certainly exist, schools play no part in their construction; that for all the fuss about girls, it's actually boys who are on the receiving end of social injustice; and that, during the schooling years, issues of sexuality are just best left alone.

Chapter 3 – *Race/Ethnicity* – addresses the final pillar of social structure and our education system. It questions the belief that race has any validity as a concept at all; that racial discrimination has all but disappeared; that race/ethnicity has virtually no role to play in determining how well we do in school; and that there is a serious and intractable 'Black and Minority Ethnicity (BME) problem' within our education system.

There is a temptation to look at modernist sociologies of education and dismiss them out of hand: 'They gloss over important intersectional differences'; 'They are overly deterministic'; and 'They create structures where none actually exists'. There is then a temptation to disparage everything they have told us about important aspects of how our society works. Although these criticisms have significant merit, the answers you get to questions are only ever as good as the questions you ask. We started out by asking some simple questions about our society (and in the context of this book, about our education system), from within a relatively simple modernist conceptual framework, and we got some simple answers. We are now asking some more complex questions, from within a more nuanced and flexible postmodern conceptual framework, and the answers we are getting reflect this shift.

SOCIAL CLASS

1

This chapter argues that, even though we all have a pretty good idea what is meant by the term 'social class', it is far from being a straightforward matter. After all, there is only tenuous agreement about exactly what it is, how prevalent it is, how it organises the life opportunities of our citizens, and how best to study it. To make it more difficult still, this is a subject that many feel uncomfortable discussing, let alone applying to themselves or anyone else.

In attempting to better understand the relationship between social class and education, this chapter will ask questions about just how equal British society actually is, how schooling success might be more likely for some than others, and why money isn't everything. In doing so, it will trace important changes in the way that the social sciences have tried to explain this phenomenon. Most notably, these changes involve a shift away from a focus on economic and structural aspects of social class, to a greater emphasis on issues of cultural practice.

Myth #1 The UK is no longer a country characterised by social inequality. *'We may have once been a class-based society, but this is no longer the case; old social and economic distinctions have gone – it's now a level playing field'.* In the twenty-first century, success in the UK is largely deemed to be based upon merit. However, contrary to this belief, the statistical evidence suggests that there remains an inequitable distribution of wealth, one that is measurably worse than in most other European countries. Furthermore, this inequality extends to gaining access to high-status jobs and well-resourced schools.

Myth #2 Schooling success is only about individual ability. *'Given we all sit the same exams, it seems perfectly appropriate to claim that education is a fair race, and that hence the winners deserve their victory'.* Research into schooling success presents a more complex picture. The dominant model – that of Critical Theory – points to the vital role that schooling plays in the processes of social reproduction. According to this reasoning, wealth buys educational success, that success guarantees more wealth, which then buys the next generation's educational success. Individual ability is only one small part of this cycle.

Myth #3 Social class is all about money. *'Many supposedly working-class people earn very good wages, therefore claims about middle-class advantage must be false'*. More contemporary theoretical approaches to social class point to a variety of forms of capital, not just economic. It is these forms of capital – cultural, social, symbolic – that help shape how people live, how they organise their relations with one another, and how much access they have to resources. It is these factors that most likely constitute our best understandings of social class.

Introduction
The Trouble With Social Class

Most of us are probably of the opinion that the existence of *social class* – the ranking of social position according to wealth, power and prestige (Weber 2012) – is not a good thing and we'd all be better off without it. Indeed, some of us might like to think that one of the many good things about living in twenty-first-century Britain is that we have left most of our social class distinctions behind – others may more accurately realise that various forms of social ranking remain, less obvious perhaps, but their effects are just as real and just as troublesome as they have always been. Curiously though, whatever your opinion on the matter, social class is something we rarely talk about among ourselves.

> Class? There is no word or concept that is more off-limits in our boundless tell-all culture right now than class. As a society, we have rapidly progressed over several generations in developing a common language to talk about differences of gender, race, and sexual orientation . . . when it comes to class, it's as if we stumble and go speechless . . . of course class differences exist, and people talk about them, but often in code and euphemism. Our discourse on class is in arrested development compared to our conversations about the other ways we differ from one another.
> (Yeskel and Ladd 2005)

It's difficult to say why social class is such a difficult, and often uncomfortable, subject. Social stratification, in all its forms, is a feature common to all societies and cultures – whether we admit it or not – and yet it's a topic that is widely regarded as failing the polite conversation test, alongside the traditional no-go areas of politics and religion. Most of us would be cautious about asking someone we had only just met what class they come from, just as we would about informing them of our own: 'Hi. I'm Gordon, and I'm upper-middle class'.

Interestingly, we can look at other cultures and societies and easily point to their various types of stratification, internal systems of ranking and forms of social differentiation, and we can develop assorted explanatory mechanisms as we go, accurate or otherwise. For example, we can scratch our heads at the seeming unfairness of the Hindu caste system, one that categorises some citizens inherently superior, and others 'untouchable' from the moment of birth, and wonder why it is still tolerated when so many suffer through its existence. Significantly, most of us would find this topic to be perfectly appropriate for after-dinner conversation – presumably as long as we're not living in New Delhi at the time.

So why can we talk about other countries' social-class systems, and yet cringe at the thought of discussing our own? Campbell (2010) rightly points to a couple of factors at play here. First, given that social class correlates directly with access to resources, power and status, most of us would be justifiably wary of admitting we are at the bottom of the social pile (or alternatively, reluctant to whinge about it), just as good manners prohibits us from pointing out that same lack of power and status in others. Second, it is normally regarded as inappropriate to talk openly about our own wealth and success, lest we are seen to be gloating, and no-one likes a gloater.

So the circumstances at both ends of the social class spectrum make any discussion of its existence, or its consequences, quite problematic. However, this doesn't mean that it therefore somehow magically ceases to exist. The evidence has long shown that all cultures have one form of stratification or another, and most have many (Reissman 1973). But even accepting this fact doesn't mean the field is clear for an unproblematic explanation of just what's going on. Social class is a complex, murky and highly contested issue, as this chapter will demonstrate, particularly as it applies to education.

Some Conceptual Problems

WHAT EXACTLY IS SOCIAL CLASS?

In a terminological sense, it is an umbrella phrase that covers a lot of ground, most frequently all the ground covered by the very similar notion of *socio-economic status*, and then a little bit more. For the purposes of this book, we'll stick with 'social class', as it lends itself to an analysis not solely focused on the more material aspects of stratification.

Semantics issues aside, what about the conceptual aspects of social class? Early *Functionalist* explanations, such as those of Durkheim (1964), regarded society as some sort of smoothly operating clock, where each of the cogs – us – have a clearly defined role to play, some of them important, others less so. The more valued the role, the higher the status attached to it, and hence the higher the social class of the cog.

This model of society, one based around consensus, has been the subject of considerable criticism over the years, and no-one really does 'functionalist' research any more, at least not if they want to get a job at a university. Criticisms of this position are many, but are mostly based around the notion that somehow we all have neatly defined 'functions'. It has also been argued that this model can't adequately account for rapid social change; after all, how do the various cogs of a grandfather clock suddenly transform themselves into the components of a digital watch?

An alternative set of explanations, generally referred to as *Conflict Theory*, see social class as a side effect of a competition for power. In a kind of zero-sum game, society is divided into those who have power and those who lack it, with the two sides locked in an ongoing struggle. This model contends that the more power you are able to mobilise, then the higher your social class. More subtle variants on this approach, mostly notably in the form of *Critical Theory*, have dominated social and educational research until relatively recently. However, just as Functionalist explanations of social class fell to the logic of Conflict Theory, as will be argued in more detail later in this chapter, so has Conflict Theory begun to flounder in the face of a concerted onslaught from various forms of *Postmodernism*: that is, a type of reasoning that seeks to reject singular explanations of otherwise complex social phenomena.

WHAT KIND OF SOCIAL AND CULTURAL EFFECT DOES SOCIAL CLASS HAVE?

So, even though there remain marked differences of opinion over what lies at its core, surely we are capable of reaching agreement over this question. Apparently not: some researchers consider that social class pretty much determines an individual's chances in life: how they'll do at school, what kind of job they'll get, who they'll marry, how and where they'll be able to live. Other researchers consider that such outcomes can't simply be read off from a person's background – that relevant factors are too complex and the causal chains too long – and at most, your social class gently whispers life suggestions to you, rather than bellows instructions. Others still, most frequently within the psychology-based disciplines, look towards individual ability as the greatest determinant of success, playing down the importance of pre-existing social factors. While there will be more on that particular belief later, it's obvious from these different perspectives that this represents a complex and contested field.

HOW DO WE GO ABOUT RESEARCHING SOCIAL CLASS?

Once again, there are different views as to the most effective way to make social class an object of knowledge. The first, and arguably dominant, approach to research has been that of *Quantitative Analysis*, which seeks to amass statistical data that can answer the 'how many' type of questions. How many people are in each social class, as a percentage? How many upper-class kids drop out of school? How many working-class kids get to university? Answers to these questions help with a *structural* analysis of our society, and help us with our understanding of who has what.

The second main approach is that of *Qualitative Analysis*, which engages in research that attempts to answer the 'why' type of questions. Why do we feel uncomfortable talking about social class? Why do some upper-class kids drop out of school? Why do middle-class kids feel more comfortable in school than those from the working-class? These answers constitute an *interpretive* analysis of our society, and add depth and texture to our understanding of the lived experience of particular social classes.

Neither of these approaches represents the *right* way to study society. Indeed, the best research most likely tries to employ both, given that this form of *methodological triangulation* promises to paint a richer, and more balanced, portrait of our social reality. In this manner, the arguments developed in this chapter are constructed from the evidence produced through both kinds of analysis. Unfortunately however, it should be pointed out that academic researchers tend to have expertise in one of these methodologies, and they often don't like the other much at all. That is, quantitative research is often characterised by its critics as the mindless assembly of vast columns of numbers, none of which bear any relation to the real life of anyone. Alternatively, qualitative research is lampooned as merely the collected transcriptions of barely interesting chit-chats, none of which bears any relation to proper research data. There are probably elements of truth in both these assertions.

All of these basic questions about social class will be addressed here, not just in relation to its impact on the social fabric of our nation, but more specifically about its effects on our education system. The most straightforward route into this analysis is to address three common beliefs about social class. As discussed in the introduction to this book, those employed in the business of researching and explaining issues of social stratification – sociologists, philosophers, historians, cultural studies academics, criminologists, anthropologists – are confronted by common-sense assertions and mythologies about this issue on a daily basis. Consequently, addressing some of these myths serves the dual purpose of (1) assessing whether they have any truth to them at all, or whether they are simply part of the background noise of a society that isn't great at admitting it has some significant faults; and (2) acting as a vehicle for an effective analysis of the complex relationship between social class and mass education.

The three myths are as follows.

Myth #1 The UK is no longer a country characterised by social inequality.
Myth #2 Schooling success is only about individual ability.
Myth #3 Social class is all about money.

Myth #1 *The UK is No Longer a Country Characterised by Social Inequality*

If we look back at the United Kingdom of the Victorian era, we see a very different country from today, and not just because we've just about stopped dying of tuberculosis, and most of us now have mobile phones. We are no longer a country of rigid hierarchies, a country of haves and have nots, a country of landed gentry tooting hunting horns and slurping Pimms, while the rest of us live in grinding urban poverty and social decay. The social and economic barriers blocking the way of those wishing to change their stars have all but disappeared.

The argument here is that while we may once have deserved our reputation as a country obsessed with social class – obsessed with the distinctions of accent, origin and education that marked us out like invisible brands on our foreheads – this is no longer the case. Certainly our regional accents may persist, but they no longer act as barriers to social mobility, any more than does having a state education. Universities are open to all, and jobs are awarded on merit.

The central questions addressed by this chapter are: how much of this rosy picture about contemporary British society is based upon fact, and how much of it is wishful thinking? And, following on from this, are our schools simply places where kids go to learn how to read and write, irrespective of their backgrounds, or are they an important part of the process by which we learn our place in the social and economic hierarchy, which, it turns out, is mostly the same one occupied by our parents?

The Comparison With Other Countries

Popular discourse here would suggest that we set a good example to other countries in terms of our social and economic equality – after all, we've got the NHS and a pretty fair tax system, haven't we? That is, the UK is not a place that tolerates the existence of a USA-style greedy capitalism, with a few ethically challenged individuals and families hogging all the wealth, with the kind of conspicuous consumption where motorised mini-Cadillacs are bought for wealthy children, while more than 45.3 million of the population live in abject poverty (US Census Bureau 2013). However, we're also not a culture that needs economic equality forced upon us, like Cuba, China or North Korea. Rather, our equity emerges from the wellspring of our own natural sense of fair play.

Fortunately, there are international statistical instruments available to test the truth of this belief. Economists employ a mathematical device called the *Gini Coefficient*, which enables the ranking of nations based upon their equality of income. The index goes from 0 (the hypothetical result if everyone is paid the same income) to 100 (the hypothetical result if all the income was paid to one person). The United

Table 1.1 In terms of income equality, where does the United Kingdom stand?

Rank	Country	Income equality (Gini Index)
1	Slovenia	23.7
2	Hungary	24.7
3	Denmark	24.8
4	Sweden	24.9
5	Czech Republic	24.9
6	Netherlands	25.1
7	Slovakia	25.3
8	Belgium	25.9
9	Montenegro	26.2
10	Austria	26.3
35	United Kingdom	32.4

Source: Central Intelligence Agency 2015

Kingdom's position on the Gini Index rankings is shown in Table 1.1. As can be seen, we don't even make the top 30 in terms of income equality. Certainly, we're not like the USA (bad), or Namibia (the worst), but just the same, with the exception of a few ex-eastern block countries, we are just about the most unequal country in Europe.

The Rich/Poor Gap in the United Kingdom

That isn't the end of the myth though. After all, even though we're somewhat more unequal than most other first-world countries, maybe the disparity in wealth in all these countries is actually relatively small; maybe the gap between what the rich and poor own still merits some kind of belief in a national, level economic playing field.

Figure 1.1 below tells a different story. The statistical evidence suggests that more than half the wealth of the United Kingdom (64%) is concentrated in the hands of only 20% of the population. In fact, the wealthiest 10% own 45% of the wealth, while the poorest 50% own just 8.7%. Currently, the richest 1% own as much as the poorest 55% (Office for National Statistics 2015). Worryingly, for those invested in the myth of equality, the concentration of wealth in the hands of the few also appears to be in the process of increasing; in 1973 the top 10% only owned 21% of the wealth in the United Kingdom – that is, in little over 50 years, the top 10% of the British population has more than doubled their percentage of the nation's wealth (The Equality Trust 2016).

In the light of all this comparative, quantitative evidence, it seems apparent that the United Kingdom is not a society characterised by economic equality. Also, to

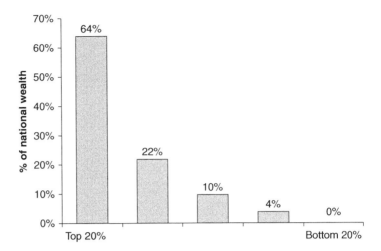

Figure 1.1 *Who has the wealth in the United Kingdom?*
Source: Office for National Statistics 2015

some extent, our cultural practices may vary according to social class, with our social and geographic background getting stamped into our accent and manners from the very beginning – an assertion that forms the basis for the third section of this chapter, and so will be dealt with then.

In spite of these differences in wealth and culture, it may still be the case that we do have a sort of *practical* equality. We all do roughly the same things, we listen to music, play a bit of sport, hang out with our friends, and sit the same school exams. Leaving aside the issues of gender, and race/ethnicity for later chapters (as well as various other important factors), the issue of us all sitting the same school exams warrants further mention, particularly since this is a book on mass education.

Hopefully, it will be demonstrated that understanding the relationship between social class and education can act as the perfect case study for understanding social class in a more general way. After all, we may well all sit for the same school exams (for those who make it through to the final year of schooling, itself a class issue), but our route to those exams is often very different.

In the United Kingdom, approximately 7% of children attend Independent schools. This covers a wide range of institutions, from traditional public schools, like Eton and Harrow, to specifically religious schools, and alternative schools; they also include a range of different sizes, organisational structures and teaching philosophies. However, what they *do* all have in common is that they cost money to attend – generally speaking, a *lot* of money. While Eton costs over £36 000 per year, the average annual fees for an Independent school in the UK in 2014 is £12 700, with a further £3000 for extras such as uniforms, meals and music lessons (boarding generally costs over twice as much). It is estimated that the total outlay for a family with two children to attend private day school, starting in 2012 and 2014, would be £526000 (Killik 2014). Obviously, even factoring in the sacrifices many families are prepared to make for their children's education, only a relatively small percentage of the population has access to this sort of money. Significantly, the evidence suggests that Independent schools are becoming increasingly out of financial reach for ordinary families; since 1990, school fees have increased by over 300% – more than four times the rate of inflation (Killik 2014).

For those for whom private schooling is not a financially viable option – a very large percentage of the British population – there remains one alternative to mainstream state comprehensive education: grammar schools. While now only 232 of these institutions exist across England and Northern Ireland (4% of the total student cohort nationally), they have always been held up as a way for ordinary children to get an elite-style academic education, as long as they can pass the 11+ exam. However, the best evidence suggests that these schools are now also dominated, in terms of enrolments, by the more affluent. An effective measure of social disadvantage is widely considered to be eligibility for free school meals (FSM). Skipp *et al.* (2013) note that while 18% of pupils are eligible for free school meals in comprehensive schools, this figure falls to less than 3% for grammar schools.

The evidence suggests that the wealthy tend to cluster within both independent schools and grammar schools. Or to look at it another way, the socially and economically disadvantaged tend to find themselves elsewhere, even if some of these other schools are now given the label of 'Academies'. It is important to note that, within each of these categories of school, there is a continuum of wealth and resourcing. Not all Independent schools are like Eton and Harrow, although most would probably like to be. Also, some state schools, generally those in high socio-economic status areas, closely resemble Independent schools in terms of ethos and expectation; as such, the effects of social class background are all the more systemically pervasive.

Of course, the effects of social class do not end at the school gates. Families may send their children to private schools for a wide range of reasons, but certainly the belief that this will increase their future employment prospects is factored into their calculations. As Figure 1.2 shows, our social class plays a large role in determining what kind of employment we're likely to obtain. Clearly, quantitative research shows that, far from the employment market being a level playing field, a private education confers an enormous professional benefit on those lucky enough to have one.

To summarise: the British class system hasn't gone anywhere. Contrary to popular myth, we remain as unequal a society as ever. Not only do a relatively small percentage of our population own an increasingly disproportionate amount of our national wealth, they attend different schools and gain more powerful employment. The next myth deals with the question: if there is this kind of class-based difference within

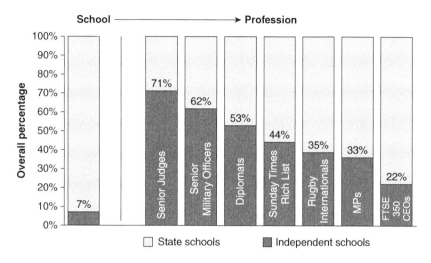

Figure 1.2 *Percentage of professions who attended Independent schools in the UK*
Source: Social Mobility and Child Poverty Commission 2014

British education, does it actually make any difference? So far, debunking the first myth has simply involved the presentation of various sets of statistical data. Myth #2 will involve a much greater degree of social analysis and interpretation.

Myth #2 *Schooling Success is Only About Individual Ability*

It's simple. Schools reward those with ability, which makes the system work. Those students who come out on top are the smart, the diligent and the determined. Those students who do poorly, do so because they lack these fundamental qualities and, as a consequence, the blame for their failure is all their own – sorry, but bad luck.

In a very important sense, this myth provides the central logic for our schooling system. Indeed, addressing this assertion has formed one of the foundational pillars of modernist approaches to the study of education. There wouldn't be much point in taking part in a sporting competition if the result was fixed beforehand, and equally we wouldn't be overly happy if we were told that the results of the final-year school assessment had been decided before the children even got into the exam room. This is the foundational logic of a *meritocracy* – a system of rule based upon the principle that success, and the power that comes with it, should go to those with the ability, rather than be given by birthright, or to those who can simply take it by force (Young 1958). With his tongue firmly in his cheek, Young organised the logic of meritocracy as an equation:

$$Success = IQ + Effort.$$

If only it were that straightforward.

Henry (2000) addresses this issue in her assessment of how best to approach the issue of social class within the education system. She cited the one phrase she has heard more often than any other during her time as a university lecturer.

> *'Yeah, but in the end, it all comes down to the individual – it's all up to the individual, isn't it.'* If I could have a dollar from every time I've heard that phrase – *it's all up to the individual* – I'd be a rich person now. It seems one of the defining ideas of our society. Yet it is a flawed idea. . . it is simplistic because it does not take sufficient account of the way society is structured. (Henry 2000, 47)

If we are to accept the claim that our education system is a genuine meritocracy, then we have to accept, as a fact, that the students who come out on top are unequivocally our smartest and most worthy. Unfortunately, that also means that we must accept that our smartest and most worthy students disproportionately attend the most elite of our private schools. The evidence for this statement can be seen in Figure 1.3 below. Any number of different data sets could have been used to make this point: disproportionate percentage of tertiary offers made to Independent school students; disproportionate percentage going to university; disproportionate percentage in the more prestigious university faculties; disproportionate percentage in the most prestigious tertiary institutions (see below), and so on.

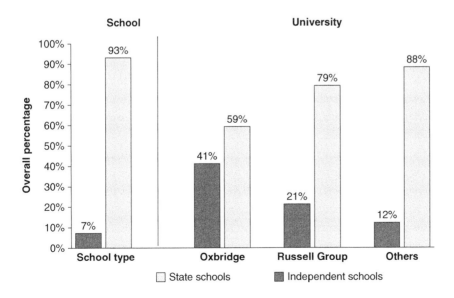

Figure 1.3 *Which types of school win the 'Education Race'?*
Compiled from Department for Education 2014a

To put it another way, if we are to accept that our education system is a genuine meritocracy, then we would also have to accept that out most privileged students are also our best; that would be quite a coincidence. As it currently stands, students from Independent schools are five times as likely to attend Oxbridge than their state school counterparts, and over three times as likely to attend a Russell Group University (ie. the top 24 UK institutions) (Department for Education 2014a). Even more starkly, Independent school students are 55 times more likely to attend Oxbridge than socially disadvantaged students (i.e. those who qualify for free school meals), and are 22 times more likely to attend a Russell Group University (Sutton Trust 2010). Let's assume then, if the whole system isn't fixed in some ludicrous, conspiratorial way – which it isn't – that something else must be going on. There must be some other, more subtle, way that social class advantages manifest themselves in terms of educational success. What are they, and how have social and educational researchers attempted to explain them?

The dominant explanatory model has belonged to *Critical Theory*, an offshoot of *Marxist Theory*. Both are premised on the contention that economic factors play the greatest role in explaining how social class works. Originally, Marxist ideas sought to divide the social world into two halves: those who owned the machinery of economic production, and those who worked on those machines. These two different statuses represented two opposing social classes, and everything else – political power, culture, knowledge, education – became a function of this fundamental division. Revolutionary ideas at the time, literally.

This early, clumsy model evolved into a more subtle form of analysis. That is, though founded on the same logic, Critical Theory went on to provide a far more nuanced account of how the world works. Gone are the two opposing classes, locked in economic war, replaced instead by a range of social classes, operating within a far more complex industrial environment. What has *not* gone, however, is the understanding that the right to exercise power is something to be struggled over, and that in the final analysis, it is still determined by economic factors. Importantly, within this logic, education is deemed to have a very special role to play in these processes.

Some of the Logic of Critical Theory

In order to best understand the relationship between social class and education, according to the reasoning of Critical Theory, the work of a number of writers needs to be briefly addressed. These writers don't tell the complete story, because there's no 'complete story' to tell, but their work provides some of the central landmarks of the position, and offers a generalised flavour of how social class has been understood within educational research from the 1960s onwards. So who should we look at?

ALTHUSSER

Althusser (1971) attempts to explain how society works by adopting the basic Marxist model of an economic base acting as the foundation for a social superstructure (that is, all the legal, political and cultural systems that define a society). Within this superstructure, Althusser delineates the 'repressive State apparatus', which includes the police, the courts, the army, i.e. all the machinery necessary to exert control by force if necessary and, of importance to us, the *'ideological State apparatus'* – all those mechanisms which exert control through the use of ideas. He argues that the ruling class (the bourgeoisie) uses the education system, more than any other part of the ideological State apparatus, for maintaining its power.

> What the bourgeoisie has installed as its number-one, i.e. as its dominant ideological State apparatus, is the educational apparatus, which has in fact replaced in its functions the previously dominant ideological State apparatus, the Church. (Althusser 1971, 103–4)

Yes, the wealthy may send their children to different schools to the poor but, according to Althusser, that's only one small part of how social class and education interact. He argues that the schooling system acts as a sophisticated filter, both ideologically and practically, one which spits out the working classes at an early stage with the belief system necessary to do what's asked of them. Likewise, the ruling classes stay on longer in school, and learn very different lessons about life, and about the exercise of power.

BOWLES AND GINTIS

Extending these arguments, Bowles and Gintis (1976) address in particular the myth of meritocracy within modern society. They argue that the schooling system is the main site for the propagation of the false belief that success in our system is based upon your intrinsic merit. Once this belief is installed in the population – largely through the usual tactics of school hierarchies, continual assessment and an overtly ideological curriculum – it legitimates the same beliefs within the wider society, in that disparities in wealth and power become explained almost exclusively in terms of personal factors, rather than any underlying social inequalities.

To put this argument more simply: once we come to believe what we've been told in school – that the reason we've done poorly is because we're stupid – it makes perfect sense to tell ourselves that the reason we also done poorly in life is because we're talentless. All of this then is nobody's fault but our own, and from this point on, we'll no longer complain about our lot. We'll become good little workers, and good little consumers, all of which allows the system to continue to tick over, generation after generation. Of course, the 'we' referred to here is not uniform across all strata of society; rather there are 'specific forms of consciousness distributed across a differentiated class structure' (Ladwig 1996, 23). That is, social elites are taught to see themselves, and the world, very differently.

APPLE

This writer examines the way the system 'keeps ticking over' in great detail. The work of Apple (1979) on education and *social reproduction* challenges another of the great myths of the schooling system: that mass education is a positive force for social change, and that an educated population is a population equipped to question its inequalities, particularly those relating to social class. Apple contends instead that schools have exactly the opposite effect; that they act to maintain the status quo, and to keep power in the hands of the lucky few.

Apple's arguments are far more sophisticated than simply pointing to the fact that wealthy and powerful parents send their kids to private schools, who then do well themselves, become wealthy and powerful, and send their kids to private school, and so on. He focuses instead upon the role that the curriculum plays in social reproduction, arguing that ideology – beliefs systems organised according to vested interests – get passed off as objective school knowledge. Internalising this 'knowledge' during their years at school renders students (and teachers) unable to meaningfully question the social order. For example, we are taught from kindergarten onwards that teacher always knows best, that it is inappropriate to question those in authority, and that truth emanates from the front of the classroom. This probably constitutes the most foundational of all school knowledge, and obviously, this mind-set doesn't exactly make for a politically active citizenry.

GIROUX

Giroux examines all those other things we learn in school without necessarily realising it. This involves not the formal curriculum of the three Rs, but the *hidden curriculum*, a curriculum comprised of all those other things we learn in school on the way through. He defines this as:

> those unstated norms, values, and beliefs embedded in and transmitted to students through the underlying rules that structure the routines and social relationships in school and classroom life. (Giroux and Purpel 1983, 47)

After all, not questioning authority isn't the only covert lesson that school teaches us. There is ongoing deference to that authority, in being quiet when the teacher speaks, and standing up when they enter the room. There's learning how to be punctual, how to work hard now if we want to succeed in the future, and how to be a good, moral citizen. All in all, it involves learning how to get ahead by learning how to fit in, and since fitting in normally means not rocking the boat, the hidden curriculum constitutes an important part of how society, or more specifically, the society's class system, replicates itself.

So What Can We Conclude From Critical Theory?

With each of these writers, there is considerable overlap in their ideas, and the decision as to which parts of their work to include could have been made very differently. In spite of this limitation, some specific conclusions can be drawn about Critical Theory, what it says about social class and education, and the insights it brings to the analysis of some of our most pervasive inequalities. Conclusions can also be drawn about the paradigm's shortcomings, and about why other approaches come to be regarded as more convincing.

First, all of these writers and, in fact, anybody who has ever studied education in a coherent way, would argue that the assertion: 'Schooling success is only about individual ability', is way off the mark. Next time you find yourself saying: 'It's all up to the individual, isn't it', pause for a moment, and have a think about exactly what that statement implies.

Second, all of these writers found their theories upon the possibility of social and educational equality. They contend that through political action at all levels – challenging some of the structures of our society, addressing educational policy and focusing on the professional actions of committed teachers – it's possible to mount a resistance to the inevitability of the classing process. Schools don't have to simply provide the rubber stamps, the credentialing, that cements your place within a particular social class. Schools can be about change.

Third, it's obvious from these writers that the nexus between social class and education remains a complex one. Educational outcomes can't be simply 'read off' from a knowledge of the social class of the student, a class determined by the school they went to, and how much money their parents earn. There's much more going on, and Critical Theory has pointed to issues such as the filtering effects of education, the myth of meritocracy, the role of schooling ideologies in social reproduction and the effects of the hidden curriculum.

It should be pointed out here that all of these remain astute observations, give or take a centimetre or two, and just because Critical Theory may have been challenged by more nuanced theoretical models, it doesn't suddenly make these observations wrong, or irrelevant. However, Critical Theory certainly has been challenged, and it has struggled in the face of approaches that have sought to frame the problem in a number of different ways, and according to some very different assumptions. To avoid the risk of needless detail, only two of those assumptions need be addressed here.

First, this approach seems to be premised upon the belief that there is a solution to the 'social class problem' within education. That is, with the right social structures in place, and the right education policies operating, we can turn schools into genuine meritocracies. The unspoken subtext to this presumption is a *teleology* – a belief that history is heading in a specific direction – which implies that the current class crisis in education is but a bump in the road on the way to an education system, indeed a society, free of the curse of social class.

Disagreeing with this optimistic presupposition isn't therefore to say that working within a social justice agenda is a waste of time; far from it. It is just that there's little evidence for a singular 'truth' of social class, one waiting to be found and cured, based on the Modernist belief that every problem has a solution if only you look hard enough. As discussed in the introduction to this book, Giddens (1990) argues that our society is characterised by continual crisis. A longstanding, endemic lack of educational equity is just one of them. And, as will be discussed in Chapter 4, another fundamental characteristic of our society is the continual failure of government to solve its problems.

Second is the contention that Critical Theory represents a reductionist and homogenising approach to social class, or to put it in simpler terms, it oversimplifies what is actually a very complex phenomenon. Just as Marx reduced society down to two ever-warring classes, in the final analysis, so too does its more sophisticated descendant, except the focus is now on a slightly different issue: power – who has it, who gets to keep it, and how. This differential access to power results in a class-based social structure, one that is real, tangible, and objectively knowable – the 'truth' of social class.

It is assertions such as the one above that prove to be Critical Theory's downfall. Ultimately, Critical Theory presents itself as a *master discourse*, a singular explanation that seeks to place all aspects of the social world within its explanatory range. The trouble is, no-one really accepts master discourses any more. The world is just too complex. In which case, where do we go from here? Perhaps the last myth will be able to offer an answer to that question

Myth #3 *Social Class is All About Money*

Blue-collar workers, like miners, plumbers and bricklayers earn a lot more than white-collar professionals, such as teachers, physiotherapists and accountants. Therefore, since social class is all about money, bricklayers must be upper-class, and teachers must be working-class – or to put it another way, all this class stuff is rubbish.

This assertion is normally used as supporting evidence for the claim that the notion of social class is, in the final analysis, simply a fallacy. After all, if we accept the proposition that social class is determined by how much money you have – and therefore what school you can afford to send your child to – it becomes very easy to start charting who earns what, and rightly observe that this doesn't necessarily follow the accepted relationship between wealth and traditional, occupationally determined notions of social class. In addition to this, research such as the work of Savage *et al.* (2013) on social class in the United Kingdom has further muddied the waters over how different groups might be conceptualised and categorised in both economic and cultural terms (they have delineated seven relatively discreet classifications) and, perhaps more importantly, how governments might then respond to these categories.

The truth is, most people's experiences of class differences don't relate directly to how much money they have in relation to others. Whatever social class is, there's a lot more to it than simply taking a student and measuring the size of their parents' wallets. We all know it's far more complex than that. As discussed at the beginning of this chapter, it's not really part of polite conversation to ask people about their social class background, or to inform people of yours. So how is it then that we are all able to make an educated guess about someone's class background after just the briefest of chats? We already know the answer to this: it's because social class is manifest in a wide variety of ways, and it is these that we pick up on. These ways might include how they dress, how they speak, the language they use, what they talk about, what they enjoy doing, where they live, how they live, and so on. All of these are cultural issues, and this means it can be argued that most of 'the stuff' of social class exists in this domain, rather than in the realm of the purely economic.

This isn't a new revelation. Previous modernist sociologies, including some operating under the broad umbrella of Critical Theory, have long pointed to issues of culture when addressing social class. This can be exemplified by two of Connell's earlier books. The first, *Ruling Class, Ruling Culture* (Connell 1977), is, at least in part, used as a case study to explore the notion of *hegemony* – Gramsci's (1971) contention that the ideas of the socially dominant eventually become the dominant ideas. In this way, social control doesn't have to occur through any kind of force, but rather it works through the shaping of the culture in ways which suit the interests of the powerful, and often most effectively, through the use of the media and the school. Indeed, much is made in the book of the role of teachers in the transmission of dominant values, but also, on a more optimistic note, in the role they can play in social change.

The second of Connell's books, *Making the Difference* (Connell *et al.* 1982, written with Ashenden, Kessler and Dowsett) focuses specifically on cultures of schooling. It examines the way that the 'hegemonic curriculum' sorts students on the basis of social class, even though it is portrayed as a neutral body of information. The curriculum does this by drawing a distinction between academic knowledge and practical knowledge, valuing the former and marginalising the latter. Moreover, the various cultural skills that the higher social classes bring to the school – more complex language use, greater skill at organising argument, a wider knowledge of high culture, and so on – become crucial to that educational success. That is, while it would be an oversimplification to state that these pre-existing cultural practices are the same as academic ability, or are mistaken for it, they are certainly the fabric from which the construct 'academic ability' is cut.

Even though both of these books stress the importance of culture in the analysis of social class, they still operate according to the assumption that class-based cultures are somehow an expression of a more fundamental organisational reality – i.e. how much money you have – and that this primary core of class division somehow lies beneath culture. However, in contrast to this, there is a body of work premised upon the assumption that, rather than class-based cultures being a direct function of underlying economic differences, such cultures constitute a relatively autonomous sphere of life. These ideas are generally associated with the French writer Bourdieu.

Bourdieu and His Four Types of Capital

So far, when analysing social class, and more specifically the relationship between social class and education, the spotlight has fallen squarely on questions of money. As previously discussed, the bedrock of social class has always been regarded as the realm of the economic – who's got the cash, who works for pay, and who takes the profit. This has constituted the essential, modernist 'truth' of a society characterised by economic classes and ideologies. Bourdieu (1986) sees it somewhat differently, and he bases his ideas around four different types of capital.

ECONOMIC CAPITAL

This has already been discussed at length in this chapter, and represents wealth in its broadest and most familiar sense. It can include money, property, shares, readily convertible possessions and investments. There's no real need to discuss this any further.

CULTURAL CAPITAL

Bourdieu argues that there are other types of non-economic wealth that can still be spent, and that have massive implications for educational success. He points to all the practices that higher social class kids bring with them to the school, just as did Connell, and notes that they form a type of *habitus*, a term he borrowed from Mauss (1973), meaning a set of socially acquired dispositions, skills and forms of conduct. At a mundane level, these might include such practices as how to walk, talk, hold the body, shake hands, particular types of gesture, dress and even haircut. All of these help mark out an individual as having a given class background, and as previously mentioned, most of us are pretty good at reading these cues, and drawing appropriate conclusions from them.

At an institutional level, schools are no different. They can also spot various types of habitus, such as those associated with the middle classes, and they 'read off' this habitus as academic ability. As such, particular embodied cultural skills (for example, linguistic dexterity, bodily self-discipline, good manners) actually have a value, a practical worth. They constitute a form of capital. Bourdieu contends that this form of cultural wealth comes in three types: embodied cultural capital, objectified cultural capital, and institutionalised cultural capital.

Embodied Cultural Capital consists not only of the kinds of physical practices described above, but also of the forms of conduct associated with a given social group. This might include going to the theatre for the higher social classes, and going to the footy for the lower. Neither of these cultural practices is intrinsically better than the other; however, knowledge of the former is far more likely to be of use within fields such as the academic curriculum. That is, this knowledge can be 'spent', and hence can be regarded as capital. These forms of capital are usually inherited from our families, and take a long time to acquire. Likewise, we pass them on to our own children as a form of tangible inheritance, one they can also 'spend' – long before they get the leftover cash we haven't spent ourselves.

An important subset here is *linguistic capital*, in that the effective use of language is one of the most crucial criteria for determining educational success. It is argued that a student's linguistic sophistication acts as important capital within the school, and that this sophistication often correlates directly with social class background (Bourdieu and Passeron 1990). This idea is also evident in the work of Bernstein (1990), who has worked on linguistic codes. He argues that *restricted codes* (forms of communication relying on shared and taken-for-granted knowledge) are more common among working-class students, whereas *elaborated codes* (forms of communication where all necessary information is included in the statement), as well as restricted codes, are commonly used by middle-class students. For example, the statement: 'I blew it – left my stuff in the back' is a restricted code, only making sense to someone with a significant amount of shared knowledge. An elaborated version of this might read: 'I've done very badly in the open-book exam. I left all the notes I needed in the back seat of the car'. Bernstein is not saying that the elaborated codes of the middle class are any better than the restricted codes of the working class, but he is saying that the ability to use elaborated codes is significantly more useful within the field of education. Consequently, middle classes can convert this ability into linguistic cultural capital, a currency readily accepted by the school.

Objectified Cultural Capital, which incorporates physical objects that give the owner status. These might include objects such as paintings, musical instruments, particular kinds of car, and so on. While these can be sold, thereby converting them into economic capital, they have value in their own right as cultural capital, in that they can speak about the owner. Arguably, owning a grand piano brings with it more cultural capital than owning a piano accordion. Owning a Bugatti Veyron arguably brings with it more cultural capital than owning a Ford Mondeo. Of course, there's more than a significant price differential between these cars, so the issue of the Veyron's associated cultural capital spills all too readily into economic capital. Perhaps then a comparison between a child being dropped off at school in a vintage MG, rather than an old Volvo 240, is more appropriate.

Institutionalised Cultural Capital, which includes the recognition associated with institutional qualifications. This often converts to economic capital directly through the labour market. After all, there are reasons of both cultural and economic capital that mean a university qualification in education is of greater value than the qualifications necessary to be a McBurger flipper, second class.

Although the notion cultural capital is probably Bourdieu's most significant contribution to an understanding of social class that extends beyond the purely economic, he delineated two other forms of capital which also add to the complexity of the issue.

SOCIAL CAPITAL

This includes all the relationships, mutual acquaintances and memberships that an individual can call upon. Often a person has social power, not simply because of who they are, but because of all the people they know that they can call upon, and the influence they can wield accordingly. Old boy/old girl networks – the old school tie – are not simply clichés about how attendance at elite schools provides a benefit long after leaving the institution itself, they represent an appropriate example of what Bourdieu means by social capital. The more people you know, and the more powerful they are, the more capital you have to spend yourself.

> The volume of the social capital possessed by a given agent thus depends on the size of the network of connections he can effectively mobilise and on the volume of capital (economic, cultural and symbolic) possessed in his own right by each of those to whom he is connected. (Bourdieu 1986, 247)

Therefore, an individual may have little economic capital, but if they have a large number of influential friends, then this constitutes an important form of capital, one that can be converted to more useable forms when necessary.

SYMBOLIC CAPITAL

This incorporates issues such as status, prestige and honour. Though perhaps less tangible than other forms of capital, it is just as significant. The right to be listened to is often determined by the many forms of ranking, both overt and covert, that exist within social groupings. In the context of the school, captains of sporting teams are frequently accorded greater status, and can wield greater power, due to the prestige of their position. This prestige can often still be spent, years after leaving the school itself. Likewise, attendance at a particularly elite school, such as Eton in England, while bringing with it obvious social capital, contains an important component of symbolic capital as well.

To summarise the discussion of myth #3: it would appear to be a gross oversimplification to claim that social class is all about money. There appears to be a far greater component of social class that is about culture. The central question here is whether class-based cultures are somehow, ultimately, a direct function of underlying economic issues – money – as more traditional, modernist sociologies tend to assert. Alternatively, are such cultures relatively independent social formations that have their own histories and momentum, with the economic constituting only one element? The work of Bourdieu leads towards the latter conclusion, take it or leave it.

Conclusion

Upon closer scrutiny, three of the most common assertions about education can't be supported. First, the available evidence suggests that the United Kingdom is not a place fundamentally characterised by equality – indeed, far from it. Second, schooling success does not appear to be only about individual ability. Instead, the various resources children bring to the school play a huge role in how well they do when they get there. The education system appears to act as a giant social filter, one filtering not solely on individual ability – whatever that means – but rather on how far through the filter the individual's parents got. Third, social class is not simply about money. Arguably the more convincing theorising on the subject suggests that if you want to understand how social class works, particularly in relation to education, the best place to start looking is within the realm of culture.

Clearly then, whatever social class is, there are a number of common misconceptions about how prevalent it is, how it works and where its boundaries lie. It seems apparent from the arguments set out here, that not only does social class have a significant role to play in structuring our opportunities, access and rewards in life, it affects our education system in very similar ways.

With regard to understanding the connection between social class and education, this chapter has discussed how earlier attempts to explain this relationship largely resulted in reductionist, teleological models promising a 'solution' to the problem of class. These models have located class as one of the three fundamental pillars of human social existence, along with sex/gender and race/ethnicity, as the next two chapters will attest. This chapter has gone on to suggest that perhaps a more sophisticated approach to social class now focuses on its existence as sets of cultural practices, and sets of lived relations, elements which in turn have significant implications for all aspects of education.

Ultimately then, rather than these practices and relations reflecting some underlying truth about a unified and objective notion of social class, perhaps these diverse and often unconnected components are all there is to the matter – all there is to the thorny issue of social class. Furthermore, if one of the central intentions of a socially just approach to education is to try and give students from the lowest of social class background a decent shot at doing well, perhaps the best way forward is to focus, not upon the large-scale, seemingly immutable, economic inequalities that characterise society, but rather upon the smaller scale, more manageable, issue of fostering cultures of learning.

GENDER

2

If we are to believe what we hear from some of our political leaders, and sections of the media, gender is now a settled issue – a battle won. However, the evidence suggests that a significant number of wider questions also still attract attention: just what is gender, and what is the best theoretical framework for approaching it? What roles do schools play in its construction? Do we still have to go down the 'men are to blame for everything' route? Why should schooling have anything to do with sexuality?

This chapter will unpack the complex and changing relationship between gender and education. In order to accomplish this, the chapter will link each of the most common myths in the area with one of the three waves of feminism that characterised the twentieth century. As with the arguments surrounding social class, it will ultimately be suggested that explanations relying upon a master discourse – not 'the economy' again, but rather in this case *'patriarchy'*: a unified system of male-domination – have had their day.

Myth #1 Sex and gender are really the same thing. *'Girls are girls, and boys are boys, because nature made them that way. Masculinity is a function of being a man, and men run society because biology determined they would be better at it'.* First-wave feminism rightly challenged this *biological determinism*, contending instead that our genders are the flexible product of a range of cultural and historical factors. We have a choice in what we become.

Myth #2 Schools are passive spectators to existing gender differences and inequalities. *'While it's true that our parents, friends and popular culture might shape our genders, schools are simply about getting an education'.* Second-wave feminism pointed to the role played by schools in the reproduction of unequal power relations. Significant issues still exist regarding the production of very particular models of masculinity and femininity, models which do not always operate in women's best interests.

Myth #3 Boys are the latest victims of the schooling system. *'Feminists have whined for so long about the plight of girls that nobody noticed it's the boys who are now on the receiving end of educational inequality'*. Third-wave feminism challenges this notion in a number of ways: simplistic notions of victimhood, questions regarding *which* boys, more nuanced understandings of gender identity. This approach no longer locates the two genders at opposite ends of a battlefield.

Myth #4 Sexuality is simply best ignored at school. *'Apart from some basics about sex education, it would be better for everyone at school if we just decided "sexuality" didn't exist. Don't ask; don't tell'*. As a society, we are past the stage of thinking that heterosexuality is right, and everything else is wrong; however, third-wave feminism (and other gender research) contends that schools remain strongly heteronormative environments, and this is problematic for all those individuals – students and teachers – who do not see themselves fitting readily into this category.

Introduction
Gender as a Topic of Educational Concern

Of all the debates over education currently being played out in the media, those with a gendered theme consistently have the highest profile. Articles concerning the high number of boys failing in school ('White working-class boys are consigned to education scrapheap' – Daily Mail 2012), or the relationship between violence, masculinity and education ('Thousands of violent primary students barred' – Times 2015), or about the supposed 'feminising' of schools ('We must stop indoctrinating boys in feminist ideology' – Daily Telegraph 2015) are familiar territory for all of us. Even those not specifically about gender often find a way of veering in that direction at the slightest opportunity. For example, recent concerns over finding employment for ex-service personnel as classroom teachers have often quickly become part of the 'What about the boys?' debate. An article in the *Daily Mail* (Gyngell 2012) champions the idea of 'troops for teachers', and bemoans the fact that one particular iteration of this policy had been refused government funding. The article concludes with the assertion that 'tough guys teaching teenage boys is what we need; not feminised men running the nappy curriculum'. Some of the responses to the article were informative:

Chris – 'It's a woman's world these days, where loony left political correctness rules.'

Ernest – 'The backlash against feminisation of boys and men is slowly but surely gaining momentum.'

Gary – 'The total removal of male teachers, corporal punishment and the phonetic teaching of reading have been part of a calculated plot to destroy education.'

Adherents to claims such as these often support their assertions with data from another of the gendered debates about education: the declining numbers of males within the teaching profession. It has been noted that although in 1980/81, 55% of all UK secondary teachers were male, by 1993/94 this number had dropped to 50% (Office for National Statistics 2010). The most recent data now puts this figure at a low of 38% (Department for Education 2015). Clearly, the 'calculated plot' is paying off.

One further topic that keeps cropping up in the newspapers concerns supposedly 'natural' differences between the brains of boys and girls. The argument here is that boys will always be better at maths than girls because their brains are wired differently. This question will be addressed at length when discussing myth #1; however, it raises the preliminary question: just what is the link between sex and gender?

So What is Sex, and What is Gender?

More often than not, these terms are used synonymously. People often use the term 'gender' because it seems less loaded than 'sex', which brings with it some uncomfortable baggage. Obviously, given this chapter is attempting to understand some of the complexities associated with the relationship between sex and gender, blurring the two into one is simply unsatisfactory.

More generally, the two terms are deemed to be part of a binary, the opposite sides of the same coin, mutually exclusive and yet somehow linked. *Sex* is generally understood as a biological categorisation, dependent upon the possession of particular sexual organs, chromosomes and hormones. More often than not, the human species is divided into two groupings according to their sex: male and female.

Different to this is *gender*. This is not a measure of whether or not you have breasts and a womb, but is rather an assessment of social factors: how you dress, how you conduct yourself, the roles you occupy, the identity you adopt. These are not inherited through our genetics, they are given to us by culture and history. Once again, more often than not, we divide ourselves into the gendered categories of man and women, although in this instance, how this can be accomplished stretches to far more than the two choices associated with 'sex'. After all, there are many possible femininities available to a women, just as there are masculinities for men, although as will be discussed when addressing myth #2, they are not all ranked equally. (Likewise, there are also different sexualities available to men and women and, as will be discussed in myth #4, these are not ranked equally either.)

As such, sex and gender form a pigeon pair, separate and yet linked, linked because specific genders are normally attached to an associated sex. The central question within the social sciences has been: what is the nature of this association?

Certainly, it has proved fruitful to distinguish the two concepts, in that it provided the initial artillery in the battle against the sociobiological contention that sex causes gender – more of that in myth #1.

Why Still Bother With Gender?

All this aside, the assertion is often made that the most important struggles over gender are now over. Aren't we all equal now? Surely no-one really thinks that women are less able than men – maybe the odd dinosaur – but the rest of us live in the twenty-first century. This equality is even enshrined in law, and women's rights are now protected, first by the *Sex Discrimination Act* 1975, and latterly the *Equality Act* 2010.

So are women equal? The evidence suggests there may be a long way to go. That is, women are now in position to apply for almost any job they want, but that doesn't mean they're going to get it. They can legitimately aspire to any career they choose, but will they do as well as equivalent men? Taking the law, for example, research suggests that in the UK, over 63% of law students are women (Law Society 2012), but only 24% make it to become a partner in a law firm (Chambers Student 2015). Within the judiciary, there is currently only one woman on the Supreme Court, out of a possible 12; also only 11% of the Court of Appeal judges are women, as compared with 52% in the rest of Europe (Pells 2014). In business, women are paid an average of 22% less than men, and while women make up 67% of entry-level management roles, they comprise only 29% of directors (Rankin 2015). Owing to recent legislation, the percentage of women on FTSE 100 companies (i.e. the big ones) has increased from 12.5% in 2011, to a still-low 23.5% in 2015 (Hope 2015). In Parliament in the House of Commons, it's a bit better, but still less than 30% of MPs are women – a poor effort, for what is the seat of our democracy.

What about education? We all know that this is a female-dominated profession, so surely this means that women get a fair go when it comes to being a schoolteacher. The latest statistics put the overall number of female teachers at 74%; more specifically, 85% of nursery/primary teachers and 62% of secondary teachers are female (Department for Education 2015). However, when it comes to leadership, females hold only 71% of head positions in nursery/primary schools, and only 36% of head posts in secondary schools (Department for Education 2013b). The issue here is that the proportions of females holding leadership positions in both cases are significantly lower than the proportions of female teachers.

Figure 2.1 sets out this information in graphic form. To put it simply, women may dominate education in terms of total number of teachers, but this dominance disappears when it comes to an assessment of who is actually running the show.

So it would appear that the entire matter of gender and education is a long way from being settled in a satisfactory and equitable manner. Furthermore, this issue is of interest to far more people than disappointed female applicants for principal's positions and education academics with nothing better to do. Those who continue to

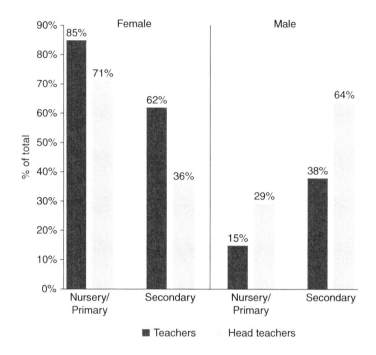

Figure 2.1 Which sex runs our schools?
Source: Department for Education 2013b; 2015

----

contribute to this debate include policy designers, curriculum specialists, main-stream teachers, concerned parents, educational administrators, politicians, and writers, researchers and activists on gender issues, to name but a few.

Theories of Gender: Three Waves

Regarding this final group, the history of women gaining full social and political rights is normally broken down into three stages, or three 'waves', each characterised by different concerns, sets of underpinning ideas and types of action and response. Although each of these will be discussed in greater detail shortly, to summarise:

First-wave feminism, during the late nineteenth and early twentieth centuries, sought the right for women to become full citizens, principally through the right to vote.

Second-wave feminism, from the early 1960s to the late 1970s, attempted to address a broad range of sex-based issues and inequalities, including reproductive rights, the family, in the workplace, and also within education.

Third-wave feminism, of the 1990s onwards, has sought to approach gender from a less fixed and deterministic standpoint – i.e. it's not all simply about men oppressing women – accepting that complex issues arise from the relations created between a variety of masculinities and femininities.

Probably more than any other area within the social sciences, common-sense assumptions about gender are often based upon everything from subtle biases, half-truths and dodgy extrapolations, right through to convenient fabrications, outright falsehoods and good old-fashioned chauvinist drivel. When it comes to gender, finding out which arguments and conceptions are actually valid is not always as straightforward as it ought to be. There are some strange players in this game (as we'll see, when we discuss sociobiology), some powerful vested interests, and several thousand years of gendered history to contend with. Any number of myths about gender could have been addressed here, but the following four should prove to be the most fruitful.

Myth #1 Sex and gender are really the same thing.
Myth #2 Schools are passive spectators to existing gender differences and inequalities.
Myth #3 Boys are the latest victims of the schooling system.
Myth #4 Sexuality is simply best ignored at school.

Conveniently, unpacking these four statements can best be done in tandem with a discussion of the three waves of feminism outlined above, as each bears directly on the logic supporting the myth.

Myth #1 *Sex and Gender Are Really the Same Thing*

Gender is just a function of sex. Our sex creates our gender. As men, we naturally do 'manly' things. After all, in the final analysis modern men are just cavemen with suits on. They are hunters, conquerors and rulers. Men spread their seed, and are good at long division. Of course, women are naturally different. They are gentle, docile, nurturing and subservient. They can't wait to have children, hang out in the kitchen and/or become teachers. It's in the genes.

Sociobiological Explanations of Gender

This is a popular point of view. So far, the *Men Are from Mars, Women Are from Venus* collection of books have sold over 40 million copies. The primary assumption support-ing these texts is that somehow our biological sex inevitably makes us socially different. Likewise, *Why Men Don't Listen and Women Can't Read Maps* (Pease and Pease 1999), with 12 million sales to its credit, also looks for biological answers to social differences, such as 'why men focus on one thing at a time' and 'why women can speak, listen and write simultaneously'. Based upon what it refers to as 'detailed scientific research', it contends that male and female brains are hardwired differently, and as a consequence of these innate, immutable neurological differences, men can't take advice and women can't parallel park.

This isn't a new explanation of the differences between men and women; far from it. Looking back at Victorian England, the reasoning is the same, only the examples are different. The central concern then appeared to be that women were thought not to be 'naturally' cut out for thinking. Mosedale (1978) details a range of wonderful nineteenth-century examples of the scientific logic used to prove women's relative stupidity. The eminent scientist George Romanes started out by correlating the smaller size of women's brains with their obviously diminished intellectual powers, and ended up by suggesting that because women are physically weaker, they clearly can't sustain the effort of prolonged brain action. An equally eminent Harvard professor of medicine, Edward Clarke, seriously contended that educating adolescent girls was dangerous because it could divert important energy from their ovaries to their brains, rendering them sterile. However, probably the most straightforward argument for the intellectual inferiority of women belonged to a certain Miss Hardaker, published in *The Popular Science Monthly* in 1882: 'The sum total of food converted into thought by women can never equal the sum total of food converted into thought by men. It follows, therefore, that *men will always think more than women'*.

It was sociobiological arguments like these that provided much of the justification for continuing to limit the rights granted to women, principally the right to property and the right to vote. Consequently, first-wave feminists had a significant vested interest in debunking the validity of this particular line of reasoning. First-wave feminism is most frequently understood in terms of the suffrage movement of the late nineteenth and early twentieth centuries. Arguably, its initial impetus came from the earlier publication of such books as Mary Wollstonecraft's *Vindication of the Rights of Women* (1792), but it was through campaigns of public education and civil disobedience that they finally managed to turn the tide of public opinion and change the law in their favour. Women were given the vote in 1893 in New Zealand and 1902 in Australia, but not until 1918 in the UK (and even then, only to women over the age of 30 who met given property ownership requirements).

Importantly, it was not just the Suffragette movement that found fault with the objective scientific evidence that supported their natural intellectual inferiority. A significant number of early-twentieth-century writers, and even scientists, seemed well aware that age-old stereotypical opinions about women had simply been trans- lated into scientifically proven facts by simple sleight of hand.

> Those who espouse a scientific superstition are still more formidable than those by whom it was created. The dogma of the inferiority of woman is so deeply rooted in the mentality of our times that the idea of attempting to dislodge it almost borders upon insanity. This is the reason that the majority of scientists appear among the most ardent advocates of the theory of the inferiority of woman. (Finot 1913, 122)

Clearly, these kinds of arguments are no longer taken seriously, hopefully by anyone. But that doesn't mean that new, more sophisticated versions haven't taken their place. That is, no contemporary scientist would give any credence to the contention that men are smarter than women, but a limited number of scientists – generally called *sociobiologists* – argued that other kinds of social difference have their origins in the natural differences deemed to exist between males and females.

For example, there exists a body of literature that explains boys' better results in maths as a direct function of differences hard-wired into the human brain. A number of articles pointed to differences between males and females in their corpus callosums, the set of nerves that connect the left and right cerebral hemispheres of the brain, in that it was said to be significantly wider in women (Gorman 1992). The outcome, it is argued, is a naturally greater level of intuition in women, and an impaired level of spatial awareness and mathematical ability. The implication here is that boys do better at maths, not because they are relentlessly pushed towards the hard sciences, both overtly and covertly (and also away from the 'girly' humanities subjects), all for heavily gendered cultural reasons, but because of a few extra bits of wiring in the brain.

Some Problems With the 'Boy-Brain vs Girl-Brain' Argument

There are, however, problems with almost every element of this argument. First, there are no longer any significant differences between British boys and girls in their maths results – pass rates for boys and girls at GCSE level are almost identical (Joint Council for Qualifications 2015) – so the entire argument is built upon a fallacy. And yet, the stereotype of the natural superiority of boys at maths persists, even though in the USA in the 20 years between 1987 and 2007, nearly 47% of all undergraduate maths degrees went to women (National Centre for Educational Statistics 2009).

Second, the assertion that the corpus callosum is larger in females appears to be false. Recent research has shown that the initial measurements, upon which the entire argument is based, haven't been replicated within later studies. The part of the brain that has supposedly doomed females to be rubbish at maths is actually the same size as in males (Bishop and Wahlsten 1997).

Third, and of greatest importance, since it has implications across a range of sociobiological arguments, is the observation that *even if* there were differences between adult male and female brains in the size of the corpus callosum, there have never been shown to be any differences in infants (Fausto-Sterling 2000). Why is this so important? It is important because if brain differences do exist, whether in the corpus callosum or anywhere, they are the *product* of gender, not the other way around. That is, if you treat a male differently to a female for their entire lives, it wouldn't be remotely surprising if you found their brains to be dissimilar – indeed, it would be surprising if they weren't. The research suggests that, from the earliest ages, boys and girls are talked to differently, played with differently, disciplined differently, encouraged differently, touched differently and presented with completely different models of what they ought to be (Gilbert and Gilbert 1998).

Fine (2010) argues that the issues raised by Finot in 1913 still apply to contemporary sociobiological 'brain' research. Countering what she calls 'neurosexism', she argues that the brain is not hard-wired from birth, as the sociobiologists would have us believe; rather the wiring is 'flexible, malleable and changeable'. Some boys develop better spatial skills because they are expected to throw and catch balls more often, reflecting dominant models of masculinity. Likewise, girls are expected to be more expressive and emotional, and hence emphasis is placed on their verbal skills. These are not innate differences; they are the product of how we raise our children, and what we expect of them. Female babies grow into young girls as the result of a 'pernicious pinkification', not because of the shape of their brains, or their genes, or their chemistry.

Importantly, if such factors are deemed to influence us at all, then that influence is very small. After all, if boys and girls are naturally different, then those differences could be seen globally across all cultures – they can't; those differences should also be historically fixed – they aren't; and those differences should result in a rigid binary between men and women – they don't.

In truth, sociobiological arguments are not widely held, either by medical or social scientists; indeed, they are regarded as rather weird, and a bit of a throwback. One place they do appear to have currency is in the popular media – 'Yes, its official, men are from Mars and women are from Venus, and here's the science to prove it' (Daily Telegraph 2014) – which in turn gives them currency within popular discourse. Consequently, anyone trying to address the possibilities of change in the field of gender is confronted by the constant presupposition that, 'in the final analysis, boys and girls are just naturally different, aren't they'. But as Roland Barthes (1972) famously wrote: 'What is sickening in myth is its resort to a false nature'.

In summary then, gender can't just be read off from sex as a causal relationship – far from it. Culture intervenes at every stage of the gender-forming process. Nicholson (1994) uses the metaphor of sex as simply a 'coat-rack' upon which gender is constructed. That is, each society superimposes a gender on an existing male or female sexed body – the coat-rack – in a manner that suits their own needs, culture and history. The coat-rack has next to no say in the cut of the gender coat that gets hung from it. So, when attempting to understand the relationship between gender and education, rather than spending all this effort focusing on any tiny natural differences that might exist between the brains of males and females, perhaps concentrating on the vast amount we have in common might prove to be more productive.

Myth #2 *Schools Are Passive Spectators to Existing Gender Differences and Inequalities*

Fortunately, education has always managed to stay immune to the effects of a male-dominated society. Fair enough, other areas of society may favour men, to some extent, but education is a fair race, with the best and the most worthy gaining the greatest success; and if that happens to be men, so be it. The school itself is a gender-neutral institution. Yes, gender differences and inequalities may exist in the wider society, but our education system is a non-combatant in the gender wars.

After the first battle over voting and property rights were won by the Suffragettes, for a while 'the sex problem' appeared to be resolved, and it wasn't until after World War II that new issues started to arise. While the men were away fighting, women had successfully occupied a wide variety of roles previously thought to be beyond their capabilities, forever reshaping what women could be, and what they might aspire to. However, when the men returned from war, women were pushed back into the home, with a vengeance, and for the next 20 years, the dominant model of femininity centred on their supporting role within the nuclear family. However, the genie was now out of the bottle.

Consequently, from the start of the 1960s through to the end of the 1970s, a new group – the second-wave feminists – sought to question what they saw as, not only the tired old arguments about the 'natural' role of women, but also the power structures that kept women in their place. Informed by such texts as Simone De Beauvoir's *The Second Sex* (de Beauvoir 1960) and Betty Friedan's *The Feminine Mystique* (Friedan 1963), they set out to challenge the entire system of male domination: the system of *patriarchy*. They noted that men called the shots in almost every avenue of life: the workplace, the home, public office, relationships, religion, the judiciary. Second-wave feminists attempted not only to raise awareness of this power imbalance, but also to do something about it.

The question now is: does this male domination extend to our education system? After all, surely if the rest of our society plays a role in the production of masculinity and femininity, as well as the power relations between them, why should schooling be any different? Answer: it isn't.

Schooling as a Gender Regime

Taylor (2004) contends that, contrary to the myth of neutrality, the school is indeed a heavily gendered site. To put it more simply, schools are giant machines for producing acceptably masculine boys and acceptably feminine girls – both in terms of gender, as will be discussed here, and also in terms of sexuality (as will be discussed in myth #4):

...gender discourses shape our behaviour, attitudes and expectations in profound and pervasive ways. It is therefore not surprising that they influence school and classroom practices in various ways as well. Schooling, as a disciplinary institution ... is a key site for re-producing gender relations, but it is also a key site where change can occur. (Taylor 2004, 91)

Taylor refers to the school as constituting a *gender regime*. This regime extends from the most direct and obvious of strategies for the production of different genders, to the subtle and the indirect. While even the most ardent of second-wave feminists wouldn't suggest that each of these factors represents an attempt to disempower women, they would likely contend that the overall effect is consistent with the logic of a patriarchal society. There are ten gendered differences outlined below (with many more for those with the time and energy to think of them).

(1) SINGLE SEX SCHOOLS

First and foremost, the sex of our children is considered so important, and the processes by which they become gendered so different, that we have set up completely separate schools for them. Within the Independent schooling system, 24% of schools are currently designated as single sex (Independent Schools Council 2015). However, in addition to this figure, many co-educational schools also separate the sexes at various points during the school day, for a variety of different social and pedagogic reasons. The Government-funded system also has single sex schools; however, they currently comprise only 12% of the total.

Various arguments are used to justify this division, but the primary rationale is that males and females gain a better education, and more comfortably engage with the process of growing into acceptable men and women, in the absence of the other. While this may or may not be true, what this separation also does is reinforce the fundamental significance of the differences between the sexes. That is, society signals in the clearest possible manner that men and women, masculinity and femininity, are not the same.

(2) SCHOOL ETHOS

Arguably, the point of single-sex schools is not simply to separate the males from the females, but to engage in different processes within those schools. Even a casual glance at an all-boys private school would generally reveal a very specific type of operating ethos, a gendered philosophy, underpinning life there. While many commonalities exist between boys' and girls' schools – likely to include valuing learning, respect, community, and so on – the dissimilarities are especially notable.

The ethos at many boys' schools is specifically about learning a given type of masculinity. School mottos can be particularly informative in this regard (Synott and Symes 1995). While some school mottos are nakedly self-serving – *Floreat Etona* (May Eton Flourish) – the mottos of other British boys' schools include *Forti Nihil Difficile* (To the brave, nothing is difficult), *Stenue Sed Aeque* (Strong but fair), *Dura Virum Nutrix* (Stern Nurse of Men), *Viriliter Age* (Act Courageously) and *Conquer We Shall*, all of which suggest a very particular understanding of what it is to be a man.

A different ethos appears to operate at girls' schools, as made manifest by mottos such as *Caritas, Humilitas, Sinceritas* (Charity, Humility, Sincerity), *Ut Prosim* (That I may serve), *Habeo ut dem* (I have, that I may give) and *Inspire, Care, Achieve*. Given the general lack of words such as 'courageous', 'conquer' and 'brave', it seems fair to assume that these institutions are out to foster very different learning environments, and very different types of student, to the boys' schools. These are institutions where 'conquest' isn't necessarily on the agenda.

It has been suggested that the ethos existing within boys' schools are one mechanism whereby a particular type of masculinity is constructed: *hegemonic masculinity*. This concept, most frequently associated with the work of Connell (2005), describes a version of masculinity that dominates the other possible options, a masculinity based upon strength, self-confidence, assertiveness and ambition; more on this shortly.

(3) SUBJECT CHOICE

Whether we are at a single-sex or a co-educational school, we are all viscerally aware that certain subjects seem to be gendered from the very start. As a result of this, by the time students arrive in sixth form, these largely covert cultural messages have been translated into increasingly clear gendered demarcations, as measured by enrolment percentages (see Figure 2.2).

These numbers are relatively predictable. Some subjects are considered 'hard' sciences, or subjects directly appropriate for dominant models of masculinity, such as physical education, and these are dominated by boys. Others are 'soft' sciences, or subjects tied to stereotypical models of femininity, such as the humanities and languages, and these are dominated by girls. Importantly, these subject choices spill over into the trajectories students take into post-compulsory education and future employment, constituting a very clear example of the social reproduction of gender.

It should also be pointed out that these figures are simply the result of boys and girls making choices for themselves about what subjects to take. At many single-sex schools, subjects deemed 'gender-inappropriate' (read 'Home Economics' for boys, and 'Technical Studies' for girls) are not even offered as part of the curriculum.

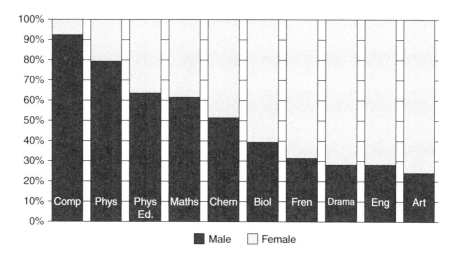

Figure 2.2 *Percentage of A-Level passes by sex*
Source: Joint Council for Qualifications 2015

(4) SUBJECT PREFERENCE

Even before students get around to making formal choices as to the subjects they will continue with and those they will drop, subjects are allocated roles to play in the formation of gender, whether they like it or not, and students respond to this accordingly.

For example, English is often marked out as a feminised subject, and male students can struggle to accommodate any enthusiasm for it, while at the same time attempting to shape a masculine identity acceptable to their peers. Indeed, belittling the study of English, and those boys who enjoy it, can form a significant component of heterosexual masculinity, as the following quote from a fifteen year-old boy demonstrates.

> This subject is the biggest load of utter bullshit I have ever done. Therefore I don't particularly like this subject. I hope you are not offended by this, but most guys who like English are faggots. (Martino 2000)

Of course, other subjects can play exactly the opposite role in the construction of masculinity. Physical education has long played a role in the shaping of men, allowing them to demonstrate physical strength, speed, courage and confidence – the very definition of hegemonic masculinity – and is hence a very popular subject with boys. Incorporating these crucial components within their identities not only marks them out as superior to other, less dominant, forms of masculinity, but also superior to girls, an attitude that can carry over into the wider world. As one male competitor said, during a strike protesting against women's participation in the famous Acapulco cliff-diving championship: 'This is a death-defying activity – men are taking a great gamble to prove their courage. What would be the point if everyone saw that women could do the same' (Bryson 1990).

(5) DISCIPLINE

Research has consistently shown that school discipline is not simply a straightforward and impartial framework that it portrays itself to be, one that allows schools to function effectively, while also producing organised and respectful citizens. The evidence suggest that social class, race and gender all play a significant role in who gets punished, how often, and for what (Wallace *et al.* 2008).

With specific respect to gender, this body of research points to the same two conclusions; first, boys are subject to greater disciplinary intervention than girls. That is, they engage far more frequently in behaviours that result in punishment: admonishment, detention, suspension and expulsion. Second, and far more interestingly, boys and girls are disciplined differently, often based upon pre-existing beliefs about what is 'natural' behaviour for each sex (i.e. back to some good, old-fashioned, subliminal sociobiology). Boys are often not disciplined for noisy, boisterous and unruly behaviour, because teachers regard this as part of some intrinsic masculinity. Girls, however, will often be punished for the same conduct, as this is deemed to run counter to the way they 'ought' to behave. As such, school discipline becomes part of a regime of moral judgement, one that succeeds in reinforcing dominant understandings of gender: confidence and assertion in boys, passivity and obedience in girls (Robinson 1992; Hart 2000; Ryan and Cooper 2010).

(6) TIME WITH TEACHER

Exactly who gets the teacher's attention follows a very similar logic to that of discipline, and in one way, boys often receive more teacher time simply because their behaviour demands it. However, more generally, boys are given more teacher time than girls, both positive and negative, are called by their names more often, have their questions answered more frequently, and are asked more complex questions (Sadker 2000, 2002). One well-known study on this issue found that boys take up about two thirds of teacher time, and if this percentage is reduced, 'they feel they are being discriminated against' (Spender 1982, 57).

The outcome of this disparity is a further reinforcement of existing gender expectations. For example, when boys call out in class (up to eight times more often than girls) they are often responded to directly, while girls are more likely to be told to raise their hands if they want an answer. Once again, such interactions succeed in cementing the notion that boys are active and forceful, while girls are placid and compliant – notions that, after years spent interacting with teachers, become part of the way children both understand themselves, and their gender (Frawley 2005).

(7) DRESS CODES

As within the wider cultural contexts, the ways in which boys and girls are encouraged, or required, to dress at school reinforces a range of dominant understandings of gender. Traditionally, boys' uniforms have been practical, durable and plain, precisely the outfit you'd want for boisterous playground activity. Conversely, girls' uniforms are generally more aesthetic and much less amenable to any kind of physical activity, either through choice of colours, or the fact that many are required to wear a skirt – the natural enemy of all things athletic.

Most co-educational schools now offer unisex clothing options, but the not-so-subtle social pressures of schooling life often make this option a difficult one. Probably needless to say, even though girls are allowed to wear traditional boys' attire, the reverse is normally forbidden, as it does not 'reflect community standards' (Hoffman 2009). Such expectations are not limited to clothing, but also encompass hairstyles, jewellery, and the use of make-up. Once again, with their short hair, make-up and earring-free faces, boys are ready for activity; girls, not so much. In the area of physical appearance, the school is not a passive spectator to existing gender differences and inequalities; it's a showcase for them.

(8) ACCESS TO RESOURCES

Not all playing fields are level, and even though resources such as computers are readily available in most schools, this doesn't mean that everyone gains access to them equally. As will be discussed in greater detail in Chapter 9, there are various types of *digital divide* – differences in the ability to access and use digital technologies – one example of which involves gender. The evidence suggests that not only are girls under-represented in ICT clubs and the use of ICTs outside school (BECTA 2008; Palmen 2011), they can struggle to gain access to computers in co-educational classroom (Blackmore *et al.* 2003). Furthermore, when they get on the computers, they are likely to face greater levels of criticism from boys, who buy into, and hence reinforce, the dominant mythology that, when it comes to ICTs, boys are simply better (Cooper 2006; Gras-Valazquez *et al.* 2009).

This isn't the only example of resourcing issues. Provision of funding for male, as opposed to female, sport has long been a matter of contention. It is, however, one of the most important ones. After all, arguing that the boys have greater access to, and encouragement towards, computers at school is of significantly greater importance than observing that the boys might also monopolise the tennis balls. ICTs now form a crucial component of most young people's social, educational and future professional life-worlds. Somehow carving this out as a male domain has massive equity implications. That said, times are changing very quickly in this area. Perhaps the next research to emerge in this area will paint a rosier picture.

(9) CLASSROOM TEXTS

Even the materials schools use to teach students have been criticised for presenting a very particular gendered take on the world, one which has traditionally fore-grounded men, and presented gender abilities and relations in predictably stereo-typical ways. As Ryan and Cooper note:

> Textbooks, other reading materials, and educational software, despite attempts at improvement by publishers and authors, often still portray females as more helpless than males. Although sexism has decreased in many texts . . . researchers argue that examples of gender stereotyping, tokenism, and omission still occur in reference to girls and women. (Ryan and Cooper 2010, 88)

A recent study by McCabe *et al.* (2011) of over 5600 children's books from throughout the twentieth century have shown that boys are represented twice as often in titles of books, and over one and a half times as often as central characters, than are girls. The animals in the books are also predominantly male, with over two and half times as many as are portrayed as female. It doesn't take much to see how being a girl has come to be understood as 'marginalised other' in so many ways. Even the storybook puppies are boys.

(10) EMPLOYMENT FOR TEACHERS

There is little need to pursue this final issue further, as it was discussed in the introduction to this chapter. Schools display all the same gender inequities of the wider world of employment. Not only are males disproportionately represented in all the leadership positions, and females find themselves clustered in those parts of the system that educate younger children (they need more 'caring'), and the 'fluffier' subject areas (i.e. those that involve reading), they are also far more likely to put their careers on hold by staying at home with a young family, than any of their male teaching counterparts. None of this goes unnoticed by students.

Some Problems With This Approach

So, contrary to myth #2, schools appear to have a huge role to play in the reinforce-ment of gender differences. While they don't necessarily overtly work for the con-tinuation of gendered inequalities, schools do play a significant role in the social reproduction of roles, practices and identities that often appear to work against women's best interests. That, however, is far from the end of the matter.

The foundation upon which these observations stand has been subject to no little amount of criticism, which doesn't mean the facts themselves are suddenly suspect, but it does mean they may need to be interpreted in a somewhat different way. The central problem here revolves around the underpinning notion of patriarchy, i.e.

the belief that society is organised around the fundamental principle of male domination. Within the logic of second-wave feminism, the ten examples of the non-gender-
neutrality of schools act as proof that we live in a patriarchy. That is, each in turn adds
another evidentiary pillar holding the concept off the ground.

The trouble is, the notion of patriarchy appears to have had its day. This approach
to gender has been criticised for a number of reasons, the following being only some
of them.

IT'S DICHOTOMISING

The notion of patriarchy divides the world into two neat halves. There are the men
who have the power, who dominate, and for whom everything is rosy. Then there are
the women, who lack power, who are subject to male domination, and for whom life is
rubbish. As discussed in the introduction to this book, this form of binary reasoning is
common within modernist forms of thought: mind vs body, culture vs nature, and so
on. Masculinity vs femininity fits right in.

IT'S REDUCTIONIST

The notion of patriarchy necessitates boiling all the complexity of social relations
down to a simple power relation. Girls wear dresses? Patriarchy. Girls don't do
Technical Studies? Patriarchy. Girls find it harder to become Head of School?
Patriarchy. It's a one-stop shop for all questions relating to gender. It makes asking
those questions kind of redundant.

IT'S HOMOGENISING

The notion of patriarchy assumes that all women are somehow the same. As such, all
men are somehow inherently more powerful than all women. It doesn't matter if you
are a high court judge, or a hillbilly living in a shack – if you are a man, you possess
some innate authority that sets you above women. Predictably, it might come as
a surprise to a Mercedes-driving, senior partner in a law firm that, just because she's
a woman, the above-mentioned toothless shack-dweller is on the winning end of life's
power equation – simply because he's a man.

IT'S DISEMPOWERING

The notion of patriarchy means that, given male domination appears to be everywhere, chipping away at one small part of it is simply delaying the inevitable. Who
cares if we finally manage to remove all traces of gender bias from our textbooks, or
make sure boys get asked to put their hands up in class, just like girls are? What's the
point if there's still this huge slant to the playing field that affects every other

component of their lives? It makes the struggle against gender inequality all but pointless. Women are victims, end of story.

It was primarily feminists themselves who articulated these criticisms (along with a few disgruntled men), thereby seeking a way to keep the debates around gender equity moving forward. Arguably, addressing the next two myths offers a solution to some of these problems, by way of third-wave feminism.

Myth #3 *Boys Are the Latest Victims of the Schooling System*

Yes, girls might have once had cause for complaint, but that was quite a long time ago now. The pendulum hasn't just swung back towards the middle, it's gone so far it's in danger of hitting the side of the clock. Boys are now being actively victimised within an education system dominated by vengeful feminists. The curriculum is biased towards girls; the teaching methods are biased towards girls; and boys aren't even allowed to be real boys any more.

This belief has significant currency, and can be found in the most surprising of places. However, if we were seeking expertise on gender equity issues, would we really consult with the headmaster of the world's most elite private boys' school?

Boys failed by education system, says Eton headmaster

Boys are being failed by the British education system because it has become too focused on girls, the headmaster of Eton has warned. Tony Little said that the different sexes required different teaching methods to bring out students' potential and that GCSEs favour girls more than boys. He also blamed teachers for failing to realise that boys are 'more emotional' than girls, despite the fact that girls 'turn on the waterworks'. (Roberts 2010)

Significantly, the initial concerns over the performance of boys in school have been taken up by two sets of commentators. The first, often referred to as *'the backlash'*, has been described as a counterattack against the ideas of second-wave feminists. Describing this phenomenon, Faludi (1992) noted how the gains made by the women's movement of the 1960s and 1970s prompted near-hysterical responses suggesting that, having gained equality, women were now taking over the whole show. Indeed, it has been widely argued that most of the 'What about the boys?' debate is part of this hysteria.

The second response to this debate came from the third-wave feminists. Third-wave feminism is a little harder to pigeon-hole than its two predecessors. Prompted by books such as Naomi Wolf's *The Beauty Myth* (Wolf 1991), this new approach also sought to challenge second-wave feminism, to the extent that, for a while, such writers were deemed part of 'post-feminism'. Their concerns, though complex and varied, largely centred upon the homogenising aspects of the notion of patriarchy. They rightly concluded that second-wave feminism had at its heart an understanding of 'woman' that was essentially white and middle class – the unspoken essence of the female. Consequently, the notion of a 'global sisterhood', so central to second-wave feminism, is simply a fable. White women are just as capable of oppressing black women as white men.

This new approach has implications for myth #3 in three separate ways.

Which Boys?

In no longer seeming to 'blame men', third-wave feminism has been more receptive to the recent discourses over the 'What about the boys?' debate. However, they note that it appears to be based upon the same faulty premise that animated earlier forms of feminism. Just as the notion of the archetypal 'girl' – forever oppressed within a patriarchal schooling system – doesn't hold water, so too the notion of the universal 'boy' is equally flawed. When we say that the modern schooling system is now slanted in favour of girls, and that boys are consequently failing, do we mean all boys? Even at first glance, this does seem like another example of a modernist binary in operation. If we begin by stating that '*some* girls' are now doing better in school, this quickly becomes 'girls', and in binary-thinking land, this must mean that the other half of this self-created binary, 'boys', must be doing correspondingly badly. That's the way that the maths works. Except that it isn't.

Vickers (2010, 227) contends: 'the proposition that boys are uniformly failing and girls are uniformly winning is seriously misguided'. She suggests that the most appropriate response to the question, 'What about the boys?' is: 'Which boys are you talking about?'. For example, an examination of the United Kingdom's PISA results for 2012 suggests that, as with previous analyses, there appear to be relatively small differences in the results gained by boys and girls in testing, with girls doing very slightly better in reading, and boys doing very slightly better in maths and science (Wheater *et al.* 2013). However, these gendered differences are much smaller than the levels of difference that have been previously evidenced between students of high socio-economic status, and those of low socio-economic status (Knowles and Evans 2012). To put it another way, when it comes to doing well in school, whether you are a boy or a girl is relatively unimportant in comparison to which social class you come from.

Of course, the problem really arises when you combine both of these factors – i.e. being a male, *and* from the working class – in which case, the big question should really be: 'What about the *working-class* boys?'. After all, what the advocates of the 'schools are conspiring against boys' position never seem to get around to mentioning, is that boys still do better than girls when it comes to getting the very best grades. In the 2015 United Kingdom 'A' level results, boys still took out significantly more of the top A* grades than did girls (Joint Council for Qualifications 2015). The truth is: boys dominate both ends of the normal curve.

Finally, a further argument in favour of the educational bias against boys – that they drop out of school in greater number than girls – may also be something of a furphy. Currently, approximately 6% more girls are involved in full-time education between the ages of 16–18 than are boys (about 75%, as opposed to 69%) (UK Government (GOV.UK) 2015). While this has been held up as additional proof of how unsuited the current schooling system is for boys, a more plausible explanation notes that poorly performing boys can drop out of school and look for a job with some confidence (via the male-orientated apprenticeship system). Equivalent girls have much more limited options, and therefore often decide to stay on (Vickers 2010).

Must We Have 'Victims?'

Foster, Kimmel and Skelton (2001, 4) address the issue of 'the problem of boys' and conclude that, within a number of educational discourses, 'boys are positioned as "victim", specifically of: single (fatherless) families; female-dominated primary schooling; and feminism, which has enabled girls' success'. Interestingly, one of the central features of third-wave feminism has been its rejection of the 'victim' status accorded to women by second-wave feminism. The all-encompassing notion of patriarchy meant that, no matter how women tried or what avenue of life they embarked upon, they were always destined to be on the losing end of male power. However, the 1990s saw the rise of a new way of understanding femininity, with a whole new range of female role models – Madonna, Xena, Buffy – all of whom managed to combine confidence, assertiveness and power, with a sexiness for which they didn't feel they had to apologise.

> . . . the new girl hero doesn't need a man to define her – she has staked her own claim to the privileges of both masculinity *and* femininity. She is not the overly emotional victimised heroine – she does her own hunting, fighting and monster-slaying. (Hopkins 2002, 3)

The issue here is that power is no longer necessarily regarded as a zero-sum game. Just because one group can exercise power within a given context, or according to a particular logic, doesn't therefore mean that someone else is automatically suffering. Besides, if this new approach teaches us anything, it's that gender domination can't just be 'read off' from social structure. Certainly, gendered issues and inequalities still exist, but it's much more complicated than that. Genders come in all shapes, sizes, colours, classes, ages, sexualities, cultures and opinions. Exactly who is dominating who? And is domination even the right word?

Also, it must be said that women haven't rightly abandoned the rhetoric of victimhood, whether in the workplace, relationships, or the school, just to see it picked up and wielded by men. Men still get the best grades and the best jobs, so it seems somewhat disingenuous to extrapolate the educational struggles of one cohort of boys into some global war on masculinity, which men are deemed to be losing.

And When We Say 'Boys'...

One of the central themes of third-wave feminism has been to address the structuring of gender identities. Part of the problem has always been that just as males and females were placed within a binary – 'the opposite sexes' – so too were genders. Masculinity and femininity are depicted as opposites: if men are strong, women have to be weak; if men are smart, women have to be stupid (and now vice versa). Third-wave feminism rejects this either/or approach.

Most writers and researchers who consider themselves third-wave feminists have now aligned themselves to far broader programmes of gender studies. These programmes don't only seek to understand the multiple, and often contradictory, ways in which feminine identities are shaped; they regard masculinity as an equally fertile ground for study. Understanding how a modern 'boy' constructs his identity, and has that identity constructed, involves far more than a grasp of the notion of 'hegemonic masculinity'. Indeed, this important concept has itself been challenged as an oversimplification of what is actually a fluid cluster of behaviours and statuses.

Therefore, just as the question 'What about the boys?' proved inadequate to the task due to its lack of social-class specification, so too is it inadequate due to its presumption that all boys somehow struggle for the same reasons within the school, and that masculinity is a coherent entity. They don't, it isn't, and sophisticated contemporary forms of gender research can help unpack the problem far more clearly.

In summary, the idea that boys are somehow the latest victims of the schooling system requires considerable qualification, in an intersection sense. Certainly, there are some cohorts of boys, most notably working-class boys, who are struggling – and are therefore worthy subjects of specific policy interventions. However, to extrapolate that to all boys, and hence make it some kind of gender-war issue, borders on the ridiculous. The discourse of 'victimhood' should no longer have a place within education for boys or for girls. Much more interesting research is being conducted into how we become one of a large range of different types of men and women, and the role that our schools play in that process.

Myth #4 *Sexuality is Simply Best Ignored at School*

Teaching is a difficult enough job without having to worry about issues of sexuality. Sure, children need to know the basics about sex, but there's no need to deal with these issues of sexuality at all, either in the curriculum or in the playground; just ignore it. After all, there's plenty of time for students to explore themselves and experiment with other identities – sexual or otherwise – when they leave school. That's what universities are for.

The problems associated with sexual identity in schools are often there for all to see, but are very often simply ignored – either deemed too difficult to address, or explained away as part of the rough and tumble of playground life. Boys teasing other boys for being 'gay', or a 'faggot', are such a common part of schooling life that it barely raises much of a rebuke if overheard. This requires some analysis.

The Failure of 'Don't Ask, Don't Tell' in Schools

While third-wave feminism and other forms of gender studies have rightly expressed concern over the inherent reductionism of a singular notion of 'hegemonic masculinity' (Connell and Messerschmidt 2005), arguably it is still useful as a heuristic device for understanding particular types of bullying. Hegemonic masculinity in schools has already been addressed in this chapter; it is a gender identity based upon the characteristics of strength, self-confidence and assertiveness. However, it is also most frequently located within a series of binaries – it is the very opposite of femininity; it is the very opposite of 'undesirable' masculinity; and, most significantly here, it is the very opposite of homosexuality. Importantly, hegemonic masculinity is often enacted through public displays, distancing itself from, or denigrating, 'that which it is not'. As Kimmel (1994, 215) notes, masculinity is largely manifest as a set of negative rules about behaviour, rules which go some way to explaining the familiar reflex homophobia so widespread in our school playgrounds.

> Never dress that way. Never talk or walk that way. Never show your feelings or get emotional. Always be prepared to demonstrate sexual interest in women that you meet, so it is impossible for any woman to get the wrong idea about you. In this sense, homophobia, the fear of being perceived as gay, as not a real man, keeps men exaggerating all the traditional rules of masculinity, including sexual predation with women. Homophobia and sexism go hand in hand.

Kimmel, a sociologist and writer on masculinity, states that he has a standing bet with a colleague that it would be possible to provoke a fight in any playground in the country, just by walking up to a group of young boys and asking, 'Who's the sissy around here?'. He asserts the most likely outcome would be various displays of masculinity, followed by violence – normally directed towards the least hegemonically masculine of the group.

The kind of heteronormative bullying outlined by Kimmel describes not only the daily social and behavioural landscape of schools everywhere, it also describes the individual life experiences of many LGBTIQ students (Lesbian, Gay, Bisexual, Transgender, Intersex, or Queer) as they progress through our education system. Research by Poteat *et al.* (2013) reveals that homophobic bullying, and the bullying of other sexual minorities, begins in the primary years, and continues right through secondary school. Of course, while boys who do not enact a sufficiently (hegemonically) masculine identity are deemed to be sexually suspect – and hence fair game for bullying – the same vulnerability exists for girls who do not follow their expected gender codes.

The issue here is relatively simple. Until recently, most schools operated according to an implicit 'Don't ask; don't tell' policy. As long any non-traditional sexual identities were kept strictly hidden from general view then there would be no problem. This was the case for both staff and students; after all, schools were not seen to be the place for 'flaunting' sexual difference. However, there are three central problems with this approach. First, ignoring the issue of student sexuality fosters an environment where it is acceptable to victimise those perceived to be in any way different. However, the repeal of Section 28 of the *Local Government Act 1988* in 2003 – a law that made it illegal to talk positively about homosexuality in schools – has meant that schools can no longer use 'the law' as an excuse for not offering students their full support and protection. Second, it excludes LGBTIQ students from genuine inclusion within the school. That is, the subtext here is that such students are welcome as full members of the school community only if they are prepared to do a good impression of being someone else. Finally, it gives these students no preparation for how they might organise their identities, their relationships and their lives when they leave the school environment. In an area as important as this, that doesn't sound like much of an education.

How Should We Best Understand 'Sexuality'?

At this point, some kind of discussion is required about what 'sexuality' is. Carpenter and Ball (2012) suggest that there are three main approaches that can be taken here.

SEXUALITY AS A NATURAL CATEGORY

This approach has largely taken shape within evolutionary biology, with its underpinning logic that human development is driven by the imperative to continue as a species; that is, 'human sexuality is seen to be rooted in biology, and thus it is easy to argue that a normal sex drive is a heterosexual one intended for procreation' (Carpenter and Ball 2012, 109). This raises the question, what then are other forms of sexuality, ones that by definition can't produce offspring?

According to this logic, it becomes easy to position non-heterosexuality as abnormality or perversion, ready to be 'cured', whether by hormone therapy, or castration, or any one of the other medical attempts that has been made in the past to make sexually different people 'better'. Unfortunately for advocates of this form of understanding, there has never been any convincing proof that sexual preference is naturally determined – no 'gay' gene has ever been found, no hormonal differences between heterosexuals and homosexuals, no differences in brain structure, no embryonic differences and no psychological differences – no significant differences at all. Nothing.

Members of the LGBTIQ community are acutely aware of the costs and benefits of this understanding of sexual difference. If it is regarded as 'natural', then it becomes unfair to deny them all the rights and privileges that everyone else in society enjoys; after all, these preferences are therefore considered to be innate and not the product some kind of 'perverted' choice. Alternatively, if these preferences are natural, then the discourse stays within the realm of normality/abnormality, and the notions of 'sickness' and 'cure' remain part of the conversation.

SEXUALITY AS A SOCIAL CATEGORY

The second approach has its foundation more in the social, as opposed to the natural, sciences. The central assumption here is that sexuality is shaped by psychological and social forces rather than biology; this leads to the presupposition that there is a 'normal' path to a 'normal' sexual development. For the psy-disciplines, this is based upon the belief that the main features of a traditional family – strong mother, loving siblings, stable relationships – will inexorably lead to healthy heterosexuality. In contrast, it is disturbances to this happy normality – maladjusted families, weak or distant fathers, psychological issues during development – that trigger the emergence of alternative sexualities.

In a similar vein, sociology looked to social and cultural factors in the environment as formative influences on sexuality. We quickly learn to make direct connections between the biological features of our sex and the dominant expectations for its associated gender (as discussed earlier in the chapter) and, from there, to make yet further connections to particular sexual desires and behaviours. That is, we are deemed to follow particular socio-sexual scripts. It is contended that sometimes these traditional scripts can be interrupted by particular kinds of pleasurable sexual experience during adolescence, which may then set the individual on course towards developing a different sexuality.

Members of the LGBTIQ community are also aware of the problems with this approach. Alternative sexualities are no longer some kind of pathology, as with the first option; however, the argument is now that these sexual preferences have become more of a social choice – and clearly, according to some voices in society, some choices are simply immoral. And what do we do with immoral choices? Simply stop. Consequently, there are now significant numbers of religious and psychological programmes promising a mental cure to non-heterosexual behaviour (Beaver 2011).

Though they appear quite different, there is one commonality between these first two approaches – they both take sexuality as a given. Sexuality is positioned as an inherent part of being human; it is an essential, unitary, transcultural 'thing' that we all have, even if that sexuality takes different forms. The last position does not share this assumption.

SEXUALITY AS AN HISTORICAL AND CULTURAL CATEGORY

Largely based upon the work of Foucault (1976b; 1987), this position contends that the notion of sexuality itself is historically contingent and culturally specific. Foucault maintains that the past 300 years have witnessed an increasing pre-occupation with sexual matters, such that they now occupy a unique position in our society. Indeed, the very ways in which we talk about sexuality are dependent upon a wide historical legacy of interrelated knowledges and practices – religious, Darwinian, libertarian, eugenic, feminist, medical, psychological, psychoanalytic, moral and so on. By refusing to assign a priority to any of these truth claims, Foucault concludes that there are no grounds for believing that sexuality exists independent of discourse, but rather that it is an aggregation of discourses concerned with sex.

So not only is the notion of 'sexuality' a relatively recent invention, so also are the categories of sexual difference that most of us take for granted (for example, LGBTIQ). As will be discussed at length in Chapter 4, a fundamental part of contemporary governance involves subdividing the population into more and more manageable categories of difference, each of which can be understood, and intervened upon, differently. This same process happened from the second half of the nineteenth century onwards with regards to sexual conduct. As Carpenter and Ball (2012, 118) state:

> Prior to the mid-19th century, men engaging in sexual practices with other men may have been disapproved of, but it was not because of the 'kinds of people' they were. Rather their stigma and criminalisation was because the acts they committed may have faced legal sanction ... However, with the development of categories such as 'homosexual', those engaging in these acts were understood differently. They now became distinct 'kinds of people' deserving different kinds of treatment.

In addition to the historical specificity of both sexual categories of difference, and even the notion of 'sexuality' itself, there is also a great deal of cultural specificity. It is important to note that in a significant number of cultures, for example in part of Melanesia, engaging in homosexual conduct is an important and expected part of eventually becoming an acceptable adult. The idea that homosexuality constitutes some kind of alternative deviant form of personal identity would make no sense to them at all.

There are two final observations here. First, unless we think that Melanesians all have some kind of 'gay' gene, or all come from troubled families with weak fathers, then the previous two sets of explanations have some serious shortcomings. Second, if we lean towards accepting that sexuality is itself a historically and culturally contingent category, then the notion of 'normal' sexuality becomes far more problematic, and sexualities themselves necessarily take on a degree of inherent fluidity. This conclusion has some significant implications for how sexuality should be addressed in schools.

Schools as Heteronormative Environments

It is probably fair to conclude that no-one actually walks around modern schools demanding hegemonic masculinity from boys and particular kinds of acceptable femininity from girls. Most of the time, the messages are far more subtle. However, just as genders are gently shaped within schools, so too are sexualities, and most of this is done simply by producing an environment where heterosexuality becomes the silent unspoken norm, and all other sexualities are quietly banished to the margins. According to Carpenter and Lee (2010), educational institutions become heteronormative in a number of ways.

First, there is a general hidden curriculum of heteronormativity. The world is understood either as asexual, or it is 'immersed in the norms of heterosexuality'. That is, there is an underlying curriculum assumption that the world is heterosexual, and other sexualities are generally only notable by their total absence. This issue is compounded by the fact that sex is often only addressed in biology, which places it within the a priori 'natural' heterosexual environment of reproduction. As Ceplak (2013, 173) observes:

> Apparent silence about sexuality conveys (or even propagates) the message that heterosexuality is the only 'normal' sexuality – by perpetuating gender dichotomy, through images of 'typical' families and heterosexual relationships, through speech on sexuality purely in the context of 'natural' biological reproduction and in contexts which are based on heterosexual relationships.

Second, even in those courses where 'diversity' is a stated component, it is often the case that this is taken to mean socio-economic, ethnic, racial or linguistic diversity. Sexual diversity is likely to be quietly ignored, as positing too many difficulties, or challenging the comfort zone of the responsible staff. Whereas this absence may have come as less of a surprise within primary and secondary levels of education, Carpenter and Lee (2010) note that this is also the case within tertiary teacher education courses.

Third, the attitudes of students and staff are already steeped in heteronormativity and this forms the context for interactions within the school. As discussed previously when addressing bullying and sexuality, there is a familiar vocabulary of ways in which daily life moves along in the schooling environment – most of these are coloured by heteronormativity. This goes far beyond commonplace insults on the school playground, it extends to what it is deemed appropriate to discuss, how people structure their work together and where social boundaries are to be set.

Finally, openly LGBTIQ students and staff are far from common. It could be that some schools actively discourage overt displays of sexual difference; for the most part it is likely to be because of legitimate concerns over social acceptance and personal safety. After all, the 'normal' student is a heterosexual student and 'displays' of heterosexuality are not displays at all, whereas 'displays' of any kind of sexual difference is likely to be positioned as gratuitous and inappropriate. Obviously there is a circularity to this last element of the heteronormative school; until enough LGBTIQ students feel both comfortable and safe enough to become a visible part of the schooling landscape, many LGBTIQ students will choose to stay under the radar, thus maintaining the levels of heteronormativity that makes them choose invisibility in the first place.

To conclude, it should also be stated that, in addition to silences in the curriculum and heteronormativity of daily life, heteronormative schools still enforce their boundaries by employing some not-so-subtle disciplinary devices. Private schools, governed as they are by contract law and not necessarily by the anti-discrimination legislation that regulates government schools, are still able to actively police how students shape their sexual identities, and who they may – and more pertinently, may not – take to school activities, events and dances (Gordon 2015; Vonow 2015).

Conclusion

Upon closer scrutiny, the first two common assertions about gender and education don't hold up to scrutiny, and the third needs significant qualification. First, gender is not unrelated to sex, but neither is it simply a function of it. Sociobiological arguments about the educational effects of brain differences or hormones weren't convincing in the late nineteenth century, and they're not convincing now. We become men and women through complex life-long processes given to us by our social background, our culture and our history. The same is true for how we learn.

Second, schools are not simply spectators to the process for gendering, quite the contrary. Educational institutions have a comprehensive role to play in the transmission of gender and sexuality. Everything from school ethos, uniforms and discipline, to resourcing, curriculum and employment structure affects the types of boys and girls we produce, and what they consider to be normal. While the evidence suggests that, historically, the school hasn't exactly been a force for gender or sexual equity, neither can it be realistically depicted simply as some kind of 'tool of patriarchy', by which females were kept in their place.

Finally, more recent approaches to gender in the school have stressed the compound ways in which schools both fail, and succeed for, their students (boys and girls), the possibilities opened up by more nuanced and contingent understandings of gender, the continuum of gendered identities and sexualities, and the need for teachers to understand them.

All of which makes the ongoing focus on the topic by academics, policy makers, educational administrators and teachers both appropriate and important. In spite of what some dominant discourses within the area might assert, this particular social issue is still a long way from a satisfactory resolution. One of the many great things about being a teacher is that they have a significant role in shaping the future, and once we abandon the notion that our genders are given to us by nature and that one gender necessarily dominates the other, or that the opposite of heterosexuality is abnormality, this leaves teachers in a better position to help create strong, confident and thoughtful citizens, regardless of their gender, sex, or sexual identity.

RACE/ETHNICITY

3

Of all the ways humans have chosen to divide themselves, none has a history as arbitrary, as spurious, and as terrible as the idea of race. This concept has significant implications for almost every aspect of contemporary human conduct, irrespective of what 'race' we are deemed to belong to, and whether we realise it or not. This is particularly so for the field of education.

In order to describe the complex issues within this important area, a wide range of interrelated terms are used, often in plural ways. Probably the most important of these terms is the underpinning notion of 'othering' – i.e. the process of deciding who's in any given social group, who's out, and why – and arguably two of the most pernicious examples of this are racism and ethnic discrimination.

Myth #1 Humanity is naturally divided into races. *'Just as there are different breeds of dog, or species of beetle, so too are there different races of people. It's just part of nature: yellow people are naturally clever, black people are naturally good at sport, and white people are naturally good at being in charge'.* None of this is true. Race is a relatively recent invention; it is one that has found a way of blaming nature for a series of socially constructed forms of discrimination. Unfortunately, though this concept is without foundation, it still has real effects.

Myth #2 We no longer discriminate on the basis of race or ethnicity. *'Sure, people who aren't white once had a rough time, but most of us now have friends with every skin-colour imaginable. No-one cares anymore'.* While hopefully there's some truth here, the evidence suggests that prejudice is still alive and well, and that discrimination extends beyond the simple and the overt, and is often at its most pervasive in its institutional and cultural forms.

Myth #3 Educational outcomes are unaffected by race or ethnicity.
'Maybe there's still some discrimination around, but the education system educates all kids equally. In the end, it just matters how smart you are'. Whether by deliberate discrimination or otherwise, some racial and ethnic minorities often still find themselves at the losing end of the education system. That said, it is also important to take into account intersectional variations in educational outcomes, within such groups, based upon social class and gender.

Myth #4 There is a 'Black and Minority Ethnicity' (BME) problem in British education. *'A greater percentage of these students lack what it takes to do well in school. Whatever their problem is, there's no ready solution'.* The fact that some of these students can struggle at school is not a BME problem, it is an issue that everyone needs to take responsibility for. Setting up the binary of 'Us' vs 'Them', employing a deficit model of educational success, and ignoring issues of underlying white privilege are not good starting points.

Introduction

If we are touchy about the issue of social class, as discussed in the introduction to Chapter 1, then the issue of race is in another league of sensitivity altogether. There are probably two main reasons for this. The first involves the long history of the appalling consequences – the world over – that could arise from being deemed to belong to the 'wrong' race in the wrong place. Up until the American Civil War, black Americans had to carry papers to prove they were free, otherwise the mere colour of their skin would make them slaves. Only a little over half a century ago, six million people were exterminated in Nazi Germany for being part of the 'Jewish Race'. In Australia, Indigenous Australians were not even counted as people in the National Census until 1967. And in the UK, it took until 1965 before the most basic of legal protections were put in place regarding discrimination on the basis of race.

The second reason for extreme sensitivity over issues of race is likely to be related to this terrible history of racial violence and discrimination, and it lies in the way we go about constructing our identities. Whereas we may well recognise that we fit the criteria for membership of a particular social class, this doesn't necessarily mean that this classification becomes a central component of how we understand ourselves. Certainly, an 'untouchable' in India, or a member of the British aristocracy, may be constantly and acutely aware of this status, and may therefore regard this as one of the most important things about themselves. In contrast however, it is unlikely that the identity of 'middle-class person' is of sufficient importance to most British people that it plays any role in shaping any kind of 'inner identity' – whatever that means. Generally, the same can't be said for issues of racial and ethnic identity. If you ask black or Asian Britons whether this 'racial' or 'ethnic' identity was of greater significance to them than any class-based identity, then the answer would almost certainly be 'yes'. This is an interesting issue, all the more interesting when compared to the likely answer given by white people to the same question, which would generally be that 'they don't have a race'. This will be discussed in greater length when addressing myth #4.

So this is serious stuff, and while coming from the wrong social class can mean you don't get access to a good education, or don't get invited to the rich kids' parties, coming from the wrong race could cost you your life; and let's not kid ourselves, even in the twenty-first century, in many places around the world, it still can.

Getting Our Terms Straight

Before having a reasoned discussion of the role of race and ethnicity in education, it is probably useful to explain some of the common terms. There appears to be a lot of terminological slippage when addressing these issues, i.e. using the same word to mean different things, or different words to mean the same thing. If there's one thing we need here, it's a bit of clarity. Even though each of these terms will be expanded upon later, not only will it be useful to provide a preliminary sketch of their meanings, it will also help to show the links between them; how one concept often leads on to the next, like falling dominoes.

OTHERING

This term is based upon a very simple premise: that we largely determine the membership of our own social groups, and its boundaries, by deciding who we are not. That is, a necessary part of figuring out who is the same as us, and why, is deciding who isn't. Although the term was popularised through the work of Edward Said (1979) on colonialism (more of which in Chapter 14), describing who 'we' were, and contrasting that construction with the lesser grouping of 'them' – the other, the native peoples.

Importantly, *othering* isn't just about peoples deemed to be of a different race, ethnicity, culture, religion or nationality, although when it came to colonialism, they were the ones that probably counted the most. Othering is the core of most unequal power relations, and can be seen every day in schools, workplaces, and in the street. You can be othered for almost any reason, not just the colour of your skin, or the God you worship. You can be othered because you are disabled (us = able-bodied, other = people in wheelchairs), because of your sexual preference (us = heterosexual, other = homosexual/lesbian), or even because of the colour of your hair (us = everyone except, other = Gingers). Othering is all about deciding, who's in, who's out, and why. No-one is immune to possible othering, and it forms the foundation of most of what is to follow.

ETHNOCENTRISM

Having sorted out the boundaries of our own social grouping – who is one of us, and who isn't – the next step appears to be to assume that *we* are somehow better than *them*. Ethnocentrism is the practice of placing your own group on an unrealistically high pedestal, and then looking down on all those who are not part of that group. Once again, this isn't just about the big ticket issues of race and ethnicity, it can be about anything.

Take rugby union, for instance. At club level, supporters of the northern clubs can look down on their southern equivalents ('self-important chinless fops') – and vice versa ('barely intelligible provincial halfwits') – right up until the national team is chosen to play in the Six Nations competition. Then, the now-united English can look down on Scots (for example) as somehow inferior ('Irn-Bru guzzling moaners') – and vice versa ('loathsome pompous twits') – right up until the Lions team is selected. Then, the now-united British can look down on the Australians (for example) as somehow inferior ('knuckle-dragging ex-convicts') – and vice versa ('Pommie bastards'). And so on.

The point is: part of belonging to a group often seems to be thinking that your group is better than all the other groups. We're great, and they're not. That's ethnocentrism, and its boundaries can slide around all over the place, depending upon who 'we' are at any given moment.

PREJUDICE

Arguably, it is the notion of ethnocentrism that forms the foundation of prejudice. Having decided that 'we' are better than you, we can start mentally finding fault with you, because, let's be honest, you are useless. Prejudice is best understood as a hostile attitude towards a person from another group, based solely upon membership of that group. Most of us probably carry around some prejudices, rational or otherwise, whether they involve the members of political organisations we really don't like (e.g. Neo-Nazis – perfectly rational), or the players in sporting teams we can't stand (e.g. Manchester United – probably not-so rational). However, for prejudice to work effectively as a concept, it needs to be teamed with another idea, one that produces a coherent target for that prejudice to focus on: stereotyping.

STEREOTYPING

There's not much point in having a prejudice against a group of people, if we then admit that the group is actually just a diverse collection of individuals with one feature in common: their membership of that group. Instead, the entire group becomes characterised without regard for individual difference – and usually negatively. Staying away from our own offensive ethnic labelling for a while, in the United States, 'Mexicans' have long been the subject of derogatory stereotyping. So, in spite of the fact that the term refers to a single characteristic (someone from Mexico, or at a stretch, someone of Hispanic origin), and in spite of the fact that 'Mexicans' do much of the truly back-breaking labour in America, they are often stereotyped as lazy and shiftless. Such stereotyping occurs when an image is formed of a 'typical' member of a group, and the assumption is made that this applies to all members of a group. These stereotypes are almost entirely context-bound, as 'Mexicans' may be 'lazy and shiftless' in the United States, but in the United Kingdom, not so. After all, Speedy Gonzales is a Mexican, therefore all Mexicans etc., etc.

Arguably, the end result of the process outlined so far is twofold: *scapegoating* and *discrimination*. An example of how this all works might be useful at this stage. Let's take an issue that currently appears to have traction in many places around the world, but in particular in the USA, Great Britain and Australia: that is, illegal immigration.

We start with 'othering'. There's 'us' who were born here, or at least came here legally; and then there are 'them', who didn't. In terms of 'ethnocentrism', clearly we're better than them, as we have homes, jobs, a stable political system, and we don't have to beg others for help. And when it comes to prejudice, easily done; we didn't ask them to come here, we don't want them, and we don't like them. And not wishing to stereotype, but one lot blew up the World Trade Centre, didn't they? All of which leads to the following.

SCAPEGOATING

We now have a group of people we can blame for all our problems. Not many jobs around? The illegal immigrants have taken them all. There are lots of drugs on the street? Gangs of illegal immigrants sell them. You live in a high crime area? Bet the illegal immigrants take everything. Are you unhappy with your life? Illegal immigrants.

Scapegoating also goes hand-in-hand, not only with stereotyping, but also with *victim-blaming*. Back to the Mexicans. Illegal or otherwise, Mexican-Americans occupy some of the lowest rungs of American society, as most avenues of social mobility have traditionally been closed off to them. As a consequence, they take many of the hardest, and lowest paid, jobs around, jobs that nobody else wants. So when the question is asked: 'why are so many Mexican-Americans living in poverty?', the answer is generally not: 'because they are badly disadvantaged from the get-go'; rather the answer is, 'because they are lazy and shiftless... and take our jobs'. The victims of the system are blamed for the problems within it.

DISCRIMINATION

The second outcome of the above process is discrimination. This is the process whereby members of particular groups are denied equal treatment, based solely upon their membership of that group. For example, if you are a black person and apply for a job, and you don't get it because someone else was better, we call that the 'economic marketplace'. If you apply for a job, and in spite of being the best candidate, you don't get it simply because you are black, we call that 'racial discrimination'. Quite rightly, it's against the law.

Discrimination comes in a number of forms – individual, institutional, cultural – all of which will be dealt with when addressing myth #2; it can also cover a range of areas – such as sex, age, religion, sexual preferences, and so on. The only two examples of discrimination relevant to this chapter are race and ethnicity.

RACE

The term race is used with confusing levels of flexibility, perhaps as a reflection of its origins as a term that simply sought to differentiate disparate social groupings, e.g. the 'English race', as opposed to the 'Irish race'. However, from the eighteenth century onwards, its meaning began to solidify as specifically referring to observable physical differences, and the notion of race came to presume that all people can be classified into one of several distinct, biological groups on the basis of their physical characteristics. However, this understanding has continued to evolve, and as will be discussed when addressing myth #1, the purely biological definition has been blurred into an explanation that involves significant social components.

> If 'race' can be defined at all today, it is a contradictory complex of vestiges of earlier 'natural' definitions that are merged uneasily with assumptions of ethniclike traits drawn from the common experiences of groups. (Doane 2003, 9)

ETHNICITY

While ethnicity is often used as a synonym for race, it is built around an entirely different logic, in that there are no necessary biological components to ethnicity, as there are with race. Certainly, different ethnic groups may vary in appearance, but this is not the pivotal issue. Ethnic classifications are based upon social factors such as nationality, culture, religion and language.

For example, most people would be unable to tell the difference between an Irishman and an Englishman, unless they were holding some kind of cultural clue, like a cricket bat, or a pint of Guinness (speaking of stereotypes). That is, there are limited grounds to accept that they belong to different races, even if we were to accept that such a concept had any validity. However, they would clearly consider themselves to have different ethnicities, certainly in terms of the elements of nationality, culture, religion and language mentioned above. After all, the notion of ethnicity does not have to refer to something exotic; some non-White 'other'. The term ethnicity is applicable to any group that shares an identity and a past.

Arguably, ethnicity is also dependent upon how tightly you focus the lens. On the lowest possible magnification, there is a British ethnicity. When we are compared with Americans or the French, we have a different nationality, a different shared culture and history, and a different past. Increase the magnification again and we have a range of ethnicities within the United Kingdom. Along with White British, we have Asian British, Black British, Chinese British and so on into the hundreds, each rightly claiming a coherent ethnic identity. Tighten the focus further still, on the Asian British for example, and you would find Indians, Pakistanis and Bangladeshis; and then again with Pakistani British, you would find Punjabis, Pashtuns, Sindhis and Muhajirs – once again, each with a shared history, identity and linguistic characteristics. Like Russian dolls, each ethnicity can form one component of a larger construct. It seems that ethnicity is often about who you are comparing yourself with.

RACISM

This is a term used in a number of different ways. The first is the most specific. It involves the belief that humanity can be organised in various groups – races – and that these groups can be ranked according to achievement, and worth. Poplin (1978, 280) defines it as 'the belief that some groups are inherently – biologically – inferior to other groups'.

The second usage is somewhat more general. It involves a generalised dislike of those perceived to be from a different racial grouping, whether manifest in terms of simple prejudice or actual discrimination. This dislike is most focused upon the colour of a person's skin (the central signifier of race), although as will be discussed in myth #2, this is often now expressed in cultural terms. Such dislike is not necessarily founded upon any underlying belief in biological inferiority.

The final definition is the most general, and is the one used within the United Kingdom's hate-speech laws. Racial hatred extends not only to a person's perceived race, but also to their colour, nationality, or ethnic origin. Therefore, it would be considered racist for an individual with a White British background to call out offensive comments to someone from an Irish or Serbian background, even though they may appear to be from the same 'race'.

Now that we have framed a basic language for approaching this area, we can tackle some of the central myths that seem to keep cropping up when looking at race/ethnicity and education. There are as follows.

Myth #1 Humanity is naturally divided into races.

Myth #2 We no longer discriminate on the basis of race or ethnicity.

Myth #3 Educational outcomes are unaffected by race or ethnicity.
Myth #4 There is a 'Black and Minority Ethnicity' (BME) problem in British education.

We now take these in turn.

Myth #1 *Humanity is Naturally Divided into Races*

Humanity is divided into different groups. Those groups – races – can be relatively easily delineated because they don't look the same. There are Caucasians, Negroids, Orientals, Asiatics, and Mongoloids... er, or is it Malaysiatics and Indigenoids... it gets a bit confusing. Anyway, the separate groups are clearly defined in nature, and not only do they look different, they have different qualities, characteristics, and abilities. History suggests that Caucasians, i.e. white people, are the best since they invented civilisation, and came to run everything. Nothing much you can do about that really, it's just the way it is. It's a scientific fact.

It's hard to know where to start with this myth really. It would be hard to think of anything else that was so 'obviously' true for so long – nearly 500 years – and yet turned out to be such utter rubbish, but in the meantime caused untold damage and suffering, and yet, even when we found out it was nonsense, still refused to go away and die. It would be laughable, if it wasn't so tragic. Probably the best way to approach the issue of race is to examine it in two sections: first, how the concept developed, and how it became a scientific fact; and second, how that fact came to be questioned, and ultimately debunked.

The History of Race

It's impossible to understand the invention of the notion of race without, at the same time, examining the history of slavery. If we say that the concept of race, as we understand it, began to take shape around 1500, we can also say that the phenomenon of human slavery is much older, probably as old as humanity itself. The Ancient Greeks certainly took slaves, but this had nothing to do with the colour of their skin, or any perceptions that they had less intrinsic worth as people. People normally became slaves simply as a result of military conquest, or having the wrong religion.

So how did we get to the position, not only where slaves were considered to be fundamentally different, but were also considered to come from a lower rung of some natural hierarchy? Writers such as Banton (1998) and Jackson and Weidman (2004) point to a number of historical issues, each of which was crucial to the final emergence of the notion of race.

SLAVERY ON THE IBERIAN PENINSULA

Between 711 and 1492, Muslims dominated what is now Spain and Portugal, and like most other cultures of the time, they took slaves – black and white. Importantly, the white slaves were worth more, as they could be more readily ransomed back to the Christians with whom they were constantly at war. This difference in value often meant that white slaves were given less onerous labour, usually domestic, while the black slaves worked outside in the heat, or down the mines. Eventually, this division became naturalised – of course whites are better at more civilised activities, and of course blacks are more suited to the brute work. Consequently, out of this division developed the first two pre-requisites of a theory of race:

(1) outer physical attributes somehow reflect inner moral worth; and
(2) physically different groups belong in a hierarchy, with white at the top.

EUROPEAN EXPLORATION

From 1500 onwards, the great European powers started to expand their power beyond Continental Europe. The underlying rationale behind this expansion, though initially military, quickly became economic. For the first time, slaves were not taken as a result of conflict, but were taken simply to provide labour; and the largest source of this labour was Africa. In a very short time, the third pre-requisite fell into place:

(3) blackness equals slavery, and slavery equals blackness.

Although the Bible was deemed to contribute a vital argument in favour of slavery – 'bringing the heathens to God' – it also contributed a second important piece of the jigsaw. At this time, the biblical belief in *monogenesis* provided the dominant model of human origins (i.e. we all come from the same starting point: Adam and Eve), therefore all physical differences between peoples must have developed later, most likely as a result of climate. Curiously though, even though North and South American Indians were more naturally suited to their environments, they died in droves soon after the Europeans turned up. As they had no understanding of smallpox or influenza, the visitors took this to mean:

(4) Europeans are superior to Indigenous Americans, as well as Blacks; and
(5) the difference is some natural, internal quality of the body.

THE RISE OF SCIENCE

The Enlightenment of the eighteenth century is credited with stimulating a number of notable social changes: the decline of the absolute power of the monarch; scientific explanations replacing those based upon tradition or theology; the belief in a notion of progress, that human civilisation would make things 'better'. Given the self-evident progress made by European civilisation, as opposed to other peoples, Europeans were clearly superior. After all, their new-found system of knowledge – Science – could be employed to explain everything, and just as science divided the natural world up into phylum, genus and species, so too could humanity be placed in convenient packages. A number of early scientists developed typologies for human difference: lists of different races, always in a hierarchy, always with white Europeans at the top. Much of this work was premised upon the heretical logic of *polygenesis*: the belief in multiple creations. This is important because it meant that white and non-white races were not necessarily related in any fundamentally binding way:

(6)   different races are like different species.

THEORIES OF EVOLUTION

Darwin's Theory of Evolution didn't just pop into the world, fully formed and uncontested by the scientific community; it had to fend off some similar, but rival, ideas first. Although Darwin's ideas immediately seemed to offer a viable explanation of how we got here, they didn't just offend some religious sensibilities, they also offended the new scientists of 'race', since Darwin was clearly a monogenesist (in that we all developed from the same, first organism... not Adam and Eve). This didn't sit well with those polygenesists now convinced the different races had fundamentally different points of origin. The solution to this problem was to construct an early version of evolution that borrowed a bit from both camps. That is, that when it came to humans:

(7)   the evolutionary 'struggle for survival' is between races, not individuals.

THE POLITICS OF RACE

Races were now deemed to be naturally at war with each other. This war manifests itself in a number of ways. First, a number of concerns were raised about waves of immigrants from different races 'flooding' into countries where the numerically and socially dominant race was white. Clearly, since whites were the superior race, the genetic result of this mass-immigration of inferiors could only be negative:

(8)   the better races can be contaminated by less worthy ones.

At this point, the political and the scientific merged within the new discipline of *Eugenics*: the science of improving the genetic composition of the population. We no longer had to be passive spectators at the slow destruction of the white race by less worthy ones; we could intervene to keep our race strong. This intervention could take any number of forms: sterilisation of the 'feebleminded', immigration laws, marriage laws (Montagu 1974):

(9)   actions can be taken to protect the purity of races.

And we know what number (10) would be, given the progression of this logic. In retrospect, it almost seems inevitable that, under the right political circumstances, someone would decide to 'remove' lesser races from the equation altogether – even though Jews aren't a race by anything other than the most deranged formulation.

Debunking Race

So there we have it; the progression of logic that lead to the invention of race. In many ways, it is the perfect example of othering: decide who *we* are, create an *other*, and then blame nature for it. And yet, in spite of its apparent scientific validation, fairly soon after the end of World War II, the entire edifice of race started to collapse; not all at once, and not in its entirety, but collapse it did. There isn't enough space here to detail all the shortcomings of race as a theory; however, it failed as an idea across three separate areas.

THE LOGICAL FAILURE OF RACE

First and foremost, it is almost impossible to construct a coherent racial grouping. All the evidence suggests that there are far, far greater differences *among* races, than there are *between* them. Take any given racial trait – height, shape of nose, colour of hair – and compare within any grouping deemed to be a race. The differences are enormous. For example, when it comes to height of the 'black race', what about the lanky Sudanese, and the medium-sized Bantu, and the stocky west-Africans, and the tiny Bushmen? Or are they all to be deemed separate races now? Even then, there are very tall Sudanese and there are very short Sudanese. The normal curve of a given trait from any race will generally overlap the vast majority of the curve of the same trait of any other race. It just makes no coherent sense.

A second notable failure in the logic of race is its self-evidently flexible boundaries, with 'whiteness' being the most flexible of them all. Given that being categorised as white has brought with it many advantages, removing that categorisation can be particularly punitive. Back to Mexicans again. Mexicans had always been regarded as white, right up until 1930. However, a social panic at the time about, you guessed it, immigration, meant that they were immediately re-categorised with the stroke of a pen as 'not white', hence less worthy, and hence much easier to kick out (Hochschild and Weaver 2007). But then, if race is really natural, surely its boundaries can't be moved around at a whim? Quite.

THE SCIENTIFIC FAILURE OF RACE

There are any number of examples of how race has failed the test of modern science. Probably the most telling involve the notion of intelligence. Gould's book, *The Mismeasure of Man* (Gould 1996) details an array of ways early scientists sought to demonstrate the superior brain-power of the white race over all others. Skull size was one early favourite, as clearly the bigger the brain, the smarter the individual (so goes the logic). By filling skulls with lead shot, their internal size could be measured. Early studies showed the expected results: whites have bigger heads. However, not only have later studies shown this to be completely false – most likely a sub-conscious fiddling of the results by researchers – but also that brain size doesn't correlate with intelligence anyway (see elephants).

IQ testing was another method that established white superiority with absolute certainty. Tests conducted for the US military around World War I showed that whites were significantly smarter than blacks, confirming everything proponents of race always knew. However, dozens of later studies have shown that IQ (assuming this concept has any validity at all, which it probably doesn't) correlates with social advantage, not racial classification. Middle-class blacks do as well as middle-class whites.

THE POLITICAL FAILURE OF RACE

This final issue proved catastrophic for advocates of racial theory. There was really nowhere to go after the Nazis. It was widely realised that dividing people into 'natural' races served no worthy social or intellectual purpose. As stated in the preamble to the *International Convention on the Elimination of All Forms of Racial Discrimination* (United Nations 1965):

> . . . any doctrine of superiority based on racial differentiation is scientifically false, morally condemnable, socially unjust and dangerous, and that there is no justification for racial discrimination, in theory or in practice, anywhere. . . (*International Convention on the Elimination of all Forms of Racism* (United Nations 1965))

Even though the notion of race is clearly erroneous and no-one really believes it any more, this doesn't mean it can't still affect people, particularly 'non-whites'. Indeed, the ghost of race seems to hang around somewhere at the back of discourses about ethnic difference, never quite going away: the ghost of nature. But we shouldn't be surprised, as just because something isn't real, doesn't mean it can't have social power. Harry Potter isn't real, but he still represents a multi-billion-dollar industry. And he never gets made to sit at the back of the bus.

Myth #2 *We No Longer Discriminate on the Basis of Race or Ethnicity*

It may have once been the case that non-whites got a rough time. People would use a variety of racist terms to describe people who were different to themselves; we all know what they are, so there's no point in listing them here. Those days are long gone, and it is only the most ignorant and uneducated now who are prejudiced or who discriminate on the basis of race or ethnicity, and given most of these people have next-to-no social or economic power anyway, I think we can say discrimination is a thing of the past. After all, does anyone really say, 'You're black, so you're not getting the job', anymore. I don't think so.

The argument supporting this myth has three elements: first, that racial prejudice is a thing of the past; second, that discrimination is something that occurs directly, when someone won't let someone else have something – a job, accommodation, entry into a pub – simply because of their racial/ethnic identity. This is a direct, individual-centred form of discrimination. The third element of the myth is that this doesn't really exist anymore anyway; once again, we are better than that now. This section of the chapter will address these three claims and, in doing so, will contend that *individual discrimination* is just one form of bigotry, and that *institutional discrimination* and *cultural discrimination* are now significantly more prevalent than this, but they are just harder to spot.

Racial Prejudice

As discussed in the introduction to this chapter, an essential precursor to discrimination is prejudice – the hostile attitude towards a member of a group, based solely upon membership of that group. A person who is racially prejudiced will dislike a person, to paraphrase Martin Luther King, not because of the content of their character, but rather the colour of their skin. It would be nice to think that no-one was racially or ethnically prejudiced anymore. The data in Figure 3.1 below suggest otherwise.

Just over 30% of the population state they are racially prejudiced – nearly one person in three. Given that prejudice, by definition, is logically nonsensical (i.e. claiming the ability to judge someone before you have even met them), this is an awful statistic – and that's before we even consider the often-terrible social and personal consequences flowing on from prejudice. The one ray of sunshine from this data is that prejudice appears to be less prevalent among the young; Gen X is about a third less prejudiced than their grandparents. The bad news is that, since the turn of the century, prejudice has increased nationally from under 25% to the current figure of over 30%. However, this increase needs to be understood in relation to specific occupational end educational categories. Figure 3.2 shows that while prejudice has decreased over the past 25 years among those in the professional/managerial occupational category, it has increased among those at the bottom end of the hierarchy. These conclusions are supported by the data relating specifically to education level (Figure 3.3).

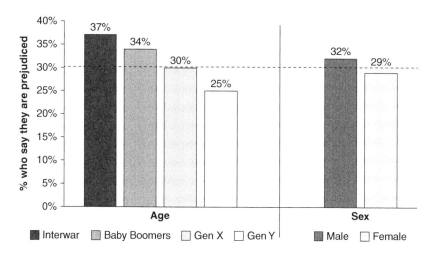

Figure 3.1 Current levels of racial prejudice – age and sex

Source: Taylor and Muir 2014, from BSA survey

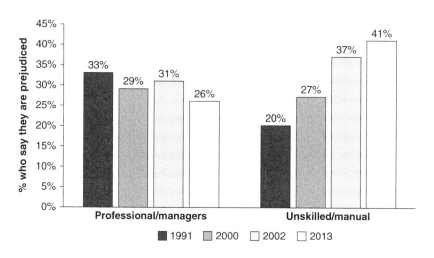

Figure 3.2 Changes to levels of racial prejudice – occupation

Source: Taylor and Muir 2014, from BSA survey

The main conclusions that can be drawn from these data are that prejudice is alive and well in the United Kingdom, and unfortunately it's currently getting worse; also, the most prejudiced among us appear to be older, less educated and less skilled males. However, by way of good news for those with a commitment to, and vested interest in, education, young people are less prejudiced than their parents, and the more educated you become, the less prejudiced you get.

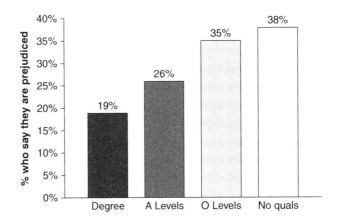

Figure 3.3 Changes to levels of racial prejudice – education
Source: Taylor and Muir 2014, from BSA survey

Individual Discrimination

If prejudice is one of the central precursors to discrimination, it does not follow that all ensuing discrimination necessarily takes the same form; indeed, there are a number of different forms of discrimination. The first, and probably the most familiar and easily identified type is straightforward, person-to-person discrimination; that moment when someone decides that the individual stood in front of them isn't going to get what they want, simply because of what they are. Myth #2 argues that this is no longer prevalent, and therefore, discrimination is all but a thing of the past. So has it gone away?

Not according to most research into contemporary discrimination, which often cites some pertinent, and disturbing, examples of the continued existence of direct individual discrimination, both overt and covert. This discrimination still occurs across the full range of human social activity, from employment to recreation, from our public spaces to our schools.

OVERT

This is where race/ethnicity is openly and directly used to deny an opportunity to an individual. Under these circumstances, there is no pretence made that any other factors may be in play. For example:

See my big brother's football team – if they found out he was a traveller, he would be dropped from it. (Pupil A, Glasgow) (Deuchar and Bhopal 2013, 743)

One Employer admitted to me during interview that if he employed me he will lose clients due to the feeling [about] people from Middle Eastern appearance after September 11 events. (Colic-Peisker and Tilbury 2007, 20)

This form of overt discrimination often spills over into the most direct and unpleasant forms of abuse and vilification:

> There was this aged man, I think he was drunk. He saw me on the bus and he said 'Hey you, Nigger, you black man. Do you have some weed on you?' I just looked away and everyone had their eye on me. He kept on asking and shouting at me. (Ghanaian student) (Brown and Jones 2013, 1011)

> The elderly lady was sitting opposite her niece and me. Her niece was a middle-aged woman, who was bitterly criticising Japan. I got on the train at Kings Cross; they got off at Newcastle. For three hours non-stop they went on about 'Yellow monkeys', 'Japs' and so on, despite being aware of my presence. I thought I had to say something. 'It is very unpleasant, so please stop it', I said. 'You know I am Japanese.' In fact, I said this twice. They shrugged their shoulders and stopped talking about the Japanese. But a few minutes later they started again. (Nishimuta 2008, 142)

These are two examples of the kind of discrimination that myth #2 is referring to. Perhaps it is on the decline; it would be nice to think so. However, there are other forms of discrimination that aren't so readily visible.

COVERT

Not all individual discrimination is so open and unashamed. Much of it is disguised behind non-returned phone calls, ignored curricula vitae, convenient excuses and silence.

> I went to an agency that was looking for someone with qualifications and experience like the ones I had. The receptionist had a hard time in accepting that fact that I was applying for that high position and, after asking me to wait while she talks to her supervisors, she came back to tell me the position was already filled even though the deadline was not until two weeks later. (Somalia man – GP and medical researcher) (Colic-Peisker and Tilbury 2007, 18)

> Dear Lara – Unfortunately we cannot accept braids – it is simply not part of the uniform and grooming requirements we get from our clients. If you are unable to take them out, unfortunately we won't be able to offer you any work. Kind regards, Sam. (letter to black university graduate) (Sherriff 2015)

This is still an individual form of discrimination, as it is still operating at a person-to-person level. It is highly unlikely that somehow policies were put in place to necessarily restrict access by racial/ethnic minorities; however, this is often the way it works out. So, as Burnett (2004a) points out, while there is clearly a need to address racism on the individual level, to focus on it too readily is to risk underestimating the pervasive effects of institutional and cultural discrimination.

Institutional Discrimination

At the risk of pre-judging the conclusions to be drawn while examining myth #3, if it turns out that some racial/ethnic minorities don't do as well in schools as white students, then this leads to one of only two possible conclusions. Either, they are naturally more stupid (and we've disposed of that possibility during myth #1), or there is something about the education system that subtly advances white students, while at the same time disadvantaging all the rest.

Of course, there are a number of possible reasons for this, reasons that are not directly about the relationship between racial and ethnic minorities and the education system, but are rather about some of the broader facts of our society. Given the continuing white dominance within cultural and economic life, and given the relationship between social class and educational success, it is hardly surprising that members of ethnic groups that often find themselves on the lower rungs of society consequently perform less well at school. More specifically, there are also forms of discrimination that directly relate to the way educational institutions operate. For example, school streaming according to 'ability' – often what is actually a misreading of cultural capital, as discussed in Chapter 1 – not only means in practice that a disproportionate number of working class and Black and Minority Ethnicity (BME) children are steered into the lowest sets, but also that those children can then be trapped within a cycle of low expectations (Rist 2000). Such schooling practices, which may well begin with perfectly well-meaning intentions, can therefore actually function as social filters, through which particular ethnic minorities end up with significantly reduced choices in life.

A further example involves the issue of testing. There exists a significant body of literature which shows – once again, often in spite of the best of intentions – that the large-scale, centralised examinations which make all education systems tick, can exhibit covert and pervasive forms of social bias (Jenks 1998). Exley (2010) provides a wonderfully simple example from Australia of the hidden cultural biases of standardised testing, using a question from the *Queensland Comparable Assessment Tasks* (QCATs). The question involves a seemingly benign written test about a little girl's lost puppy; the children from the Torres Strait island of Tortol did not do well on the QCATs, but did particularly badly on this specific 'puppy' question. Exley shows that, at almost every level, the story makes no sense to the islanders: first, puppies aren't kept as pets at all; also, puppies aren't fenced in, so the notion of being 'lost' is incomprehensible, particularly on a relatively small island; and working dogs, not puppies, become companions of boys nearing puberty; and crucially, young girls simply do not own dogs within Tortol culture. So no wonder the islanders struggled on the question; they couldn't understand it, let alone write creatively about it.

Of course, similar – and far more subtle and hence hard to spot – versions of this argument can readily exist for most racial and ethnic minorities within British education. Most of those who write the test questions are likely to have their origins within the dominant white, middle-class British culture. However, this is not the only way in which cultural difference can affect the outcome of high-stakes testing.

> Culture is not merely a body of knowledge and skills. It is also a set of strategies for dealing with the unknown and with tasks that seem difficult. Culture can affect people's willingness to think about unfamiliar questions, their strategies for seeking answers that are not obvious, their motivation to persist in the face of frustration, their confidence that such persistence will be rewarded, and their interest in figuring out what the tester thinks is the right answer. (Jenks 1998, 69)

It is important to realise that there is no 'perfect test' out there that succeeds in including all cultural groups equally. What we end up with is an unspoken privileging of the white, middle-class majority (see myth #4), and often a subtle, and not so subtle, institutional discrimination occurring against all those who do not share this background.

Cultural Discrimination

One final form of discrimination merits a mention. When looking specifically at issues of racial discrimination, whether individual or institutional, the essential point of reference has always been the notion of race itself – obviously. However, the goal-posts seem to have moved somewhat, and it is increasingly rare to witness race as constituting the focus of discriminatory discourse. That discrimination now appears to be cut from the fabric of culture instead.

As Burnett (2004a) points out, the familiar phrase, 'I'm not racist, but... ' is no longer generally followed by the individual outlining some spurious argument about why a particular racial grouping is less physically/intellectually/morally worthy than their own, rather it is now almost always followed by some measure of that group's lack of *cultural* worth. That is, those with an interest in doing so no longer point at the colour of someone's skin to explain why they don't fit in here, instead they point to the fact that they still have arranged marriages, or that they cover their heads in a veil.

> What is important is that although race remains the primary signifier of difference, the notion of difference and associated claims of incompatibility are now expressed in cultural and, increasingly, religious terms. (Burnett 2004a, 106)

So of course, we're largely still talking about the same people – pick your minority – it's just that we've found a new rationale to justify our discrimination.

Myth #3 *Educational Outcomes Are Unaffected by Race or Ethnicity*

Haven't we been through this before with the issue of social Class in Chapter 1? So maybe there's still some discrimination around, even if the really obvious stuff isn't as common as it used to be, but this doesn't necessarily mean that the education system doesn't do its job and educate all British kids equally. In the end, it doesn't matter what your racial or ethnic background is, it just matters how smart you are.

This doesn't need to be a particularly long section. The evidence is out there for those who wish to look. Just as the game appears to be stacked in favour of those from higher social classes, so too does the game favour white people – people who are unequivocally part of the dominant British culture. After all, as Welch (2010) rightly observes, the hidden curriculum of the school still succeeds in perpetuating mono-cultural values and practices, which in turn significantly benefits those from that culture.

Ethnicity and Educational Outcomes

The issue of teaching students of a wide variety of ethnic backgrounds is just one of the factors that make the profession both complicated, and yet rewarding. While notions of 'good' teaching are open to almost endless debate, most commentators would probably agree that an ideal school teacher in a multi-cultural environment would seek to organise a welcoming and pastoral classroom, foster a wide range of important student attributes, develop a full complement of relevant curricular skills, tailor their teaching with regard to cultural differences and differences in learning styles – while all the while keeping a wary eye out for racism and stereotyping. And none of these is, by any means, necessarily an easy task.

Even so, if all educational professionals were able to structure their teaching according to principles and practices like these – and most teachers across the country try as hard as they can, every day, to get it right – the evidence still suggests that our education system would struggle to produce equitable outcomes. Figure 3.4 shows, in quite a straightforward manner, that educational outcomes are clearly affected by race/ethnicity. The evidence suggests that white students do better at every single stage of the education process, from early primary school to university graduation, than do their black peers.

To reiterate, it is important to remember that we have already disposed of the possibility that this might be the outcome of 'natural' differences in ability between 'racial' groupings. Such groupings have absolutely no ontological validity, and they certainly don't have different levels of intellectual ability.

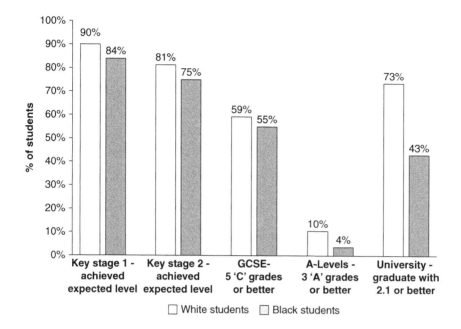

Figure 3.4 Educational outcomes by ethnicity (2011/2012)
Sources: Department for Education 2011, 2012a, 2013c, 2014a; Equality Challenge Unit 2012

Unfortunately, this type of differential outcome is not limited to academic results. Figure 3.5 provides further evidence that race/ethnicity has a significant role to play in shaping how various aspects of the internal machinery of the school are deployed, and from there, what kinds of outcomes can be expected. The figure demonstrates that black students – both African and Caribbean – are far more likely to be excluded from schools, than are equivalent white or Asian students.

The point here is that if educational outcomes, whether academic or disciplinary, are genuinely unaffected by the colour of your skin or your ethnic background, as myth #3 suggests, then Figure 3.5 would be flat, as would each element of Figure 3.4. However, just as race and ethnicity have a significant role to play in who does well at school, they also appear to have a role to play in determining who is likely to get kicked out.

The question now is, why do these differences occur, differences that affect both academic and disciplinary outcomes? Rhamie (2014) suggests that, in addition to broader structural issues about disadvantage and access, which apply not only to black students but also to those from low socio-economic backgrounds, the evidence suggests that teachers have an important role to play in the educational disadvantaging of black students. It has been argued that, in the vast majority of cases, this is not a function of overt and deliberate discrimination by teachers, rather it is as a result of

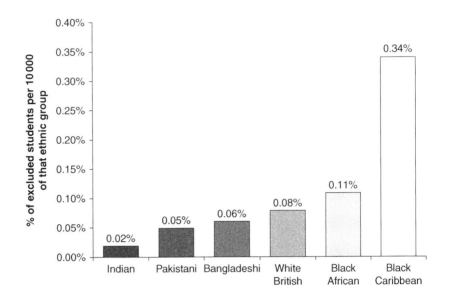

Figure 3.5 School exclusion by ethnicity (2009/2010)
Source: The Poverty Site 2015

----

how teachers interact with, and respond to, black students within schooling contexts.

> Teachers have reported that they treat all pupils equally, but there were subtle and persistent differences in how they treated black pupils... Whereas this has historically been the case, what is becoming clear is that despite a plethora of past research in the area, current research is returning to the same fundamental themes of labelling, stereotyping and low teacher expectations. (Rhamie 2014, 55)

However, Gillborn (2008, 63) takes his assessment of the exclusion of black students one stage further, when he concludes that 'there is compelling evidence that the over-representation of African Caribbean students in exclusions is the result of harsher treatment by school, rather than simple differences in behaviour by students'.

It's important to point out that it's not all doom and gloom here. First, not all non-white groups are the same, having the same educational experiences and the same outcomes. For example, the data on Figure 3.4 are limited to a comparison between white and black students – in order to most simply and directly debunk the myth of race and education equality. Research suggests that while black, Pakistani and Roma/Traveller students may not do as well as white students, Chinese, Indian and Bangladeshi students actually do somewhat better (Department for Education 2012a, 2013c). The point here is that being a BME student is not some kind of educational prison sentence; it's far more complex than that.

Second, the research also suggests that some of the inequalities of outcome outlined above are in the process of improving. For example, at GCSE level, the gap between white and black students has narrowed by 3.3 percentage points since 2007/2008 (Department for Education 2013c). Similarly, since 2003/2004 overall exclusions have fallen by about 40%, and although black students are still over-represented within these statistics, arguably it's all heading in the right direction (The Poverty Site 2015).

Finally, the figure outlining black educational attainment levels is a significant oversimplification in another important way, and not just because it does not include other ethnic minorities. By having a grouping based solely upon racial/ethnic identity, i.e. 'black', this glosses over a range of other important variables, most notably those of social class and gender.

Intersectionality

It would make our job as social analysts so much easier if each of the three pillars of modernity – class, gender and race/ethnicity – could be understood and addressed in isolation. We have already addressed some of the more important effects of class and gender on education in Chapters 1 and 2; however, studying these factors independently is actually something of an explanatory artifice, as it is with race/ethnicity. There are no 'middle-class people' who don't also have a gender and a race/ethnicity. This is also true in reverse: all the issues of race and ethnicity discussed so far in this chapter are mediated in various ways by social class and gender.

For example, Figure 3.4 in this chapter has shown how black students are consistently disadvantaged throughout the schooling system, from primary school to graduation from university, as compared with white students. Who are these 'black students' and 'white students'? Certainly, the research suggests that they are not homogeneous groups. Chapter 1 of this book points out that social class has a huge role to play in educational success; given this fact, it is highly likely that middle-class black students are going to outperform working-class white students, and this is before gender is even brought into the picture – which makes it even more likely, given that when it comes to doing badly at school, no-one does it quite as well as white, working-class males (Wilson, Burgess and Briggs 2005).

In addition to this, the question 'Who are these black students?' requires answers that also speak to the issue of gender. Black Caribbean girls perform 12.5 percentage points better than their male counterparts (Department for Education 2012b). Likewise, when it comes to issues of school exclusion, black students may well be far more likely to be kicked out of school, but it needs to be noted that this figure relates primarily to boys, who are three times more likely to be excluded than equivalent girls. It is also worth noting that in the intersectionality of school exclusion, a disadvantaged black Caribbean boy with special educational needs, is 168 times more likely to be excluded from school than a regular middle-class white female (Office for the Children's Commissioner (OCC) 2012).

Importantly, the effects of social class, gender and race ethnicity can't simply be 'read off' in a simplistic and summative way. White middle-class male? That's +3 points for you; black, working-class female? That's –3 points for you, and so on – it's far more complex and context-bound than that. For instance, the effect of social class on educational achievement varies between different racial/ethnic groups. Whereas social class makes a major difference with respect to 'White British' and 'Irish' students' academic outcomes – i.e. white kids at private schools do significantly better than white kids at state schools – it makes far less difference for 'Chinese' students whatever their background is, or what kind of school they go to (Stevens and Crozier 2014).

Probably the best example for the complexity of these overlapping forms of potential disadvantage concerns the very first specific deployment of the notion of intersectionality: the work of Crenshaw (1991) on race and gender within the US criminal justice system. She notes that, when it comes to being black, and it comes to being female, the criminal justice system places both those groups at a comprehensive disadvantage. However, when it comes to being black *and* female, *and* the issue is rape, then these two forms of disadvantage don't add up to –2, they add up to –22. That is, this they act as *compounding* forms of disadvantage.

> The racism and sexism written into the social construction of rape are merely contemporary manifestations of rape narratives emanating from when race and sex hierarchies were more explicitly policed ... A study of rape dispositions in Dallas, for example, showed that the average prison term for a man convicted of raping a black woman was two years, as compared to five years for the rape of a Latina and ten years for the rape of an Anglo woman. A related issue is that fact that African American victims of rape are less likely to be believed. (Crenshaw 1991, 1268–9)

Immigrants and Refugees

It is probably timely for a very brief mention of educational outcomes for immigrant and refugee children. Probably needless to say, some sections of the media have painted a dire picture of the educational consequences of their arrival ('Mass migration is a threat to our children's education' – *Daily Express* 2015), speculating that 1600 new schools will be needed over the next decade to cope with the 'vast influx'. These newcomers compromise our 'sacred duty' of providing 'access to a high standard of education'. Curse those migrants and refugees!

The hard evidence suggests otherwise. Coughlan (2015), citing OECD statistics, notes that there is no link between the numbers of migrant children and the performance of the host school systems – including the UK. Indeed, migrants were more likely to be an 'asset than a liability' for school standards. Geay, McNally and Telhaj (2012) found that recent arrivals, most specifically from Polish backgrounds in this case, did not hold back their British peers in reading and writing, and in fact they had their results boosted in maths. They also point out that first- and second-generation immigrants tend to be better educated than the native population, perhaps due to the elevated education levels of their parents, which can eventually compensate for any early language difficulties.

Refugees can present a somewhat different picture. Those refugees from conflict areas, particularly from Africa, continue to struggle in our education system. Not surprising really, given that many of them may have lived in refugee camps for years, they may have had next to no formal education at all, they may be illiterate in their own language never mind English, and they may have witnessed terrible events that no-one should ever have to see, let alone children. The complexity of this issue is compounded by the age at which the refugee enters the schooling system. If they are young, there are reasons to be positive; if they are older, their prognosis within formal education can often be bleak.

Myth #4 *There is a 'Black and Minority Ethnicity' (BME) Problem' in British Education*

Many BME students struggle in our education system. We've tried our hardest to deal with this issue, but in the final analysis their cultures are often just too different from ours. They often seem to lack whatever it is that enables ordinary kids to do well in school. These students have a problem, and there doesn't really appear to be a satisfactory solution.

It's hard to know where to start with this myth. There are so many assumptions, generalisations and misconceptions built into the statement above, that it needs to be unpacked piece by piece in order to find some solid ground to build upon. Unfortunately, it could be argued that a number of existing sociological approaches to race/ethnicity in education contain many of these same errors, errors similar to those we've already seen in the preceding chapters on Social Class and Gender. For example, there is the homogenisation of cultures, the prevalence of simple binaries, a zero-sum understanding of power, and an unshakable belief in their own objectivity. It will be argued here that a more nuanced understanding of race/ethnicity in education can open up a range of new and productive possibilities.

In terms of a very preliminary analysis, there are four issues and presuppositions inherent within the myth outlined above that immediately warrant discussion: (1) the belief that the 'problem' is self-evident, and there's a single way of understanding it; (2) the understanding that 'they' are somehow outsiders to 'our' education system; (3) the notion that many BME children fail in the education system because of some kind of cultural 'deficit'; and (4) the understanding of the dominant white culture as neutral in the entire process of 'problem' creation.

(1) Theoretical Approaches to Race/Ethnicity and Education

It is important to realise that there isn't just one conceptual way of approaching issues relating to race/ethnicity and education. Just as theoretical understandings of gender have evolved through successive waves, as discussed in Chapter 2, so too have different conceptual tools been brought to bear on this particular educational area. There are several reasons for this. First, the field itself is constantly shifting. Tomlinson (2008) charts the changing terrain for race and education within the UK from the 1960s onwards, from the early assimilationist ideologies regarding the importing of willing labourers for low-level jobs, through an increasing acceptance of cultural pluralism in the early 1980s and the rise of a less compliant generation of young immigrants wanting access to all levels of UK society, to contemporary concerns over religion and the full establishment of a multi-ethnic society. Each of these shifts in the social fabric of the nation has reorganized – to some degree – how the issue of race/ethnicity and education might be best understood.

Second, as with all research areas, different theoretical understandings of the central issues have held sway at different times. Stevens and Crozier (2014) point to a series of consecutive shifts in the academic landscape, arguing that research had initially been dominated by psychological models, which sought to explain disparate educational outcomes in terms of cognitive differences, and the 'deficits' that some BME cultural groups innately possess – the significant flaws with this approach will be discussed shortly. From this point onwards, the focus shifted to a more sociological approach, one that emphasised social background characteristics, which then in turn gave way to a greater investigation of the role of perceived ability in the construction of educational inequality, such as streaming and the concomitant development of anti-school cultures. The rise of the 'new sociology of education', coupled with the impact of feminism, then turned the focus to the role of school processes within the complexities of social reproduction. Most recently, conceptual frameworks such as Critical Race Theory, and more postmodern approaches, now seek to chart the field. It is important to note that none of these are unequivocally the 'right' way to approach the issue, although it is probably fair to say that some of them, particularly the earliest frameworks, are now deemed to be pretty much unequivocally 'wrong'.

Finally, different questions are often being asked of the relationship between race/ethnicity and education. For example, if the question concerns the demographics of educational disadvantage – as this chapter has, in part – then Stevens and Crozier (2014) point to the utility of the positivist, largely quantitative 'Political Arithmetic' tradition within educational research. However, if the question concerns how BME students experience specific forms of disadvantage within schooling environments, the 'Racism and Racial Discrimination' tradition is probably more useful. An important issue here is that this tradition is committed to not simply charting the existence of racial/ethnic inequality, it ties these inequalities to specific forms of individual, institutional and cultural discrimination, and from there adopts an overtly anti-racist political research agenda (Crozier 2014). Questions may also concern race/ethnicity and school effectiveness, or culture and education outcomes, or school markets. Each has the potential to generate a different approach to the problem.

(2) Us vs Them

Many discussions of the issues surrounding BME student education seem to operate from within a familiar modernist binary. First of all there is the unspoken 'us', normally constituted as the white, middle-class owners of the system: the writers of the curriculum, the teachers of the knowledge, the most familiar faces in the classroom. Those who consider themselves part of 'us' not only feel at home in the system, they *are* the system. It is this reasoning that validates the statement: 'BME students often struggle in *our* education system'.

In contrast to this of course, having first homogenised 'non-us' into various conceptually manageable pieces – blacks, Asians, Travellers – we can then roll them all together into a single grouping: 'them' – the other, social and cultural outsiders, visitors to our sensible system from a different planet. Importantly, much as we may try to integrate 'them' into 'our' classroom – and certainly, they are more than welcome there – this doesn't alter the fundamental fact, that 'we' have organised the life-world of the classroom in our own image; they are just guests within it, and have to make do the best they can. This is a familiar situation that any number of 'othered' groups find themselves in.

There are any number of issues worthy of discussion here, however we will only address two of them: the first, which will be discussed at length in Chapter 13, concerns the notion of *integration*. Within the integrated classroom, students who lie outside the mainstream, (whether culturally, physically, sexually or linguistically) are brought inside the big tent, and they are taught how to fit in (Uditsky 1993). We know we have succeeded when they become just like us. Arguably a far more preferable approach to dealing with difference involves the notion of *inclusion*. Within the inclusive classroom, the cultures and abilities of all students are valued equally, and the variations they bring with them are incorporated into the fabric of the learning environment (Topping and Maloney 2005). One culture does not exert its hegemony over all the others, such that they can either march in step, or sit at the back of the class – or sit somewhere else altogether (Slee 2011). An inclusive classroom tries very hard to do away with 'us' and 'them', and focus on working towards a 'we'. Given the many covert and subliminal contexts within which the 'we/them' binary operates, this has not proved to be an easy task.

The second is more conceptually complex. Hall (1992) notes that it is no longer possible to operate according to simplistic and essentialist notions of race and ethnicity, or more specifically, a singular 'black' subject position that can somehow operate in opposition to dominant white identities.

> What is at issue here is the recognition of the extraordinary diversity of subject positions, social experiences and cultural identities which compose the category of 'black'; that is, the recognition that 'black' is essentially a politically and culturally *constructed* category, which cannot be grounded in a set of fixed trans-cultural or transcendental racial categories and which therefore has no guarantee in nature. (Hall (1992, 443)

The point here is that not only is the 'us' vs 'them' binary an oversimplification of epic proportions, but also that even once BME students have been broken down into various more appropriate cultural categories, these categories themselves – such as 'black' – no longer represent any kind of coherent subject position.

(3) The Deficit Model of Education

As a continuation of the arguments above, having artificially rolled all Blacks, for example, into a single ball and labelled it 'them', we quickly note that 'they' aren't doing too well within our education system. The answer to this is simple: there's something wrong with them. This is a very common argument, and it is normally called the *Deficit Model* of educational failure. The answer to why working-class students don't do as well as their middle-class counterparts is often to look at working-class lifestyles, language, and ways of learning, and to contend that they are somehow not as good. The same happens with some racial/ethnic groups. Once we believe in the objectively neutral character of our education system, those who fail to succeed there must shoulder the burden of responsibility for that failure themselves – BME students included. It's a meritocracy, after all.

Actually, this seems like a pretty good example of *victim-blaming*, discussed in the introduction to this chapter. We set up a school with a whole series of subtle cultural biases ingrained within it, and when other cultures fail to do particularly well there, we hold them responsible. That is, we rarely think to examine the various components of the school that might pre-determine this failure: an irrelevant curriculum, inappropriate instructional practices, unsuitable disciplinary codes and authority structures, out-of-place organisational arrangements, the list goes on.

The contention that specific cultures or students – if we really want to head back to the discredited racial theories of myth #1 – lack what it takes to fit into mainstream schools is bunk (Valencia 1997). If some BME students struggle to find a place for themselves within our schooling system, the issue doesn't pivot upon what they 'lack', or what's 'wrong' with them. The debates need to focus around issues of difference, not absence.

(4) White Race Privilege

The great thing about the deficit model – at least, the great thing for those who are part of the dominant culture – is that it absolves the rest of us, and the education system we created, from any real responsibility for the 'BME problem'. As discussed, this understanding is based upon an erroneous belief in the cultural neutrality of our schools. Failure is deemed to be, first and last, an individual matter, and if a BME student fails, maybe they should take a good long look in the mirror.

However, the issue of erroneous neutrality extends beyond the boundary of the school, into the very essence of how those members of the dominant, white culture see themselves. There is a significant body of literature concerning *White Race Privilege*, which examines 'whiteness', and its place – or rather, its invisibility – within debates over race. For most whites, race is something that other peoples have: black people, yellow people, brown people, red people. To be white is to not have to regard race as an issue (Kendall 2006).

However, there's more to it than that. Not only is whiteness *not* neutral, it also brings with it some very real advantages. McIntosh (1997, 291) contends that being white is like owning 'an invisible weightless knapsack of special provisions, assurances, tools, maps, guides, codebooks, passports, visas, clothes, compass, emergency gear and blank cheques'. As a general rule, white people don't have to worry about their race limiting access to important resources, or whether their race will be depicted positively in the media, or whether their children will face discrimination on the basis of their race.

> White people need not wonder, for example, if their achievements (a job, an award, a scholarship) will be seen as happening because of their race; they need not worry that if they fail, their failure will be used to judge their race. Whiteness just is; no white person is seen as representing their race. Indeed, most white people do not even think of themselves as raced subjects. (Anderson 2003, 26)

Proponents of *White Race Privilege* suggest that white kids enter schools with a thousand invisible little advantages under their belt, and not just in the big issues concerning curriculum content and dominant teaching styles, but also all the little ones: assumptions about how well they'll do, language codes, shared history, familiarity, and the confidence born of insider status. To somehow suggest that non-whites are given social or educational advantages, as can often be read in the more conservative newspapers and other domains of shared ignorance, is to suffer from one of the most pernicious forms of colour blindness: the inability to see what whiteness means to those who have it (Rosenberg 2004).

So, as long as those in the dominant culture continue to regard themselves, and the institutions they create, as simply passive bystanders to the unsatisfactory relationship between many BME students and our schools, nothing much is ever really going to change. This isn't about finding someone to blame; it's about finding a way forward.

Conclusion

It would appear then that none of the myths outlined here have much basis in fact at all. First, humanity is not naturally divided into separate races. Any divisions we have made between peoples are almost entirely social in origin. Unfortunately, just because we now know race isn't real, doesn't mean that its effects have all gone away. The notion of race somehow still seems to haunt our popular discourse and imagination. That's not good.

Second, racial and ethnic discrimination hasn't gone away either. Even though there are some grounds for supposing that the worst elements of individual racism are becoming more of a rarity, institutional and cultural discrimination are still part of the landscape. Unfortunately, these are often significantly more difficult to spot, although being aware of their existence is the first step in the process of doing something about it.

Third, educational outcomes are most certainly affected by racial and ethnic background. Although some ethnic minorities actually do better in school than those from the dominant white background, many also do significantly worse. This is especially the case for those who came here as refugees, and the later they came, the more they will struggle.

Finally, to say there is a 'BME problem' within our schools is to consent to placing blame where it doesn't belong. Many BME children don't succeed in the same numbers as white children, largely due to the structure of our education system, the way that system is policed, the way knowledge is organised and delivered, and the measures that are used to assess success. These reduced rates of success cannot be simply accounted for by some imagined 'deficit', either in terms of intellect or culture.

Of the three topics covered in the first section of this book, issues raised by this chapter on race/ethnicity perhaps lend themselves to the greatest degree of optimism. Certainly, there are legitimate concerns that the white middle-class is slowly and quietly withdrawing from schools with high BME student numbers, resulting in a situation where – as a number of commentators have stated – we are 'sleepwalking towards segregation'. However, for those invested in a career within the education system, most of us would rightly think that at the heart of racial and ethnic discrimination, and the educational inequalities that flow from it, lies ignorance. And if anyone's in a position to do something about that, it's teachers.

PART **II**

THE FOUNDATIONS OF
AN ALTERNATIVE
APPROACH: EDUCATION
AND GOVERNANCE

Making the move from modern to postmodern forms of social analysis is not the only option open to those unhappy with the shortcomings of the traditional social class/gender/race approach. It is possible to step out of this paradigm, and to address mass education, and society in general, from another direction altogether. Part II will explore the possibilities associated with this alternative direction. Not only does this alternative approach ask different questions, it also asks them about largely different elements of the social fabric, and it underpins its ideas within entirely different domain assumptions.

The theories outlined in Part I – even those more clearly postmodern in orientation – tend to ask questions about who has what, and who is exercising power over whom, while focusing primarily upon issues of disadvantage and inequality. This model is built upon a coercive understanding of power, one that describes struggles over resources and access, one which notes who wins and who loses, and one which positions mass education as ground zero in the ongoing battles between classes, genders and races,

The approach taken in Part II is very different. Largely based upon the work of Foucault, the questions it asks focus more upon the ways in which institution like the school produce particular kinds of individuals, both as objects of knowledge, and as objects of governance. Power is no longer regarded as necessarily coercive; rather it is usually productive; it brings new ways of understanding, and new identities, into being. As will be discussed in Chapter 4, governance is about how categories of difference are created and managed; it is about the strategies through which particular populations are normalised; it is about 'the conduct of conduct'. According to this logic, mass education is not principally about the social reproduction of advantage and disadvantage; it is about distributing and classifying individuals for the purposes of social administration.

Chapter 4 – *Governance* – addresses the central premise of the part, that mass education has a crucial role to play in managing the conduct of the population. It questions the common-sense assertions that individuality is the same now as it was 300 years ago; that schools have nothing to do with social administration, being there solely for educational purposes; and that the internal structure of the school – its organisation of space and time – isn't really that relevant.

Chapter 5 – *Subjectivity* – investigates the rise of psychology, and its role in the governance of subjectivity. It questions the view that psychology is solely about uncovering the mysteries of the human mind; that the human mind remains largely ungoverned; and that the categories of difference we now take for granted – such as ADHD – were simply uncovered by psychology, and the discipline itself had no role in its emergence

Chapter 6 – *Pre-Adulthood* – examines the ways in which various categories of pre-adulthood have been organised, and the role they play in governance. It questions the belief that categories such as 'childhood' and 'youth' exist as natural stages of life; that these categories have nothing to do with contemporary social governance; and that these categories have natural characteristics, such as 'innocence', that determine how those placed in these categories will necessarily behave.

Chapter 7 – *Big Data* – addresses the advent of giant data sets, and the consequences of this for governance. The chapter investigates the size and utility of these data sets, and examines some of the areas they are currently affecting; it investigates how such large amounts of data are changing our education system; and it looks in particular at standardised testing.

The central point of this approach – certainly in the context of a book on education – is to show that contemporary mechanisms of rule are not really about the authority of 'the State', or the instilling of unquestioning obedience to the law, or figuring out who has power and who does not. Rather, we are ruled (and rule ourselves), in large part, through the techniques of governance made possible through institutions such as the modern school.

GOVERNANCE

4

It will be argued here that the modern school isn't just about 'education' in some abstract, humanist sort of way. Rather, it will be contended that schools have an essential role to play in how we govern our society. It is tempting to think that the process of teaching children has always been pretty much the same, and that mass schooling emerged as a result of greater concern for the well-being of the young. The evidence paints a somewhat different picture, a picture wherein mass schooling formed a crucial component of a new form of social regulation, one based upon an increasing focus on individuality, one where the school subtly conforms to the requirements of the State, and one where the disciplinary management of the population is made possible through continual surveillance, and through the close regulation of space, time and conduct.

Myth #1 Society has always been simply a collection of individuals. *'Whether 300 years ago, or in the present day, we have always regarded ourselves as individuals, part of a population, but each of us different in thousands of ways'.* Modern governance – and indeed individuality itself – really only became thinkable when we changed from being a mob into a population, a change that came about as a result of new techniques of information gathering, allowing for the construction of endless new categories of difference. Importantly, with each new category, came new possibilities of intervention and regulation.

Myth #2 Schools are primarily about education, not regulation. *'Schools aren't about the exercise of power, or about population control, they are simply about giving children an education'.* With the demise of sovereign power throughout the eighteenth century, liberal forms of governance sought less intrusive ways to regulate the population. One of the most effective strategies was to 'govern at a distance' through relays like the mass school. All the required capacities could be inculcated into the population without the Government seeming to be involved.

Myth #3 The structure of the school isn't really that important to the education process. *'It doesn't matter where we educate our students, or how, it's just the knowledge that counts; the organisation of the school is ultimately irrelevant'.* The mass school is an example of a disciplinary society, a society based upon continual surveillance, the close regulation of space and time, and the detailed management of behaviour. This new institutional logic, with its three-fold process of individuation, differentiation and normalisation, soon proved so successful that it spilled out of the school ground, and came to organise society in general.

Introduction

This chapter is, first and foremost, about the history of mass education: what schools used to be like, how the modern school arose, why it emerged at the time it did and why it took its current familiar, all-pervasive form. However, the interesting issue here isn't really a curiosity concerning how schools once were – fascinating though that might be – rather the central purpose is to better explain why things now are as they are. This approach has often been referred to as writing a *history of the present* (Foucault 1977, 31), a method that will, in this instance, not only tell us a great deal about how our education system works, it will also go a long way towards explaining some of the most important ways in which our society is governed.

Two Foundational Historical Myths Regarding Education

This chapter, like all others in this book, is based around a number of commonly held myths about a given topic area within education, in this case, the rise of the modern school. Before addressing these myths, two preliminary sub-myths will be addressed in passing here in the introduction. These do not warrant the status of 'full myth', as debunking them doesn't represent much of a challenge; in truth, they operate more at a subliminal level, and a brief trip through virtually any book on the history of education would amply demonstrate their invalidity. Also, the three myths warranting a section each in this chapter will shed a far more valuable light on issues of contemporary social governance.

(1) A CLASSROOM IS A CLASSROOM, IRRESPECTIVE OF WHEN AND WHERE

It is frequently assumed that teaching is a relatively unproblematic activity: one person has some knowledge – the teacher – and a small group of generally younger people – the pupils – gather around them to acquire that knowledge. It is also assumed that this process is, with a few minor historical and cultural provisos, pretty much universal. The contemporary school is simply an effective, modernised extension of the same story. Of course we should organise our learning in the way we do, with the emphasis on teacher–pupil interaction, formalised learning spaces, a graded broadly based curriculum, timetables of activities, various forms of assessment, and a clear hierarchy of authority. These features of the education system merely reflect the fact that this is self-evidently the best system available. After all, how else could education possibly be organised?

The answer to this question is: in many, many different ways. In the centuries leading up to the establishment of the mass education system, what was understood as 'schooling' often operated according to very different systems of reasoning, social purposes, accessibility, spatial arrangements and practices of instruction (Maynes 1985). For example, there is nothing fixed or inevitable about the desirability of children receiving a broadly based general education; schooling has often only been about religious knowledge, or specific skill training. Equally, most people, for most of Western history, didn't get to go to school at all; access to education was often a direct function of social status. Even the modern Western school is not as clear-cut and unproblematic an institution as it might first appear. Just what is the modern school? Is the school some kind of blanket attempt to introduce important principles of social equality? Is it a mechanism for allowing children to reach their 'full potential' – whatever that means – or to achieve intellectual enlightenment? Or is none of this accurate? After all, in his excellent text *Rethinking the School*, Hunter (1994) suggests that, in reality, the contemporary mass school is simply a piecemeal, improvised device that emerged out of education's previous social functions of pastoral care and citizen-building.

Likewise, the notion of 'the teacher' and of the act of 'teaching' has had very different meanings in the past to its current connotation (Verger 2003). For example, teachers haven't always sat at the front of the class, keeping an eye on their pupils, indeed in the past much of the actual instruction was done by the older children. This 'monitorial' method permitted far larger numbers of children to be taught by the same number of teachers: the teachers instructed the older children, who then acted as relays to pass that instruction on to the younger pupils, as well as acting as disciplinary agents within the classroom (Jones and Williamson 1979). As will be discussed shortly, significant elements of such earlier hierarchical arrangements remain within our current education system. In addition to this, and in contrast to today, teaching itself wasn't even regarded as a profession until relatively recently; even in the late nineteenth century, little was really expected of teachers. It was only with the 1902 Education Act that the move began towards college and university educated teachers, finally signalling the end for the old pupil–teacher system (Robinson 2006).

The point here is that there is nothing natural about our education system. There isn't a *teleology* – an inevitable, underlying purpose – that has shaped the way we've chosen to organise our schools. Our system of mass education developed the way it did, not because it unequivocally represents the best way to educate, but because of the historically contingent social, cultural and governmental forces that shaped it, forces that will be discussed at length in this chapter

(2) MASS SCHOOLING AND THE CIVILISED SOCIETY

Preliminary myth #2 involves probably the most frequently told story charting the rise of mass schooling. This story normally centres around the post-Enlightenment social changes of the late eighteenth and early nineteenth centuries, and details how society slowly became more caring and more humane, and how we all decided that rather than simply being fodder for the mills, all children – including those from the working classes – had the right to an education. The more 'civilised' we became, the more we pushed back the school leaving age, until we eventually developed schools that clearly reflected the values and ambitions of the wider community.

Once again, there is no teleology here; instead it will be argued that our schooling system did not emerge as an inevitable by-product of our increasingly civilised society, rather the structure of the modern school came about due to the possibilities it gave for more effective social governance, with its associated rationales of a ranked and differentiated population, mass literacy and numeracy, and the productive needs of a disciplined national workforce. Indeed, the evidence suggests that far from schools coming to reflect the logic of the wider 'civilised' society, in many ways society came to reflect the logic of the school. That is, the forms of disciplinary organisation that developed inside the new institutions of the early nineteenth century, such as the mass school – timetables, record-keeping, surveillance – spilled out into the general management of the population, such that they now constitute fundamental foundations of our broader society.

This chapter will seek to address these issues by asking the following questions. Why is schooling organised in the way that it is? Or rather, what were some of the historical circumstances that led to the shaping of what constitutes a 'normal' education? Furthermore; why is the notion of 'discipline' so central to this? We can answer these questions by focusing on how various disciplinary practices came to constitute a central strategy, not only for the running of schools, but also for the governance of society itself.

A Different Perspective on Governance

If we look into the past, it is often easiest to imagine it populated with individuals who understood themselves in pretty much the same way as we do now. While we in the twenty-first century now live longer, have different kinds of houses and clothes, do different jobs, eat different foods, and entertain ourselves differently from our medieval forebears, surely the more crucial elements of individual consciousness have remained constant? This would include how we understand ourselves as autonomous beings, and our relations to, and differences from, other people. Surely they are the same? Well . . . very probably not.

It has been argued that, over the past 200 years, there have been a number of significant changes in the way in which society is governed. These changes have not only affected how schools sought to educate their pupils, but also actually reorganised the way in which people conceptualise who and what they are, as individuals. At the risk of oversimplification, three interrelated issues will be addressed here as being of greatest significance to the formation of contemporary mass schooling.

THE POPULATION

The first myth in this chapter involves the invention of the notion of a 'population', and the belief that we have always been the kinds of individuals we are today. It will be argued that we haven't always been the organised, regimented and knowable bunch of people that we now see around us. Most of us know the population of the country, as well as the city/town we live in, give or take a few thousand; most of us would know our approximate life expectancy, based upon our sex, occupation and lifestyle; we would also generally know the various risk-factors for threats like skin cancer, HIV/AIDS and heart attack. However, this was not always the case. It was only a couple of hundred years ago when we didn't know much about ourselves at all, either as individuals or as part of a society.

It all started to change towards the end of the eighteenth century. A new set of processes of governance started whereby the social body was transformed from an undifferentiated 'mob', into a workable and more readily governable 'population'. This population was comprised of differentiated individuals, each with increasingly discernable capacities and characteristics. Separating people out in this manner radically increased the possibilities of targeted, effective governance. Importantly, for the purposes of this book, much of this new social regulation was to take place within the new institutions of the mass school.

LIBERALISM

The second myth concerns the purpose of schooling, and the contention that it is all about 'education', in the sense of some kind of intrinsic personal growth. Sure, there may be some governance involved, but that's just the price we pay in order to get the best out of our children. It will be argued instead that the *central* role of schooling is that of governance, and that our schooling system came to be seen as the perfect vehicle for the effective production of particular types of citizen.

The crucial change here relates to rise of liberalism. The Enlightenment signalled the beginning of the end of the absolute power of the monarch, and this triggered a series of debates about the extent of the legitimate power of the state. Liberal philosophy held that the State ought to be involved in issues such as law enforcement and international affairs, but stay out of, for example, the running of the marketplace and the raising of children. However, it was soon decided that producing the next generation of citizens was far too important to be left to chance, and the State began to involve itself in the process 'at a distance', once again most notably through the new medium of the mass school.

THE MODERN INSTITUTION

The third myth involves the birth of the modern institution. Surely the structure of the school – the internal architectural arrangements, the organisation of the curriculum, the management of the classrooms – doesn't matter that much? Surely, it's what we teach the children that matters? We've always had schools; whatever their form, they are simply the places in which education occurs. It doesn't make any sense to suggest that the design of the school is somehow crucial to how modern education functions.

Actually, it does. While schools, prisons and hospitals obviously weren't invented at the end of the eighteenth century, their forms were radically transformed, and all according to the same underpinning reasoning. As such, new school designs meant that pupils could be placed under constant surveillance, and hence their conduct more closely and effectively governed; indeed, the emphasis shifted from governance to self-governance. Within such institutions, through the threefold processes of individuation, differentiation and normalisation, and through a pervasive regimen of disciplinary management, acceptable citizens could be shaped and regulated.

In summary, the taken-for-granted effects of each of these three historical changes – the rise of the notion of 'the population', the advent of liberalism and the birth of the modern school – can be best addressed through an analysis of three commonsense assumptions about the relationship between governance, citizenship and schooling. The three myths are as follows.

Myth #1 Society has always been simply a collection of individuals.

Myth #2 Schools are primarily about education, not regulation.

Myth #3 The structure of the school isn't really that important to the education process.

Myth #1 *Society Has Always Been Simply a Collection of Individuals*

People are just people, irrespective of when they were born. There's no real differ-ence between a person from 300 years ago, and someone who lives now. Physically we're the same, mentally we're the same, and in terms of outlook, we probably see the world in pretty much the same way. We may now drive cars, watch TV and know the world is a sphere, but ultimately we're all simply individuals trying to find out about ourselves.

Most of us know a great deal about the society in which we live – how many of us there are, what part of the country the majority of us inhabit, what kinds of things we do, how long most of us live – and we take that kind of knowledge for granted. Importantly, such knowledge not only informs us about our com-munity, it informs us about ourselves. We know where we stand in relation to others: we know if we are smarter than national averages, or heavier, or wealthier, or drink more.

Such knowledge, however, has not always been available. In Europe, prior to the nineteenth century, the vast majority of the people, including those who ruled, would have known very little about the demographics of their social surroundings, quite simply because the mechanisms did not exist to accumulate the necessary information. We might then legitimately ask: how do you rule a country about which you know next to nothing? This is an interesting historical question, not least because it helps shed light on our past, but also because it goes to the heart of how we have come to govern.

A New Model of Rule

The philosopher and historian Foucault (1977) famously begins his book *Discipline and Punish: the Birth of the Prison*, with a comparison of the horrendously brutal execution of Damiens the Regicide in 1757 (the price for trying to kill King Louis XV), with an example of the exercise of power from only 80 years later – a set of rules from the House for Young Prisoners in Paris, rules structuring daily tasks according to tightly regimented subdivisions of time and conduct. Foucault is making a very clear point here: that within the space of only 80 years, something significant had changed about the way in which we govern.

Damiens' punishment served a very clear purpose. That is, by executing him with such ferocity, in front of thousands of people, the King was symbolically reinforcing his own authority in the clearest possible terms. Public execution had always served this function: *challenge the power of the sovereign, and this is what you get!*

However, with the decline in sovereign power during the eighteenth and nine-teenth centuries – along with the advent of a more complex, industrial society (among other reasons) – new ways of governing were sought. It would no longer be enough to simply execute a few people every now and again, to keep the rest of the mob in line; a new approach was needed, one based upon the acquisition of social information (Kay-Shuttleworth 1973). With this realisation came the first use of statistics in social governance; indeed, the word *statistics* comes from the German, meaning 'the science of state'.

This process began with the deployment of relatively modest devices, such as a simple national census, early versions of which enabled disparate organs of government to sketch out a preliminary map of some of the most important contours of community life. These contours included, for example, how many people lived in a particular country, how they were employed, where they lived and for how long. Then, as the nineteenth century progressed, more and more statistical information was gathered about almost every conceivable aspect of existence, what Hacking (1982) referred to as 'an avalanche of printed numbers'. With this knowledge developed the notion of a population, complete with 'inherent' characteristics, features and categories.

For instance, no longer were there just 'thieves', to be caught and publicly punished in the name of the sovereign. Sufficient data were gathered to break this category down into a large number of sub-categories, each of which could be addressed and managed in their own way, a process out of which developed the science of criminology. Likewise, the nebulous character of 'the pauper' began to be subdivided, giving way to a series of well-delimited categories based upon perceptions of their relative idleness ('good poor', 'bad poor', 'wilfully idle', 'involun-tarily unemployed') (Foucault 1984). Modern medicine also developed largely as a result of new forms of information gathering, recording and categorisation. New categories of illness were invented, burgeoning throughout the nineteenth century (and which still continue to burgeon), each more specific and targeted than the last (Wright and Treacher 1982).

Importantly, the school also became a fundamental site of social calculation. All children were now placed within the system of mass education, to be counted, numbered, and measured across an array of different axes – intellec-tual, physical, behavioural, and moral. The 'avalanche' of data produced by this ongoing measurement began to form the basis of the increasingly important and complex governmental identity: 'the modern child'. And just as with the 'thieves', 'paupers' and most of modern medicine, this evolving identity rapidly became divided into a plethora of sub-categories of child, which themselves were subject to subdivision, each of which could be targeted for intervention and management in different ways (Rose 1990). This will be discussed in greater detail in Chapter 6.

The Rise and Rise of Individuality

The important issue here is that people were no longer part of an unknown and unknowable mob. Instead, they had become part of a population, a new and pivotal phenomenon that was soon to replace the wealth of the sovereign as the central *raison d'être* of government. That is, prior to this time, government – the exercise of State authority – had, in a sense, been its own purpose, operating almost exclusively in the interests of the ruler. It now began to be directed at the population. This occurred both directly and indirectly, not simply in improving its conditions, but also in managing its habits, aspirations and interests. Government would therefore become 'the conduct of conduct' (Gordon 1991, 2).

One of the most significant side effects of the creation of a population, certainly for the purposes of this chapter, was the exponential growth in the notion of individuality. Prior to this time, individuality wasn't really that important. People tended to regard themselves, first and foremost, as members of particular communities. If *individuality* is the number of ways we know we differ from others in that community, prior to the advent of 'the population', people could barely be regarded as individuals at all. As Foucault states:

> For a long time ordinary individuality – the everyday individuality of everybody – remained below the threshold of description. To be looked at, observed, described in detail, followed from day to day by an uninterrupted writing was a privilege. (Foucault 1977, 191)

Foucault is making two points here: the first is that only the wealthy and important were deemed worthy of separate, recorded identities. The vast majority of us – the poor and the common – passed under the radar of relevance, remaining simply part of an undifferentiated mass. Second, in comparison to the intensely individuated beings we are today, individuality barely existed. It was only through Hacking's avalanche of printed numbers, the manic counting first begun early in the nineteenth century, that first tens, then hundreds, then thousands of new categories of being were brought into existence. These categories were medical, social, criminological, intellectual, moral, physical; indeed, they covered every human capacity imaginable, and it was from this new palette of difference that individuality first took shape... and then grew, and grew, and grew.

Returning to the myth at the beginning of this section: the historical evidence would suggest that people aren't the same, irrespective of what era they came from. Prior to the mid eighteenth century in Europe, people did not regard themselves, above and beyond anything else, as individuals, clearly and endlessly different to others around them. Neither the mechanisms, nor any kind of desire, to measure those differences were in place. It took the widespread use of social statistics to make those differences visible. Significantly, as we will soon find out, it also took the advent of mass schooling to provide suitable sites for much of this measurement to occur.

Of course, most significantly of all, as soon as all this measurement took place, and almost endless new categories of difference were created, each of these new categories could be intervened upon differently. This is the point. The possibilities of governance had now been increased exponentially. You can't really govern a mob, but you can most certainly govern a population.

Myth #2 *Schools Are Primarily About Education, Not Regulation*

Schools aren't about the exercise of power, or about somehow producing a manageable population; schools are about giving children an education. We educate our children because we want them to reach their full potential, not because of any grand scheme of social regulation.

The Advent of Liberalism

The second significant change to the way we govern involved the effects of an important change in eighteenth- and nineteenth-century society: the advent of liberalism. The Glorious Revolution of 1688, in which James II of England was removed from the throne of England – not by force of arms, but by the will of the people – signalled both the beginning of the Enlightenment, and the beginning of the end of absolute monarchy. This left a clear problem: the monarch had always had total power; since this was no longer to be the case, how should the exercise of power be understood? Absolute rulers could do what they liked, but surely we hadn't replaced one form of despotism, with the rule of an equally despotic State? What should the State be allowed to do? Where should its power begin and end? It is questions such as these that form the fundamental foundations of liberalism.

These concerns over how to determine the limits of government were articulated principally within the philosophical writings of John Locke and David Hume, as well as the economic theories of Adam Smith. The publication of Smith's *The Wealth of Nations* resulted in both a change in political and economic thinking, but more importantly, a shift in ideas about how society ought to be governed. Liberalism depends upon a certain distance from matters of State, a State with inherent limitations in its ability to know. It also expresses a scepticism about the ability, or the right, of the State to know perfectly and in all details the reality to be governed (Burchell 1993). This is particularly significant because, as was discussed in the previous section, the State now had at its disposal an array of new tools for finding out ever-more information about the population. But could it ever find out everything it needed to know? And should it? All in all then, liberalism has rightly been characterised as:

...a doctrine of limitation and wise restraint, designed to mature and educate government by displaying to it the intrinsic bounds of its power to know. Liberalism undertakes to determine how government is possible, what it can do, and what ambitions it must needs renounce to be able to accomplish what lies within its powers. (Gordon 1991, 15)

To put it more simply, liberalism took as its central problem the demarcation of the governable from the ungovernable, and of those areas of necessary State intervention from those of autonomy. For example, it was argued that while it was still appropriate for the State to organise the defence of the nation, as well as the judgement and punishment of criminal conduct, it should stay out of the economic marketplace, and leave families with the right to raise children as they see fit – an understanding of government that is now, more or less, taken for granted.

This all sounds great. The unlimited power of the monarch has become a thing of the past. The State would intervene only where it was deemed necessary, and it was widely held that children would be none of the State's business. So did this mean that large portions of society were just to be left to their own devices? After all, this had certainly worked in pre-industrial, undifferentiated societies where any kind of close management of the citizenry was impossible, but times had changed. The State now had the potential not only to find out about its population, but also to begin the process of shaping it. But how could this happen, given that the doctrine of liberalism had placed this kind of interference beyond its legitimate powers?

Government at a Distance

The answer to this question: with a great deal of subtlety. Some of those domains where governmental intervention was deemed inappropriate, such as those responsible for the raising of children, were to be organised by far less direct forms of management, mechanisms of government which 'operate at a distance' (Rose and Miller 1992). That is, the state would not be administering the internal conduct of the population based upon such clumsy and direct coercive mechanisms as laws, decrees and regulations; within the new governmental philosophy of liberalism, this would be far too obvious, and would be seen as overstepping the mark. Rather, it now sought to regulate the raising of future citizens – far too important a process to be left to chance – while not appearing to do so at all. The State could *appear* to step away, while still getting what it wanted through two important relays: the *family* and the *school*.

With regards to the family, rather than commanding parents to act in certain ways through the force of the law, the raising of children could be effectively managed through the power of *expertise*. This expertise would be associated with such disciplines as family guidance, welfare, psychology, community medicine, counselling and pedagogy (Rose 1985). In this way the family could at once be private and autonomous, while at the same time being tightly regulated as one of the most important sites for instilling the capacities, aspirations and habits required of the population (Donzelot 1979). This has often been referred to as the *pedagogic family*.

As part of the pedagogic family, expert knowledge also constructed the identity of 'the good mother', an ideal shaped within the discourses of the associated knowledges, one that can easily be contrasted against its evil twin, 'the bad mother' (Rock, 2007; Logan 2012). Mothers would be subtly recruited into the various processes of self-shaping necessary to become 'good'. This serves a number of social and governmental purposes:

> . . . it ensures that women take in child rearing, it ties women's identities to their role as child raisers and nurturers of others. More generally, it regulates families and family life, it controls the reproduction of the next generation of citizens, it is also implicated in shoring up the dominant culture and driving nation-building agendas. (Goodwin and Huppatz 2010, 6)

In addition to the family, the school also became one of the most important sites where this 'government at a distance' was to occur. The expertise of the teacher became a vital component in the management of an entire segment of the population (Rose 1990). Schools would no longer be places where a few, wealthy children went to acquire the cultural capital necessary to maintain their social status; schools would now be put in place for everyone, regardless of background. Crucially, within these new mass institutions, the population would be assessed, shaped and regulated in ways deemed necessary for the common good – with teachers providing both the expertise and the moral guidance to accomplish this governance – all while giving the appearance that the State had nothing to do with it. The school would become a relay, an intermediary device for producing the kind of citizens needed, without seeming to break its own rules of non-intervention.

This is an important issue, particularly in relation to the myth at the beginning of this section. Schools are often regarded simply as places where children learn the knowledge we consider especially important, and to some extent this is true. However, this is not why mass education has become the most important of all our institutions. It is because of the role they play in social regulation. If you want to understand how we govern contemporary societies, the first place to look is the mass school.

Liberalisms

It should be noted that, although the central principle of liberalism has remained constant – that is, setting limits to government – government itself has experienced a number of important modifications. Rose and Miller (1992) outline two of the most important of these modifications to classic liberalism.

First, they argue that the late nineteenth and early twentieth centuries witnessed an increasing conviction that classic liberalism was failing to produce the kind of society that many desired; there were high levels of poverty and social disadvantage, and very limited social mobility. In response to this dissatisfaction, many Western societies became welfare states. This did not signal the founding of a new form of state altogether; rather, it initiated a new mode of rule. Welfarism attempted to transform the State into a more interventionist entity, one which, while retaining some distance from those domains in need of intervention, still succeeded in their effective management.

The second change involves the rise of neo-liberalism from the mid 1970s onward. As with classic liberalism, neo-liberalism concerns itself primarily with setting limits to governmental intervention; however, it characterises welfarism in terms of a counterproductive expansion of the State. Because the State is deemed to be inherently unable to deal with the marketplace, it should therefore all but leave it alone. Furthermore, the principles of the market should be applied more widely within society, even to the level of the construction of a particular type of subjectivity. That is, within the logic of neo-liberalism, 'the rational principle for regulating and limiting governmental activity must be determined by reference to . . . the free, *entrepreneurial* and *competitive* conduct of economic-rational individuals' (Burchell 1993, 271).

So, whereas welfarism attempted to govern through the concept of 'society', neo-liberalism governs through managing the choices of individual citizens, within a market governed by 'the rationalities of competition, accountability and consumer demand' (Rose 1993, 285), a culture 'driven substantially by notions of self-development, personal progression and self-actualisation' (O'Brien and Osbaldiston 2010, 174). Ball (2012, 132) sums up the effects of neo-liberalism on education perfectly.

> At its most visceral and intimate neo-liberalism involves the transformation of social relations and practices into calculabilities and exchanges, that is into the market form – with the effect of commodifying educational practice and experience. Neo-liberalism is made possible by a 'new type of individual', an individual formed within the logic of competition . . .

Given the ever-increasing levels of individuation discussed earlier in this chapter, this final element of neo-liberalism shouldn't come as any surprise: as we have become more and more individualised, liberalism has too.

Myth #3 *The Structure of the School Isn't Really That Important to the Education Process*

It doesn't really matter where we educate our students; for us it just happens to be the modern classroom. It's the information, the knowledge, that counts, and even that can be presented in any number of different ways. Likewise, we don't have to keep student records, or our students under continual surveillance, or engage in continual assessment. It isn't crucial; it's just convenient.

Following the work of Foucault (1977), it will be argued here that the major social institutions that developed into their current forms during the nineteenth century – the school, the prison, the barracks, the hospital, the asylum and the factory – all share a similar structure and logic. These similarities didn't come about by chance. These institutions developed as they did because they enabled the effective management of the individuals contained there, whether they were pupils, inmates, soldiers, patients or workers, and each is organised according to a fundamental underlying principle: *discipline*.

According to O'Farrell (2005), discipline is a mechanism of power that regulates the behaviour of individuals within the social body. It regulates the organisation of space and time, people's activity and behaviour, and is enforced with the aid of complex systems of surveillance. As such, schools are examples of a 'disciplinary society'. That is, rather than the current structures of schools being simply a random convenience – rows of desks, timetabling, a progressive curriculum. . . all just a quirk of history – those structures are absolutely fundamental, not only to what schools can accomplish, but also to the way we have come to regulate our wider society (Gore 1998).

Disciplinary Societies

This term describes the form that modern institutions came to adopt. Largely following the reasoning of utilitarian philosophers such as Bentham, it was realised that a series of architectural and organisational changes could result in new sets of possibilities about the role that institutions could play in the modification of human conduct (Symes and Preston 1997). The most crucial components in such 'disciplinary societies' are as follows.

THE PANOPTICON

Arguably, all modern institutions are founded upon the possibility of continual surveillance. The reasoning behind this is simple. While the modern State had already moved social governance far beyond the notion of periodic symbolic execution as the principal method for the exercise of power, the panopticon took the process one stage further, in that the emphasis was to move from governance, to self-governance.

Once again, it was Foucault (1977), in his book on the history of the modern prison, who sought to demonstrate that, through the use of architectural devices like the panopticon (where all prisoners were continually visible from a central observation point), it became possible to enlist prisoners in the process of their own reformation. Since the prisoners would never be sure if they were under surveillance, they would have to keep their conduct in check at all times, thus becoming, in essence, their own gaolers. The discipline imposed by this surveillance would become self-discipline, and regulation, self-regulation.

The use of panopticons was not restricted to the prison. Educational institutions quickly adopted this system of organisation, and it soon became the norm for all classrooms. Take a look around any lecture theatre: the speaker will almost certainly present from a single vantage point from where all students are visible at all times, and thereby one lecturer can regulate the conduct of 500 students. This did not just happen by accident. Likewise, in the school classroom, teachers can continually surveil the conduct of their all pupils, and consequently – so the theory goes – university students and school pupils alike (and prisoners and factory workers) all learn to govern their own behaviour.

The process does not stop there. More often than not, just as the pupils are watched by the teachers, so too are architectural and administrative mechanisms in place such that teachers can themselves be surveilled (Wilkins and Wood 2009). From there the teachers are watched by the head of department, who is watched by the deputy principal, who is watched by the principal, who is watched by the Department for Education. This is called *hierarchical observation*, and it forms the core of a disciplinary society. However, in addition to this new disciplinary mechanism, is the threefold strategy of individuation, differentiation and normalisation.

INDIVIDUATION

As was discussed in myth #1 in this chapter, the possibilities of effective govern-ance increased exponentially with the society from an unknowable mob, into a modern population – an entity composed of distinct individuals, each with their own measurable, and governable, characteristics. While this came about as a result of new methods of counting and analysis, it also came about as a result of the architecture of the new mass institutions. Within these institutions, each prisoner/patient/pupil was now to be allocated their own space. No longer could they be treated as part of a mob, moving around without restriction. Instead they were to be individuated – prisoners were placed in specifically allocated cells; patients were allocated to a particular bed, within a given ward; pupils organised into rows and columns in particular classrooms – each knowing their place, and in turn being known.

As an example of the success of the process of individuation, we now take it for granted that a competent head of school can pinpoint the whereabouts of any given student, at any given time, almost to the desk. It is as if the panoptic 'eye' of the school extends beyond a direct 'line-of-sight', into an all-seeing administrative visi-bility. Each individual is now an identifiable 'case', to be placed on a specific seat with a metaphoric 'empty folder' attached to it, a folder than can now be filled with an almost endless amount of information about that person.

DIFFERENTIATION

The question now is: how do we start filling that folder? The most obvious answer is through continual, systematic and wide-ranging *assessment*, a fact most readily observable within the disciplinary society of the school. Through such testing, it is now possible to identify particular characteristics, skills, capacities and weaknesses of any pupil, and thereby to *differentiate* them from their peers. This is a twofold process: first, the results of these tests – from potentially hundreds of thousands of students across the country (and beyond) from within the same cohort – are then used to construct normal curves. Second, after contributing to the construction of any given normal curve with an individual result, any student can then have their result located on that curve. And this process happens across an almost innumerable range of areas – academic, physical, behavioural, ethical, disciplinary, and so on. Taking just one small example: students are not just tested on how good they are at maths in relation to their peers, they are compared across dozens of different types of maths, for every year they are at school, and not just against others in their own school, they are differentiated from all the other students in the country. All of these forms of testing produce normal curves, and students are differentiated on the basis of all of them.

Add to this testing the effective keeping of records, and new identities started to emerge, identities with far greater depth, texture and permanence than was previously possible or even thinkable. These are not just identities such as 'good at maths', or even more complex identities such as 'in the top percentile at advanced calculus, for a fifth-form student'. As will be discussed in Chapter 6, identities such as 'ADHD student', 'OCD student' and 'ASD student' are now a common part of our pedagogic vocabulary. Students are now intimately and densely documented as part of what is considered to be good practice in education. Of course, now that the folder on each chair is brimming with information, and places on the normal curve allocated, it is now possible to begin the process of intervention and correction.

NORMALISATION

Probably the most significant aspect of this process was that it has now become possible to normalise the population in ways that were previously inconceivable. By divining ever-increasing numbers of measurable capacities within children, and by constructing endless sets of norms from this data, children could be assessed against their peers, their shortcomings documented, and the relevant forms of intervention set in motion. These interventions are also not restricted to the daily efforts of classroom teachers. There now exists a vast array of other therapeutic agents, knowledges, mechanisms and processes that can be wheeled out by the school (and other organisations) when necessary to gently push those children on the lower ends of any normal curve back towards the middle.

This has become a comprehensive process. Students are no longer to be normalised on just their punctuality or their spelling. Instead a densely saturated *corrective* apparatus has been put in place, an apparatus that normalises everything from speech to sports, from attitude to arithmetic. We have become an intensely normalised population; that is – incorporating all three elements of the process – by individuating students, they can be differentiated, and by differentiating students, they can be normalised. And a normalised population is a manageable population.

MANAGING TIME

Space was not the only thing to be subdivided into manageable units within a disciplinary society. Such disciplinary societies are, in part, also characterised by techniques for taking charge of the *time* of individual existences. This does not simply extend to the rigorous demarcation of the working day. Rather, it is composed of a minute positioning in relation to the pervasive division of time – the organisation of time into successive or parallel segments; the arrangement of these segments into a graded, cumulative series of increasing complexity; and the connecting of these series into an overall developmental plan. The disciplinary management of time is especially evident within contemporary schooling.

> It is this disciplinary time that was gradually imposed upon pedagogic practice – specialising the time of training and detaching it from adult time, from the time of mastery, arranging different stages, separated from one another by graded exam-ination; drawing up programmes, each of which must take place during a particular stage and which involves exercises of increasing difficulty; qualifying individuals according to the way they pass through these series. (Foucault 1977, 159)

Society as a Reflection of the School

Common sense would normally suggest that societies produce education systems that are a reflection of themselves, a small reproduction of the larger whole. The most self-evident features of a culture – its forms of organisation, its structures of authority, its mechanisms of socialisation – ought logically to find their way into the schools, just as they most likely find their way into all other forms of communal life.

Only in this instance, that isn't the way it happened; in fact, in many ways, it was quite the reverse. The features of the disciplinary societies that emerged in the great institutions of the nineteenth century proved to be so successful as techniques of population management, they spilled out of those institutions and into the wider society, where they started to shape a new way of governing the entire social body. We now take it for granted that we will be surveilled, that CCTV cameras will be placed at regular intervals throughout our cities, in police stations, in shopping malls, and in their basement car parks. We know that extensive records are kept about us detailing our health, our financial status, our purchasing habits, our educational achievements and our automotive transgressions. We also know that we will be differentiated into virtually endless categories of existence: sexual categories, medical categories, professional categories, socio-economic categories. Finally, we expect that we will be normalised, that if we are found to have shortcomings in some aspect of our lives – how we behave in public, how we treat our children, how we drive, how we interact with each other – we expect to be subject to various forms of targeted social intervention, and to have our conduct steered back towards what has been deemed normal. All of these familiar techniques of governance had their origins within institutions such as the school.

Conclusion

The central purpose of this chapter has been to show the essential role that mass schooling plays in the governance of contemporary society. This role is not simply about giving everyone a good education, such that they can all behave relatively reasonably and get themselves a job, thereby maintaining the status quo. The role of mass schooling is far more fundamental than that. It constitutes probably the most important site for shaping and managing the conduct of the population. Indeed, it was probably the most important site for the notion of the population to emerge. Furthermore, with the decline of sovereign rule, the school provided a vital relay through which the new 'liberal' forms of governance could guide the shaping of the citizenry while still appearing to mind its own business. Finally, the school constitutes a 'disciplinary society', which, through continual surveillance, endless testing and category-production, acts as a vast normalisation machine.

Three further points are of note here. The first is that this chapter has not sought to describe some kind of 'big brother' society, where we are constantly surveilled by the malevolent, panoptic eye of the State, where the State is a singular, oppressive entity – what Nietzsche (1891) referred to as 'a cold monster'. Arguably, the State, far from being a single entity, is better understood as a loose cluster of often-contradictory agencies, institutions and assemblages, often with no singular governmental strategies or set of policy goals in mind. And while the exercise of power most certainly can be coercive and repressive, it can also be productive and organisational, producing particular types of citizen, with specific capacities and abilities. For the most part, the arrangement of our disciplinary institutions fits this latter model; we are not really *coerced* into participating in our system of mass education, we are willingly *recruited* into it, through the promise of what it can offer. To put it another way: the intention here has not been to argue that our contemporary governmental society – or the disciplinary mass school – is either somehow a bad thing, or a good thing. It's just a thing.

The second is that the various forms of the exercise of power raised here – sovereignty, discipline, governance – should not be regarded as mutually exclusive. The blunt instruments of sovereign rule, with its laws, decrees and regulations, did not simply disappear when discipline started to emerge in the seventeenth and eighteenth centuries, before really taking hold in the nineteenth century. Likewise governance, within its all-pervasive 'conduct of conduct', did not simply trump all that remained; or to put it another way, discipline did not replace sovereignty, only to be replaced itself by government. Rather, 'one has a triangle, sovereignty–discipline–government, which has as its primary target the population. . . ' (Foucault 1991, 102). As a society, we are regulated in complex ways, and in our explanations of that regulation, we should always resist easy oversimplifications.

The final point is that it is often assumed that governance and disciplinary management occur only in obvious and visible ways. That is, the disciplinary technologies already discussed here – panopticons, timetables, specified seating arrangements, individual records, and so on – are most usually associated with the primary or secondary classroom. This leads to the assumption that other educational environments, for example the kindergarten or the playground, are somehow 'zones of freedom' where the notion of discipline takes a secondary position behind the 'real' life of children. This would be a mistake.

As previously mentioned, along with the pedagogic family (i.e. the *new* family, the family that willingly bore the burden of responsibility for producing good and healthy future citizens), mass schooling became one of the most important and convenient mechanisms for implementing specific forms of self-cultivation and distributing them to a mass population. However, these ends could not be satisfactorily realised solely through the mechanisms available at the beginning of the nineteenth century – that is, either the strict regimen of monitorialism or the pastoral care of the Sunday school. David Stow (1850), a nineteenth-century Scottish educational reformer, argued for a form of schooling that allowed a greater level of freedom than previously possible within the monitorial school, and yet which still permitted the subtle imposition of required social norms. This 'child-centred' pedagogy successfully combined the strategies of pastoral care with those of social administration. It also promoted a sympathetic relationship between teacher and pupil, in the form of the concerned teacher who observes and directs the moral development of children. However:

> The move to overcome 'mechanical' teaching and the remoteness of the classroom from 'life' through a new 'child-centred' pedagogy was, therefore, no fundamental opposition to the disciplinary normalisation of whole populations. Quite the reverse: it was the means by which the latter could be most successfully achieved. (Hunter 1993, 25)

Even in educational sites like the playground, pastoral care is combined with social management. Within this remodelled school (which is still the dominant contemporary form of education), children move between the playground and the classroom, playing and discussing their play, beneath the benevolent, but all-seeing gaze of the teacher. Consequently, the 'freedom' of the playground and the 'discipline' of the classroom do not represent a 'fundamental opposition', but rather two tactics, which form part of a wider strategy aimed at the correct training of young people.

In support of this contention: the correct training of young people provides the focus for much of the work of Tyler (1993) on the kindergarten – supposedly a site of self-expression and freedom, but within which there operates a variety of subtle techniques of measurement and surveillance. The measured organisation of bodies in space permits the teacher to assess each child against graded developmental norms at a glance, while a number of unseen observation posts are often incorporated into the standardised design of the buildings themselves. Furthermore, careful records are kept of each child, detailing even the smallest elements of daily conduct, life and learning.

It is not, however, only the external actions of children that are now governed within the school, whether in the playground, the kindergarten or the classroom. Although the technologies and practices associated with the implementation of a disciplinary society effectively manage daily conduct – who does what, when and how – it has now become possible to administer an entirely new domain of life: that of the mind. As will be discussed at length in the next chapter of this book, the rise of psychology, with its ability to regulate the subjective experiences of citizens, has proven to be a crucial new tool within the field of social governance.

In summary, the central features of the modern school are so familiar to us that we often don't even notice them any more – timetables, academic records, rows of desks, playgrounds – of course they should be there; how could education possibly be otherwise? However, the evidence suggests that these features are neither inevitable, nor did they appear merely by chance. Instead, they are the most important components of a new type of institution altogether, one inexorably tied to the goals of government.

SUBJECTIVITY

5

This chapter argues that our subjective experiences – how we experience the world, and understand ourselves within it – are just as closely governed as our objective conduct, discussed within the previous chapter. Whether they realise it or not, contemporary teachers are expected to play a significant role in this form of regulation. After all, teachers are now not simply responsible for transmitting a given curriculum and keeping children in line, they are de-facto psychologists, responsible for the mental health, regulation and development of their pupils.

Myth #1 The sole purpose of psychology is to understand the nature of the human mind. *'All societies have mentally ill people. Psychology began by explaining the workings of the normal human mind, and why some people were different. From there, the discipline eventually came to be used in schools'.* 'Mental illness' is a relatively new way of understanding forms of conduct associated with 'unreason', and regardless of its function today, psychology originated not as an attempt to know the normal human mind, but rather as a system for finding and managing those unlikely to fit into the new, mass school.

Myth #2 My conduct may be governed, but my mind remains free. *'Disciplinary societies like the school certainly regulate our conduct, but they can't control our minds. That is, the power of the school may cover our bodies, but it doesn't extend inside our heads'.* Just as contemporary forms of governance have rendered our objective conduct amenable to regulation and normalisation, so too has the discipline of psychology made our subjective lives – our desires, motivations, intellectual capacities, perceptions, systems of thought – open to rigorously structured intervention and regulation.

Myth #3 Psychology simply discovers new behaviour disorders; it plays no role in creating them. *'Psychology reveals new facts about the* *human mind. It has recently found, existing in nature, a wide range of behaviour disorders affecting children's performance at school. It has also developed a range of treatments for these conditions'.* Just as other forms of governance operate by subdividing the population into manageable, bite-sized categories, each of which can be intervened upon differently, so too does psychology, and it is unrealistic to think that psychology had no part to play in the creation of these new pathologies. After all, when new ways of seeing are employed, new realities come into being. 'Behaviour disorders' are a perfect example of this.

Introduction

It is important to make a particular point here, so important that it will be made again in the conclusion. This is not an anti-psychology chapter. Psychology is an interesting, useful and worthwhile discipline that contributes much to our understanding of what it is to be human. It is also a vital tool in the armoury of all teachers; indeed, you probably couldn't be much of a teacher without it. However, it is the role psychology plays in social governance that lies at the heart of this chapter, as it will be argued here that social governance is really what psychology is all about.

The first question that should now be asked is: why is this chapter titled 'Subjectivity', rather than 'Psychology', given that psychology seems to be its main focus? There are two main reasons for this. The first is that psychology is not the only discipline that deals with the governance of human subjectivity, rather it is just one of several, including psychiatry, psychoanalysis and psychometrics. As a group, these have often been referred to as the *psy-disciplines*. Certainly, in a text on mass education – and certainly within this chapter – psychology may well be the main player, but it is never quite alone.

The second reason is because this chapter sets out to examine the governance of subjective experience, the regulation of how we see the world, and how we go about seeing ourselves. While it examines in detail the role that psychology has played – and continues to play – in this process, the central focus here remains on the 'government of the self', the realisation that our inner selves are just as regulated within the schooling environment as is our behaviour.

Understanding the Human Mind

On the surface, this whole topic area seems very straightforward. Psychology is one of the most important discipline areas within the field of education. Of course we should spend a significant amount of time and energy trying to better understand what goes on in our students' minds – how they subjectively relate to the world. After all, not only will this help us create more effective environments for them to be educated in, and organise the delivery of the curriculum in ways that make it easier to learn, it will also help us know what to do when those minds don't work quite in the way we'd like them to.

In many ways, this justification for the central role of the psy-disciplines – both within our education system and within our wider society – is premised upon a couple of important assumptions, assumptions that will form the basis of myth #1. The first is that there exists a relatively neat distinction between those minds that work as they should – that are normal, and that will function appropriately within the context of the school – and those that are not. Those that fall into this latter category are deemed to suffer from various forms of pathology – natural afflictions – whether they are a full-blown mental illness, or simply any one of a large range of behavioural disorders.

Having once accepted this foundational proposition, the second assumption is that we are lucky to have developed an unproblematic and objective way of explaining how the human mind works, and why sometimes it doesn't. The psy-disciplines themselves play no role in giving shape to the pathologies they uncover. They simply sit outside the problem, and make objective observations and assessments of what the issues are, and how they should be treated.

It will be contended here, when addressing myth #1, that the situation is much more complex than this, and that the medicalisation of mental differences should not necessarily be regarded as a logical *fait accompli*, but rather that this came about for very specific historical reasons. Also, the psy-disciplines did not develop as a way of mapping the human mind in a detached and objective way, rather they emerged primarily as forms of educational administration for dealing with those children who didn't fit the mould; it was a management tool for managing difference. As Foucault (1976a, 74) states: 'It is not psychology that tells the truth of madness, because it is madness that holds the truth of psychology'.

Schools, Psychology and the Management of Difference

In the previous chapter, it was shown how the very architecture of the school, along with its internal forms of organisation, was able to produce differences among pupils, which could then be effectively and acutely managed. Students learned to govern themselves; how they sat, when they talked, how and when they moved around the school. Individual differences were manufactured, and then utilised. It will be argued in myth #2 that this was only half the process. That is, the notion of 'difference' now permeates the children themselves, wherein it is just as tightly regulated – and arguably, this has been made possible through the deployment of the discipline of psychology.

It is psychology that has provided the largest girders in a conceptual framework built around the humanist mantra that all pupils are individuals, each with individual needs, responses and abilities. This understanding of the teaching process regards the individual as the foundational unit of analysis; this is the primary point of departure, and the bedrock upon which everything else is built. Therefore, according to this logic, the fundamental task of educators is to variously accommodate, encourage and refine such differences so as to produce the whole and self-actualised individual – problems with this account of individuality aside (Mauss 1985; Hirst and Wooley 1985).

Therefore, it will be argued here not only that the school plays a huge role in the shaping of individual self-identity, but also that, far from leaving the subjective experiences of students to remain 'free', the school actively regulates and normalises student subjectivity, just as it seeks to manage and normalise their conduct. After all, they are not unconnected.

Education and Pathology

The rise of the inclusive school – that is, institutions where special needs students are to be given full access to, and involvement in, the daily life of the classroom – has now placed the teacher at the centre of diagnosis and treatment of a wide range of learning and conduct disorders. Teachers are now expected to be able to intervene upon a wide range of educational differences. These differences are no longer either below the threshold of intervention, i.e. regarded as relatively unimportant, or simply part of the human condition. Instead they are now deemed to constitute objective pathologies to be identified, categorised and normalised. It is this assertion that forms the substance of myth #3.

It is within the context of the inclusive school that the most significant differences between contemporary teachers and their historical predecessors can be seen. Modern teachers can now almost be regarded as de-facto psychological therapists, and whereas once significant conduct or learning difficulties would be the trigger for either expulsion or removal to special schools, teachers now, with the guidance of experts, have been recruited into the ongoing management of 'problem' students (Lane 1990; Tyler 1993).

This management involves a number of elements: first, it requires a working knowledge of a lot of discipline areas, from pedagogy to psychology, from counselling to child welfare, and (increasingly) from paediatrics to pharmacology. Second, it necessitates a constant process of keeping up with developments and 'discoveries' within those discipline areas. It is not enough for teachers to know that certain forms of shyness have now been pathologised as Anxiety Disorders (American Psychiatric Association (APA) 2013), it also helps to be aware of some of its subdivisions – such as Selective Mutism (Cline and Baldwin, 2004; Viana *et al.* 2009), Social Phobia (Lopes and Albano 2013), or Separation Anxiety Disorder (Ehrenreich *et al.* 2008) – as well as how to recognise them, what to do with them, and how to organise your classroom practices accordingly. Third, these developments and discoveries are normally manifest in terms of a burgeoning array of student differences, to the extent that education has become (curriculum transmission aside) the effective management of those differences.

The question here is: to what extent does psychology discover these disorders within the fabric of the natural world, and to what extent does it play a role in bringing them into existence? According to myth #3, phenomena such as Attention Deficit Hyperactivity Disorder (ADHD) have always existed, we just were unable to spot them, to realise that they were illnesses in their own right, in need of intervention and treatment. It was the rise of psychology that finally allowed us to see with sufficient clarity to produce a valid diagnosis. As with the first two myths, it will be argued here that there are other ways of interpreting the recent appearance of a swathe of behaviour disorders, and that it has far more to do with the process of governing through the creation of categories of difference, than it does with triumphalist accounts of the steady march of scientific reasoning.

To summarise, the three myths to be dealt with in this chapter are as follows.

Myth #1 The sole purpose of psychology is to understand the nature of the human mind.
Myth #2 My conduct may be governed, but my mind remains free.
Myth #3 Psychology simply discovers new behaviour disorders; it plays no role in creating them.

Myth #1 *The Sole Purpose of Psychology Is to Understand the Nature of the Human Mind*

We didn't really understand much about the human mind before psychology came along. There had always been mentally ill people, but it was only when psychology started to explain how the normal human mind worked that we could begin to figure out why some individuals were different. From there, psychology came to be used in the school – always with the primary intention of helping individuals within the system.

There is a very familiar story concerning madness and the rise of psychology. It normally has two interrelated elements. The first is that mental illness is as old as humanity itself. There were people in ancient Greece who were mentally ill, just as now; there is no difference – after all, sick is sick. Examples of these mental illnesses can be seen throughout the ages, but it has only been with the rise of modern forms of assessment and treatment that we are finally able to do much about them, a gradual progress of learning what to do.

The second element of the story involves the birth of psychology. The history of dealing with these mental illnesses generally involves descriptions of a wide range of often-bizarre forms of intervention and treatment. With the benefit of perfect hind-sight made possible through the rise of modern scientific reasoning, these interventions were little better than forms of guesswork based upon superstition and ignorance. Then along came psychology, and we were finally able to base our treatments upon a solid foundation of real knowledge. Born towards the end of the nineteenth century, psychology developed from a long line of attempts to understand the workings of the normal human mind. Fortunately, it was able to shed an equal amount of light on abnormal minds.

This myth can be addressed in two parallel ways. First, it will be argued here that there is nothing natural and inevitable about the notion of 'mental illness'; the subject matter of the psy-disciplines is very much a social creation. The second point is that psychology has its own history, one not based in the pure, benevolent desire for knowledge about the human mind, but rather based in the mundane imperative to manage school children who failed to measure up to expectations.

The Great Confinement

Contrary to popular belief, those deemed to be mad have not always been regarded as 'sick'; citizens to be separated out from the rest of us, 'othered' (as discussed in Chapter 3) and made subject to all manner of interventions and cures. There is nothing natural and inevitable about this particular response to the various forms of conduct that we may find strange, or that does not meet our expectations. Rather, the best evidence suggests it came about as the end result of a series of social and administrative changes in Europe from the sixteenth century onwards. In the book *Madness and Civilisation*, Foucault (1965) charts the rise of contemporary ways of understanding and dealing with the mad. He begins by noting that during the Middle Ages, madness was largely an 'undifferentiated experience' (1965, ix), one where the mad formed part of the general fabric of society, cared for by their communities, or else wandering between towns. Foucault suggests the initial impetus for change from this model of madness to our own can be found in two historical events.

The first is the disappearance of leprosy across the Western world. The disease that had terrified Europe for over 1000 years all but died out by the fifteenth century. This left behind two things: a void where the great 'other' – the leper – used to be, the blighted space beyond the margins of society, and also nearly 19 000 leprosariums across Christendom with nobody left in them. The second impetus for change came in 1656. During a time of social upheaval and famine, it was decreed in Paris that all those incapable of contributing to the common good – the poor, the sick, the unemployed, the indolent, prostitutes, libertines and, of course, the mad – would be incarcerated, banished from society, held away from the rest of us, thereby purifying the social body. Within a few months, this 'Great Confinement' resulted in one in every hundred residents of Paris being locked away: the ultimate act of social othering. From there, this practice quickly spread across Europe, made all the easier by the availability of space left for them by the disappearance of the leper – not only in the metaphorical sense of a new group to loathe and fear, but also the physical sense of thousands of empty buildings with a new use. Indeed, the Great Confinement had begun in the *Hospital General* in Paris, itself in part an old leprosarium.

For the next 150 years, the mad were incarcerated within these great institutions (until they were 'discovered' by scientists such as Pinel and Tuke), innocents 'lost' among those otherwise deserving of their imprisonment. From 1800 onwards, the mad quickly became subjects of general scientific interest within what quickly became quasi-medical establishments, but always from within the perceptual framework that was the legacy of their initial forced confinement. That is, the mad were now to be regarded as fundamentally different to the rest of us and, as modern-day lepers, they were also to be feared.

WHY IS THIS RELEVANT?

Of the many arguments that Foucault makes in *Madness and Civilisation* (Foucault 1965), two are of interest here. The first is that there is nothing inevitable about the current understanding of madness; instead it is the product of history. That is, the notion that madness (and by extension, subgroupings such as behaviour disorders) has an objective reality, a timeless truth, defined in terms of 'sickness', is very much a product of the forms of knowledge that eventually took charge of it. If this had not happened the way it did, we would now understand mental difference very differently.

In spite of the relative success of the dominant, medical model of madness, there has been no little dissatisfaction with elements of the labelling processes associated with 'mental illness'. Seminal work by Hollingshead and Redlich (1958) notes that an individual's chance of being committed to a mental institution varied in relation to their social class, a variable surely irrelevant to an 'objective' illness. Some writers, such as Szasz (1961, 1973), suggest that any understanding of 'insanity' as an objectively valid category needs to be abandoned. A number of 'objective' mental illnesses have already had this status questioned, such as split personality (Hacking 1986) and anorexia nervosa (Tait 1993). Furthermore, it is not just the more intangible regions of 'mental' illness that have had their self-evidency challenged. Just like mental illnesses, it has been argued that 'obvious' physical diseases, such as syphilis, asthma and tuberculosis, are not permanently fixed and labelled in nature, and hence have had their objective standing disputed (Fleck 1979; Gabbay 1982; Wright and Treacher 1982). This will be discussed in more detail when addressing myth #3.

Foucault's second point is that the medicalisation of madness isn't necessarily something that we should be celebrating. He suggests that there are significant moral implications associated with allowing any form of truth-claim – scientific or otherwise – to decide who is sane enough to be considered normal and who isn't, and hence should be called sick.

> We have yet to write the history of that other form of madness, by which men, in an act of sovereign reason, confine their neighbours, and communicate and recognise each other through the merciless language of non-madness. (Foucault 1965, ix)

He is talking about psychology.

Schools and Psychometrics

Not all disciplines begin in the way in which most of their practitioners imagine. For example, modern physical education in schools did not spring, directly and fully formed, with the purity of purpose of the ancient Olympics, and the romantic rigor of the playing fields of Eton. Physical education in schools developed largely as a set of disciplinary practices targeting the body; lines of pupils swinging their arms in time – individuated, differentiated and normalised – docile bodies to be governed for the national good (Kirk 1993).

The history of psychology is much the same. In his book *The Psychological Complex*, Rose (1985) suggests that psychology developed, in large part, not as a detached and unbiased attempt to understand the normal human mind, but as a set of governmental practices for dealing with the newfound problem of the 'feeble-minded', concerns largely driven by the logic of eugenics. The eugenic movement – founded upon the belief that, through selective breeding, based upon race and intelligence, the risk of 'degeneracy' could be reduced (see Chapter 3) – was highly influential towards the end of the nineteenth century, remaining so for a further 50 years (O'Brien 2013). Advocates of this reasoning perceived a threat to the well-being of the nation due to the excessive breeding habits of the genetically less-worthy (i.e. generally the poor). However, mass schooling had inadvertently revealed a new and unexpected menace to the gene pool.

'THE FEEBLE-MINDED'

Prior to this time, the subdivisions of mental abnormality had been relatively simple. 'Lunatics' were those for whom a cure was possible; 'idiots' and 'imbeciles' were those with congenital problems that doomed them to their condition. Unlike with lunatics, it was always deemed possible to spot idiots and imbeciles from their physical appearance:

> The idiot . . . *was visible*. The mark of idiocy was impressed upon the surfaces of the body, in physical signs and external stigma. Idiots might pose a problem of economy, a problem of order, a problem of philanthropy, pedagogy or treatment, but they did not pose a problem of detection . . . (Rose 1985, 97)

In the new mass schools, lunatics and the idiots could be excluded from the very start. Likewise, the deaf, blind and dumb were denied entry to the classroom, unable as they were to benefit from a 'normal' education. And so the problem was solved. . . except that a proportion of the schooling population seemed unable to learn much at all. They had all their senses, and were clearly not physically marked out as idiots, so what on earth was going on?

A new category, halfway between the normal and the idiot, was speedily required, and the social and governmental obsession with feeble-mindedness began. Clearly new techniques of mental measurement were going to be needed if these feeble-minded people weren't going to be allowed to sneak through the net, mixed in among all the normal people, and breeding even more feeble-minded people. What a potential genetic disaster!

A very small, relatively insignificant group of loosely connected doctors and academics claimed the necessary testing expertise. The *psychometricians* began the process of IQ testing school children to see who should be excluded from the normal classroom. In doing so, they founded a new discipline, and began calling themselves psychologists. Interestingly, they quickly discovered that there were millions of children to be assessed, and hardly any of them (the psychometricians). Consequently they needed to recruit quasi-experts to help them with the mental testing, mini-psychologists who could collect the data, even begin any diagnostic processing needed, before passing the information on to fully trained psychologists when needed. These quasi-experts quickly became known as 'professional teachers'.

In summary then, psychology came to be the dominant discipline it is, not because it answered questions about 'normal' people like us, but because it provided strategies for dealing with people who weren't like us at all, and were causing disruption. Psychology was always, first and foremost, a form of social governance. This will become more apparent when addressing myth #2.

Myth #2 *My Conduct May Be Governed, But My Mind Remains Free*

We may have our conduct closely regulated within a disciplinary society like the school – where we sit, how we are permitted to act, how our time is to be spent – but in spite of this social control, my thoughts remains as free as ever. The school may be able to surveil my body, but it can't surveil my mind. There are some basic limits to the reach of government; its authority does not extend into my head.

Following on from the previous chapter, it is fairly undeniable that schools have a huge role to play within contemporary social governance. However, all the practices, techniques and forms of organisation discussed there are about our *objective* conduct; about how we appear to an external viewer. As discussed, they include where we sit, what we learn, how our bodies are physically regulated, and how we are moved about in space and time. All this may be true, maybe our bodies are tightly managed, and our behaviour governed, but at least our minds remain zones of freedom. This is a democracy; surely we are free to think how we like. The evidence suggests otherwise.

Psychology and Governance

As discussed in the last section, psychometric testing emerged as a way of ascertaining the existence of feeble-mindedness in circumstances where those mental deficiencies were not visibly written onto the surface of the body. The school became the perfect place for this form of evaluation: first, because it was a place where all future citizens were compelled to attend; and second, because an entire new population of professionals – teachers – could be recruited into assisting with that testing. As a result of this, feeble-mindedness very quickly became established both as an objective condition, part of nature that had always been there, and also as an administrative category, a reason for excluding children from school. However, the implications of this testing went far, far deeper.

THE KNOWABLE INDIVIDUAL

There were a number of other important social and governmental consequences of the rise of mental testing around the beginning of the twentieth century. Sutherland (1984) notes that the testing did not stop at the boundaries of the abnormal. Psychologists such as Binet quickly noted its potential for assessing the far wider range of mental abilities than just the pathological – making what Rose (1990, 142) refers to as 'a device for creating a hierarchy of the normal'. This is a crucial leap, as psychological testing was now to be relevant for everyone, not just those who worried the Eugenicists.

From there, the German psychologist Stern resolved to make the entire testing process more user-friendly and accessible to the lay audience (teachers, among others). He created a single scale, upon which everyone could be ranked, accomplished by dividing a person's mental age by their chronological age, and then multiplying by 100. The resulting *Intelligence Quotient*, or IQ, quickly gained widespread acceptance, and helped cement the belief that there exists a singular measure of mental capacity – a highly contentious assertion, at best. The British psychologist Burt and the American psychologist Terman then standardised the tests to permit their effective usage within schools. Furthermore, they organised the tests into written form (they had previously been oral), such that they could be administered and marked by the less highly trained (teachers again).

One of the most important implications of the new standardised measure of mental capacity – the IQ – is the easy comparison that could now be made between one child and another. What may have once been a vague, guiding teacher's intuition that one student was more capable than another, was now transformed into a rigid, quantifiable fact, a numerical value perfectly suited for ranking and streaming students. It became the ideal tool of governmental differentiation.

Of course, the IQ test was only the first of an array of forms of intellectual differentiation that arose from the new discipline, both formal and informal: these include various aptitude tests, subject tests, mental health tests, attitude analysis, as well as tests for adjustment, motivation, employability, morale, ethics and so on. Once again, each of these moved what would have previously been somewhat vague and insubstantial estimations, if they had been thinkable at all, into tangible, statistical realities. These are realities not only crucial to us all becoming more and more focused upon our own subjective experience, but also making the whole domain of individual difference more amenable to government. As Rose (1988, 187) notes:

> One fruitful way of thinking about the mode of functioning of the psychological sciences ... might therefore be to understand them as *techniques for the disciplining of human difference*: individualising humans through classifying them, calibrating their capacities and conducts, inscribing and recording their attributes and deficiencies, managing and utilising their individuality and variability.

THE NORMAL CURVE

There is no better demonstration of how a simple technique of governance can potentially reorganise the way in which we understand ourselves, and regulate our society, than the use of the normal curve. This is especially the case when addressing the rise of psychology. Rose (1990, 141) discusses how, in the latter half of the nineteenth century, Galton sought a way of making the rather abstract notion of human variability more thinkable, and hence more easy to act upon. As the concept of 'the population' was becoming more central to social management, the processes of differentiation occurring within institutions, such as the mass school, created more and more new categories and capacities. As such, the need to measure and calibrate these human variations became increasingly apparent; after all, what is the point of putting all that administrative effort into creating something like IQ, if you can't put it to any practical use?

Mathematically, the normal curve allows for a comparison of the respective amounts of an attribute possessed by members of a population. In simple terms, what it permits represents the Holy Grail of population management: the 'mathematicisation of difference'. Furthermore, the normal curve provided all the evidence that psychologists, as well as assorted educational administrators, needed that student variability is governed by natural statistical laws, and better still, that all this information could be reduced to a single graph that could be applied to anything. If a disciplinary society is based upon the threefold process whereby we individuate, so that we can differentiate, so that we can normalise, the normalising component of the process had found bedrock, and could now claim validation by nature. The brilliance of the normal curve – much like Stern's IQ – was the simple way it permitted an easy and accessible visualisation of the subject matter. They were both as much successful models of marketing, as they were scientific advances. It is probably fair to say that, at the bottom of almost every example of social governance you can think of, now lurks a normal curve.

DEVELOPMENTAL PSYCHOLOGY

As can be seen, the rise of psychometric testing provided one of the cornerstones of the normalisation of childhood. Its widespread deployment of the normal curve meant that any capacity could be calibrated, and any given student measured, not only against their peers in a classroom, but also against some abstract notion of human nature itself. It provided a snapshot of any capacity, an instant judgement, and institutional administrators loved it.

But more was to come. Why settle for a snapshot when you can make a movie? Psychometrics compared students against normal curves that were fixed in time. This provided a very static way of understanding the distribution of capacities within a population, and an equally static way of ranking a student's abilities. It soon became apparent that the normal curve had a far greater potential than simple, one-off comparison. Why not make a series of sliding scales? Why just have a normal curve measuring, for example, a child's spatial awareness? Why not have an entire set of normal curves, based upon a child's age, against which their spatial awareness can be measured? It would then be possible not just to say whether a child was normal or abnormal when it came to this particular capacity – as with psychometrics – it would now be possible to say whether they were advanced or lagging; ahead of their age, or behind. This realisation represented a whole new dimension of governmental possibilities, justifying an encyclopaedia of new forms of intervention and normalisation. It also signalled the birth of a new sub-discipline: *developmental psychology*.

Importantly, as discussed in the previous chapter, this form of governance – indeed, the entire discipline of developmental psychology – could not have come into being without the pre-existence of the new administrative and architectural arrangements of the modern school.

> Developmental psychology was made possible by the clinic and the nursery school. Such institutions had a vital role, for they enabled the observation of numbers of children of the same age, and of children of a number of different ages, by skilled psychological experts under controlled, experimental, almost laboratory conditions. They thus simultaneously allowed for standardisation and normalisation... (Rose 1990, 145)

Psychology, Misconduct and Risk

Rose (1990) goes on to make an interesting point about the types of education that are available to parents, a point that could well have been made in Chapter 1 of this book on the issue of social class. He suggests that two main models can be discerned: one model of education for the wealthy, and a different one for the working class. Importantly, psychology is been able to play a foundational role in each, which has probably contributed to its ongoing success as a discipline.

For the wealthy, education seeks to produce the best possible adult, with all their capacities honed, and their potential capitalised upon. Parents are recruited into this process from birth, with each pedagogic choice scrutinised and justified, and each test result assessed and acted upon. Psychology has dovetailed neatly into this approach, permitting ever-greater scrutiny of students' abilities, and the promise of being able to inch those students up each and every normal curve throughout their educational career.

For the working class, the central issue has always been to minimise the threat they are deemed to pose to the social order. This has included a wide range of strategies, from the education of mothers in the 'correct' way of raising children, to the close policing of conduct in school, searching for signs of delinquency and its inevitable path to future dangers. Importantly, psychology quickly became especially good at this, and hence now underpins both the new disciplinary strategy of *behaviour management*, as well as the entire industry surrounding the notion of the *'at-risk' youth*.

BEHAVIOUR MANAGEMENT

The old models of intervening into unacceptable conduct – physical punishment, periods of confinement and repetition of tasks – have now long since been replaced by the far more subtle forms of intervention and guidance advocated by behaviour management. Uncooperative students are now identified, targeted and managed, recruited into their own self-reformation as part of a new tactic of governance, one founded in the individuating logic of psychology.

The suggestion here is not that this is necessarily a bad thing; the suggestion is solely that psychology has managed to place itself at the front and centre of the disciplinary life of the school. This has significant consequences for how problems within the school might be understood. Traditional structural explanations of misconduct – poverty, social disenfranchisement, hegemonic masculinity, lack of English as a first language, lack of parental education, lack of breakfast – are all far more likely to be considered irrelevant within a paradigm that locates the problem solely within the individual. You are messing up in class? Well it's not because the academic curriculum might be meaningless to you, or the teacher is boring, or the room has only one window, and you've been sitting in there all day, and you're starving. No, it's because you are naughty; the problem necessarily lies within you.

Behaviour management is an excellent way of organising and regulating the contemporary, individuated classroom. All teachers need it in their toolkit. However, it comes at a price in terms of who gets the blame.

THE 'AT-RISK' YOUTH

The implications of psychological management now extend far beyond the boundaries of the school. Not only has the education system had its focus sharpened in recent years as an instrument for the production of employable citizens (Gee, Hull and Lankshear 1996), the school is now also widely regarded as one of the central sites for some of the most important aspects of ongoing social management. Children at risk of anything from unemployability to criminality are now targeted while still at school (McCallum 1993; Prior and Paris 2005), and the central mechanism by which this future social programming occurs, is the production, identification, organisation and treatment of difference. Young people can now be measured against a graded and cumulative set of normal risks, both by their age category, and by the severity of the risk involved. Just as the disciplinary school has become characterised by the minute division of space and time, risk has also become an important indicator in the grid of governmental knowledge.

Once again, this all acts to significantly increase the scope of government. Whereas more traditional forms of surveillance require the spatial arrangement of the target population under a central, panoptic gaze, the new strategy of risk almost entirely avoids the need for such direct scrutiny. After all, the focus now falls not on a given subject, but rather upon a set of abstract risk factors. For example, if a student has the personal demographics of a working-class background, just one parent, and English is their second language, as well as the psychological risk factors of low aptitude scores, poor adjustment, and a diagnosis of ADHD, alarm bells will be ringing all over the place. Castel (1991) argues that the deployment of risk in this manner permits a virtually limitless expansion of the possibilities of government, based primarily upon unlimited suspicion. Indeed Castel argues that:

> Prevention in effect promotes suspicion to the dignified scientific rank of a calculus of probability. To be suspected, it is no longer necessary to manifest symptoms of dangerousness or abnormality, it is enough to display whatever characteristics the specialists responsible for the definition of preventative policy have constituted as risk factors. (Castel 1991, 288)

For Ewald (1991, 199) 'anything can be a risk; it all depends upon how one analyses the danger, considers the event'. The reach of risk is now endless, and hence nothing remains beyond the reach of possible governmental intervention. Once again, it should be emphasised here that intervention is by no means necessarily a bad thing – far from it. The vast majority of governmental intervention is organised with the best of intentions, whether successful or otherwise, whether justified or otherwise. However, what this does illustrate is the depth of the role that psychology continues to play in the governance of populations.

Myth #3 *Psychology Simply Discovers New Behaviour Disorders; it Plays No Role in Creating Them*

We are fortunate to have found a system of investigation – psychology – that has enabled us to discover otherwise-hidden truths about nature; more specifically, it has recently uncovered an ever-growing range of behaviour disorders that always existed, but that we were unable to see. Psychology is managing to peel away layers of ignorance, and shine an objective light into dark recesses of the developing human mind, finding more and more children with mental conditions, and helping them by pointing this out.

In the introduction to the book *The Problem of Medical Knowledge*, Wright and Treacher (1982) contend that scientific knowledge is always presented as objective, benevolent and teleological. The truths of the natural world are relentlessly uncovered, with the individual researchers merely perceptive observers to whom these truths are passed. They contend that this understanding, particularly of medical information, not only legitimates the pre-eminent status of these disciplines, but also acts to support the validity of their truth claim and the categories they produce. However, they suggest medical categories don't really deserve this status, as they are essentially social constructs – conceptualised, produced and enacted in social ways.

Exactly the same is true of psychological categories. While it is often reassuring to imagine that they exist as 'natural facts', timeless entities that we have merely uncovered, the evidence suggests otherwise. A brief review of our not-so-distant past reveals 'objective' categories of psychological difference that we now rightly regard as utterly ridiculous – clearly the product of the social views of the time. The 'hysterical woman', a well-defined pathological category, was the product of an explanatory system that regarded women as innately weak and unstable. Female behaviour was generally understood as an extension of their reproductive capacities (hence, hysteria – *hysteros*, Greek for uterus). In practice, hysteria became a conveniently ambiguous term covering all forms of physical and mental stress, and which could be applied to anyone, as long as they were female and middle class.

Those psychologists invested in the possibility of objective categories of difference might simply say, 'Well yes, clearly that category was complete rubbish, but the ones we have now are true'. The real issue here is not whether categories are true or false (although clearly, some are utter junk), the issue is more about the realisation that *all* categories are the product of specific social, historical and intellectual forces. Attention Deficit Hyperactivity Disorder (ADHD) is a pretty good example.

The Rise and Rise of ADHD

From its first appearance in 1987 – then as Attention Deficit Disorder (ADD) – the following quote is fairly typical of the way in which Attention Deficit Hyperactivity Disorder has been presented within the literature, and by those with an interest in its acceptance as a valid and objective category.

> ADD is an inherited neurobiological disorder which becomes evident in early child-hood and usually continues throughout a person's life ... There is no doubt in the scientific community that ADD is real ... ADD is not a new phenomenon, it has always been with us but has not always been recognised. (Sosin and Sosin 1996, 6–7)

It is evident here that the disorder is understood as an objective condition, an indisputable fact of nature. In addition, it is deemed to have existed long before its identification by the clear-eyed and perceptive scientists who brought it to our attention, thereby dispelling the former erroneous explanations for the same conduct, and long before it became a familiar element within the schooling landscape. In contrast, superseded ways of understanding and healing are presented as superstitious, ignorant and/or barbaric. With the benefit of hindsight, psychologists argue, ADHD can now be delineated long before it is formally diagnosed. In fact, many texts point to the work of the paediatrician Still in 1902, who made some early observations on hyperactivity, and they often note that prior to the diagnosis, ADHD children were simply regarded as naughty and uneducatable (Hurley and Eme 2004). Medical history is thereby presented in triumphalist terms: the heroic unmasking of the hidden realities of nature, the shedding of light into the mysteries of the human body and mind, and the identification and control of independent disease entities.

There is, however, significant literature that understands the process of producing medical and psychological classifications very differently. Arguably then, there are four basic problems associated with this approach to behaviour disorders and, more specifically, ADHD. First, there is far from universal support among psychologists regarding the validity of the diagnosis of ADHD. Indeed, a growing number of mental health professionals, not to mention teachers and parents, remain sceptical that a disorder that was rarely mentioned before 1980 could now exist in what is almost plague proportions (Cohen 2006). This concern aside, an even greater number of those professionals are uncomfortable with the use of amphetamines, such as Ritalin, as the central form of treatment.

Second, ADHD rates vary widely, depending upon the country of diagnosis. If ADHD is truly is an objective biological disorder, how is it possible that the UK level of ADHD among children is now at 1.5%, while in America it is close to five times greater (Russell *et al.* 2014)? Are we somehow a genetically superior people here in Britain? If so, you have to admire the French, whose ADHD rate currently sits at about 0.5%. Wedge (2015) suggests that the most logical explanation for these differences actually lies in the fashionability of the disorder in the USA – in addition to the hegemony of the drug companies there, offering instant pharmacological 'cures' – along with simple mundane social differences in areas such as parenting, diet and educational policy.

Third, and from a more philosophical perspective, this approach is largely premised upon the unproblematic existence of objective, natural categories of difference, ones that endure irrespective of human opinion or belief. As previously discussed, this assumption rests upon the shakiest of philosophical ground. In addition, as Barthes (1972) has pointed out, positioning a problem within the realm of nature removes that problem from social debate or social responsibility. Locating student misbehaviour within nature itself means that no further justification is required, and all those issues most frequently associated with student misbehaviour – social class, masculinity, school violence, educational failure, delinquency – can be considered irrelevant.

Finally, as has been contended throughout this chapter, the discovery of categories such as ADHD is driven, first and foremost, by the broader governmental practice of dividing the population up into ever-more manageable sub-units. Categories such as ADHD are a primary element within the fundamental functioning of a disciplinary society. By differentiating populations into smaller and smaller groupings, it becomes possible to target, with ever-increasing acuity, specific forms of governmental intervention into conduct. Not only does this permit ever more effective normalisation, but it also renders the population more knowable within the broader web of governmental intelligibility.

The issue here is not really ADHD, in and of itself. The issue is that ADHD is now just one of hundreds of categories of psychological difference, across which children (and increasingly adults) can be measured, assessed, found wanting and normalised.

Behaviour Disorders by the Hundred

As Tomlinson pointed out as early as 1982, this appears to be part of an ongoing and exponentially increasing process. After all, within the realm of educational difference/handicap, there were only two classifications prior to 1890: idiot and imbecile, quickly followed by 'feeble-minded', as discussed in the previous section. This had swelled to eight by 1913 (including divisions such as moral imbecile, and mental defective) and on to 12 in 1945 (with severely subnormal, maladjusted and delicate) (Tomlinson 1982). Currently, the list of such differences is enormous – in excess of 300 – each with its own treatment, prognosis and educational implications (Tait 2010).

As previously mentioned, contemporary pupils are no longer simply too shy. They now have Social Phobia, Separation Anxiety Disorder, or are Selective Mutes. Nor are they simply too lively; they were first to be reclassified as hyperactive, and now as suffering from ADHD, ODD or CD; and pupils are no longer simply unpopular or obnoxious, they are reclassified as Borderline Personality Disorder (BPD), or Antisocial Personality Disorder (APD). They aren't greedy, they have Binge Eating Disorder (BED); they aren't lazy, they have Motivation Deficit Disorder (MDD); and if they punch someone who happens to annoy them, they probably have Intermittent Explosive Disorder (IED).

Clearly, this process has a number of significant implications for how difference can be managed within schools. After all, the ever-increasing pathologisation of students exposes them to a vast new range of interventions, which in turn exponentially increases the effectiveness of the range of governmental strategies aimed at normalising young people. For example, identifying, organising and treating non-conforming children as ADHD and ODD sufferers serves a dual purpose: first, there are significant administrative benefits to be gained from keeping children in line by simply giving them a pill – ethical issues aside. Second, there is a greater social acceptability for a child to be suffering from a medical condition, than there is for one who might otherwise be regarded as wilfully naughty. As Meadmore (1998, 1) states: 'It is better for everyone for the child to be "sick" rather than "bad"'.

The issue here is not to suggest the rejection of such pathological categories of difference outright. Instead, the point is that when new canons of judgement are employed, like psychology, new realities come into being. As a result of the rise of contemporary forms of governance, teachers are now confronted with a range of such new realities. Simply refusing to accept the veracity of disorders such as ADHD is ultimately of little use. The decision as to its 'truth' will be made in locations other than the school, and by knowledges other than those produced by educators. It should also be pointed out that it is not just new canons of judgement that produce new realities, so too do new forms of social administration. After all, medicine and psychology alone were not responsible for the production of ADHD; so too was the individuating/ differentiating logic of the contemporary school itself.

That said, there is still perhaps a place for some healthy scepticism over the seemingly endless production of new categories of difference. As previously mentioned, it is part of the ongoing processes of government to keep finding new 'objective' classifications within which to normalise targeted sections of the population. Surely then, it is appropriate not to accept immediately, dutifully and uncritically every new personality and learning disorder that emerges. Perhaps longevity should be regarded as the primary test of veracity. Dyslexia has survived as a disease entity for in excess of 30 years, and still appears to operate well and validly within its definitional criteria, whereas the jury is still out on ADHD, and is likely to be so for some considerable time yet. However, questions are still to be asked over entities like ADHD because of the social and administrative *function* they appear to serve within the classroom. That is, suspicions will inevitably arise over the objectivity of such categories when their central purpose appears to be the maintenance of good order within a context as artificial and historically contingent as the modern classroom.

Conclusion

This chapter has not set out to undermine the discipline of psychology. As stated at the very beginning of this chapter, psychology is an incredibly useful tool within the knapsack of all teachers, and offers one particular type of truth about the life-worlds of pupils in school: why some succeed and some don't; why some fit in and others don't; why some are happy and others not. However, it is also important to understand the role that psychology plays within contemporary governance; indeed, that is precisely where the discipline has its origins. Psychology has a huge role to play in regulating the subjectivities of the population, both at school and in the wider community. Our inner thoughts, desires, emotions, motivations and aspirations are now all open to assessment, intervention and normalisation – for better and for worse.

All that said, and in spite of emphasising the fact that this chapter is not simply a cheap swipe at psychology, most people with experience in the field would have discerned an ongoing tension between psychologists on the one hand, and philosophers/sociologists on the other. This is nothing new; academic and professional life is full of such disciplinary rivalries – the traditional enmity between mathematicians and physicists provides an even more vivid example. The important question is: why does this tension exist?

Bearing in mind that this book is written from a philosophical/sociological perspective, there are probably three reasons that are worth mentioning here. Addressing these in terms of increasing importance: first, there is disagreement over the romantic story told by psychology of its own foundation. As discussed here, the best evidence appears to suggest that the discipline emerged largely as an effective way of sifting out the feeble-minded from the normal population; i.e. it was simply a very effective form of social administration. Interestingly, this isn't really a damning indictment; the same sort of claim can probably be made about most social sciences.

The second point of tension generally revolves around psychology's claim to objective analysis (and the concomitant production of objective categories of difference). This really shouldn't come as a surprise. As science became the dominant mode of truth production within the era of modernity, its success was based upon its much-lauded status as a neutral observer, an impartial describer of the natural world. This was probably a practical necessity, given it was trying to set itself apart from previous ways of determining 'truth', ones largely based upon religious belief, sovereign command and half-baked opinion. As a science then, psychology has often understood itself in similar ways. For the sake of fairness, it should be pointed out that many modern scientists and psychologists do not unquestioningly share this understanding of their disciplines, or the 'reality' of the knowledges they produce. The problem lies with those that do.

Finally, and of by far the greatest importance, is the disciplinary disagreement over what constitutes the primary unit of analysis. Philosophers and sociologists tend to start with society, and then explain individuality, and individual circumstance, from there. Indeed, this entire section of the book is really an analysis of how modern understandings of individuality have been created by contemporary forms of governance and disciplinary management. Psychologists generally start from the other end, in that they begin with the individual and work out from there. The constant banter between the two camps is that psychology underestimates the importance of social influences – thereby coming uncomfortably close to the 'it's all up to the individual' line, critically discussed in Chapter 1 – while philosophy/sociology underestimates the importance of the individual. The best answer to this issue is probably to reiterate that *how you look determines what you see*. Different disciplines produce different kinds of truth; decide for yourself which you find the most convincing.

Of course the flip side of this question is: having been given a philosopher's/sociologist's take on the issues, how would psychologists explain the tensions? There is obviously the same issue of what you take as your primary unit of analysis, the social or the individual, but other than that. . . you'd probably have to ask them.

PRE-ADULTHOOD 6

This chapter argues that educators need to have a good grasp of all the various forms of pre-adulthood we take for granted, such as 'the child' and 'the youth'. These categories are the focus of a range of different disciplines, most of which found their explanatory models in nature itself. As such, the behaviour of children and youth may be deemed to require explanation, but not the very existence of the categories themselves. The issues raised in this chapter concern the degree to which childhood and youth are actually socially constructed categories, categories serving particular social functions. Of greatest interest here are the ways in which childhood and youth are both artefacts of, and vehicles for, social governance.

> **Myth #1 'Childhood' and 'youth' are facts of nature.** *'We didn't invent children or youths; they have always been here. These aren't socially constructed categories. They exist in all cultures, and have existed in all eras'.* The evidence suggests that childhood and youth are both social inventions, childhood emerging from the fifteenth century onwards, and youth appearing in the early 1950s. It has also been suggested that childhood is now in the process of disappearing again, with youth expanding to fill its place.

> **Myth #2 The categories of 'childhood' and 'youth' have nothing to do with governance.** *'Though not the product of nature, the notions of childhood and youth developed as they did for purely cultural reasons. These reasons have nothing to do with social governance'.* These categories of pre-adulthood are both the products of government, and the vehicles for its effective operation. They are shaped most thoroughly through the governmental sites of the mass school, and the pedagogic family.

> **Myth #3 'Childhood' is characterised by its innocence, 'youth' by its natural resistance to authority.** *'Both childhood and youth have innate*

characteristics; young children are naturally innocent, and youth are naturally rebellious. Youth cultures are always oppositional in both content and purpose'. Both childhood innocence and youthful rebellion are products of the way in which the categories developed and came to be conceptualised. The idea of childhood innocence arose from the Romanticism of the eighteenth century, and concerns over youthful resistance can be traced, in large part, to the theoretical framework employed to explain youth subcultures in the 1970s.

Introduction

Within books of this type, categories like 'the child' are often taken for granted. They are the objects that social forces act upon, such as social class or gender, they are the targets of strategies of intervention, as with the law or disciplinary rules, and they are the focus of moral concern, discernable within analyses of the media and popular culture. What rarely happens is that the substance of these categories gets picked apart and discussed in its own right. That is the purpose of this chapter.

Teachers in particular have a large investment in pre-adulthood. Even in the era of lifelong learning, the notion of education is almost always associated with people who have yet to be granted the full status of adult. Whether these people are called infants, children, adolescents, teenagers, or youth, they have been made the focus of an entire profession, and whether the teacher is in early childhood, primary or secondary, they are each expected to know the 'nature' of their students, down to the smallest biological, psychological and intellectual detail.

However, it seems that these various categories of pre-adulthood don't represent a fixed target. How are teachers supposed to make the best of teaching 'youth' when the parameters of the group won't stay still long enough to allow any kind of consistent understanding? Arguably, the ways in which childhood was conceptualised, and in which children acted, even as late as the 1960s, bears only limited resemblance to current models of childhood. Children were dressed differently, even accounting for the vagaries of fashion, and occupied themselves differently, even accounting for the effects of technological advancement (Postman 1994). The question is: what are we to make of this? Or, more specifically, how thoroughly do we need to theorise these categories to make sure we do the right thing by them?

What Are Children? What Are Youths?

Sometimes, when we become so sure that the circumstances of our lives couldn't possibly be any other way, we ascribe those circumstances to nature. This gives them a certainty – a truth – and it means we no longer have to worry about justifying them. The best example of this has always been gender (see Chapter 2). We take something that *does* belong in nature (our sex, male or female) and wrongly conclude that the social formations roughly correlating with them (our gender, masculine or feminine) are also part of the natural order.

The issue here is whether popular understandings of concepts like 'childhood' are making the same error in logic. The inference we generally draw from our depiction of the young is that 'children' are simple facts of nature, and have been around for as long as we've been modern human beings; after all, even the Flintstones had a child (Pebbles). This reasoning suggests that you can't have adults without having children; they are a stage of life, one we mature out of on our way to becoming fully grown. The same is true for 'youth', who exist as a transitional stage between the total dependence of 'the child' and the finished product of 'the adult'.

The evidence suggests that the truth may be a little more complex than this. A number of writers have pointed out that artistic depictions of the very young in early medieval times appear to have fully mature faces, as if the young were just regarded as little adults. Other writers have noted that the term 'youth' doesn't appear anywhere describing a discreet stage of life before the early 1950s (Talburt and Lesko 2012; Buckingham 2014). Prior to this time, it was just an all-purpose word meaning 'young'. Surely, if these were timeless categories with historically fixed meanings, such confounding examples wouldn't exist?

Is Governance Relevant to Any of This?

Whether or not 'the child' is grounded in nature or otherwise, the historical evidence suggests that the new disciplinary apparatus of the mass school has certainly made children the focus of the widest imaginable array of management strategies: continual surveillance, rigorous location in space and time, extensive keeping of records, the production of categories of difference, normalising intervention. The same is the case for 'the youth' at the upper end of the secondary school; it is also individuated, differentiated and normalised. Furthermore, the school is not the only site wherein this 'government at a distance' occurs. The new *pedagogic family* plays a significant role in governance, particularly of 'the child'.

The issue here is whether the relationship between categories of pre-adulthood is more complex than this. That is, are these categories simply the target of governance, or are they more enmeshed in it than that? It could be argued that the various techniques, practices and forms of organisation associated with government constitute the very instruments that have produced 'childhood' and 'youth' in their current forms. This means that 'the child' is not simply the focus of governance; it is also an *artefact* of it. More than that, having produced such categories, as well as innumerable associated sub-categories, they then become the vehicles through which governance can occur more effectively.

Shaping the Capacities of Pre-Adulthood

Finally, the problem of understanding the dispositions of various categories of pre-adulthood needs to be addressed. Should teachers premise their pedagogy upon well-known natural elements of childhood, such as their innate innocence? After all, if this is a fixed and immutable element of 'the child's' makeup, then perhaps it could act as the solid foundation for all teaching practice, much as Descartes' *Cogito Ergo Sum* – 'I think therefore I am' – has acted as the foundation of Rationalist philosophy for 500 years. But if this is not the case. . . then what? How much of our understandings of childhood and youth, their 'natural' capacities and their pre-dispositions, are actually just social and historical inventions? If so, how liberating might this be for teachers?

To summarise, the three myths to be dealt with in this chapter are as follows.

Myth #1 'Childhood' and 'youth' are facts of nature.
Myth #2 The categories of 'childhood' and 'youth' have nothing to do with governance.
Myth #3 'Childhood' is characterised by its innocence, 'youth' by its natural resistance to authority.

Myth #1 *'Childhood' and 'Youth' Are Facts of Nature*

Childhood is a fact of nature. We didn't invent children; they have always been here. Part of living is growing from childhood, through our youth, into full maturity, and from there, eventually, to old age and death. You can't avoid any of these stages now, any more than you could in ancient or medieval times. These aren't somehow socially constructed categories. They have existed in all cultures and in all eras.

There is something vaguely comforting about the notion of childhood. It is presented as a time of almost infinite potential, a time of innocence before the realities of the real world take hold; it is a stage of life that we all eventually outgrow, a smaller but purer version of ourselves; it is the colourful little caterpillar, before we turn into big ugly moths. The caterpillar analogy is a fair one, since it implies that somehow children are naturally different to ourselves; a separate type of being. Fair enough, unlike caterpillars and moths, children might look like tiny versions of us, but they are still somehow not the same. After all, the difference between a 10 year old and a 20 year old is not the same as the difference between a 50 year old and a 60 year old. Ten year olds occupy a different category of existence; they are children. This difference has always existed, and it will always exist.

Most writers in the field would disagree with both of these assertions. They suggest instead that childhood is a relatively recent cultural development; it is a new way of understanding the young, one grounded in neither nature nor necessity.

The Invention of Childhood

ARIES – *CENTURIES OF CHILDHOOD* (1962)

Aries (1962) advances the proposition that before the sixteenth century, the category of the child simply did not exist. Pre-adulthood consisted solely of being an infant – a category that lacked any real importance – and upon reaching the age of six or seven, they were immediately accorded the full status, rights and obligations of adults. Those too fragile to be considered adult simply did not count. From the sixteenth century onwards, he argues, the single status of adult started to fragment. Young people from the upper classes began to be represented distinctively in art, not just in the structure of their faces, but also in that they were clothed in a different manner from adults. Eventually, a separate status of child was demarcated from the broader status of adult.

Aries argues that the idea of *coddling* provided the focal point around which childhood was eventually to crystallise, in that children became a source of amusement and relaxation for the women who looked after them. While this occurred within the family circle, however, a parallel set of imperatives began to impinge upon the new space of childhood from outside the family, in that an assortment of churchmen and social moralists also began to take an interest in childhood. However, rather than lauding it for its simplicity and sweetness, they regarded the child to be in need of safeguarding and reformation. The family was deemed the appropriate place to provide protection and instruction for what were, indeed, future adults. Consequently, children were no longer to be dressed and treated as miniature adults; instead they were conceived of as a form of property to be admired, cared for, disciplined and, especially, protected.

POSTMAN – *THE DISAPPEARANCE OF CHILDHOOD* (1994)

Aries has not been alone in arguing that a time existed when 'the child' did not. Postman (1994) argues that the ancient Greeks and Romans had some embryonic notions of childhood, and while they were by no means the same as ours, they did share some foundational ideas. The most important link can probably be traced through the centrality of education – and, in particular, learning to read – to the concept of childhood, and when the Roman Empire fell and Europe entered the Dark Ages, education, literacy and the notion of childhood, all fell with it.

Postman goes on to contend that childhood began the process of flickering back into life in the fifteenth century with the arrival of a seemingly unrelated invention:

Guttenberg's printing press (see Chapter 10). In the Medieval world, prior to the advent of print, everyone shared the same information, and hence the subordinate category of childhood was not required. However, alongside all the other social changes the printed word triggered, Postman suggests that this device came to create a different kind of adult, one that required new skills, aptitudes and forms of consciousness, largely based upon a new breadth and certainty of knowledge. These quickly turned out to be a vital element of a new world, ones that could not exist in an almost entirely oral culture. Consequently:

> From print onwards, adulthood had to be earned. It became a symbolic, not a biological achievement. From print onwards, the young would have to *become* adults, and they would have to do it by learning to read, by entering the world of typography. And in order to accomplish that they would require education. Therefore, European civilisation reinvented schools. And in doing so, it made childhood a necessity. (Postman 1994, 36)

Two issues are of particular importance here. First, there began to develop specific indicators of childhood, symbolic markers that we now take for granted, but which came to delineate 'children' from 'adults'. For example, children started to develop their own games and forms of entertainment, whereas previously they had joined in with adult pastimes without reservation, such as gambling. They also came to be dressed differently, a fashion that reached its zenith during the Victorian era, where boys might be dressed in little sailor outfits, and girls as dolls.

The second issue involves the development of adult knowledge. As previously stated, prior to the rise of print, everyone shared the same information. Those children witnessed all the daily activities of life without censorship; the idea that there were certain kinds of knowledge to which the young should have no access, did not exist. Importantly, this included sexual knowledge. However, since only adults had access to print, a world separate from children, the idea soon developed that there were certain things that only adults should know, that were inappropriate for children to be exposed to. From there, it was only a short step to understanding the child as innocent, and in need of protection. This will be discussed further in myth #3 in this chapter.

CHILDHOOD COMES, CHILDHOOD GOES

The second half of Postman's argument is as interesting as the first, and is even more relevant to those involved in education. He suggests that, after its birth 500 years ago, and after half a millennia of development, the category of childhood has, over the past few decades, begun the process of fading away. He uses several examples to make his case, citing not only the 'adultification' of children, but also the 'childification' of adults, or to put it another way, the merging of these two categories. He notes that younger and younger children are being dressed in adult styles, and that the domain of children's games has all but disappeared, being replaced by quantified and bureau-cratised mini versions of adult sports. While children still occasionally play Bulldog, Red Rover and Brandy, the important space these games once occupied has been taken over by organised activities; children now join soccer leagues from the age of five, with uniforms, referees and play-offs. Postman also points to the reciprocal issues of adults playing computer games, and eating hamburgers, to show that the process works both ways.

According to Postman, the reason the distinction between children and adults is breaking down revolves around the same issue that caused the split in the first place: access to knowledge. The suggestion here is that it has become increasingly difficult to maintain the distinction between those things that everyone should be allowed to know, and those that only adults should be privy to – and yes, we're largely talking about sex. To put it simply, children's increasing access to sexual knowledge is rendering the category of 'children' redundant.

CRITIQUES OF THESE ARGUMENTS

While these ideas have been very influential for those studying childhood, they have not been without their critics. It has been suggested that while Aries certainly makes a good point about the relative lack of 'child-like' faces in medieval art, according to some writers, they weren't missing altogether. Given the interpretation of art is always a subjective process, this is hardly damning evidence, but it does suggest that some degree of caution might be called for when claiming that each and every element of contemporary notions of childhood was utterly absent prior to the sixteenth century (Heywood 2001; Coster 2007).

Postman has also been subject to some criticism. One reading of Postman has been that he is bemoaning the disappearance of childhood, lost to a perceived rise of sexual permissiveness that is in the process of swallowing what was once the most innocent and beautiful stage of life (Prout 2005). If this is the case, the criticism is probably justified, since – whatever your opinion on the issue – this is a moral, rather than a historical, argument and hence should be made elsewhere. It also makes a number of unspoken assumptions about what is 'natural' for contemporary child-hood, assumptions which hold little water given the descriptions of what was 'natural' for a seven year old from the fifteenth century. Still, if Postman's argument is taken in strictly historical terms, it is a fascinating one: once, we invented child-hood, and now we are in the process of dis-inventing it.

The Gap Between Children and Adults

There is perhaps one further problem with the general understanding of the Postman position. His work seems to suggest that as the boundary of childhood gets younger and younger, then so too does the lower limit of adulthood. This is clearly not the case, as there is now a third category in the equation, one that acts as an intermediary between the child and the adult.

THE YOUTH

This third category is, of course, youth. After all, those young people who have reached an age where they no longer wish to be regarded as children, are not therefore aspiring to move directly into adulthood. There is the whole world of youth culture, and youth identities, waiting for them to explore.

Like childhood itself, there is nothing natural or innate about the category of youth. It also developed as a result of otherwise mundane social changes. Cashmore (1984) has argued that the notion of youth first emerged in the early 1950s as a consequence of the widespread demise of national military service, whereby entire cohorts of young people suddenly found themselves at a loose end, as well as the advent of hire-purchase, such that the relatively affluent young workers of the time (historically speaking) were able to acquire previously unattainable goods like fashionable suits and Dansette record players. This new purchasing power of the young was almost immediately translated into the development of a specific youth market, and the rest fell into place from there: youth fashions, youth music, youth culture and a specific and identifiable, intermediary category of existence, independent of both childhood and adulthood.

Though youth itself had a traceable history of its initial appearance, as did childhood, it actually developed from a series of other categories of pre-adulthood, which childhood did not. In the nineteenth century, childhood arguably began to fragment into other functional sub-categories, such as the 'problem child' and the 'juvenile delinquent'. These in turn later went on to produce 'the adolescent' and 'the teenager', which were the direct precursors of 'youth'.

THE ADOLESCENT

Of these pre-youth groupings, adolescence was the most influential. Although some concerns had been expressed over adolescence during the latter part of the nineteenth century, these did not assume any coherent shape until the publication of G. Stanley Hall's massive study (Hall 1904). Hall's adolescent was firmly rooted within the realm of biology; the book contained numerous chapters on subjects such as physical growth, instincts and (as a result of Hall's intellectual debt to Darwin) evolution. Furthermore, his emphasis on storm and stress came to form one of the central foundations of ensuing depictions of the adolescent persona.

Unlike the notion of the 'innocent' child, the adolescent was also a personage to which the psy-disciplines attributed an active sexuality. Not surprisingly, Hall's adolescent reflected most of the dominant theoretical understandings of sexuality of the time. Male adolescents were seen to develop in terms of strength and aggression, while the development of female adolescents was interpreted predominantly in terms of preparation for maternity.

Despite the continuing pervasiveness of the category of adolescence within certain types of research (Roberts 2007), retrospect suggests that it was simply the product of the intellectual milieu of the time in the field of psychology, along with Hall's own eclectic background, rather than anything more concrete. Smith (1989) suggests that the adolescent was:

> an amalgam of neurological research, literary romanticism and nineteenth-century American child rearing advice – an amalgam which did not succeed in forming its constituent elements into a coherent object. With the somatic base of much of Hall's evidence discredited ... the adolescent became abstracted as merely a figure of storm and stress, without any determinate content upon which educational policy or technique could be formulated. (Smith 1989, 8–9)

In summary then, categories such as childhood, adolescence and youth are not natural facts, inevitable stages of life existing in all cultures and at all times. Instead, all emerged at particular historical moments, and for particular historical reasons, and as we shall see, all have a huge role to play in contemporary social governance.

Myth #2 *The Categories of 'Childhood' and 'Youth' Have Nothing to Do With Governance*

The notions of childhood and youth may not have been given to us by nature – indeed, they may just be social categories that have developed over time – but they developed as they did for purely cultural reasons. Children may be the subject of governance, but childhood itself is not shaped by it. Governance occurs in schools; children just happen to be there.

Yet More About Governance

In Chapter 4, it has already been pointed out that the contemporary notion of individuality was made possible by the widespread use of various techniques of government, like the census; that the rise of liberalism led to government at a distance, through the medium of expertise; and that institutions like the mass school became disciplinary societies, effectively regulating space, time and conduct. On top of this, in Chapter 5, we've seen how psychology developed as an effective mechanism for managing those who appeared normal, but did not fit well into the environment of the modern classroom; how psychology permits our subjective experiences to be governed; and how this governance often occurs through the production of endless new categories of mental difference, such as behaviour disorders. Surely 'childhood' and 'youth' are just social descriptions of stages of our life, and they have nothing to do with governance. According to the reasoning that underlies all of Part II of this book, they most certainly do.

CHILDHOOD AND YOUTH ARE FUZZY CATEGORIES

Two issues need to be understood before unpacking this myth any further. The first is that these categories of pre-adulthood – 'the child' and 'the youth' – can't be understood as singular, coherent objects, unitary facts in themselves. As will be discussed shortly, the notion of 'the child' gets mobilised in a wide range of different sites, and by a plethora of diverse knowledges; likewise 'the youth'. 'The child' of criminal law – normally focused round *doli incapax*, the age of criminal responsibility – is not 'the child' of physiology, based upon growth plates and hormone levels, which is not 'the child' of product marketing, based upon cultural tastes and parental spending power, and so on, almost *ad infinitum*. The same logic applies to 'the youth'. There is no single object at the heart of all these depictions. Rather, these notions are plural, fuzzy clusters of *family resemblances*, lacking an essential core, but still permitting a generalised conception to occur; they are threads, composed of thousands of individual fibres (Wittgenstein 1952).

CHILDHOOD AND YOUTH ARE BOTH ARTEFACTS, AND VEHICLES, OF GOVERNANCE

Second, in stating that the categories of childhood and youth are all intimately tied to social governance, this occurs in two ways. First, these categories are the product of governance – artefacts – created by various systems of management and intervention, systems put in place to achieve specific ends within given contexts. For example, statistical analysis of the results of tens of thousands of psychometric tests, when plotted on a normal curve, produced a new artefact of governance: the 'gifted child'. This particular artefact illustrates the point made in the previous section quite well, since even within a fixed sub-category of child – such as 'the gifted' – precisely who gets to be called 'gifted' varies according to precisely who is making the assessment: psychologists (about 6% of the schooling population); parents (about 98% of their own children).

However, and second, as well as being artefacts of governance, upon creation such entities immediately become vehicles through which governance can occur. For example, as soon as the 'gifted child' is brought into administrative existence, it acts as a mechanism – a hook – upon which any number of governmental programmes and forms of intervention can be hung. 'Giftedness' can now justify variations in budgetary allocation, implementation of curricula changes, new forms of specialised testing, re-evaluation of teaching techniques, strategies for social management, the formation of links with other centres of 'giftedness'; the list goes on (Robinson *et al.* 2007).

Having set out these initial, underlying elements of the link between pre-adulthood and governance, it would now be useful to examine other, more specific, aspects of their working relationship, starting with 'childhood'.

Childhood and Governance

Childhood is the most intensely governed sector of personal existence. In different ways, at different times, and by many different routes varying from one sector of society to another, the health, welfare, and destiny of children has been linked in thought and practice to the destiny of the nation and the responsibilities of the state. (Rose 1990, 123)

Throughout the nineteenth and into the twentieth centuries, 'the child' became an increasing focus of legislation. Laws were enacted that attempted to reduce child abuse and suffering, to create better working conditions, and to improve the health of the young. These Parliamentary instruments had some success; however, it would be a mistake to think that such interventions were the only, or even the main, mechanisms by which the lives of children were to be managed. The difficulty arose because, as discussed in Chapter 4, the liberal State was now expected to keep its nose out of the business of child-rearing. Therefore, if the State was going to have any control over the shaping of future citizens, it would have to do it by stealth – 'governing at a distance' – by subtly managing those sites where children were raised: that is, the school and the family.

THE SCHOOL

We have already discussed how the school manages its pupils. Children are subdivided in space and time, they are continually surveilled, and their conduct is regulated and normalised, all crucial elements of a disciplinary society. The issue here is that children are not simply sat in classrooms with this disciplinary regime going on round them, they are actively shaped by it. Or, to put it another way, schools are in the business of producing particular types of children.

There isn't just one category to be dealt with here – the child – a single, self-evident stage of life; rather, there are countless. Some of these are familiar: the problem child, the gifted child, the disordered child; all of these are subject to intervention and management. Then there is the diligent child, the easily distracted child and the obedient child. In more specifically educational terms, there is the child who is good at sport, the female child who is good at maths, and the male child who is good at English. The whole point of this can be summed up in one sentence: the child is something you *make*.

Of course, this idea stands in opposition to the dominant model of childhood. The idea that the child arrives at the school in a natural state, innocent and yet fully formed, has provided the basis for a great deal of education research and that strand of philosophy that traces its origins to the philosophy of Rousseau. As A. S. Neill, the most well-known advocate of free schooling, states in the influential *Summerhill*: 'the whole idea of Summerhill is release: allowing the child to live out his natural interests' (Neill 1962, 114).

Tyler (1993) understands the role of the school somewhat differently. In an article titled 'Making Better Children', she discerns within child development literature an exhortation towards helping children achieve rationality, autonomy, and self-regulation, and yet these qualities are simultaneously deemed part of the child's nature. That is, 'the child' is simultaneously a natural fact, a fixed entity, and yet also something that you have to work at making better.

The point here is that the school isn't just a holding pen for children. It plays the important role of producing particular kinds of future citizens. Those future citizens are shaped with very specific goals in mind, and those goals are best realised through the production not just of any old child, but the 'good' child. Once again, the 'good' child is not comprised of a single 'good' thread, but is rather made up of innumerable fibres formed throughout the entire schooling process.

THE FAMILY

In addition to the school, a number of historians have pointed to the modern family as an equally important organ of governance. For example, Donzelot (1979) argues that a very specific creation – the *pedagogic family* – became a crucial component in 'governing at a distance'. This new type of family was to be regulated by a range of medical, educational and psychological experts, and these experts linked the inner workings of the family unit with the broadest objectives of government. By what Donzelot (1979, 169) refers to as 'the subtle regulation of images', it became possible to construct desirable and effective norms of family life, and these images recruited mothers into becoming 'good' mothers, a necessary pre-requisite for the parallel production of 'good' children. In this manner, the family became crucial in establishing the capacities and aptitudes expected of the socially and pedagogically acceptable child.

Although Donzelot's analysis is concerned with French history, these same arguments have wider application. In all contemporary Western societies, including Great Britain, the family became enlisted as an effective mechanism through which to govern at a distance. In particular, motherhood came to be depicted as a skill that required learning. No longer were women deemed to be innately possessed of the ability to raise children, rather maternal common sense was something that had to be taught.

With the institutionalisation of the infant welfare movement, 'mothercraft' had emerged as a new domain of knowledge, now under professional control and ready for popular dissemination through the women's magazines and feature pages of the newspapers. The major theme was that of maternal ignorance and the need to educate parents and mothers in particular, because ... they're 'on duty unremittingly night and day.' (Reiger 1985, 128–9)

Women were deemed to need expert guidance in order to fulfil their maternal responsibilities, now deemed a vital element in shaping 'good' children. To repeat: 'good' children don't just develop by themselves; they have to be *made*.

Youth and Governance

Precisely the same arguments that have been made about the governmental construction of various types of child can also be made about youth. The category of youth is the product of innumerable forms of assessment, intervention and normalisation, as well as the vehicle for achieving a range of social and governmental objectives. In addition, youth is not a singular entity, but rather an entire range of sub-categories: the 'delinquent' youth, the 'subcultural' youth, the 'at-risk' youth.

This latter category is particularly relevant. If the entire classification of youth concerns the transition from childhood to adulthood, then the sub-group of 'at-risk' youth delineates those in danger of not making this transition successfully. The 'at-risk' youth itself is comprised of any number of other 'risk' categories, all the subject of research and management: youth 'at-risk of committing serious violence' (Loeber *et al.* 2005), youth 'at-risk of criminal behaviour' (Hine and Williams 2007), youth 'at-risk of social exclusion' (Squires and Stephen 2005), and so on.

Given the breadth of the category of youth, the 'at-risk' youth is also managed extensively through the existing governmental and disciplinary structures of the school. Indeed, from its inception in the mid 1980s, the notion of 'risk' has quickly become woven into the fabric of the school, and young people can now be measured against a graded and cumulative set of normal risks, both by their age category, and by the severity of the risk involved. So, just as the disciplinary school became characterised by the minute division of space and time, 'risk' has also become an important indicator in the grid of governmental knowledge. Importantly, it provides a versatile rationale for intervening in the conduct of those categorised as 'at-risk' youth, whenever it is deemed necessary.

While the 'at-risk' youth provides a useful example of the way in which youth is both an artefact and vehicle of government, the notion of youth is also more complex than just the label of a category; it is also an identity, and one that requires self-governance.

YOUTH AND SELF-GOVERNANCE

Young people are not just placed in administrative categories, and from there they are left to get on with their lives, subject to whatever management strategies are targeted at them. The categories are more pervasive than that, in that they become part of our identities, and this requires work. A good example of this is the array of governmental programmes that have targeted the gendering of young people, programmes that have attempted to construct 'appropriate' male and female youth. A great deal of effort has gone into the production of these particular categories: gender specific curricula, codes of conduct within schools, rules for appropriate attire, and even single-sex schooling.

However, the important issue is that becoming a 'female youth' involves far more than being required to wear a skirt at school; it is an *identity*, one that requires ongoing and wide-ranging forms of self-governance. Two points are of importance here. The first is that young people are recruited into this self-management. In the same way that mothers are persuaded to become 'good' mothers, so the young are persuaded to do specific kinds of work on themselves, out of which 'appropriate' genders are shaped. That shaping is guided by far more than the resources available within the environment of school. Manuals of self-formation are to be found in a wide variety of places; one good example of this within the context of 'female' youth, are young women's magazines. These provide a vocabulary of ways for young girls and women to learn how to 'make' themselves; to regulate their identities.

The second point is that this regulation takes a number of forms, some of which might involve embracing particular styles of dress and musical tastes, adopting given attitudes, interests and ways of thinking, and acquiring specific bodily practices – all of which constitute a *habitus* (see Chapter 1). After all, there is much more to making yourself a female youth, than simply being 15 years old. These forms of self-governance have been called *practices of the self* (Foucault 1987).

The issue of acquiring specific bodily practices is an interesting one, particularly with regards to young women's magazines. Research has consistently shown that the successful acquisition of femininity is not a *fait accompli* for all teenagers; rather, becoming the kind of young woman that particular magazines consider appropriate requires hard work (McRobbie 1982; Tait 2003). Among other things, this hard work involves learning to use the body in certain ways, as *Cosmopolitan* points out in an article entitled 'The walk that drives men wild':

> Your head is up, shoulders are back, and you lead with your boobs. Your arms swing loosely back and forth while your hips swivel from side-to-side. Your weight is more in your heels. It may take practice to make it your go-to gait, so repeat this mantra to yourself when you walk: 'Shoulders, hips, heels ... '. (Miller 2010)

In summary, the categories of 'the child' and 'the youth' are by no means unrelated to matters of governance. They are both given their general shape by various administrative practices of government, and yet at the same time, these new entities act as vehicles through which governance can occur. This happens most effectively within the sites of the mass school and the pedagogic family.

Myth #3 'Childhood' Is Characterised By its Innocence, 'Youth' By its Natural Resistance to Authority

Even though it is fairly clear that childhood and youth are not natural, timeless categories, they still have some innate characteristics that can be seen across all cultures. Young children are innocent, and youth are naturally rebellious. In fact, part of being a good secondary teacher is to be able to manage teenage children, who always seem to be testing the boundaries. When you think about it, youth culture is pretty much set up in opposition to accepted ways of doing things.

The first myth in this chapter addressed the notion that childhood and youth are somehow natural categories, and the best available research suggests that this is a mistake. No such timeless, trans-cultural classifications exist; instead they are social creations. However, just because childhood and youth aren't natural, doesn't mean that they can't possess some natural characteristics, common features that can be discerned within everyone of the right age. After all, don't we all know that young children are innocent? Don't we all know that teenagers are difficult and defiant, and that their cultural practices are primarily based upon their natural desire to thumb their noses at adults?

In spite of how broadly held these beliefs often are within Western societies, there are good reasons to think that they have limited grounding in reality. Rather, both viewpoints have historical starting-points; we started to regard children as pure and innocent only with the rise of Romanticism in the eighteenth century, and youth eventually became tied to inner turmoil and cultural resistance as a combined result of Hall's adolescent from the start of the twentieth century, and more recently, the success of youth subculture theory in the 1970s.

Childhood As Innocence

Christian belief had always painted a very particular picture of the nature of humanity. The doctrine of Original Sin claimed that we are all born into a state of sinfulness, a legacy of Adam and Eve's brush with the snake in the Garden of Eden. This belief had far greater reach than just religious canon, it also informed a range of philosophical thinkers, most notably Hobbes in the seventeenth century. Hobbes held that humans are naturally selfish, and that it is only the rules of society that hold our instincts in check. Without those rules, as he famously stated in *Leviathan*, life would be 'solitary, poor, nasty, brutish, and short' (Hobbes 1994, 12). This analysis of innate selfishness did not exclude children; they were just as bad as the rest of us.

One of the first – and certainly the most important – thinkers to reject this understanding of children was Rousseau (dealt with in greater depth in Chapter 10). One of the founders of Romanticism in the eighteenth century, he took the opposite point of view. In the influential novel *Emile*, he set out the basis for this element of his philosophy, in that he concluded children were actually naturally innocent, and that it was society that eventually led them to a state of corruption (Rousseau 1991).

The question then became: how were we to best understand this innocence? Principally as a result of the central importance the Christian church had started to place upon sexual morality – curiously enough, prior to this time the focus had fallen mostly on the morality of diet (Tait, 1993) – the initial separation of the child from the adult came to be based largely round the notion of sexual innocence. That is, since sexually immoral people were now considered as being of the greatest concern, the innocence of children was therefore best conceptualised in terms of their total lack of sexual knowledge.

That children were naturally innocent, and needed to be protected, came to form a defining part of the relationship between childhood and sexuality, and this characterisation of the child reached its high point within the world of the middle-class family (Finch 1993, 70). Since children were now deemed to be intrinsically pure and innocent, by shielding them from the corruption of society (a corruption most normally characterised by the lifestyles of the working classes) for as long as possible, they could be equipped with the necessary moral faculties to cope by themselves (Weeks 1981, 49). Aries also contends that the idea of childhood innocence resulted in a particular approach towards childhood; that is, 'safeguarding it against pollution by life, and particularly by the "sexuality" tolerated if not approved of among adults' (Aries 1962, 116).

The point of all this is that there is nothing natural and timeless about the depiction of children as inherently innocent – rather it came about as a result of the rise of Romanticism, and increasing levels of concern over sexual morality. Even though more recent approaches to childhood have discerned in infants an active sexuality, and the same strengths and weaknesses of character as the rest of us (Freud 2005), the notion of innate innocence still haunts most discussions of children.

> ...the discourse of innocence works in conjunction with the sacred status of the child, to produce childhood as a moral rhetoric. Children and childhood function to explain and legitimize any practice or opinion as right while removing the necessity to provide reasons: children are the reason. (Meyer 2007, 85)

Youth As Resistance

During the mid 1970s, youth briefly became *the* central topic within social analysis; more specifically, it was the spectacular youth subcultures that pricked the interest of researchers – Skinheads, Mods, Rockers, Punks, Teddy Boys, and Goths – all seemed to demand some kind of immediate sociological explanation. That explanation came in the form of the highly influential *Subculture Theory*, whose effects are still being felt in terms of how youth is conceptualised.

The theoretical framework that underpins this position, arguably best represented by texts such as *Resistance Through Rituals* (Hall and Jefferson 1976) and *Subculture* (Hebdige 1979) – both from the Centre for Contemporary Cultural Studies (CCCS) in Birmingham – positioned large numbers of young people within discrete categories, each with specific codes of behaviour and ways of relating to the outside world. The theory consists of three main components.

(1) *Generational consciousness*: the belief that young people had started to perceive themselves to be intrinsically different from the parent generation.
(2) *Style as discourse:* discussed briefly in the last section, understanding fashion and self-shaping as a form of communication.
(3) *Counter-hegemonic struggle*: the belief that young people attempt to resist the dominant social order, and create their own cultural space instead. It is this element of the theory that is relevant here.

COUNTER-HEGEMONIC STRUGGLE

As discussed in the brief introduction to this section of the book, arguments about governance have arisen, at least in part, as a rejection of the dominant understanding of power, an understanding where its exercise is necessarily coercive, where if one person has power, someone else necessarily lacks it. Subculture theory is an example of this type of reasoning.

Subcultural theory argues that the defeat of the labour movements of the 1920s had led to the total domination of the working classes in the 1930s. However, after the watershed period of World War II and the ensuing social reconstruction, the 1950s saw the rise of popular ideologies centred around notions of increased affluence, consensus and embourgeoisement. Unfortunately, by the late 1960s and 1970s, the promised affluence had failed to materialise, and the working classes were forced to recognise the relative permanence of their position at the bottom of the social hierarchy. As they lacked the means to effect any real change, the solution many working-class young people chose was the 'magical' resolution of their problems within youth subcultures. In this manner, they conducted a struggle (albeit indirectly and symbolically), against the dominant social order.

The relationship between social class, symbolic resistance, and the winning of cultural space, is exemplified in Jefferson's analysis of the Teddy Boy subculture of the 1950s (Jefferson 1976). He argues that with its mock upper-class uniform of drape coats, crepe-soled shoes and bootlace ties, and its violent reputation, the Teddy Boy subculture was a coded working-class response to declining status, and encroachments upon its territory. This encroachment involved both actual loss of land to postwar developers, and also the cultural encroachment of the loss of kinship networks and communal space. Thus, the Teddy Boy subculture was a form of symbolic resistance through which working-class male youth won back some of this lost cultural space. Very similar arguments were also made about the Skinhead subculture, and their symbolic resistance against the fragmenting of post-war working-class communities. For more on youth cultures, see Chapter 9.

The important point here is that just as the logic of subculture theory came to dominate youth research, so too did its underpinning reasoning come to dominate our perceptions of young people themselves. That is, even though there already existed the belief that there was something of a natural 'storm and stress' present within youth (courtesy of Hall's questionable version of adolescence), subculture theory then added to this the associated idea that youth are naturally predisposed to contest authority. This understanding of youth is by no means a global one, and to assume that our own models of growing up are shared by other cultures, that resistance to authority can be seen wherever you look at the cultures of young people – that this is 'natural' – is to make a serious conceptual error (Bucholtz 2002).

SUBCULTURES AND GOVERNANCE

As discussed in the introduction to this section of the book, the coercive model of power isn't the only option available, and hence youth does not have to be understood in terms of resistance to authority. If a model is adopted wherein power is understood as productive, rather than coercive, youth subcultures begin to look very different, as does the whole category of youth.

To spell this out further: as discussed in myth #2 of this chapter, it can be argued that the category of youth has been formulated as an object of knowledge within a series of diverse disciplines that have posited 'youth as problem'. For example, youth has been constructed and operationalised as a category through the different mechanisms and knowledges associated with law enforcement. Youth is defined as the object of expertise in areas ranging from psychology to orthopaedics, social work to sociology. Youth is the centre of a multitude of regulatory practices and techniques associated with pedagogy, and it is situated and interpreted in relation to the labour market by economists. Each of these knowledges plays a part in youth being positioned as the object of government

Understanding the manner in which the category of youth is produced, in part, as an artefact of government, allows for similar conclusions to be drawn about youth subcultures. Subcultures are not constructed as forms of resistance to the exercise of power; instead they can be best understood as the by-product of particular forms of government. Along with those already mentioned, these might include rationales and knowledges behind inner city planning; various demographics of immigration; the rise of particular types of reporting and styles of media coverage; and specific technologies of marketing. Hebdige takes this even further.

> The category 'youth' gets mobilised in official documentary discourse, in concerned or outraged editorials and features, or in the supposedly disinterested tracts emanating from the social sciences at those times when young people make their presence felt by going 'out of control', by resisting through rituals ... When young people do these things ... they get talked about, taken seriously, their grievances are acted upon. They get arrested, harassed, admonished, disciplined, incarcerated, applauded, vilified, emulated, listened to. They get defended by social workers and other concerned philanthropists. They get explained by sociologists ... (Hebdige 1988, 17–18)

Of course, youth subcultures can also be partially located within the logic of a differentiating form of government. As has been discussed at length throughout the last three chapters, by classifying individuals into categories along an increasing number of axes, it becomes all the more possible to create a domain of government, enabling power to be exercised in a far more comprehensive and targeted manner. In our society, there tends to be a strong process of individualisation of those upon whom it is exercised; those who do not conform to accepted social norms are the subject of the greatest attention. That is, 'the child is more individuated than the adult, the patient more than the healthy man, the madman and the delinquent more than normal and non-delinquent' (Foucault 1977, 193). It is through the construction and demarcation of pathologies – such as the 'juvenile delinquent' – that social, legal, psychological and medical norms can be reinforced. This process is especially evident when addressing the young: 'It is around pathological children – the troublesome, the recalcitrant, the delinquent – that conceptions of normality have taken shape ... Normality is not an observation but a valuation' (Rose 1990, 131). As such, the focus on delinquent youth, and the categorization of some of them into subcultures, is part of the broader processes of measurement and judgment against various sets of accepted social norms.

In summary, even though categories such as childhood, adolescence and youth cannot reasonably be considered facts of nature, it has been suggested instead that these groupings have 'natural' qualities to them: innocence in childhood, inner turmoil in adolescents, resistance in youth. Once again, the best evidence suggests that this is not the case. All of these beliefs have historical starting-points, and as such they are neither fixed nor permanent. In the future, we may understand the 'nature' of these categories in different ways, or we may invent new ones altogether.

Conclusion

This chapter has drawn three main conclusions about categories such as 'the child' and 'the youth': the first is that they are not natural, transcultural and transhistoric stages of life. The evidence suggests that they developed at specific historical moments, incidental by-products of social, technological, and domestic changes. Writers like Aries and Postman paint a very historically contingent picture of the advent of childhood, and Postman goes on to suggest that, just as it once emerged out of the previously undifferentiated status of 'adult', it is currently in the process of disappearing again.

The second conclusion is that categories such as 'the child' and 'the youth' are both closely tied to imperatives of government. This social management occurs within both the mass school and the pedagogic family, where these categories of pre-adulthood are both created as artefacts of governance, yet are also vehicles through which that governance occurs. Importantly, such imperatives don't work simply by putting a policy in place and then waiting for the expected changes to happen, rather they work by recruiting members of those categories into doing work on themselves.

The third conclusion addresses the assertion that categories of pre-adulthood have 'natural' qualities to them, irrespective of whether they are essential categories themselves. These 'natural' qualities – innocence in childhood, inner turmoil in adolescents, resistance in youth – turn out to all have their own histories. The main implication of this is that our widely shared social conceptions of these categories are fluid, and therefore open to change.

So where do these arguments leave us? There are probably three issues to reflect upon here. The first is that, given the historically flexible nature of these categories, educators need to be aware of how these categories work, as reflected by equally flexible teaching practices. After all, many older secondary teachers, who once taught 14-year-old 'children', would now be teaching 14-year-old 'youths', with all the social differences that might entail. The second is that, given there is nothing 'natural' about the various categories of pre-adulthood, or the qualities that are attributed to them, we are free to either ascribe new qualities to existing categories – perhaps coming to regard adolescents as inherently vulnerable, or disorganised, or just plain annoying – or to create new categories altogether; the possibilities there are endless. The final issue is that abandoning the notion of 'natural' predispositions within children or youth, may well lead to more open and adaptable approaches to education practice for teachers. Surely questioning some of our ingrained ideas about what constitutes age-appropriate pedagogy wouldn't be a bad thing.

BIG DATA

We are now in the era of Big Data and standardised testing. It will be argued here that, as a consequence of this, the possibilities of social governance are currently in the process of increasing exponentially. Contemporary governance has always been about the management of data, whether this involves making particular populations intelligible through continual assessment, or constructing ever-increasing categories of difference. However, the recently developed ability to instantly correlate almost unfathomable amounts of data means that we are no longer subject to 'an avalanche of printed numbers', as in the early nineteenth century, but rather a worldwide tsunami. The potential of governance is consequently moving far beyond that envisaged within earlier iterations of individuation–differentiation–normalisation outlined in Chapter 4. As such, the possibilities of correlation, differentiation and intervention are now almost limitless.

> **Myth #1 Big Data isn't that big, or that important.** *'We've had computers around for ages now. They've always dealt with data. The computers are just getting bigger'.* It is now possible to analyse exabytes of data, from huge numbers of disparate sources, in ways that were utterly unthinkable until very recently. Big Data isn't just big, it's stupendously enormous ... and it's important. Obama's effective use of Big Data in micro-targeting the American electorate in the 2012 presidential race has been widely credited with giving him the edge over Mitt Romney. That's about as important as it gets.
>
> **Myth #2 The rise of Big Data has no implications for the field of education.** *'So what if we can now correlate anything with just about anything else. Our schools are still based upon good teachers, a sensible curriculum, and fair assessment – end of story'.* While these factors will always be important to systems of education, Big Data has the potential to reshape those systems, for example, radically increasing levels of feedback, offering greater individualisation

of curricula, and more effective student tracking. However, it also promises a seemingly endless educational culture of standardised testing, raises ethical questions about privacy and appropriate implementation, and further reduces students to a collection of numbers.

Myth #3 SATs and School League Tables are the best thing to happen to education since the invention of chalk. *'How can it be a bad thing to know how well your children are going in school? And how can it be a bad thing to know if your school is any good?'* While it isn't a bad thing to know how your children are doing at school, it may be less than desirable if that testing causes them unacceptable levels of anxiety for no real reward, or if teachers are forced to focus large portions of their teaching on those tests just to ensure the school looks good, or if those tests don't really assess what we think they do. Also, it's less than desirable if we start comparing schools in ways that have almost nothing to do with the actual data, or drawing spurious conclusions because important contributing variables are being ignored.

Introduction
What Is 'Big Data'?

> Big Data is a type of supercomputing for commercial enterprises and governments that make it possible to monitor a pandemic as it happens, anticipate where the next bank robbery will occur, optimize fast food supply chains, predict voter behaviour on election day, and forecast the volatility of political uprisings while they are happening ... So many seemingly diverse and unrelated global activities will become part of the big data ecosystem. (Needham 2013, 1)

'Data' are nothing new. As will be discussed in Chapter 10, the world is full of data; and our schools are full of data. Some of these data immediately seem important to us: how well the students do in their exams, what percentage of students actually turn up each day, how many students get hurt each year during PE lessons... all useful. However, almost all available data seem utterly unimportant: how many peas are there on an average lunch plate, how many molecules of helium are there in the chemistry lab, what is the mass of each book in the library. The digital world – by definition – is also full of data. Some of the data are useful, but most are seemingly equally irrelevant. Who cares how many emails have to pile up in the school secretary's junk folder before they get deleted, how often students have to backspace after pressing M instead of N on the keyboard, or how long they pause before answering a particular multiple choice question?

This is where the notion of Big Data enters the picture. Within the context of this chapter, the term will be used in two closely associated ways. The first is as a more generalised descriptor for large-scale statistical analysis, such as the kind required for standardised educational testing. In many ways this is the more familiar use of the term. It is Big Data that forms the foundation for Standard Assessment Tests (SATs); it is Big Data that provides the content for the School Performance Tables. When teachers quietly complain about the professional ethics of seemingly endless rounds of educational testing, what they are really complaining about is the relentless incoming tide of Big Data. It is this more generalised meaning of the term that will be employed in the final myth of the chapter, specifically regarding SATs and School League Tables.

However, since about 2012, the term Big Data has also started to gain a more focused meaning. The rise of new technologies and software platforms – such as Hadoop – means that it is now possible to record unimaginably vast stores of data, for example the digital trivia suggested above, whether they seem relevant or not, and to run statistical analyses on them. Such stores are now being mined for information, correlating previously unconnected bits of information, drawing new conclusions and making predictions. No longer do we have to take small samples of data from given populations, and extrapolate our assumptions and predictions from there; we can sample everyone, about virtually anything. The complexity and density of this new information are very likely to have a profound effect, not only upon our education system, but upon all aspects of society. For the most part, it is this more specific meaning of the term that will be employed when we examine the first two myths of this chapter.

So How Is Big Data Tied to Governance?

In Chapter 4, there is a discussion of the rise of contemporary forms of governance. The central tool of this new form of regulation was to be the science of statistics, which worked on the 'avalanche of printed numbers' that quickly gathered pace as the nineteenth century progressed (Hacking 1982). These numbers provided the middle plank of the individuation–differentiation–normalisation triumvirate that forms the conceptual core of contemporary governance. That is, with each new set of figures, it became progressively more possible to subdivide the population into smaller, more specific and more manageable categories of difference.

Fast-forward a century and a half, and the avalanche of printed numbers has now turned into a tsunami, and not a run-of-the mill tsunami either; we're talking about a continent-swamping tsunami. Still, irrespective of this massive adjustment in scale, the central theoretical principles remain the same. That is, as more and more data are deployed, the grid of governmental intelligibility grows tighter and tighter. Importantly, this is not just in terms of the ability to create ever-more specific categories of difference – each of which, of course, can be targeted for regulation in their own way – but also in terms of another crucial governmental possibility: that of *prediction*. The oceans of numbers that constitute the 'Big Data ecosystem' hold out the promise, according to its enthusiastic advocates, of highly accurate predictions of future conduct. Those deemed to be at risk of future academic failure, or truancy, or teenage pregnancy, or criminal conduct will be identified early and intervened upon. . . and perhaps even excluded before the problems arise.

While Big Data is widely held to be the future of international big business (Kolb and Kolb 2013), it clearly also has much to offer social governance. Managing current conduct, and accurately predicting future conduct, is one of the foundational aspirations of all governance. However, as will be discussed later in this chapter, there are significant ethical issues raised by these new possibilities. After all, having the potential to exclude someone for something they haven't done yet (but are highly statistically likely to do) sounds uncomfortably like Tom Cruise in *Minority Report*. Is that where we want to go, as a society. . . even if we can?

It's Pretty Big. . . and Important

Myth #1 of this chapter will address the questions: how big is Big Data, and why should we care? As just stated, the world's full of data, and we all use it to make decisions, both at a personal level and at a governmental level. Why the panic all of a sudden? Obviously there are over 7 billion of us now, and we simply have more efficient ways of communicating, recording information and acting upon it. While this is true, the real issue is we have a *lot* more data, and we can now act on these data quickly and pervasively, and this is starting to alter how we conduct ourselves, what we accept as normal, and where our society is heading. It took just a relatively small amount of statistical information about early-nineteenth-century society to begin the process of turning the unknowable and ungovernable mob into an embryonic population, as discussed in Chapter 4. It is difficult to speculate with any precision what the precise effects of Big Data will be; however, most commentators in the area consider that those effects will be profound.

As will be discussed in myths #2 and #3, Big Data is certainly important within education. This is particularly, but not exclusively, the case regarding the matter of standardised testing, both at an individual level and for the schools who increasingly rely on standardised testing results to market themselves against their competition. But this is only the tip of the iceberg, both in terms of size and importance. Big Data will affect how businesses work, it will affect our employment practices, how our sports are played, how our health resources are distributed, and even how our elections are decided. It is already having implications in terms of our basic rights as citizens – as the Edward Snowden case perfectly illustrates. That is, in relation to the augmented possibilities of surveillance associated with Big Data, many now accept that it is perfectly appropriate for the state to record everyone's personal phone calls, texts and emails, store them in giant data warehouses and run them through complex forms of analysis looking for keywords and patterns – all in the name of national security. Others do not accept this, and do not consider this type of surveillance to be appropriate within any kind of liberal democracy worth its name (Lyon 2014).

The Consequences for Education

It is fairly easy to see how the rise of Big Data is important for the world of business. It has the potential to affect everything from the identification of new markets and the better distribution of inventory, to more accurately assessing and servicing customer needs and the speeding up of response time. Likewise with many aspects of government functioning; one of the foundational elements of macro health management is the effective use of available data, indeed it has been argued that modern medicine was born from the effective gathering and analysis of hospital statistics (Foucault 1973).

It is not quite so easy to predict its effects upon various types of learning. Consequently, myth #2 will examine some of the most likely ways that Big Data will reshape systems and practices of education, particularly in the era of massive online units. In terms of positive effects, it has been suggested that it has the potential to radically increase levels of student feedback, allowing commentary not only upon final scores, but also every conceivable element of the process; it has also been suggested that it can offer greater individualisation of curricula, adapting to account for where progress has been made, and where help and further practice are still needed; finally, the contention is that it can offer more effective student tracking, in both in terms of success/failure, as well as drop-outs (Mayer-Schonberger and Cukier 2014).

However, there have also been some significant concerns raised about the negative effects of Big Data upon education. The first, and most obvious, is the worry that it will add to the already seemingly endless educational culture of standardised testing, providing yet more national and international benchmarks against which teachers will be required to measure their students. In addition to this, it certainly adds yet another few hexabytes of data to the argument that our students have been reduced to a mere collection of numbers. Finally, deploying all these new forms of analysis over every piece of data from a student's educational history extends concerns over excessive surveillance in myth #1, in that it raises ethical questions about information privacy and appropriate policy implementation.

SATs and School League Tables

Most of us are now acclimatised to the fact that every 11-year-old child in England now undergoes comprehensive standardised testing, under exam conditions, so that they can be ranked against every other 11-year-old child in England. SAT data are amassed from hundreds of questions, structured across a range of different areas, from hundreds of thousands of children, year after year. Furthermore, those data can be compared with the data sets from other countries, or added to them, to create even more massive data sets. We're talking stupendous amounts of information, and that's just within one small part of the totality of the educational dataset, and education constitutes just one small element of the 'Big Data ecosystem'.

The main question here is: in terms of a tactic of governance, what should we make of all this? Obviously if a particular child is struggling with literacy, it's better to be aware of that fact, and to be able to intervene accordingly; it seems like a no-brainer. However, myth #3 points out that there's a lot more to it than that. While this is supposed to be relatively low-stakes assessment (after all, it's not their A-levels), the practical truth is that a lot of pressure is put on children to do well in these tests. Not only are the results used as filtering mechanisms for school entry, the schools themselves also have a lot riding on the outcomes. The neo-liberal environment of contemporary education means that schools are forced to compete against each other just to survive. If their results are consistently poor – irrespective of the complexity of the reasons – there is the possibility that a particular staff member will bear the brunt of the blame, putting their jobs at risk, and that parents may even start to abandon the school, putting its viability into question, or that the school may even be formally closed, and converted into something else.

In summary, the three myths addressed in this chapter are as follows.

Myth #1 Big Data isn't that big, or that important.
Myth #2 The rise of Big Data has no implications for the field of education.
Myth #3 SATs and School League Tables are the best thing to happen to education since the invention of chalk.

Myth #1 *Big Data Isn't That Big, or That Important*

There's nothing new about using various forms of data to make informed decisions; even the ancient Egyptians used seasonal data to better manage the irrigation of their fields. We've had computers around for decades now, and they're simply devices for the speedy use of data – they're not doing anything new, they're just doing it quicker. And the computers are getting bigger, so we can use the data more even efficiently. The notion of 'Big Data' is just more of the same.

Big Data and the Changing Face of Sport

Cricket is a game where statistics matter. It would be hard to call yourself any kind of cricket fan without knowing that the Australian Don Bradman has the best-ever test batting average of 99.94, although you might have to be a bit of a cricket fanatic to know that England's best-ever test batsman is Herbert Sutcliffe, with an average of 60.73. However, in terms of an obsession with statistics, cricket pales into insignificance when compared with the sport of baseball. Entire American subcultures exist around being able to demonstrate an encyclopaedic knowledge of the results of various types of analysis of hundreds of billions of bits of baseball data: hundreds of players' batting averages, at bats, home runs, runs batted in, on base percentage, walks-to-strikeout ratio, and so on (Kuper 2013). Strangely enough though, for a sport so focused on data, and with such huge amounts of money at stake, the processes by which players have always been scouted by the major league clubs have generally had a much more subjective element to them: in addition to their batting average, scouts asked themselves: do they *look* like an athlete? How aesthetic is their swing? Is this a confident person?

The movie *Moneyball* centres upon this particular hiring culture within baseball, and the attempts by the Oakland A's to find a way to win the World Series in 2002, while using only the cheaper players that other clubs didn't really want, i.e. those who didn't meet the above criteria of what a good baseball player ought to look like. The approach they took was to use some of the oceans of available data to try and better assess what *really* matters when it comes to baseball success. Although they were ultimately unsuccessful, their approach (referred to as 'Sabermetrics') quickly became the norm within the sport, and every major league team soon adopted it. Success was no longer to be based upon 'scouting intuition'; it was to be a function of effective data analysis – and the more data, the better the analysis; colossal amounts of data, all directed towards the goal of increasing the chances of winning.

Interestingly, 10 years later, this level of data analysis was suddenly made to look positively primitive. Whereas the (relatively limited) statistics of *Moneyball* were all recorded by direct observation, the times have changed.

> The amount of data being generated today is mind-blowing. In fact, one baseball game is close to generating up to 1TB of data. This is all possible thanks to new technologies dedicated to data generation . . . for example, about 20 different pieces of data are recorded with every pitch, ranging from pitch velocity to the angle of the pitcher's arm. While generating that much data in one game may sound impressive, it's really only scratching the surface of big data's true potential, with some experts predicting advances will push data generation to as much as 7TB per game. (Delgado 2014)

Every game generating 7 terabytes (TB) of data, and this is just one game, in one league, in one sport. However, while American sport may be leading the way in Big Data technologies and usage, it is not alone. World football is already heading in the same direction (Rosenbush 2014), as is almost every other sport where people want to get an edge on their opposition (ie. all of them). For example, rugby league teams have been using GPS tracking systems since 2008 (Johnston, Gabbett and Jenkins 2014), and their use of Big Data is growing every season. While in the grand scheme of things, sport may not be that important, it illustrates just how utterly immense Big Data already is... and it's getting bigger.

Big Data, Privacy and the Reach of Government

We don't have to look around too far to see issues relating to Big Data that are *very* important. Certainly the traditional liberal concerns over the reach of the State into individual citizen's lives, as discussed in Chapter 4, would fit that category. We have come to expect a degree of privacy in our lives, specific zones that we assume are free, *a priori*, from governmental scrutiny. It turns out that Big Data is in the process of rapidly shifting the terrain in this area, as the Edward Snowden case clearly illustrates.

Edward Snowden was a system administrator with the American Central Intelligence Agency (CIA). In 2013 he leaked classified information from the National Security Agency (NSA) to the Guardian newspaper. The information he leaked concerned the existence of a number of global surveillance programs, mostly run by the NSA, but with the cooperation of other governments and several telecommunications companies. Though regarding himself as a whistleblower, Snowden was forced to flee the United States to avoid charges of violating the Espionage Act, and he currently has temporary asylum in Moscow.

> Whatever Snowden's fate... his actions have sparked a firestorm of debate around surveillance, security, and privacy. But one thing's for certain: none of the NSA's alleged programs would have been possible without the rise of so-called 'Big Data', and all the storage and analytics platforms that come with it. (Kolakowski 2013)

The programs in question concern the ability of the government to record and analyse the electronic communications of everyone in the country – phone calls, texts, emails, internet searches – all in the name of national security. These communications are then not only subject to 'meta-analysis', where patterns of behaviour and association are delineated, but also where particular 'persons of interest' can be isolated and tracked.

The claim by government is that the entire process is perfectly legal, and that ordinary citizens have nothing to fear from this Big Data program, only those with malevolent intent. However, a recent finding by the UK's Investigatory Powers Tribunal has ruled that regulations covering access by the Government Communications Headquarters (GCHQ) to data intercepted by the NSA breached human rights law (Bowcott 2015). In many ways, the dispute hinges over the difference between the 'bulk interception' of electronic communications, which the NSA (and, let's be honest, every other government with the capability to do so, including the United Kingdom) admits to carrying out, and 'mass surveillance', which they say they do not.

The issue then becomes not one of whether we should have Big Data relating to communication; it's already out there, and is growing every day at an exponential rate. Instead, the issue becomes one of how it can be utilized, and by whom. Even if the telephone metadata program gets shut down, there is so much Big Data out there that it would only be a matter of time until the government finds other streams of data to mine or, as Vladeck (2014) wryly notes on the presumption that this is already the case, until we get to find out about it. Stockman (2013) puts it another way:

> So the issue is not really how to protect privacy in the age of Big Data. Privacy, in the old fashioned sense, is already gone. The question now is: How can we be sure that the Big Data out there will be used only for good?

Big Data and Democracy

If Western democracies are currently faced with a set of ethical dilemmas over the relationship between Big Data and personal privacy, they are also faced with an equally important set of concerns over the relationship between Big Data and the most fundamental of our democratic processes: elections. Many of us still retain the almost quaint notion that elections simply consist of us putting a tick in the box every five years for the party we hate least; if only it were that straightforward in reality. Once again, the best example here appears to be American, although the United Kingdom is rapidly heading down the same electoral path (Coppola 2015).

Obama's victory in the 2012 American election has been credited, at least in part (and by both sides), to his far more effective use of all the advantages afforded by Big Data. This is thought to have happened in three primary ways, all of which are applicable to the British context. First, Big Data helps raise campaign funds – in the case of Obama, one billion dollars. For example, (at a very simple level) through an analysis of political donation patterns, it was discovered that the largest category of donors to the Democratic Party is women between the ages of 40 and 49, and while looking for ways to leverage money from these women, a Big Data analysis of social media revealed the one thing these women appeared to want more than oxygen – George Clooney. Fortunately for Obama, George is a committed Democrat and was more than happy to host large parties that very wealthy, west-coast women were prepared to pay huge amounts to attend (Scherer 2012).

The second advantage offered by Big Data involves an augmented ability to maximize the reach of those increased campaign funds. Very specific information can be gained by those who have the technology to find it, information about media consumption patterns, local and regional variation in issue importance, specifics of micro-demographics, and so on. It is no longer a case of simply being able to buy advertising time on the most popular programmes at peak time. Big Data can break the market down in ways that were previously impossible.

> 'We were able to put our target voters through some really complicated modeling, to say OK, if Miami-Dade women under the age of 35 are the targets, [here is] how to reach them,' said one official. As a result, the campaign bought ads to air during

unconventional programming, like 'Sons of Anarchy', 'The Walking Dead' . . . How much more efficient was the Obama campaign in 2012 than 2008? . . . 'On TV we were able to buy 14% more efficiently'. (Scherer 2012)

The third advantage involves being able to target the electorate with vastly improved levels of specificity. It is no longer the case of getting campaign workers to knock on every door and hope for the best. Big Data allowed the Democratic Party to try and identify, register, mobilise and turn out every single potential Obama voter in the entire country on election day. Each voter in America was given a score between 1 and 100 on their likelihood of supporting Obama, and another score on their likelihood of actually turning out to vote; the greatest efforts were then to be placed on those with a high first score and a low second score. The point here is that such elections are no longer best understood as macro-events, played out over a large map of America. Instead, as Google chairman Eric Schmitz, who advised Obama's team, stated, 'a successful campaign is highly, highly local, down to the zip code. The revolution in technology is to understand where the undecideds are in this district and how you reach them' (Schmidt, cited in Balz 2013).

Obama's use of Big Data did not end with his election. By way of emphasising its size and importance, it should be noted that Obama has put $200 million in the 'Big Data Research and Development Initiative'. This initiative involves more than 85 different projects across a range of different areas, including education. They included the CyberInfrastructure for Billions of Electronic Records (CI-BER), and NASA's Global Earth Observation System of Systems (GEOSS), which is a collaborative, international effort to share and integrate Earth observation data. The White House called the initiative 'a big bet on big data' (Scola 2013). This wouldn't be done unless coming to grips with Big Data was deemed to be very important

Myth #2 *The Rise of 'Big Data' Has No Implications for the Field of Education*

'Big Data' might be useful for producing better weather forecasts, or for getting you to buy more breakfast cereal, but it has no real impact on education. So what if there's an almost infinite amount of data out there, just waiting to be mined; this has nothing to do with schooling. In the grand scheme of things, the professional quality of our teachers, and the availability of resources, will have far more impact on our education system than any facts some statistics nerd can come up with.

We keep coming back to the pervasive mythology that as long as teachers are able to do their job, then the effects of social demographics – class, race, gender – or any other governmental, technical or philosophical variables, are all ultimately irrelevant.

It's the brains of individual children, and the commitment of teachers, that count. A computer program called Hadoop, sat on some mainframe somewhere, isn't going to make a dot of lasting difference to education, for better or for worse. Common though these beliefs are, there are many, many good reasons to think that this is not actually the case.

Some Possible Educational Benefits of Big Data

Each year teachers are expected to do more with less (McKenzie *et al.* 2014). Working on the principle that the best indicator of future behaviour is past behaviour, this trend is only likely to continue. Consequently, it is fair to assume that those pedagogies which involve dealing with a large number of students, while minimising teacher input, will be looked upon favourably. Of course we're talking about large-scale, online teaching here; it's already dominating the university environment, and there is potential for similar programs to become the norm in schools.

Tertiary institutions have a range of online offerings. There are the run-of-the-mill units with online components and resourcing; there are those where the assessments are all online; there are units that are completed entirely externally/at distance; there are MOOCs (massive online open courses); there are SPOCs (small private online courses), there are alternative organisations running large-scale courses, such as *Coursera, Udacity*, and *edX*, and so on. According to Mayer-Schonberger and Cukier (2014), all of these have the potential to benefit from the effective deployment of Big Data. Interestingly, all of those benefits can be understood in terms of more effective governance. They contend the benefits are threefold.

(1) GREATER DIFFERENTIATION/NORMALISATION

It can already be assumed that by the time students have enrolled for a university course, they have been adequately individuated, in a governmental sense. They have been separated from their peers, given their own metaphoric number and desk, and their own file to record their results. They are no longer part of a mob, but rather they are an identifiable member of a specific population. Big Data doesn't really add anything to that part of the process. It is with regard to differentiation and normalisation that things start to get interesting.

The argument here is that there is something 'Fordist' about traditional education – like a car production line. We have a curriculum, and students find themselves placed somewhere on a normal curve according to their ability to work their way through that curriculum successfully. We may give lip service to individual learning but, in reality, it's still one-size-fits-all. Given the massive amounts of data now produced by every single person taking a given test, most of them previously ignored – how long each question takes, how long students hover their clicker over each answer, which clusters of errors are made, which questions are avoided – it becomes possible to tailor that test to better facilitate individual learning.

To put this in specifically governmental terms, suppose a particular student gets Question No. 12 of their online maths drills correct. There's a limit to the information that could previously be ascertained from this fact, i.e. they understood the specific subject matter of this question. But suppose that student took five times as long to answer the question as the average of everyone else, and they hovered over a specific wrong answer for most of that time, or they tried a variety of answers before plumping for their final choice. Here is an ocean of previously neglected data that can be mined for ways to far more accurately differentiate that student within any chosen population. From there, individual question sets can be better adapted to reinforce those areas of knowledge that require work. As a result of this, that student can be far more efficiently normalised. It's a win-win for effective governance.

(2) GREATER PROBABILISTIC PREDICTION

Mayer-Schonberger and Cokier also suggest that Big Data will augment the predictive powers of governance within the sphere of education. This extends the arguments set out in Chapter 5 about risk, wherein government seeks to correlate the existence of a series of factors against the likelihood of future conduct, or future outcomes. For example, it may well be the case that if a child is raised in a certain level of poverty, if one or more of the parents is in jail, and if that child has already come to the attention of the police, then there may be a 90% risk that they will not complete Year 11. As a consequence of this risk status, various types of intervention may well then be put in place to try and improve their odds. This is a case of using prediction for governmental purposes.

With the rise of Big Data, the possibilities of this kind of governance increase exponentially. Continuing on with the student who got Question No. 12 correct on their maths drill; by correlating all the data they produced against the numbers generated by all the other students who have completed the drills, any number of different predictions could be made. It could well be that 90% of all students who took longer than three times the average time to answer this question, and who also chose at least one wrong answer before choosing the correct one, have a 75% chance of getting the answer wrong on this topic in the final exam. Further investigations can then be done to find out exactly what lies at the root of this risk – i.e. is there a lack of understanding of a particular part of the mathematical process? – and from there, targeted remedial intervention can be organised. As such, it can be seen that the ability to make probabilistic predictions from Big Data vastly increases the possibilities of governance.

(3) GREATER CURRICULA FEEDBACK

The first two prospective benefits of Big Data to educational practice described above are direct, in that they impact immediately upon any given individual. The final benefit is somewhat more indirect, in that it involves feedback loops into improved curricula. Making changes to devices like online maths drills is normally a slow and somewhat *ad hoc* process. As teachers, we normally hold students accountable for their grades, and perhaps tend not to turn our scrutiny upon ourselves, and our teaching materials, as often as we should. Big Data may help with this process.

If a very large proportion of the students fail their maths drills, this undoubtedly gives the teacher something to think about. However, it is often difficult, with the information available, to know precisely what the problem is. In the era of Big Data, far greater levels of feedback are available. If more than 50% of the students hover their clicker over the alternative answers to Question No. 12, a far higher percentage than any other question, it may well be the case that there is a problem with the knowledge base in this area. Other data may also support this conclusion. Alternatively, it may well be that the question is simply badly worded, or needlessly confusing. All manner of correlations are possible: it may well be that only NESB students struggle with the question, and once again, the wording may need to be altered. It may well be that only women struggle on the question because some of the assumed knowledge is slightly gendered; or people from rural backgrounds, or who have a particular tutor. The possibilities for feedback are all but endless.

Of course, at this stage these three benefits primarily apply to large-scale online courses, and as stated, such courses may well be the future of mass education (or at least, one quadrant of it). That doesn't mean to say that this constitutes the full extent of the educational implications of Big Data, far from it. The ability to correlate huge amounts of data will feed back into the governance of students in much smaller classes, and into the teaching of the subjects they study.

It's Not All Good

While Mayer-Schonberger and Cokier (2013, 2014) appear to be relatively enthusiastic advocates of the use of Big Data in education, they are also aware that it is something of a double-edged sword. This chapter has already alluded to a number of potential problems with Big Data – ethical, administrative and professional – and these need to be fully articulated before heading down a pedagogic path that may have more significant disadvantages than it does benefits. Arguably, there are four potential problems with the Big Data/education/governance nexus that require further discussion and assessment.

(1) FURTHER DOWN THE 'STANDARDISED TESTING' PATH

As will be discussed in detail in the next myth, 'standardised testing' has become a pivotal part of most Western educational cultures; it certainly is in England. This testing involves the comprehensive comparison of all children within given age cohorts, both against national norms of ability and against each other. However, the giant pool of data that currently feeds national standardised testing is miniscule in comparison with the bottomless ocean of numbers that is Big Data; so, if such testing is currently regarded by many educators as a significant problem, things have the potential to get much worse.

The question is, what are regarded as the main problems with standardised testing? The answer here depends upon who you ask, but four particular concerns appear to be very widely held (Maggiano, in Strauss 2014). First, for all the rhetoric of tests such as SATs not being *that* important, the reality is that they are; they matter to the school and they matter to the students. Consequently, teachers are forced to use up valuable classroom time preparing students for those tests, and other, arguably more important, parts of the curriculum receive significantly less attention than they should. Education becomes 'test preparation'. Second, the reason these tests become important is because they are used, often in spurious ways, to rank schools against each other. Not only are these rankings often a case of comparing apples with oranges but, increasingly, a school's very survival can hinge upon doing well. Likewise, individual teachers are measured by their students' results, and isn't it strange that most of the really good teachers turn out to be at high SES schools. To put it another way, there is a correlation between high standardised test scores and teacher job security. Standardised tests aren't just about the governance of children; they are equally useful for the governance of professional staff. Third, for all the talk of increased individualisation with Big Data, the curriculum actually becomes less varied, rather than more so. If certain topics are known to be on the tests, why would you bother exploring anything different? And if certain approaches pay dividends in terms of general exam success, why risk experimenting with alternative pedagogies? Finally, standardised tests don't necessarily test what students have learned, often they simply test how well students can deal with stress and anxiety. Is it appropriate to put children as young at seven on the exam treadmill? Does this form of disciplinary management have to start quite so young?

(2) THE PROBLEM WITH PREDICTION

Probabilistic prediction is generally regarded as a very positive element of 'governance by Big Data'. As stated above, accurately predicting the conduct of the population is one of the holy grails of social management. Knowing what particular individuals are capable of, and likely to do, long before they've actually thought of doing it, might be an effective way of optimising effort and ability. Surely there's no point in trying to be an architect when you leave school if 20 petabytes of educational data, taken over the previous 15 years, state with 95% statistical certainty that you don't have the spacial awareness or design capability to pass second-year university architecture exams, especially when that same data say you'd make a great doctor.

That may be fair enough, but what about if the predictive capacities of Big Data continue to improve, and we start to be able to draw accurate conclusions about seven year olds, based upon their Year 2 assessment? 'Sorry Johnny, the data say there's only a 3% chance you could ever make it to university, so let's forget about learning to read, shall we? Apparently, you'll make a great abattoir worker'.

> These constant forecasts of our likelihoods in areas big and small will not only affect our behaviour, but will forever change what the future holds – transform it from a wide-open landscape to a terrain as predefined and immutable as our past. Would this not push our society back into a new form of caste system, an odd marriage of meritocracy and high-tech feudalism? (Mayer-Schonberger and Cokier 2014, 566)

These problems only increase when we start to use probabilistic predictions in areas such as criminology. If the data state that a particular individual has a 98% chance of committing a murder later in life, what do we do?

(3) PRIVACY AND APPROPRIATE IMPLEMENTATION

All the best cultural and historical evidence suggests that there is nothing innate about the desire for privacy, but we have it, and most of us are happy with that; however, precisely what we mean by 'a right to privacy' is by no means fixed. While most of us would agree it means that no-one should have the right to peer in our bedroom window, does it also mean that all our financial records should not be open to general public scrutiny, or those from our time at school?

This is precisely the debate that needs to occur over the use of Big Data, particularly with regard to education. Given that digital records are permanent, and instantly accessible, the risk now is that every single element and incident within an entire schooling career can be accessed and scrutinised by a future employer, a university admissions officer, or the police. The fact that you threw a sandwich from your lunchbox at someone in Year 1 (propensity to violence?), or that you got caught copying off that brainy kid in Chemistry in Year 4 (untrustworthy?), or that you had to retake parts of your Algebra 3 times in Year 6 (a bit stupid?) can all be immediately retrieved and either directly held against you, or correlated against any number of other forms of conduct, or statistics from the data pool. This hardly seems to be a fair and appropriate use of your otherwise long-forgotten personal history. It is unlikely you are the same person as you were when you were in Year 1; you probably haven't thrown a sandwich at anyone in months.

Craig and Ludloff (2011, 10) state that a number of questions need to be asked regarding the relationship between Big Data and personal privacy. The first question is, who owns the data, and what are they entitled to do with it? Are your school academic and disciplinary records yours, or does the school have priority rights over them, giving them to other organs of governance, or even selling them? Second, what assumptions can we make about the personal data we now share online? Should our future employers have a right to trawl through our Facebook pages? Finally, and probably most importantly, what are legitimate government uses of digital data in a democracy? For example, does the notion of 'security' simply trump all other personal and ethical concerns? The answers to these questions are very important, and may well come to shape what remains of our conceptions of privacy.

(4) STUDENTS... NOTHING BUT NUMBERS

There is a very positivist presupposition that underlies the belief that numbers can tell us everything about a person. Whereas current notions of individuality have certainly been the product of contemporary forms of information gathering, as discussed in Chapter 4, it would still be abhorrent to most of us to think that we could be reduced to a collection of numbers, regardless of how stupendously large that collection. The rise of Big Data adds significantly more weight to the assertion that we are, at a governmental level at least, just an assemblage of scores on a normal curve. Whereas businesses still interview prospective employees, many universities no longer interview students for places, and while there are certainly important issues of scale here, the truth is that everything they need to know is considered to be right there, among the data, on the student transcript.

In summary, Big Data appears to have something to offer our education systems, at least – at this stage – the large-scale, online components of it. However, this also comes with some risks; in particular, many have already expressed concerns over the 'testing culture' that exists in schools, as well as the ongoing matter of privacy regarding the use of personal data. These important issues are not going to resolve themselves without a significant degree of further public debate. One thing is certain; none of us should accept the argument that this is all just 'trivial stuff... nothing to worry about'. These are two crucial issues that go to the very heart of both our education system, and our society.

Myth #3 *SATs and School League Tables Are the Best Thing to Happen to Education Since the Invention of Chalk*

Given we are going to be assessed all our lives, we might as well start young. After all, how can it be a bad thing to know how well your children are doing in school? If there's a problem, surely it's better that we find out early. And if it turns out that everybody there's doing badly, then it's probably down to the quality of that particular place. Shouldn't we all have the right to know if our children are going somewhere rubbish.

Mirroring a global trend towards standardised testing (Lingard 2010), Standard Assessment Tests (SATs) were introduced in the UK between 1991 and 1998, following the Education Reform Act of 1988. The initial intention was to test seven-, 11- and 14-year-old children against agreed national standards. In England, the tests for seven-year-old and 14-year-old students (at the end of Key Stages 1 and 3) were eventually replaced by teacher assessments, leaving only the national standardised assessment for 11-year-old students (at the end of Key Stage 2) – testing three areas: reading; spelling, grammar and punctuation; and maths. However, in 2003 Scotland abandoned national testing of students between the ages of five and 14 altogether; Wales followed suit in 2004, only to reintroduce national standardised testing for each age group between Year 2 and Year 9. While fearful of creating 'crude league tables', Scotland is now also moving back towards standardised testing for Years 1, 4, 7 and 10 (McIvor 2015).

As a consequence of the annual accrual of this type of educational Big Data, the state now has *some* kind of statistical picture – accurate or otherwise – of both how the nation is travelling in terms of the three Rs of its younger citizens, and how almost every child has performed at an individual level. Importantly, parents now also know how their child has done (and even more importantly, how their friend's children have done: 'Meredyth got a 5C in the SATs; we're very pleased. . . so how did yours do?'). From there, in England at least, the data from National Curriculum Assessments (NCA) – including Ofsted inspection reports, etc. – are then published in the form of the School and College Performance Tables, available on the Department for Education website, which enables the direct comparison of educational institutions.

After nearly two decades of standardized testing in England, the question then needs to be asked: to what degree has this data-driven approach improved our educational standards? If the desired goal has been to significantly improve our national literacy and numeracy levels, where do we now stand in relation to other countries when it comes to reading, writing and counting? Surely, after all this rigorous national testing, standardisation and accountability, we must be some kind of international powerhouse by now?

Unfortunately not. The latest international league tables, released in 2013, organised through the Programme for International Student Assessment (PISA), only placed England twenty-first for science, twenty-third for reading and twenty-sixth for mathematics, out of 65 participating nations – well behind educational and economic giants such as Liechtenstein, Estonia, Vietnam and Slovenia. So in terms of moving us up the table of nations, the relentless focus on standardised testing does not appear to be achieving its intended goals, quite the reverse in fact, as it could be argued that we are even marginally declining (OECD 2012).

However, improving the basic aptitudes of the students was only one of the goals of SATs and school league tables. One of the central intentions of the Education Reform Act of 1988 was to improve accountability and transparency of schools and school systems. Certainly, it can be argued that this has been accomplished, at least to some extent. The issue here is: at what cost?

The Unintended Consequences of Government

It's hard to argue with the ideas behind national testing instruments, such as the SATs. If students are falling behind in important educational areas, such as their ability to read, write and count, then it's best we know about it; once we know about it, we can intervene and try and get them up to standard. This is the core of governance: get each child to take the test (individuation), find out who has short-comings in any given area (differentiation), and then target specific types of remedial intervention in order to reach the desired level (normalisation). What could possibly be the problem with such a straightforward form of governance?

The problem is that governance is never straightforward. It is always the subject of ongoing dissatisfaction and reassessment. Indeed, Wickham (1993) argues that a perpetual dissatisfaction with government is actually essential to its continued operation. While not decrying the many mundane achievements of contemporary government – such as testing the entire nation's children for numeracy and literacy – he suggests that government is necessarily never complete, never totally successful. It is through the continually disappointed reassessment of governmental outcomes that more effective programmes are introduced, in time only to be replaced them-selves by newer and even more successful programmes. Wickham is not alone in his assessment. Rose and Miller (1992,190) also consider government to be a congenitally failing operation. They note that the very nature of governmental programmes often make them ambiguous, contradictory, partial and inexact, which ultimately results in the targets of government 'refusing to respond according to the programmatic logic that seeks to govern them'. The question now is, in what ways might the SATs – and by association the website – be considered a 'failing operation'? Why might it be the subject of a 'disappointed reassessment'?

Concerns have long been expressed about some of the 'unintended consequences' of the national standardised testing/league tables binary. These concerns were even-tually taken up within parliament, and the House of Commons Children, Schools and Families Committee (2008, 3). In their report 'Testing and Assessment', the committee stated:

> We find that the use of national test results for the purpose of school accountability has resulted in some schools emphasizing the maximization of test results at the expense of a more rounded education for their pupils. A variety of classroom practices aimed at improving test results has distorted the education of some

children... we find that 'teaching to the test' and narrowing of the taught curriculum are widespread phenomena...

The evidence suggests that these concerns, among others, are widely held by many of the stakeholders within British education, and there now exists a significant international literature on precisely these unintended consequences.

Some Problems With SATs and School League Tables

Myth #2 in this chapter discusses some of the apparent problems with Big Data's arrival in the field of education. This was predominantly an analysis of the more specific meaning of the term 'Big Data' – the 'Hadoop-platformed, tsunami of numbers' version of the phrase. The central problems there were deemed to be, in addition to the further expansion of standardised testing, some ethical issues with probabilistic prediction, data privacy and usage, and the further reduction of students to numbers. While all of these concerns are still applicable to any analysis of SATs and School League Tables, the problems raised in this next section are somewhat more specific.

There have been a number of excellent analyses of the strengths and weaknesses of regimes of national standardised testing, both in the United Kingdom and elsewhere – for example, Polesel *et al*. (2012) and Hutchings (2015). Interestingly, the problems with such enormous, data-driven forms of macro educational governance appear to be both familiar and recurring. These analyses point out a number of main areas of concern.

(1) THE POST-SAT CURRICULUM

National standardised testing has tended to focus exclusively upon the three Rs. This is not an inherent flaw, *per se* – it isn't possible to test for everything on the curriculum at the same time. However, as SATs have become more and more high-stakes, the pressure for the school to do well in the tests means that the curriculum is being slanted towards subjects that *are* testable, and the extra time is found by reducing the time given over to non-testable subjects (Polesel *et al*. 2012). The issue here is that while curricula *should* be flexible, that flexibility should be there to service changes made for pedagogic reasons, not for purely instrumental ones.

Thompson and Harbaugh (2013) note that the consequences of this are potentially far greater than simply losing a bit of time from the more creative subjects, like art, music and drama. While these subjects are beyond the direct scope of national standardised testing, the creativity and individuality fostered in these areas support the development of high-order thinking skills. Therefore, reducing the time spent honing these skills in the classroom is likely to have the consequence of adversely affecting students' ability to reason their way through the more difficult SAT problems. Cutting art and drama to practice maths and literacy might seem the best way to good scores, but the reverse might actually be true.

Thompson and Harbaugh also note that this kind of *ad hoc* instrumental tinkering with the curriculum can result in the fragmentation of what is otherwise a carefully planned and weighted set of documents; in order for a curriculum to maintain its long-term coherence, it cannot readily be broken down into 'test-sized' pieces. Consequently, the desire to do well in the SATs, and to adjust the curriculum accordingly, may be counter-productive, both in the short and the long term.

(2) TEACHING TO THE TEST

In recent decades, teaching styles have become significantly more dialogic and student-centered in their approach. The old model of 'teacher out the front, students sitting in silence taking down notes' has become much less prevalent than it once was; student-centred learning is now generally deemed to be the most appropriate and effective pedagogy (Cornelius-White, 2007). Unfortunately, one of the principal side-effects of increasing the pressure upon teachers for their students to do well in their SATs – and to please the Ofsted inspectors – is for classrooms to undergo a reflex reversion to a more teacher-centred approach to instruction.

Part of the problem here lies with the notion of 'good teaching'. Most of us will have some fairly coherent ideas as to what a teacher has to do to be considered good. Indeed, we can probably look back in our own educational past and remember teachers who richly deserved this label. The cluster of traits and aptitudes may vary somewhat, but they would probably include some of the following: engaging, kind, enthusiastic, funny, organised, diligent, supportive, knowledgeable and trustworthy. According to Thompson and Cook (2013; 2014), an important characteristic of high-stakes testing is that it erodes more traditional understandings of 'the good teacher', replacing them with an 'audit culture', where a teachers' value is determined by their ability to 'achieve an optimal pattern of data-points' on their student's examinations.

One side effect of this audit culture is that teachers now know they are at greater risk of getting the sack if they can't get close enough to the 'optimal pattern of data points'. All those other traditional elements of 'the good teacher' lack the inherently measurable components of the students' SAT scores. As such, the buzzwords of neo-liberal education – efficiency, accountability and performance – have now been provided with a domain wherein they can all be readily quantified.

Thompson and Cook (2014) also note the rise in the number of schools and teachers resorting to 'cheating' in standardised testing. This professional response to the audit culture takes a number of forms, almost all involving data manipulation. Some of this manipulation is deemed (almost) acceptable, such as down-playing KS1 results to improve later KS2 comparisions, and some is deemed unacceptable, such as collusion between staff and students. The point Thompson and Cook are making is not one of moral judgement here, but rather locating such data manipulation as a predictable reaction to the 'new rules of the game'. When the only thing that appears to matter are the educational numbers, both schools and teachers will adjust their survival strategies accordingly.

(3) STUDENT LEARNING

There are a number of issues in play here. Whereas preparing for SATs can give a certain structure to learning, the contention is that it can also teach children that the most important thing in education are the scores they get in an exam. While they are clearly not unimportant, an excessive focus on outcome measures, such as SAT scores, can lead to an inherent under-emphasis on the intrinsic processes of learning and knowledge-acquisition (Polesel *et al.* 2012). Most academics are already familiar with the 'is this going to be on the exam?' syndrome: answer 'No', and you can empty a lecture theatre.

In terms of the kinds of thinking privileged by standardised assessment, it has been contended that SAT-style tests lead to shallow, superficial reasoning (Australian Literacy Educators Association (ALEA) 2013). The argument here is that the kinds of multiple choice protocols most frequently utilised are unable to measure otherwise-important attributes like critical thinking, curiosity, empathy and self-discipline. Deeper levels of understanding – untested by the SATs – are required if students are to progress beyond the stage of initial decoding.

A further important issue regarding standardised testing and student learning involves issues of social equity. Arguably many middle-class students will thrive in the setting of standardised tests. Comber (2012) notes that standardised testing takes time away from other curriculum areas, often those important for maintaining students' long-term engagement with schooling (where this may be a problem), such as art and physical education. In doing so, it is likely that students from low socio-economic and culturally diverse backgrounds will ultimately pay the highest cost (Hutchings 2015). As Au (2009, 3) states: 'the weight of the high-stakes testing environment falls heaviest on the shoulders of low-income students and students of colour.'

(4) STUDENT/STAFF WELLBEING

In his study of teachers' attitudes towards standardised testing, Thompson (2013) found that the general perception is that it increases stress, pressure and anxiety, not just for students, but for the entire schooling community: teachers, principals and parents. As discussed earlier, this is perhaps not surprising, since we start the process when the children are very young; and it is self-evident, even to such students, that this is important stuff, especially given the lengths many primary schools now go to in order to do well, thereby finishing ahead of their rivals in the rankings. Hutchings (2015, 5) observed that:

> Children and young people are suffering from increasingly high levels of school-related anxiety and stress, disaffection and mental health problems. This is caused by increased pressure from tests/exams; greater awareness at younger age of their own 'failure'; and the increased rigour and academic demands of the curriculum.

These physical and mental outcomes are not restricted to the United Kingdom's SATs. In their study of over 8000 Australian teachers' experiences of their version of standardised testing, Dulfer *et al.* (2012) also found that 90% of teachers found pre-test stress among their students, which generally manifests itself in the form of crying, sickness and sleeplessness. Lending more weight to the argument that testing disproportionately harms the disadvantaged and the lower achieving, it was also noted that full-cohort testing can damage the self-esteem of these students, which then has knock-on effects on their confidence regarding the possibility of success in other areas.

(5) THE RELIABILITY OF THE DATA

The first issue with the data is to question whether they actually reflect the relative abilities of the students in the way they claim. Polesel *et al.* (2012) point to a number of concerns, from the suggestion that the data from standardised testing always have the potential for unreliability in terms of the allocation of grades to specific children, to the argument that the individual results are only of limited use, both to parents as an information source and to teachers as a diagnostic tool. Whatever the case regarding the veracity of the data, what is certain is that they don't represent some perfect, positivist mirror of the state of the real world.

In addition to these concerns over the reliability of the data at an individual level, there are also concerns over the data when presented at a school level. There are two elements to this. The first is to improve the likelihood of attaining good results by manipulating the data. The second is the inappropriate use of the data to rank schools. Let us take these in turn.

It has been suggested, somewhat paradoxically, that one way to improve the appearance of the national end-of-KS2 SATs is to artificially reduce the scores in the teacher-administered end-of-KS1 tests – thereby allowing the school to improve their KS2 value-added scores. As Allen states,

> This isn't cheating as we have seen in the US, where people get a rubber and they erase the things that children have written. It is asking people to apply subjective judgments knowing that the decisions they make are going to be critical to the success of the school in a few years' time – in the way that they are judged by Ofsted and by everybody else. (Allen, cited in Stewart 2015)

This kind of data manipulation is relatively innocuous in comparison to other countries and their own versions of standardised testing. For example, in Australia, where their SAT-equivalents (called NAPLAN) are not compulsory, Thompson and Cook (2014) have reviewed various ways the school population can be controlled over the testing period. Although this is a relatively complex procedure, it can be reduced to the twofold process of identifying those students who will have a negative impact on the school's results and eliminating them, and identifying those students who will have a positive impact and making sure they turn up, and turn up well prepared. It is suggested that the most common strategies of exclusion are suspending 'trouble-makers' for relatively minor infractions; encouraging parents of students with learning difficulties, Indigenous students, and NESB students to keep them home to 'protect them' from negative results; and rejecting applications for enrolment from students with previous low testing scores. Alternatively, for the higher achieving students, schools can organise free breakfasts during testing, as well as free transport to the school; they can also encourage parents to ready students for the tests, including special courses and preparation material (Thompson and Cook 2014, 136). In effect, schools have to learn how to game the system in order to succeed; to a lesser degree, English schools game the system as well.

The second, and final, issue regarding the data relates directly to the School League Tables. On the Schools and Colleges Performance Tables website schools are compared against other schools in the local area, and around the country – more often than not, allowing 'good' (usually wealthier) schools, to be compared with 'bad' (usually poorer) schools. As the entirety of this book will attest, our schools and our education system are incredibly complex, layered and context-bound institutions, so to reduce their respective values to a single list borders on the absurd. Yet even so, every year our newspapers will print league tables of our 'best' schools, tables which never place their information in any kind of appropriate context – just a long stack of schools going from 'the very good' to 'the very bad' – and which can represent the death-knell for schools placed too low on those lists, or at least the start of a death-spiral. This is not useful or fair at any level, and can give the most simplistic and one-dimensional measure of what ought to constitute a 'good' education.

In summary, finding out how well children are doing at school, where their strengths and weaknesses lie and how they can be improved – particularly in foundational areas like reading and maths – is the very definition of contemporary governance. However, governance always brings with it unforeseen consequences. Standardised testing and School League Tables may have been introduced with the best of intentions; however, they are very far from perfect, and if we accept that governance is necessarily a continually failing process, one which requires continual revisitations and reassessment, then such educational practices – as they currently stand – fall well into this category.

One recurrent suggestion for improving the relationship between student learning, SATs and School League Tables, may be to separate out tests according to purpose. As Hutchings (2015, 7) states, we should ensure that 'tests intended to measure pupils' progress and attainment are not used for school accountability'.

As has been demonstrated in this section, using the same Big Data for both these purposes can cause far more educational problems than it purports to solve.

Conclusion

The central purposes of this chapter have been to understand just what Big Data is, and the extent of its potential in relation to contemporary governance; to see what it can bring to the field of education, in both a positive and a negative way; and to examine one particular example of the Big Data/education nexus within the British context, that of the SATs and School League Tables. As with the previous two chapters, this chapter acts as a case study of governance. That is, Chapter 4 has set out the central framework of understanding, and Chapters 5, 6 and 7 have given practical examples of how it works in different ways.

In spite of the many concerns expressed in this chapter about the rise of Big Data, the suggestion is not to turn the clock back and somehow do away with it all; Big Data is not going anywhere anytime soon. The main reasons for this are twofold. The first is that too much money can be made from it, and if the history of humanity has taught us anything, it's that nobody – not individuals, not business, not nations – is willing to give up something voluntarily if it makes them rich. The second is that we all like what Big Data can offer us too much. We like it when our smart phones give us the quickest way home through rush hour traffic; or when we get fabulously cheap hotel rates online; or when shopping coupons mysteriously appear in our letterboxes for something we actually want to buy. All of these, and a thousand other things too, are the result of Big Data. And as we have discussed, it's only getting bigger.

Given these facts, what can be done? In reality, the best we can hope for is to better manage its arrival. Big Data use should be transparent; the extent of its potential and its reach means that, as a society, we should always be informed of how and when our data is being used. Big Data use should be subject to ongoing scrutiny and criticism; it is also important for us to know what its costs and consequences are. Big Data use should be tightly regulated; our data should not be part of an economic and governmental free-for-all, even when the magic words 'national security' are involved.

PART III

CULTURAL CONTEXTS OF CONTEMPORARY EDUCATION

Having addressed some of the theoretical foundations of education, both from within the familiar modernist paradigm – though with some ground given to the logic of postmodernity – and also from within a Foucault-inspired governmental approach, the next part of this book examines some of the cultural issues, concerns and contexts impacting upon contemporary education. While there is no direct, correlative link between the culture of a society, and the kind of schools it contains – where the latter is simply a function of the former – it would be a mistake to think that there are not important connections between the two. Indeed, a better approach might be to not consider them as discrete entities at all.

Chapter 8 – *The Media* – addresses the relationship between education and the news media. It questions the assertions that 'media studies' is not a serious subject, and doesn't belong in the school curriculum; that media messages need an education to decode properly; and that the media is not responsible for whipping up moral panics, whether to further specific political ends, or to simply sell papers and gain viewers.

Chapter 9 – *Popular Culture* – investigates recent concerns over the increasing presence of popular culture in the classroom. It questions the common view that all popular culture is rubbish, unlike 'high culture'; that teachers need to be popular culture experts if they are going to connect with their students; and that the classroom is no place for popular culture, as it has absolutely no educational value.

Chapter 10 – *Technology* – examines the rise of digital technologies and their implications for mass schooling. It questions the belief that these technologies represent the solution to many of education's enduring problems, such as limited access to information, particular kinds of social-class disadvantage, and inconsistent standards of education; and that digital technology spells the end for traditional teaching, since learning resources can be accessed instantly from almost anywhere, and students now have access to virtually limitless information.

Chapter 11 – *Globalisation* – addresses the emergence of a global economy, as well as global cultures and global forms of politics, and makes connections between these phenomena and our education system. Contrasts are drawn between the common view that globalisation is simply Americanisation by another name; specific changes to education are discussed in the light of the rise of global systems of management, transnational economics and employment patterns; and global environmental issues are examined through attempts to implementation issues of sustainability within the curriculum.

Two points are of particular note here: first, there is a significant overlap between the four chapters, not in terms of the content of this book, but rather in terms of the topics themselves. The subdivision of Part III into The Media, Popular Culture, Technology and Globalisation is, in many important ways, an artifice. After all, digital devices such as the iPad and iPhone are significant global cultural artefacts in and of themselves, irrespective of their digital properties, and they are also important mechanisms for the consumption of media. As such, they could legitimately have been discussed in all four chapters; actually, they aren't discussed anywhere, but the point is made.

Second, all four of these areas have already given significant ground to post-modernity, and it would be setting up something of a 'straw man' argument to suggest otherwise. It would be unlikely that you could read any contemporary book on any of these topics and find simplistic, modernist descriptions of how media messages are encoded – the 'truth' of the message – without parallel discussions of the plurality of ways they can then be decoded. Likewise, analyses of popular culture are no longer likely to be underpinned by the unspoken presupposition that most of the content is relatively worthless, and that we'd all be better off if everyone just turned off their televisions and started listening to classical music.

However, in spite of this, the evidence suggests that all four areas are often still asked to frame their conclusions in terms of modernist binaries, certainly when applied to broader educational debates. Is the media a positive or a negative force in the lives of children? Does popular culture belong in the school classroom, yes or no? Is digital technology a good or a bad thing for education? Is globalisation good or bad, either for education and for society? As will be seen, the answers are far too complex for either/or answers.

THE MEDIA

8

It is important, for students and adults alike, to understand the pervasive, corporate, global and continually developing nature of our news media. The news media does not occupy a realm somehow removed from our schooling system; indeed it impacts upon education in a wide range of ways, both directly and indirectly. However, for much of the time, most of us barely pay attention to the thousands of media messages we are exposed to every day, and even when we do, we generally assume that those messages are both objective and neutral. This is a mistake.

Myth #1 We do not need pointless subjects like 'media studies' in our already crowded curriculum. *'Children need to learn to read and write, and until they can do that properly, we can do without media studies; it doesn't add anything'*. On the contrary, understanding the media represents a new and important form of literacy for the twenty-first century. In addition to contributing to critical thinking skills, it contributes to the production of active, global citizens, and it helps them understand the workings of one of our most important contemporary institutions.

Myth #2 With the news media, you don't need to think, you just need to read and listen. *'You don't need to "decode" the news media; there's nothing mysterious or ambiguous about it. It tells us what's going on, nothing more, nothing less'*. The news media is not simply the objective and transparent communication of current events to a unitary audience. News gathering and selection is a subjective process, and those items selected generally have specific elements – negativity and conflict ranking high among them – and these stories can often support a given agenda, the conservative media campaign against 'progressive education' providing a good example.

Myth #3 The media doesn't create moral panics, but even if it does, this doesn't affect education. *'Even though the news media is under pressure to be entertaining, they aren't responsible for whipping up public hysteria when it happens'.* The evidence suggests that from time to time, the news media can create highly visible 'folk devils', not only to sell newspapers and garner viewers, but also to reinforce the boundaries between 'us' and 'them'. The treatment of 'asylum seekers' by some elements of the media has often taken this form, and this can have significant implications for how minorities are treated in our schools.

Introduction

The term 'the media' refers to a very broad set of concepts, practices, agencies, technologies and forms of representation; however, for the specific purpose of this chapter it will largely mean the *news media*. Within this more limited version of the term, there is still a wide range of possible issues to look at, all of which impact upon our understanding of mass education, both directly and indirectly. For example, one important topic might be the matter of ownership, and more particularly, the issue of media monopoly. In the era of the Murdoch-owned News Corporation – i.e. when a huge percentage of our mainstream news media appears to be in the hands of a very limited number of people – questions arise about the role of such organisations in presenting particular versions of the world for public consumption, versions which suit the political and economic interests of those owners (Herman and Chomsky 1994).

An associated issue might involve the specific subject matter of the news. Those topics deemed worthy of reporting are not chosen at random, and neither are the approaches taken to those topics, rather they generally reinforce dominant representations of, and structures within, British culture. It is perhaps not surprising then that, for example, women's sport receives less than 5% of the sports coverage, as compared to men, in British newspapers (Packer *et al.* 2014). To put this figure in context, the sporting activities of horses receive greater media attention.

Another topic might concern the significant changes that the news media is currently undergoing. Traditional commercial newspapers are struggling under the twin onslaught of free newspapers, supported solely by advertising, and of the news available on the internet (Kuhn 2010). Likewise, traditional British television network news, such as BBC, ITV and Channel 4, have lost market share to their cable news equivalents. This is particularly the case in the USA, where News Corporation's ultra-conservative Fox

News has gone some way to breaking the stranglehold of ABC, CBS and NBC, with all the political implications that flow from this.

All of these, and many more, are common enough topics within any analysis of the media, and it would appear that issues relating to 'News Media and Education' don't really get much of a look in. However, this would be incorrect, and for three main reasons.

The Importance of Media Education

First: there is considerable disagreement over the best way to introduce the media into the education curriculum. That is, education gets a look in because we appear to have trouble agreeing over the best way to educate *about* the media, or even whether we should educate about it at all. As will be discussed in myth #1, this debate has often been constructed as a modernist binary: i.e. the media isn't a problem, so we don't need to learn about it in the curriculum, vs the media is a problem, and children need to understand how it works. That is, more conservative commentators frequently bemoan the teaching of media studies, stating that this somehow represents the death rattle of traditional education.

> Some schools abandon the more traditional academic subjects altogether and do not teach them at all... schools will have children take drama, PE, or media studies, abandoning history, physics or French to do so, and our so-called progressive thinkers rejoice... (Birbalsingh 2011)

Opponents of this position point to the importance of the media in giving students a window into the world, and in making active, informed citizens, citizens who can reason effectively, and who can participate in the shaping of our society in what is an increasingly global context.

Educating About the Media

Second, it is also suggested that it is important to teach students to 'decode' the media, to help them understand that the news is not impartial, and that the shaping of opinion through the media often comes with a range of different agendas. While the newspapers are full of domestic politics, world events, local issues, sports reports, cultural reviews, and adverts – likewise with television news coverage – at first glance, education doesn't seem to feature very often at all. However closer scrutiny not only reveals a fairly consistent stream of education-related topics in recent years – the school building programme, funding levels for private schools, multicultural education, literacy standards and practices, postmodernism in the classroom, drugs and violence in schools – it also reveals a very particular set of stances on these topics.

It is not a huge leap to suggest that schools are often portrayed as hotbeds of drug abuse, violence and political sedition (Henry 2009); and that staff are depicted as being almost as illiterate as the children they teach (Smith, 2014). Myth #2 will address the manner in which one recent debate has been handled in the news media: the issue of student literacy. It will point to the importance of equipping students with the capacities necessary to understand that, to use the title of the book by Burton (2002), when it comes to what's going on in the media, there's *More Than Meets the Eye*.

The Media and Moral Panics

Third, other than simply pushing certain agendas within the field of education, as will be discussed in myth #3, the media frequently plays a significant role in whipping up moral panics within our society, panics that have both direct and indirect consequences for education, and which feed back into public policy and determine our perceptions of what is going on in our schools.

Though the notion of a moral panic is most frequently associated with the activities of young people, it can apply to a wide range of issues and groups. It could be argued that the conservative media campaign against progressive models of literacy education shared many of the characteristics of a moral panic – engendering widespread hostility towards teachers, a disproportionate response to the problems at hand, and so on – but a better example probably involves ongoing representations of 'asylum seekers' arriving in Britain, particularly, for example, as depicted within the pages of *The Daily Mail*. This has repercussions that have spilled out of the newspapers, directly into our classrooms.

To summarise, the three myths to be dealt with in this chapter are as follows.

Myth #1 We do not need pointless subjects like 'media studies' in our already-crowded curriculum.

Myth #2 With the news media, you don't need to think, you just need to read and listen.

Myth #3 The media doesn't create moral panics, but even if it does, this doesn't affect education.

Myth #1 *We Do Not Need Pointless Subjects Like 'Media Studies' in Our Already-Crowded Curriculum*

How many times does the point have to be made? Schools aren't there as part of some ongoing experiment on our children's minds. The traditional curriculum survived for so long simply because it deals with precisely what's needed: the three Rs. We don't need each new, trendy social issue to be given space in the classroom. What are you going to take out, in order to find space for 'media studies'? Kids watch enough TV as it is.

One thing most certainly *is* true. There aren't an endless number of hours in the school day, such that everything we'd *like* to teach, we *can* teach. Anyone who has spent time in a school would know that constant battles are fought over various aspects of the curriculum: what gets taught, when, who has to teach it, which subjects get priority (either overtly or covertly), which subjects get more funding, which subjects become part of the school 'branding', which subjects become dumping grounds for underachieving students; and these are only school-level disputes. Wider debates are also fought out at national level about what should be taught in schools, and how.

Many subjects can make strong claims to a higher profile within British education. Given our obesity rates, advocates of daily physical education can mount a very strong case. Those who argue for compulsory second language education rightly point to the arrogant parochialism that can go with thinking you only ever need to be able to speak English. Part IV of this very book, in addition to arguing that a knowledge of philosophy is essential for making sense of mass education, also attempts to make the case for its re-introduction into the school curriculum. Where does it end?

In spite of this competition for space, there are a number of arguments that support giving school children a better understanding of the media – and specifically the news media – as part of their formal education. These arguments vary in their approach, and their significance, but they all reach the same conclusion: the subject is far too important to ignore.

(1) Finding Space in the Curriculum

The first question here is a purely practical one: do we have to kick out another subject in order to make room for media studies in the curriculum? The debate is often framed in such binary terms, and largely for reasons of rhetorical effectiveness; after all, who would really argue that we should abandon maths or history to do so? Nobody, except a straw man.

This generally leaves two options which, relatively unproblematically, represent the current situation within the curriculum. The first is to offer media studies as a stand-alone subject, both at O- and A-level. This leaves the central problem of the subject remaining optional, and hence – within the context of a broader educational environment where traditional subjects still retain the intellectual status – unstudied by the majority of school students.

The second is to embed the study of the media from primary school onwards within a subject such as English and/or citizenship. For example, given the flexibility of the contemporary curriculum to address a wide range of texts – while still examining issues of narrative, perspective, context, genre, and so on – it has become obvious that English doesn't always have to be about Shakespeare. 'Literacy' can take many forms, and there is plenty of evidence to suggest that media literacy has become just as important as the others (Hobbes 2007; Bazalgette 2010).

(2) Critical Thinking

Maths teachers would argue that maths isn't just of value because it teaches you to count; they would also contend that it teaches you to think in an orderly fashion, to organise your premises well in order to reach a valid conclusion, to reduce problems to their functioning elements and to find some certainty in areas where there previously may have been none.

Those who see value in media education would make similar kinds of claims, suggesting that the conceptual skills required to better understand the media bring benefits beyond the boundaries of the discipline itself. Media studies as a discipline represents an ongoing exercise in critical thinking. That is, addressing the way news messages are assembled and disseminated, appreciating how audiences can receive and negotiate those messages, and thinking through the nature of the forces that give rise to those messages in the first place, all these processes of criticism and reflection result in the production of more intellectually competent, flexible and insightful citizens (Share 2002). This belief in the intrinsic value of media studies is supported by Hart (1991, 1), who states the following.

> When we are able to evaluate media messages with confidence and respond critically to them, we are much less likely to rely on the opinions of others and more likely to become autonomous rather than automatons. In learning how meaning is made in the media, we can gain more understanding of the world in which we live. We can be determined not to be determined.

(3) Media Literacy and Active Citizenship

Hart is making a good point here. Not only is a better understanding of the media good for intellectual ability and confidence, it also makes us more independent, questioning thinkers, which in turn has implications for the way in which we act as citizens who can effectively participate in our democracy. There is much more to a democracy than simply having the right to vote; citizens have to have access to accurate and appropriate public information, such that they can make informed choices – choices about candidates, parties, issues and the future direction of their community.

Schirato *et al.* (2010) contend that the concepts of 'citizenship' and 'community' are not as straightforward as they might first appear, and that the media has always played a vital role in linking the two together. Citizenship concerns the rights and obligations we have as members of a community, but how do we form that community? After all, we have only met the tiniest fraction of the British population, and that doesn't constitute a sufficient basis to form any kind of valid group identity. This is where the media is of importance, in that through the circulation of various forms of knowledge and information, *imagined political communities* can be established, allowing people to think about themselves, and their relationships to others. Without agencies such as the media then, the conceptual bonds that form the fabric of the community would quickly begin to dissolve.

The point here is that – ideally – citizenship is not a passive status. The public space, in which ideas are debated and opinions aired, only operates when citizens are both free to participate, and willing and capable of doing so. The media – the Fourth Estate (after the executive, legislative and judicial branches of government) – has the historical role of holding the government to account. Students in a democracy need to learn the importance of that process, and to participate in it, as soon as they can.

(4) Global News, Global Citizenship

The implications of this now go far beyond the borders of the United Kingdom, as will be discussed in Chapter 10. We now live in a global economy, and no country is entirely immune from the financial difficulties that might beset any other – with the possible exception of North Korea, which shouldn't be a point of envy. This inter-reliance extends beyond the realm of the economic, into a broader convergence of ideas and identities. The notion of the 'global citizen' comes into its own here; the notion of global warming, with everyone equally at risk irrespective of nationality, provides a perfect example.

Significantly, it was writers on the media who were the first to foresee the rise of a global culture. McLuhan and Fiore (1967) noted that the advent of new forms of communication technology had overthrown the constraining factors of 'space' and 'time', and that, as a consequence, we had begun to live in a *global village*. McLuhan and Fiore's claim is important for two reasons. First, it is no longer sufficient for students to know only about their immediate social and political environment. As well as issues of global climate change, there is the matter of global terrorism, the global economic crisis, an ongoing global refugee crisis, risks of global pandemics, geopolitical issues ranging from the rise of China to the troubles in Europe, global repercussions of the Arab Spring, and the list goes on. All these issues impact upon the UK, directly and indirectly, and students now have to be both equipped to understand their implications and, as future global citizens, to begin to participate in the process of finding effective solutions.

The second reason involves the global nature of modern news organisations. Such news organisations are not new; agencies such as Reuters, AFP and AP have long gathered news internationally, which they then sold on to clients around the world. The more recent changes that have occurred involve the rise of media conglomerates like News Corporation, the blurring of the boundaries between national and global news agencies, and the boundaries between news, opinion and entertainment, as is arguably the case with Fox News (Boyd-Barrett and Rantenen 2010).

(5) Understanding One of Our Major Social Institutions

This latter point is important because it addresses the issue of the major institutions that organise the lives of all of us in the UK, regardless of age. While we are aware of the civic importance of educating our children about our central legislative and judicial institutions – the Crown, the House of Commons, the House of Lords, the Supreme Court – as well as the functioning of major institutions such as the military, our education system, and the Civil Service, this list generally excludes one of the biggest, and the most influential: the media.

Burton (2002) points to a number of associated reasons as to why we should study the media, as a set of institutions. He suggests the extent of the media's power and influence enables it to shape our ideas about the world according to its own agendas. He suggests that its economic power gives it almost limitless reach to achieve its ends, and he also notes that the sheer scale of the media's operations means that few are unaffected by its messages. Indeed, its diversity and concentration enable it to reach virtually any audience it chooses to target. Given the breadth of media forms, it now acts as one of our central mechanisms for gathering information, and can present, and re-present, that information in any number of credible and persuasive ways.

This is not to say that media institutions should then be understood in a simple, modernist, cause-and-effect manner, such that a singular thing – 'The Media' – with a unified agenda and mode of operation, induces a predictable response within an equally unified audience. Rather, the entire equation is far more piecemeal, contingent and unpredictable than that. Media messages may be encoded with one idea in mind, but decoded by different audiences in entirely different ways. For example, just because the makers of news put together an item highlighting the dangers of train-surfing, doesn't mean that some 18-year-old risk-taking youths won't read the very same news item as a 'how-to manual'. This notion of 'decoding the media' provides the final, and perhaps the most important reason for studying the subject.

(6) Decoding the Media

In suggesting that students need to be able to decode the media, this is not to jump headlong into what Share (2002, 8) calls the *protectionist approach* to the media, where we regard it as some kind of evil ogre from which citizens, young and old, need safeguarding; and that by educating against its manipulative tricks, we can avoid simply being passive victims of media indoctrination. The situation is far more complex and nuanced than that, but certainly there's a lot more going on than is apparent at first glance.

Rather than regarding the news media as a straightforward source of objective information, to be communicated and understood in a singular, unproblematic way, most media commentators would argue that the news we receive is neither neutral nor transparent. As Branston and Stafford (2006, 194) rightly note:

> News is a globally important media form ... and modern democracies depend on accurate news to give adequate accounts of a complex world, even though this is far from always being the case. It matters greatly that news is understood as being 'made' and not 'natural' or 'given'. It matters what kind of news is made, under what conditions, what spaces and budgets it occupies, and the support or criticism it is given by its audiences.

Indeed, it matters so much, that the next two myths are devoted in their entirety to the need for citizens to be able to decode the news media; to realise that the newspapers they read, and the TV news programmes they watch, often have agendas all of their own.

Myth #2 *With the News Media, You Don't Need to Think, You Just Need to Read and Listen*

Reading a newspaper or listening to the news isn't an overly complex business. They simply tell you what's going on in the world around you; they don't just make stuff up – not the important stuff anyway – and if they don't make stuff up, what they are telling us must be true, so what's the problem? If it's true, you can't complain about not liking it. If the news tells us that kids in schools can't read like they used to, or that illegal immigrants in boats are swamping the country, well. . . facts are facts.

It would be nice and simple if there were only two options regarding the news: either, the provision of Goebbels-like misinformation and propaganda, so easy to see through that a child wouldn't be fooled; or alternatively, utterly objective material, informing the audience with neither distortion nor omission. Unfortunately, this isn't the case, and for two main reasons.

First, as will be discussed in Chapter 14, the concept of 'truth' isn't a matter of black and white. Indeed, the belief that something can be unequivocally, eternally and objectively 'true' exists on very thin philosophical ice. This isn't to say that the falsehoods Goebbels constructed about the Jews can somehow be considered true – they can't – but it does mean that truth can be assembled in many different ways, depending upon what evidence is used, how the argument is constructed, the context that argument is placed in and what conclusions are drawn. For example, if some children produce disappointing results in their literacy tests, can we conclude from this – as *The Telegraph* and *The Daily Mail* have suggested on a number of occasions – that this is because our schooling system is overrun with left-wing teachers bent on destroying traditional education because of their ludicrous ideas about how best to read?

> Changes will be made as part of sweeping reforms designed to boost the quality of teaching in English schools and raise standards of state education. Under the proposals, ministers are also planning to slash the number of students on university-based courses over the next three years – shifting would-be teachers towards on-the-job training … coalition insiders also insist the plan was intended to weaken the influence of left-wing training institutions that have filled generations of teachers with 'useless' education theories. (Patton 2012)

Not surprisingly, the idea that teachers are somehow causing most of the nation's literacy problems due to their choice of pedagogy is not a view remotely shared by the vast majority of British teachers themselves, or the hundreds of dedicated university lecturers responsible for their 'substandard' teacher education. However, this has not stopped the government introducing a raft of changes to teacher training – such as on-the-job, school-led programmes – organised with the primary intention of lessening the pernicious influence of university academics on future generations of teachers. In addition to this, it can also be argued that this 'apprenticeship' model of teacher education will have a significant impact on the ability of teachers to retain their current status as 'professionals'.

Second, as we shall see, there is no such thing as totally objective news. Burton (2002) rightly points out that news always comes in a particular form – a genre – and as such follows specific conventions in the way it is organised. The process of news gathering and selection is also necessarily subjective, and a function of perceived 'newsworthiness'. Furthermore, particular news values impact on whether an item is deemed newsworthy. Is the story negative? Is it simple to understand? Is there conflict involved? Also, language is often used in very particular ways, ways that relate to issues of authority and credibility. Underlying this, there are questions relating to the kinds of agendas that are operating. Is the item impartial, or are particular views of the world being pushed? Finally, is the media trying to whip up a panic over a given issue in order to further its own ends, and to sell more papers/gain more viewers? While these constitute only a fraction of the ways in which the news media can be decoded, they provide a good place to begin.

'The Reading Wars'

For many years, article after article has been published in the UK's more conservative newspapers, pointing to what they see as the self-evident failure of contemporary education. The themes have been relatively consistent: (1) children are being defrauded of a proper education –'Education system failing pupils' (Editorial, *Daily Express* 2012); 'The traditional way to a sound education' (Editorial, *Daily Mail* 2011);

and (2) traditional approaches to teaching are under attack from babbling left-wing ideologues – 'Left-wing thinking still prevails in schools' (Pearson 2014); 'The malignant left-wing pathology of educational academics' (Hilton 2013).

The point being made here is that unbeknownst to the vast majority of us, our schools have become a 'battleground' in the ongoing war between the left and the right, and some newspapers feel it is their responsibility to point out both how this battle is principally being fought – i.e. through the teaching of reading – and precisely what is at stake. This 'battle' is by no means limited to the United Kingdom; similar 'Reading Wars' are apparently being fought in the United States, Canada, New Zealand and Australia, to name but a few.

There is nothing new about concerns over student literacy (Dooley 2004); however, in her book *The Literacy Wars*, Snyder (2008) details how the teaching of reading, an important but seemingly politically innocuous element of every primary teacher's professional responsibilities, somehow became transformed into something much, much more. The underpinning logic here is that the conservative voices champion the teaching of *phonics*, the traditional method of sounding out parts of words, as opposed to *whole-language* teaching, which involves memorising whole words, and which is associated with the broader educational philosophy of *constructivism*. Snyder suggests that by shaping this as a choice between two apparent polar opposites, and by associating whole-language teaching with loony left-wing faddism, it has become possible to create a 'Literacy War' out of next to nothing.

At the risk of spoiling a good story, Snyder notes that good teachers actually appear to employ both methods in their classroom. She cites the research of Louden *et al.* (2005) who revealed that highly effective, highly regarded teachers:

> ... employed a wide repertoire of practices, some of which appeared decidedly whole language – process writing, reading groups and contextualised practice skills – and some of which appeared skills-orientated – explicit phonics lessons, sight word practice and comprehension instruction strategy. (Snyder 2008, 67)

Louden is not alone in pointing out what almost all teachers already know: that is, good reading teachers use phonics in their classroom all the time, but as a part of a wide vocabulary of learning strategies. Ewing (2014) argues that there is no single correct, one-size-fits-all approach to teaching children how to read; children are complex creatures, and being an effective teacher involves a lot more than just reciting a phonic checklist. Teachers need to master a repertoire of strategies and approaches to learning. To put it simply, 'the "phonics versus whole language" debate is pointless' (Andoniou 2013).

So the question arises, how is it possible to construct a 'war' out of thin air? Or to ask a different question; using the example of the 'Reading Wars', what might a very basic framework for decoding media messages begin to look like?

Decoding the News Media

There are a number of entry points into an organised analysis of the news media. Below are just some from Burton's framework (Burton 2002) for media analysis, but they provide a good place to start.

GENRE

News comes in a variety of different forms, each with their own rules and features. News does not flow to us from the outside world, free and unimpeded; it is funnelled through particular types of media product. For example, television news is almost always organised in the same familiar way: two talking heads, both exuding gravity and trustworthiness, various reporters in the field, live feeds from trouble spots, little obvious editorialising other than by story selection, and a clear ranking of those stories, ending with sport and the weather.

Newspapers are no different; they follow familiar codes that we have come to recognise and expect. Broadsheets like the *Daily Telegraph* and the *Sunday Telegraph* follow somewhat different codes to tabloid newspapers, taking more seriously their role as civic guardians, and providing forums for debate. As such, the *Telegraphs* (*Daily* and *Sunday*) support the conservative teaching methods, such as phonics, through straightforward articles such as 'Punishing traditional teaching has to stop' (Gibb 2014). In contrast, the tabloid *Daily Mail* feels no such responsibility. In pieces with titles such as 'Ideologues of illiteracy: the terrible damage wrought on our schools by left-wing educationalists' (Hastings 2010), teachers are depicted as ideological zealots, happy with schools full of illiterate children, who are all but held prisoner in their socialist-inspired classrooms, doomed to lives of under-achievement – all thanks to 'egalitarian claptrap'. The *Daily Mail* goes even further down this path with the frankly unhinged suggestion that, 'The National Association of Head Teachers has undertaken an evil conspiracy to create an illiterate Britain' (Pandya 2012).

Editorialising is also generally accepted by the readership, with particular newspapers tilting to the left or the right in their coverage of issues. For example, the *Guardian* and the *New York Times* are both left-leaning newspapers. The two *Telegraphs* and the *Daily Mail* tilt significantly to the right. That said, the right to a political perspective all too often spills over into blind partisanship and outright distortion.

Therefore, the *Telegraphs'* campaign against progressive teaching can be read in terms of genre. The information is presented via editorials, opinion pieces and news articles, each with their own formats and conventions. The items are all composed of familiar elements that give the pieces their weight, and authority and resonance. For example, stock characters (in this case, 'vulnerable children', 'left-wing fanatics' and 'right-minded Brits') are set within stock situations (yet one more defence of traditional British values), both of which are then continually repeated, and continually reinforced.

NEWS SELECTION

For every news item chosen by a newspaper's editors for publication, a vast array is ignored. Likewise, for every bandwagon a newspaper decides to jump on, any number of other possible bandwagons are allowed to roll past. That is, decoding the news is as much about what has been left out of the selection process, as what has been put in.

> News, like any kind of media product, is the result of a process of selection and construction. Items are selected in or selected out. Newspapers or news programmes are artefacts that are put together. In effect, meaning is constructed into them ... For example, the reporter or newsreader interprets events for us. As soon as they talk about 'confrontation', they are actually interpreting what has happened. They are asserting that there has been a confrontation, where someone else might have talked about 'disagreement'. (Burton 2002, 182)

Interestingly, foregrounding the notion of 'confrontation' is clear in the piece on education by Gove (2013a) in the *Daily Mail*, not just with the title 'I refuse to surrender to the Marxist teachers destroying our schools' but also words and phrases from the piece itself, such as 'enemy', 'fight' and 'battle'. There are alternative words that could have been chosen to describe the disagreements over the best way to teach literacy within schools: 'ongoing discussion', 'healthy professional disagreements', or 'debate' for instance, but of course, none of these are as effective when attempting to sell newspapers.

Unfortunately, the term 'debate' may not be an appropriate term within the context of much of the conservative newspaper coverage of the literacy issue, as it only seems interested in giving voice to the anti-progressive education side of the conversation, a fact which leads on to an associated issue: that of *agenda*. News content is not selected at random, nor solely in terms of how pertinent it might be considered by the readership. It is also selected because it fits within a given narrative; part of a political and cultural agenda pushed by the paper, in this instance, the conservative belief that everything was better in the good old days. This will be discussed again in the subsection on 'Editorialising and Bias'.

NEWS VALUES

In order for news items to be deemed newsworthy, it is widely preferred that they contain specific elements – values – and if they are not immediately present, an angle must be found where any trace of these elements can be expanded upon and foregrounded. After all, does anybody really want to read that British children are doing quite well in global literacy tables, and that teachers are hard-working profes-sionals, who employ a range of diverse pedagogic strategies, in what is a very difficult task, within an ever-changing, multicultural society? No, you probably don't.

Generally speaking, items are far more likely to be selected – or once selected, regarded as effective pieces of news – if they exhibit most of the following criteria. In no particular order, they are as follows.

Negativity: bad news sells. The rosy picture painted above is regarded as far less interesting than the alternative notion that we are producing a nation of virtual illiterates; worse, even the teachers can't read and write properly; and worse again, our university lecturers are embarrassing morons – 'Academics chastised for bad grammar in letter attacking Michael Gove' (Flood 2013).

Simplicity: good articles are ones that can spell the issue out easily. A complex picture of the nuanced and context-bound use of differing teaching strategies for literacy is nowhere near as journalistically desirable as the image of bad teachers using left-wing gobbledegook in the classrooms to the detriment of our children – 'British education is a con' (Hitchens 2015b).

Conflict: this is an easy combination of negativity and simplicity. Why depict the subtle nuances of a debate between loose clusters of interest groups, theoretical positions, and practising teachers, when you can construct the entire issue as a straightforward battle between good and evil? It seems far more exciting that way, and excitement sells newspapers. In 'Now is the time to break forever the stranglehold of the teaching unions over British education', Gyngell (2012) states:

> NASUWT and NUT have declared war. They have thrown down the gauntlet and Michael Gove has no option but to pick it up – and take them on. Mrs Thatcher did it with the miners; Rupert Murdoch did it with the Print Unions . . . a 'reading war' over the reintroduction of phonics has been waged by teachers with a Taliban style zealotry.

The Taliban? Really? Teachers and their unions, who simply favour a mixed approach to the teaching of reading, are now presented as quasi-terrorists, engaged in a war against the rest of us – all the 'right-minded' people.

Human interest: one of the most effective ways of driving home a story is to tie it to the lives of specific individuals, to the 'victims' of the conflict; pointing out gener-alised caricatures of the good guys and the bad guys only goes so far. A good news item then is likely to include the case of little Johnny, the primary school child, who, after five years of being taught with whole-language methods was completely illiterate, and now, after only one month with phonics, he has a reading age of 63; or the noble teacher, battling against the forces of 'whole-language' darkness:

> In October 2007, the Daily Telegraph reviewed a Channel 4 documentary called 'Last Chance Kids'. In the programme, an inspirational teacher named Ruth Miskin turned one young boy's life around using a teaching method called

'synthetic phonics'. 'Within two weeks' the Telegraph reviewer wrote, 'previously illiterate Christian was reading to a mother weeping with joy at the transformation.' As Christian said at the end of the documentary, 'It has changed my life.' (Gibb 2014)

NEWS AND DISCOURSE

Language, and the manner and context of its use, is never neutral, and the news media is no exception. Just as using the terms 'enemy', 'fight' and 'battle' sets a conceptual tone for coverage of the literacy debate, so too do other aspects of newspaper discourse. Through the presentation of news items in seemingly authoritative and credible ways (as opposed, perhaps, to more 'tabloid' newspapers), publications like *The Daily Telegraph* are able to trade upon that credibility to add weight to their arguments within their opinion pieces and editorials. Consequently, when *The Telegraph* claims there is a crisis in education, people are more likely to believe it than if it was published in *Viz* Magazine.

In addition to the aura of authority and credibility emanating from broadsheet newspapers like *The Daily Telegraph*, a further associated strategy involves the use of 'experts' to bolster their arguments. Allocating the status of 'expert' need not be based upon anything other than that they possess educational qualifications and agree with the newspaper's agenda, but it still adds weight to their overall argument. Interestingly, none of the 'experts' used by *The Daily Telegraph* appear to be employed by faculties of Education within British universities.

EDITORIALISING AND BIAS

While there is an expectation (largely misplaced) that television news will remain politically impartial, and simply present the day's happenings in a neutral and objective manner, the same code of conduct does not necessarily apply to the print media. As discussed, many readers expect newspapers to have a gentle political slant – particularly the editorials – although if this is handled subtly enough, and it also aligns with the readers' own politics, then such a slant is often regarded as 'sensible, right-thinking', in contrast to other newspapers with which the reader doesn't agree politically, which can be dismissed as 'overtly biased'.

Two points are worth making here. First, it is important for all audiences to be aware that such biases exist; this forms a crucial component of media literacy. All newspapers have a slant, and sometimes just knowing who owns the title will be enough to let you know what that is (assuming it isn't self-evident). Second, understanding and accepting that there is a slant, is not the same as tolerating distortion, either as a one-off portrayal of a specific incident/issue, or as part of an ongoing campaign in support of a particular political position.

The campaign was relentless – the populist press running anti-teacher and general education-decline themes day after day over periods of weeks during the whole year. Government ministers, Right-wing press, the usual 'expert' pundits and the shock jocks – all mobilised and remaining firmly 'on message'. The education profession was demonised and Ministers and editorial writers were able to portray themselves as the saviours of the nation's schools. (Sawyer 2006, 237–8)

In summary, the idea of 'totally objective news' is a myth. At one level, this is not a criticism; the very process of gathering and selecting news, the familiar categories into which it is shaped, the choice of aspects that are deemed to make something newsworthy, and the forms of discourse that become attached to the stories (indeed, the very notion of a 'story' itself) make the notion of 'objectivity' necessarily illusory. However, the ability to decode the effects of these elements is important, as is the ability to understand that other, less benign factors affect the objectivity of news. The ability to decode the media also includes, when such issues arise, the ability to recognise specific media agendas, to recognise overt and covert political bias, to recognise simplistic solutions to what are complex problems, and to recognise organised campaigns of disinformation.

Myth #3 *The Media Doesn't Create Moral Panics, but Even if it Does, This Doesn't Affect Education*

The media isn't in the business of whipping up public hysteria. It may use colourful language occasionally, and it may try to present news in exciting and engaging ways, but so what... it's a business after all. If your news isn't interesting, people will turn the TV over and find news that is. If the line is crossed every now and again, and the media lays it on a bit thick, this is only about things like Bikie Gangs, and a bit of a moral panic about them is probably justified. None of this has anything to do with education.

There seems little doubt that the media does exaggerate when it suits them, just as it engages in very selective representation, often with its own agenda, as was discussed in myth #2. Certainly, some parts of the media seem more responsible than others, almost as a matter of genre, and you often know what you're going to get before you even start reading or watching. For example, the *BBC News* or *Panorama* seem much more concerned with journalistic accuracy, fairness and objectivity than do *Good Morning Britain* or *Mock the Week;* likewise with broadsheets, as opposed to tabloid newspapers.

The question now is: what kind of implications can these less desirable forms of media conduct have? Is it just a matter of rolling our eyes – thanks to our new-found decoding skills – and accepting that all news media is, ultimately, part of the entertainment industry? Or are the social consequences of sensationalistic news reporting too far-reaching, pervasive and pernicious to be dismissed so lightly?

Moral Panics

In 1972, Cohen wrote the book *Folk Devils and Moral Panics*, a seminal text on the role played by the media in mobilising the public against perceived threats to the social order. Cohen analysed the spectacular fallout that occurred from a minor brawl in the small seaside town of Clacton in the UK in 1964. Such an event would normally have barely warranted a mention in the national media, but this time it was different. The media picked up on the fracas, and ran with it. In line with the values of a good news story (negativity, simplicity, conflict) the protagonists soon became magically divided into two discrete warring camps, The Mods and the Rockers – modern day *Folk Devils* – and a national moral panic began in earnest.

> The headlines are self-descriptive: 'Day of Terror by Scooter Groups' (*Daily Telegraph*), 'Youngsters Beat Up Town – 97 Leather Jacket Arrests' (*Daily Express*), 'Wild Ones Invade Seaside – 97 Arrests' (*Daily Mirror*)... editorials began to appear, together with reports that the Home Secretary was being urged (it was not usually specified by *whom*) to take action... Feature articles then appeared highlighting interviews with Mods and Rockers. Straight reporting gave way to theories especially about motivation: the mob was described as 'exhilarated', 'drunk with notoriety', 'hell-bent for destruction'... (Cohen 1980, 30)

Having invented the phenomenon, the news media then salaciously reported the copycat riots that followed in other seaside towns; with equal glee, they then pointed out the terrible threat posed by the gangs of Mods and Rockers that had immediately established themselves within every town in the UK. Mods and Rockers were a threat to the nation's way of life; Mods and Rockers needed stamping out.

Cohen raised a number of interesting issues. The first, and the most obvious, is that the media is not simply a passive observer of news; rather it is instrumental in organising both its creation, and its impact. He discussed how the media *exaggerated and distorted* the news, in terms of the significance of the events, the manner in which they were described, and the threats they posed. He examined the way in which the media used *prediction* as a vehicle for keeping the story alive: 'When will they strike next?', 'Who is in most danger?'. They loudly anticipated riots with each new holiday, which quickly became self-fulfilling prophecies. He also addressed the *symbolic* role played by such media inventions. The terms 'Mod' and 'Rocker' became larger than themselves; they came to represent all that was wrong with the country. Even their clothes and their haircuts became endowed with particular new types of (negative) meaning. The Beatles' loveable mop-tops were no longer quite so loveable.

Now this is all very interesting, in a recent-history sort of a way, but what has this got to do with us in the twenty-first century? And what does it have to do with education? The point here is that, arguably, this synthetic process of *moral panic* creation, and the associated construction of *folk devils*, still happens on a relatively regular basis, and that it affects our education system, both directly and indirectly.

It affects education directly, in that some moral panics are actually about education. The concerns over literacy described in myth #2 most likely rises to the level of a moral panic – complete with its own associate folk devil: the radical left-wing teacher. Importantly, moral panics also affect education indirectly. A good example involves the issue of 'asylum seekers'. This can be examined through the framework set out within a more recent, but equally useful, approach to moral panics.

The *Daily Mail* and Asylum Seekers

When it comes to conducting a case study of a contemporary moral panic such as 'asylum seekers', it should be pointed out that this could be done in a number of different ways. The same set of themes could be addressed if all forms of media were to be analysed within the country, or if the analysis were limited to just one type of media, or, as with the approach adopted here, just one particular newspaper.

The *Daily Mail* is the United Kingdom's second biggest-selling daily newspaper, having an average daily readership of 3 600 000 (Newsworks 2015). Founded in 1896, the paper has adopted a consistently conservative editorial policy across a range of issues: limited government, tough on law and order issues, climate change scepticism, anti-EU sentiment and anti-immigration.

Regarding this final issue, the paper has been consistent in its opposition to all forms of immigration into the UK. In 1938, in the article 'German Jews pouring into this country', the then pro-Fascist paper famously supported the deportation of Jews fleeing Nazi persecution. It has maintained a similar 'anti-foreigner-in-Britain' stance ever since. Welch and Schuster (2005) point to a consistent and generalised pattern of moral panic generation regarding immigrants within the *Daily Mail*, citing articles such as 'Warning over the new influx of gypsies' (1997), and 'Handouts galore! welcome to soft touch Britain's welfare paradise' (1997). They note the use of emotive language to describe those arriving in the UK – tides, waves, floods, swamps – which, they argue, serves to both dehumanise the migrants and exaggerate the scale of the issue. They also point out the recurrent theme of 'bogus' or 'illegal' asylum seekers. This is an important issue, since it is not possible to be an 'illegal' asylum seeker.

To clarify this matter, it would probably help to define our terms. According to Article 14 of the 1948 Universal Declaration of Human Rights, everyone has the right to seek asylum – to become a refugee. The status of 'refugee', as well as the kind of protection to which they are entitled, is set out in the 1951 Convention, and the 1967 Protocol, relating to the status of refugees. Importantly, the United Kingdom is a signatory to both these documents. A refugee is defined by Article 1 of the Convention as any person who:

> owing to well-founded fear of being persecuted for reasons of race, religion, nationality, membership of a particular social group or political opinion, is outside the country of his nationality and is unable or, owing to such fear, is unwilling to avail himself of the protection of that country.

However, an 'asylum seeker' is someone who is seeking international protection, but is yet to have had their claim for refugee status assessed. Importantly, 'What may be considered an illegal action under normal circumstances (e.g. entering a country without a visa) should not, according to the convention, be considered illegal if a person is seeking asylum' (Refugee Council of Australia 2014). Accordingly, using the term 'illegal' within the context of asylum seekers is not only inappropriate, it is also so heavily loaded with negative connotations that the question must be asked if those who continue to use it, do so for their own social and political reasons, none of which have anything to do with truth or accuracy.

The news media, but in particular the *Daily Mail*, have depicted asylum seekers – 'Illegals' – as welfare dodgers, queue jumpers, potential terrorists, disease carriers and as liars. To put it another way, they are depicted as a threat, to us as individuals, and also to our prosperity and the British way of life. Such depictions, and the consequences of those depictions, can best be understood through a variant on Cohen's model: the five-part moral panic framework as set out by Goode and Ben-Yehuda (2009). Let us take each of these in turn.

(1) CONCERN

There must first be increased levels of concern over the behaviour of a particular social group, as well as the consequences of that behaviour. This concern need not always be experienced in terms of fear; however, there must generally be a sense of threat, a threat that produces a widespread sense of anxiety. For example, media portrayals of the supposed conduct of Mods and Rockers produced levels of social unease that went right to the highest levels of government.

Contemporary concerns over 'asylum seekers' have become now widespread within the British popular consciousness, and the media has a huge role to play in this. *Daily Mail* articles such as 'Asylum: you're right to worry' (Brogan 2005), and 'The "Swarm" on our streets' (Ellicott and Wright 2015) generate a series of anxieties over the 'overwhelming' presence of a generalised, ethnically and religiously different 'other' growing within British society. Of course, this other is to be feared due to both its inherent nature (i.e. different to 'us'), and its size ('swarm' – these aren't humans, they're locusts).

In addition to the fostering of fear, there is also resentment. There have been numerous articles spelling out the full price of our hospitality – that is, the unwarranted economic burden of their continued presence on our welfare system. In the *Daily Mail* article 'Asylum seekers' summer fun with your £1 m', Butler (2002) states:

> The asylum seekers will be envy of many British families as they are treated to sports coaching, seaside excursions, music and arts events. Those in London can look forward to visiting top tourist draws including Madame Tussaud's and the Tower ... Tory spokesman Oliver Letwin called it an indictment of the shambolic state of the asylum system that more money was being thrown at a problem which already cost over £1billion a year.

In addition to this kind concern – the wasting of our money on 'them' – other kinds of resentments are also fostered: 'Patients lose GP surgery to asylum seekers' (Wilkes 2002) and 'Lock your doors. Your holiday hotel's full of asylum seekers' (Tweedie 2015). In the *Daily Mail*, mention is never made of the fact that, in looking after asylum seekers in humane and appropriate ways, we are simply fulfilling our obligations under international law, and that the concerns continually articulated – asylum seekers are getting more than 'ordinary' British citizens, asylum seekers are all simply economic migrants playing the system – are largely and demonstrably false.

(2) HOSTILITY

After initial concern about the behaviour of the social group in question, comes increasing hostility towards that group, hostility stoked by the tenor of the news coverage they receive. As Goode and Ben-Yehuda (2009, 36) state:

> Members of this category are collectively designated as the enemy, or an enemy, of respectable society; their behaviour is seen as harmful or threatening to the values, the interests, possibly the very existence of the society; ... a division is made between 'us' – good, decent, respectable folk – and 'them' or the 'other' – the deviants, bad guys, undesirables, outsiders...

The *Daily Mail* consistently raises community hostility towards immigrants in general, and asylum seekers in particular, across the widest possible array of topics. Some of these areas are relatively predictable: 'True toll of mass migration on UK life' (Slack 2013), 'Foreign workers get 3 in 4 new jobs' (Walker 2011). Others are seen as little more than an attempt to blame asylum seekers for anything they can think of: 'As thousands of servicemen are made redundant, how many will be turned away from homeless shelters that are packed full of immigrants?' (Mallinson 2012), or even, 'Swans killed and fish vanish as "migrants pillage river for food"' (Levy 2010).

Some areas can be significantly more inflammatory than others. Predictably, to engender maximum hostility, the *Daily Mail* positions asylum seekers as a sexual threat to the general population: 'Asylum bid by Libyans in sex rampage' (Levy and Brown 2015), 'Refugee who raped girl, 12, wins battle to stay in the UK' (Whelan and Slater 2012) and '4,000 foreign murderers and rapists we can't throw out' (Shipman and Doyle 2013). Closer scrutiny of pieces such as these can often reveal a considerable level of duplicity. For example, the last article is referencing government papers concerning the number of foreign nationals in the UK under deportation orders – which are often subject to legal challenges over issues of documentary confusion and concerns over the safety of return destinations, hence the delays. At no point does the government paper concerned ever detail the crimes for which they are being deported – i.e. murder and rape; this was just made up to increase the inflammatory effect of the article. From this point, the headline can now dovetail neatly into the *Daily Mail*'s general narrative about foreigners and asylum seekers being murderers and rapists. Interestingly, when the *Daily Mail* was finally pressured into apologising for this front-page story, that apology was buried at the bottom of page 4, underneath yet another article about the undesirability of migrants.

(3) CONSENSUS

For the moral panic to take hold, and to generate significant social consequences, there must be widespread agreement that 'the problem' is worth worrying about. If concerns about 'asylum seekers' were limited to *Daily Mail* readers, this might not constitute much of an issue, but when it is echoed within other news media, on our radios and in our popular magazines, and even within the discourses of our parliament, then the necessary critical mass has been achieved. The Refugee Council UK (2015) notes that:

> According to the opinion polls, asylum continues to be one of the most important issues for the British public. It is rarely out of the newspapers and is the subject of intense political and public debate. Reporting and commentary about asylum seekers and refugees is often hostile, unbalanced and factually incorrect.

The Refugee Council cites the example of the claim in the *Daily Mail* (2005): 'Asylum seekers sent to more affluent areas'. The Refugee Council state that the reality is that most asylum seekers' accommodation is in deprived areas, in poor quality housing and often where they are more likely to face racial harassment. Likewise, the *Mail on Sunday* (2005) stated: 'Asylum seekers given votes to get loans'. The Refugee Council states that asylum seekers are not allowed to vote, or to get loans; they are not allowed to work, so they are largely forced to live in poverty, most experiencing hunger and lacking the basic ability even to buy clothes and shoes. Consequently, the manufactured consensus that asylum seekers are a threat, and are getting it easy, is largely based upon demonstrable falsehoods – for which the media rarely seems to be held to account.

(4) DISPROPORTION

An important part of the notion of a moral panic is that the threat is perceived as far greater than it actually is in reality, that is, in terms of an objective assessment of the risks posed by the 'folk devils' in question. In Cohen's study, Mods and Rockers were widely represented as a threat to the British way of life, a potent symbol of national decline. With hindsight, they were simply relatively innocuous subcultural fashion statements; in fact, they represented little more than two different types of musical taste, transportational preference, and choice in bad haircut.

The same is true of 'asylum seekers'. After all, why is it that the UK has to take so many of the world's refugees? Why do we have to do so much more than our fair share? Given the endless panic in our media – and in particular, the *Daily Mail* – what percentage of the world's refugees do we take? Thirty percent? Forty percent? Fifty percent? We are going to be utterly swamped by other ethnicities, religions and cultures; the United Kingdom as we know it is at an end...

The truth is nothing like this. While these figures are subject to rapid change, particularly given the situation in Syria as of 2015/16, according to the British Red Cross (2015) there are more than 13 million refugees worldwide; 80 per cent of the world's 13 million refugees are currently hosted by developing countries – Jordan has 2 500 000 refugees, Pakistan has 2 300 000, Turkey has 1 600 000, Lebanon has 1 200 00, Iran has 1 000 000, Kenya has 650 000, and so on. The United Kingdom, one of the world's richest countries, has accepted only an estimated 126 000 refugees – which is less than 0.2% of their total population. In terms of asylum seekers accepted per head, the UK is ranked only sixteenth out of the 28 EU countries. According to Harding, Oltermann and Watt (2015), citing the UN's refugee agency, over 4 million refugees have already fled the civil war in Syria; Germany was expecting to take over 800 000 asylum seekers in 2015 alone; the UK has taken 166. Given these figures are actually so small then, relatively speaking, this should only increase our questioning of why asylum seekers are continually demonised in the way they are.

(5) VOLATILITY

An important issue with moral panics is that they are never permanent; they arrive, cause lots of trouble and anxiety, and then they fade away, to be replaced by some other social concern. Panics over Mods and Rockers were soon replaced by others involving football hooligans (Pearson 1983), Punks (Hebdige 1979), Goths (Tait 1999), and even latterly, children who underachieve at school (Miller 2008). Each serves the function of both selling newspapers and garnering viewers, but also legitimating the targeting of those groups for demonisation and then punitive intervention.

The moral panic concerning asylum seekers appears to be somewhat different to the norm. While it certainly appears to be volatile – in that the panic appears, gains momentum, occupies centre stage in the news cycle for a few months, and then fades away – it differs from other moral panics in that the story doesn't end there. The moral panic over asylum seekers/immigrants has tended to reappear in one form or another in an ongoing way. It seems that engendering a fear of 'the other' – whether Jewish, Muslim, West Indian, Bangladeshi, or Eastern European – continues to serve a very useful political purpose. It does us no credit as a nation.

Having outlined the five elements of Goode and Ben-Yahuda's theory, it should be pointed out that moral panic theory is not without its critics. Given that all the chapters in this section detail concern over the modernist tendency to shape the debate into *binary oppositions* (the news media is good/bad, popular culture is good/bad, digital technology is good/bad), it doesn't necessarily help to employ a conceptual tool that appears to act as a *master discourse* (a single theoretical device that explains everything within its scope), which is a further foundational aspect of modernism. So, much as moral panic theory is a useful mechanism for conceptualising some of the ways in which the news media can shape and mobilise public opinion, often to the detriment of particular social groups, there is a tendency to homogenise the process somewhat. That is, the questions should always be asked: is the moral panic uniform throughout the social body? Is it actually unreasonable? Are there important differences within the 'folk devils'? Are there loud voices rejecting the substance of the moral panic altogether? In the case of the recurrent moral panic over asylum seekers, let's hope so.

The 'Asylum Seeker' Panic and Education

When it comes to asylum seekers, the *Daily Mail* makes it evident that there is more to fear from them than the taking of 'our' jobs and sexual assault mentioned earlier. Asylum seekers have been demonised in a range of other ways, ways which have a more direct impact on how the young might be understood, and hence treated. For example, asylum seekers have also become a synonym for disease carrying, bomb carrying and queue-jumping. Let us take these in turn.

With regard to risk of infection, *Daily Mail* articles such as 'Migrants blamed for diseases' (Amory 2003), and 'Sickly immigrants add £1bn to NHS bill' (Doherty 2011), explicitly link immigrants and asylum seekers to diseases such as HIV, Hepatitis B and C, and tuberculosis. Both articles involve 'worst-case scenario' speculation about the effects 'overwhelming' numbers of unwelcome disease-carrying foreigners. Significantly, this orchestrated scare-mongering is not supported by the facts.

> A Government TB screening pilot in Dover tested around 5,000 asylum seekers over a six-month period and found not a single case of symptomatic TB. What doctors did find however was much evidence of maltreatment and torture – evidence of the very reasons why they were fleeing their country of origin. (Bristol City Council 2010, 13)

Likewise with the issue of terrorism: it has been suggested by the *Daily Mail* that hiding among the refugees trudging their way across Europe are a very large numbers of IS terrorists, simply biding their time before launching attacks in major cities: 'How many are genuine?' (Reid 2015). While this type of assertion has been largely ridiculed by counter-terrorism experts (*Sydney Morning Herald* 2009) – why, after all, would you want to spend that amount of time and effort getting to your target, with no guarantee of final entry, when you can simply fly into the nearest airport – such absurd claims still have the effect of demonising both asylum seekers in particular, and the Muslim community in general. Significantly, for the *Daily Mail*, who knows how young these terrorists could be? ('From clean-cut students to poster boys for terror' (Reid 2015).)

And not only are asylum seekers all potential disease-carrying potential terrorists, they are breaking the most fundamental of all British conventions of politeness: in not applying for visas in the normal way they are simply queue jumpers, usurping the places of the more deserving and the more civilised. Needless to say, the Daily Mail finds this particularly unacceptable: 'Did Jesus really say "blessed are the queue-jumping knifemen?"' (Hitchens 2015a). As for queue jumping, this is the greatest misconception of all: *there is no queue*. Refugees by definition have left their country of origin, and have entered another country to seek asylum. Besides, the UN resettlement system does not work like an orderly queue, such that if you join the end, you are guaranteed to reach the front if you wait long enough (Refugee Council of Australia 2014). Rather, it is more like a lottery, being based upon perceived need (which can change at any time, depending upon who arrives at the camp), and worse, many refugees actually lack access to the resettlement processes altogether. For many then, the only option is to set off, and hope for the best.

The important issue here is that this relentless tide of negative articles is not just of academic importance, providing evidence for some abstract theory about moral panics. The campaign managed by newspapers, such as the *Daily Mail*, is instrumental in colouring the way asylum seekers are understood and treated within our country. As has been discussed, not only are they depicted as job-stealers and sexual predators, they are disease-carrying, queue-jumping proto-terrorists, not to mention homeless shelter-hogging swan-killers; all this has significant consequences for people's lives.

D'Onofrio and Munk (2004) addressed attitudes towards asylum seekers within the British community, interviewing both locals and the asylum seekers themselves. Given the tenor of the newspaper coverage of the issue, some of the results are perhaps not surprising. For instance, asylum seekers themselves are aware of how they are portrayed in the media.

> When I see (the news), it is always 'asylum seekers are doing this, asylum seekers are doing that, they are doing all kinds of things'. In the news, mostly bad things are

coming out, I feel. It is not the good things that are coming... Always they say 'asylum seekers are bad'. (Female asylum seeker, from Sri Lanka)

The interviews also suggest that the locals adopt the negative media messages regarding asylum seekers relatively uncritically. For example, as the following quotes illustrate, it appears widely accepted that asylum seekers are likely to be carrying all manner of diseases, and that they receive government benefits that locals do not – neither of which is supported by the evidence.

Now I have got a 2 year old who goes in creche, and I think there should be something like immunisation or test done... there is this disease and that disease, then they should be tested and immunised so that it is not causing problems in the area. (Single mother, Newcastle)

They are getting thousands of pounds for cars, they get mobile phones, they get computer... they get everything... So we say, 'Well, how do the asylum seekers get it? That's what annoys people. That's what gets a lot of people's backs up. (Young woman, Newcastle)

Research by the British Red Cross (2015) demonstrates that there is a 'reality gap' between what most people think is true about asylum seekers and the demonstrable facts, perhaps not surprising given the kinds of articles regularly published in the *Daily Mail*. Most likely as a consequence of these kinds of articles – or at least in part – further research suggests that the UK public is now more opposed to asylum seekers and immigrants entering their country than any other nation in Europe (Migration Observatory 2015). As stated previously, the deliberate construction of folk-devils such as the 'asylum seeker' has wide-ranging consequences for those depicted in this manner:

You can't go in a bar in this area. I tell you now. I have been here next to this place. They nearly killed me. Nearly. They broke their glasses and they nearly killed me and I said 'Excuse me, I go home now'... He (a local) said: 'Go out, don't stay here, here is not your country!' Something like that, and I said 'Okay, excuse me, I go out.' (Male asylum seeker, Iran)

Finally, and probably needless to say, these attitudes inevitably spill over into our schools. A recent survey by Show Racism the Red Card (2015) of 6000 schoolchildren found similar kinds of misconceptions about asylum seekers and immigrants as those outlined above. For example, the average estimate for the percentage of foreign-born people living in the UK was 47% ('The "swarm" on our streets') – the actual figure is 13% – and the average estimate of the British population who are Muslim was 36% – the actual figure is 5%. In addition to this, 60% thought that asylum seekers and immigrant are stealing our jobs, and 31% thought that all asylum seekers and migrants are here illegally. Interestingly, 29% of the children reported seeing the *Daily Mail* in their home; 52% reported seeing *The Sun* in their home, which has a similar attitude to asylum seekers as does the *Daily Mail*.

Importantly, broader social attitudes and bigotries, as so obviously articulated in some of our newspapers, can easily spill over into our schools. Research by the BBC has found over 87 000 racist incidents recorded in British schools between 2007 and 2011, a figure the anti-racism charity Show Racism the Red Card called 'the tip of the iceberg' (Talwar 2012). Biddle and Priest (2014) contend that this kind of abuse in school has a couple of serious consequences: first, those students often feel as if they are not part of the schooling community. That is, they were 'othered' from the very beginning of the educational process; the boundaries are all neatly drawn, and they are placed on the outside. Second, they can lose the desire to go to school at all. Given the language and learning difficulties often faced by migrant and refugee children, it can be hard enough to succeed in school without adding the issue of hating the place altogether for what happens to them there.

In summary, the media is more than capable of whipping up a public outcry when it considers it useful to do so, or when it sees a way to improve its bottom line; often both. Though moral panics are generally not about education directly – with the occasional exception – many of them impact upon education indirectly. Most commentators would agree that the conduct of some elements of the news media has been appalling in relation to its coverage of asylum seekers, and their ongoing vilification into 'folk devils'. This has implications not only for our education system, but also for our status as a civilised and decent nation.

Conclusion

The news media plays a very important role within our society. Not only does it keep us informed of all the most important events within what is now a global community, as the Fourth Estate, it is also responsible for keeping our organs of government under close scrutiny. A healthy press is often a good sign of a healthy society.

That said, for the most part, the news media is now a business. This has two central implications. First, as a business, the news media is necessarily subject to market forces; or to put it another way, for all the history and idealism that underpin the news media, it now has to make money. As such, the line between news and entertainment no longer exists in the way it once did (or the way we thought it once did), and journalists have to compete for an audience. With this competition comes the temptation to pander to the worst aspects of our natures; bad news sells, conflict sells, simplicity sells. . . so perhaps it is not surprising that we get so many stories with simplistically drawn villains, in constant struggle with 'good' people like ourselves. So what if it's neither fair nor accurate?

The second implication is that *as* a big business, the news media is owned by powerful corporations, run by powerful individuals. Such individuals have their own agendas and political affiliations, and almost by definition, they have the means to influence public opinion in ways the rest of us can't. This takes the already tenuous notion of 'media objectivity' and makes it almost meaningless.

The truth is, there's not really very much that any of us can do about either of these issues; they reflect the nature of the society we live in. What we can do, however, is to educate ourselves, and our children, about the way the news media works. We can recognise its importance, but equally, understand its frailties, and identify those areas where it often fails to meet our expectations. Just as the media serves the function of holding many of our most important social institutions to account, it is equally important that we also learn the necessary skills to hold the media to account.

POPULAR CULTURE

9

This chapter argues that the relationship between popular culture and the classroom remains a contentious issue. Its presence has been used as a symbol of how much our culture has declined, and how educationally corrupted our schools have become, while its absence has been used to suggest our schools are out of touch with their primary constituency – young people. This is not a simple issue to address; even the notion of 'culture' itself is subject to considerable disagreement.

Myth #1 Popular culture is rubbish – in terms of taste, it's awful; as an object of study, it's irrelevant. *'Even though most of us consume various forms of popular culture on a daily basis, we still know it's the media equivalent of junk food; it's not really worth eating, and it's certainly not worth studying'.* The division between 'high' and 'low/popular' culture is largely a false binary, but still one that has significant implications for how we approach our most familiar cultural forms. It is fair to say that the label of 'high' culture is often more about its audience than its content, and that some popular culture can be of great value. Significantly, the academic study of popular culture can tell us much about ourselves as a society.

Myth #2 Teachers need to be up to date with student cultures. *'If you want to connect with students, you have to be able to communicate with them on their cultural terms. If you can't do that, then you won't be an effective teacher'.* This myth operates through the false binary of teacher culture and student culture as mutually exclusive entities. Both groups are consumers of popular culture, and there exist significant areas of overlap as audiences. That said, it is probably useful for teachers to be familiar with various elements of some student cultures, but without therefore having to be consumers of those elements themselves.

Myth #3 Popular culture has no place in the classroom. *'Students get enough of "The Simpsons" at home, so the last thing they need is yet more mindless tosh in the one place where they ought to be learning about the best our culture has to offer'.* This is the final false binary: i.e., either we stick with recognised classics in a traditional curriculum, or we just adopt every bit of popular culture that comes down the pipe. Arguably, popular culture has a place in the classroom if it is used deftly; it can be used to engage students, to develop general learning and reasoning skills, and to illustrate to students how aspects of their identities are often formed from within a vocabulary of cultural choices.

Introduction

In recent years, there has been significant debate concerning the types of text that should be taught in our English classroom. In 2014, the then-Secretary of State for Education Michael Gove presided over the dropping of several US literary classics from the UK's GCSE, books such as Steinbeck's *Of Mice and Men*, Miller's *The Crucible* and Lee's *To Kill a Mocking Bird*. Ostensibly, the removal of these familiar works was to more easily comply with the Department for Education's requirements that students should study a range of 'high quality' texts, which must include at least one play by Shakespeare, at least one nineteenth-century novel, a selection of poetry since 1789, including representative romantic poetry, and fiction or drama from the British Isles from 1914 onwards (Department for Education 2013a). Plenty of classic, 'high quality' British texts to read; no need to stoop to the (ex) colonies.

The two sides of the debate lined up in predictable ways. Writing in the conservative *Daily Telegraph*, Gill (2014) supported Gove's decision, labelling *Of Mice and Men* 'boring' and *To Kill a Mockingbird* 'too obvious a moral parable', thereby positioning the decision as aesthetic, rather than simply ideological. On the other side of the argument, the left-leaning *Guardian* cited a range of academics who regarded the decision as a rejection of the important cultural and literary landmarks of the late twentieth and twenty-first centuries, 'a return to the syllabus of the 1940s', and proof-positive that the 'union jack of culture' had now been hoisted over the GCSEs (Kennedy 2014).

Interestingly, in a 2010 speech, Gove set out the kind of books that he thought ought to constitute the UK's English curriculum. He stated that British literature is 'the best in the world', and that it is every British child's birthright to learn about 'the great tradition of our literature – Dryden, Pope, Swift, Byron, Keats, Shelley, Austin,

Dickens and Hardy – (which) should be at the heart of school life'. However, as Olive (2013) points out, not only is this great domestic literature almost exclusively white and male, the authors have, on average, been dead for over 206 years.

It could be argued that this list of writers presupposes an answer to two associated questions: not only, what kind of texts belong in our English curriculum, but also, what kind of texts best represent our collective culture? In a 2013 speech, Gove showed little doubt; 'Stephenie Meyer cannot hold a flaming pitch torch to George Eliot. There is a Great Tradition of English Literature – a canon of transcendent works – and Breaking Dawn is not part of it'. Clearly, high cultural texts such as Elliot's *Middlemarch* are deemed to have intrinsic and timeless value, while artifacts of popular culture such as Meyer's *Twilight Trilogy* are fundamentally ephemeral and disposable. Olive (2015) further addresses Gove's distaste for popular culture evidenced in a speech to Cambridge University on liberal education, when she noted the following.

> He unfavourably compared William Gladstone's penchant for talking Shakespeare, Virgil and Dryden with labourers and miners to Tony Blair's reference in the House of Commons to the soap opera *Coronation Street*. He then proceeded to criticize Gordon Brown's declaration to the public that he is a fan of the Sheffield indie-rock band, the *Artic Monkeys*. . . for Gove, it would seem, to admit knowledge, let alone enjoyment, of popular culture, or advocate that it had a role in public life and education, is to confess ignorance, childishness and general bad taste. (Olive 2015)

It would appear then that this issue is often organised as a perfect modernist binary opposition: *either* we have a 'traditionalist' English curriculum full of tiresome old classics, *or* we have a 'progressive' English curriculum involving the serious study of *Twilight*, the scripts of *EastEnders* and the lyrics of *One Direction*. And this is by no means the only binary evident within the field of popular culture and education. Not only is there the explicit division between high and low culture, they are also allocated the status of either good or bad, which leads to the contention that popular culture either has no place within modern education, or, since it represents the lived culture of the young, it should form the foundation of modern classroom practice.

One of the central problems here is, however, with all this concern over 'culture', we are often in complete disagreement as to what we mean by the term. There is probably no other concept within the social sciences that can be understood in as many different ways, and causes such discord – a response not limited to university lecturers; as the Nazi poet Johst (1933) once wrote: 'When I hear the word culture, I reach for my gun'.

What Do We mean By 'Culture'?

The answer to this question is often based upon the specific discipline from within which it is asked. For example, the most general understanding can be found within anthropology, in which 'culture' is understood as the totality of a society's way of life. Tyler (1871, 1) offered one of the first definitions, when he stated that culture was 'that complex whole which includes knowledge. Belief, art, morals, law, customs, and any other capabilities and habits acquired by man as a member of society'. To put it more simply, according to this approach culture is virtually everything that is passed on from one generation to another that isn't biological.

A somewhat more specific usage is to be found within the discipline of sociology. In essence, culture refers to the systems of meaning that arise from within a society. That is, all societies have institutions relating to the family, the law, economics, politics and so on: their *social structures*. How these structures are interpreted, and how patterns of meaning are organised, vary considerably; the specifics of these variations constitute the society's culture, and would include systems of belief, ethics, rituals and aesthetics (Lee and Newby 1983).

A further influential understanding of culture can be found within Marxism, and its intellectual successor, Critical Theory. According to these approaches, culture is given its shape by the economic structures and relations that form the foundation of any given society. Importantly, culture is not just a 'given' that emerges fully formed from this foundation, rather is it the product of struggle, in that the culture of the powerful is continually forced to reassert its domination over the cultures of the weak. Apple (1982, 41–2) makes this very point when addressing the role played by mass schools in social reproduction.

> They help maintain privilege in cultural ways by taking the form and content of the culture and knowledge of powerful groups and defining it as legitimate knowledge to be preserved and passed on . . . Schools, hence, are also agents in the creation and recreation of an effective dominant culture. They teach norms, values, dispositions, and culture that contribute to the ideological hegemony of dominant groups.

The final understanding of culture to be addressed here relates to the assemblage of practices, tastes, and forms of expression that carve out a relatively distinct realm – 'Culture' – largely separated from the rest of social life. Williams (1981, 11–12) points to the '*informing spirit* of a whole way of life, which is . . . most evident in "specifically cultural" activities – a language, styles of art, kinds of intellectual work'. As such, he is clearly delineating this understanding of culture from the broader focus evidenced within other approaches, and it is this understanding of culture that will largely be used within this chapter.

High and Low Culture

An important proviso needs to be added to this final understanding of culture. What is normally being referred to here is the notion of 'high culture'. Someone is generally regarded as cultured if they can play an instrument of status like the piano – not the piano accordion – and you also need to be able to play pieces on that instrument that are allocated cultural weight, pieces that reflect refinement and taste; it doesn't count if all you can play are drinking songs.

Underpinning this logic is the binary premise that some cultural forms have intrinsic 'quality', and others, the culture of the masses – *popular culture* – is shallow and vulgar. Myth #1 addresses the widespread belief that, whatever popular culture is, it isn't really worth worrying about too much. After all, there's Shakespeare and Beethoven, and then there's *Big Brother* and the Eurovision Song Contest.

This myth is extended into the realm of social analysis. After all, who would want to waste their time investigating popular culture? For example, what can we possibly learn from an analysis of the tripe that often passes for entertainment on our TV screens every day? Shouldn't we really be investigating issues of power, governance and identity? Perhaps we can do both.

Youth Culture

It would be a mistake to assume that just as culture can be divided into two opposite values, so too can their audiences, with 'high' and 'low' cultures being consumed by 'cultured' and 'uncultured' audiences respectively. Other divisions also appear to mark out the field; one of the most important is the apparent split between the dominant culture, and 'youth culture', which almost by definition, is deemed to form the central currency of the mass school.

Myth #2 addresses the belief that, as a result of the existence of this entirely separate and somewhat mysterious phenomenon of 'youth culture', teachers need to school themselves regularly in its ever-changing characteristics if they want to do their jobs effectively. If teachers aren't up to date with what kids are watching on TV, how can they find sufficient common cultural ground to establish an effective pedagogic relationship?

There are a number of assumptions built into these claims; that there is a clear boundary around youth culture; that schools are populated by two categories of person, the young and the old; that the best way to relate to pupils is through utilising elements of their external cultural life; that school children even *want* you to know about the TV they watch and the language they use. After all, is there anything worse than finding out your dad likes the same band you do?

Popular Culture and the School

This represents the final major binary associated with this area; the binary alluded to in the start of this introduction. Myth #3 asserts that low culture – popular culture – has no place within the school. Schools should be about coming to terms with the highlights of the Western canon, with the complexities of human nature as laid bare by the great writers and artists of the last 500 years. Students get enough popular culture outside the boundaries of the school. They don't need any more, and besides, there is absolutely nothing of value to be learned from *Twilight*.

Arguably, this is not an either/or situation, in spite of the way the debate is often presented in the media. Popular culture can find a place in the classroom, not necessarily at the expense of more familiar staples within the English curriculum, for example, but rather as an addition. Popular culture can be used to engage students where they otherwise may be uninterested; it may be used as part of the process of decoding what students see and hear, as discussed with the news media in Chapter 8; it may also be used as part of illustrating how contemporary identities, including the identities of the students themselves, are shaped by the various elements of the cultures they consume, and with which they interact (White and Walker 2008).

To summarise, the three myths to be dealt with in this chapter are as follows.

Myth #1 Popular culture is rubbish – in terms of taste, it's awful; as an object of study, it's irrelevant.
Myth #2 Teachers need to be up to date with student cultures.
Myth #3 Popular culture has no place in the classroom.

Myth #1 *Popular Culture is Rubbish – in Terms of Taste, it's Awful; as an Object of Study, it's Irrelevant*

Even though most of us probably watch a fair bit of television, for the most part, we know it's generally depressingly lowbrow – after all, South Park isn't exactly Shakespeare. The same goes for the music we hear on the radio; it's formulaic rubbish; some of it may be catchy, but it's hardly going to stand the test of time. Besides, all you need to make it is three chords and a drum machine. And surely our university academics have better things to do with their time than investigate what is, for the most part, just faddish drivel.

We all know that there are some great novels out there: Joyce's *Ulysses* (1922), Proust's *Remembrance of Things Past* (1927), Tolstoy's *War and Peace* (1886). These are long, complex and nuanced works of art; most of us have never read any of them, but we know they represent something important. They are deemed to be part of a canon of literature, representing the best of Western culture. Wildly popular though they are, Brown's *The Da Vinci Code* (2003) is not on this list, and neither is Collins' *The Hunger Games* (2008). They are considered to be something else. They are manifestations of a lower form of culture – popular yes, but lacking the beauty, depth and originality necessary for the novels to be considered works of art, to be considered genuine timeless classics.

We may take this division for granted, but who gets to make this assessment? Who gets to say that *Ulysses* is 'literature', and *The Da Vinci Code* isn't? Indeed, what does this division even represent, and where does it come from? Is it *real*, in any objective sense of the word?

The Invention of High Culture

Nearly 2500 years ago, when Plato set out the subject matter for an appropriate education in *The Republic* (1974), he not only listed those areas crucial to a good education, such as astronomy, geometry and gymnastics, he also made it very clear as to what should be left out. There would be no place in Plato's idealised society for poets and painters, as their endeavours were not focused on the search for truth; rather, they were simply engaged in the act of *imitation*. That is, the emphasis on appearance lacks the philosophical weight of a genuine quest for truth, and hence they should be banned from the city. Weaver (2009, 3–4) regards this as a vital moment in the development of contemporary understandings of culture:

> It is with Plato's quest to ban poets and painters from the Republic that marks the first attempt to demarcate between Culture and popular culture ... For Plato, the poet offers nothing to elevate society, instead he will only pander to the lowly tastes and desires of the masses.

Weaver goes on to note that Plato is far from the only great philosopher who shares distaste for the cultural pursuits of 'the masses'. He cites Rousseau, Kant and Schiller, who, at various times, have all expressed concern over the corrosive and stupefying effects of what might now be called 'popular culture'. Kant (1979) was particularly pointed in his observations, regarding the masses as too ill-educated and base to be able to tell the difference between cultural forms with legitimate aesthetic and intellectual value, and those that, while entertaining, are ultimately worthless.

Probably the most influential text speaking to the divide between high and low culture is Arnold's *Culture and Anarchy* (1963). Written in England in 1869 at the height of the industrial revolution, Arnold was horrified by both the rise of a new type of society that seemed only interested in wealth and power, and by the most conspicuous leaders of this new social order, the newly rich merchants and mill-owners, whom he regarded as 'barbarians'. Arnold wrote about the civilising power of culture, by which he meant 'a pursuit of our total perfection by means of getting to know, on all the matters which most concern us, the best which has been thought and said in the world' (Arnold 1963, 3).

Arnold's ideas on the value of high culture have proved to be both durable and influential over the ensuing 150 years. Not only do they continue to lay the foundation for the emergence of texts such as *The Closing of the American Mind* (Bloom 1987) – a best-selling book that bemoans the abandonment of traditional high cultural forms by America's elite, and champions, in the style of Arnold, a list of 'great books' that must be read – they also continue to influence media discourse on the subject of popular culture and education in the UK. As already discussed, Gove's campaign for 'traditional education' stresses the vital importance of the English literary canon.

In part, the issues appear here to be twofold: first, that when classical literature is found in the school curriculum, it is often no longer to be simply read and appreciated, as was once the case; it is now subject to the undignified, progressive process of postmodern 'deconstruction', wherein the text is interrogated for all manner of hidden elements. Second, other less worthy texts are finding their way onto the curriculum, texts which can only be described as part of 'popular culture'.

The Arrival of Popular Culture

The notion of 'popular culture' is just as complex and as contested as its larger sibling, 'culture'. Whereas apprehension over the cultural shortcomings of the working classes has a very long history, as discussed above, the first theoretical concerns over 'the culture of the people' became manifest with a focus upon 'folk culture', an idealised version of quasi-rural life, focusing on the songs, stories and rituals of ordinary, non-elite life (Burke 1996). In many ways, this creation differs markedly from the notion of 'popular culture'. 'Folk culture' generally conjures up images of medieval dancing, traditional craftwork, and songs with phrases like '*Fie diddly oh*' in them. These cultures are romantically regarded as having emerged organically from their host societies, passed down through generations – and centuries – and as such the cultures have specific meaning and resonance.

Arguably, 'popular culture' represents something else altogether. It is the product of new types of social organisation and technology. Through the rise of radio, movies, and eventually television, individual examples of particular cultural forms – songs, films, television programmes – could be popularised almost immediately, and almost globally, in ways that were impossible at the beginning of the twentieth century. For example, within days of becoming popular in America, George Cohen's song *Give my Regards to Broadway* could now be hummed by people in Manchester, Sydney and Auckland, by people who didn't even have the faintest idea where Broadway was. This leads on to another important point about popular culture – it is no longer rooted within the host culture itself, rather it can trace it origins to a far wider set of influences and sources. Of course, many of these are American, but as will be discussed in Chapter 11, this is a long way from the suggestion that popular culture and American culture are the same thing.

Of course, popular culture also extends beyond *The Da Vinci Code*, and rock 'n' roll; it takes an incredibly wide range of forms, extending from the relatively obvious, to the subtle and the indirect. Popular culture extends beyond self-evident components such as fashion styling, television programming, and the content of magazines, it is also evidenced through less tangible elements, such as in the choice of leisure activities (dance styles, or beer selection), the embracing of particular types of belief (*One Direction* are the most attractive and talented human beings who ever lived), and the adoption of particular codes of speech ('Australian Questioning Intonation' – i.e. continually raising vocal pitch at the end of sentences – or saying 'like', instead of 'um'). Arguably, all of these are part of contemporary popular culture, or are directly constituted by it.

Having drawn some conclusions about the origins and parameters of popular culture, other questions begin to arise: how can we conceptualise this relatively new phenomenon? What are the theoretical tools available to us? How can we place it in relation to other associated concepts, such as 'high culture', consumer society, social class and postmodernity?

Some Theories of Popular Culture

When addressing the question 'So what is popular culture?', the most obvious answer is: those cultural forms which people like. Clearly, this doesn't really take us anywhere. More complex and satisfying answers have been proposed utilising a wide range of theories, from within an almost equally wide range of disciplinary starting points – cultural studies, sociology, philosophy, psychology, history, English – and all continue to have something to say about the subject. This section will address four of the most influential.

POPULAR CULTURE: THE 'OTHER' OF HIGH CULTURE

The ideas of Arnold, discussed earlier, eventually spawned a coherent theoretical approach usually referred to as *Leavisism*, after its driving intellectual force, F. R. Leavis. In books such as *Mass Civilisation and Minority Culture* (1930), Leavis argued that the social elite – who had always dictated cultural tastes, indeed, they had regarded themselves as 'the guardians' of culture – were no longer venerated by their social inferiors, as had traditionally been the case. One of the consequences of this decline in respect for the ruling classes was a parallel decline in respect for the cultural forms they championed. Importantly, these forms of culture were regarded as 'better' than those enjoyed by the uneducated masses. As Leavis and Thompson (1977, 3) state:

> Upon the minority depends our power of profiting by the finest human experience of the past: they keep alive the subtlest and most perishable part of tradition. Upon them depend the implicit standards that order the finer living of an age. . .

Leavis believed it possible to discern objectively, for example, which literature meets the necessary criteria to be considered of value. All the others could then be grouped together as 'popular culture' – the mindless dross of the common people, pandering to the simplest of emotions – and the rise of which, according to Leavis, clearly represented a culture in intellectual and moral decline. It is the limited social access to 'high culture' that ties in with Bourdieu's notion of cultural capital, discussed in Chapter 1. That is, those who understand high cultural forms, who have the background to appreciate it and to use it, are able to translate this capacity into social and educational advantage.

Probably needless to say, the Leavisite position – 'high culture is better' – has been subject to considerable criticism; indeed, it acts as a counterpoint to almost all the approaches to popular culture. Many would argue that this theory is underpinned by a romantic nostalgia for a largely mythic past, and yet in spite of this fundamental flaw, it has constituted a remarkably persistent theoretical position, struggling only recently in the face of explanations emanating from cultural studies (Patterson 2008).

POPULAR CULTURE AS MASS CULTURE

A second theoretical position on popular culture in some ways takes an almost diametrically opposite viewpoint from that of the theory above. The most logical way to disagree with Leavis surely would be to reject the notion that there exist objective criteria for assessing the worth of cultural forms. However, the advocates of the 'mass culture' position do not specifically disagree with the Leavisite contention that popular culture is mostly formulaic nonsense; their disagreement lies in their assessment of the implications of mass culture.

The Leavisites regarded popular culture as a threat to the power of the ruling classes. Popular culture was seen to represent a rejection of not only the high cultural forms of the ruling elites, it also represented a rejection of the authority that underpinned those forms. The 'mass culture' position argues the opposite. Writers like Adorno and Horkheimer (1979) suggest that the stultifying and conformist aspects of mass culture produce a desensitised, depoliticised and easily manipulated population. These arguments are paraphrased by Storey (2003, 29), 'Work under capitalism stunts the senses; the culture industry continues the process'. Thus the magazines, music and movies that constitute the bulk of popular culture are not designed to stimulate thought; they are there for passive consumption. Artistic and creative merit is all but irrelevant. The issue is conformity.

This understanding of popular culture constitutes a perfect example of a modernist approach to social analysis. There is a single truth to be uncovered, from within a single explanatory framework, a framework that can explain everything – a *Master Discourse* – and consequently this explanation has been criticised for all the reasons modernism has been criticised: it is reductionist, it is deterministic, and it is homogenising.

POPULAR CULTURE AS RESISTANCE

The writers of the influential Centre for Contemporary Cultural Studies in Birmingham (CCCS) did not accept that the population were simply victims of some kind of 'popular culture conspiracy'. While they agreed that there was certainly a mass culture industry, they contended that different groups found space for themselves within these prevailing models, and by struggling against their *cultural hegemony* – their often-unspoken cultural dominance – they gained some measure of autonomy. It should be pointed out that they did not see popular culture as any kind of real threat to the social order, as did Leavis, and they certainly didn't think that high culture was somehow intrinsically better.

As discussed in Chapter 6, the CCCS focused mostly upon youth culture. They contended that youth subcultures were stylised responses to the dominant social order, and through the process of *bricolage*, such cultures could take bits and pieces from the dominant culture and endow it with new meaning: the Union Jack worn by Mods in the 1960s had little or nothing to do with patriotism. Consequently, popular culture is not 'the other' of high culture, and neither is it 'the opiate of the masses', rather it can be understood as offering the potential for a form of cultural independence, a place where non-elites can, in part, take material that appeals to them, and shape a culture of their own (Stack and Kelly 2006).

This approach does not escape all of the criticisms levelled at the mass culture model; however, it moves some distance from the reductionist position of Adorno and Horkheimer. As was argued in the Chapter 6, equating youth with resistance brings with it problems of its own, and suggesting that popular culture somehow necessarily contains the seeds of resistance, when taken outside the realm of youth subcultures, can be regarded as equally problematic.

POPULAR CULTURE AND POSTMODERNITY

As has been discussed at various points throughout this book, postmodernity offers a viable alternative to the approaches taken by modernist sociologies, and the issue of popular culture is no exception. Rather than looking for the truth of popular culture, for an objective standard by which it can be measured, or for the key to understanding how its messages are to be interpreted, those studying popular culture from this perspective face a more difficult task.

Postmodern accounts of popular culture can be understood as having a number of features. First, there is no single explanation of popular culture to be had; postmodernism did not criticise the master discourses of modernity, only to then replace them with one of its own. Postmodern accounts are necessarily contingent, dynamic and partial, after all, arguably there is no fixed, stable and complete story to tell.

Second, postmodernism argues for the abandonment of the binary between high and popular culture. Not only are high and popular culture now relatively arbitrary categories, they can also lead to the questionable conclusion that high culture is somehow good, and popular culture is inevitably bad; this is by no means the case. There are forms of popular culture that could arguably pass any kind of Leavisite test of inherent quality, whether this involves popular music (*The Beatles, The Rolling Stones*), Hollywood movies (*Casablanca, Pulp Fiction*), or television programs (*M.A.S.H., The Sopranos*). Insert your own favourites here. Or, to make matters even more complex, as Beethoven and Chaucer slowly fade from view, perhaps debates will increasingly be about 'high' popular culture vs 'low' popular culture, with people talking about the 'timeless beauty' of Stevie Wonder vs the 'mindless drivel' of Britney Spears (Greene 2012).

Third, postmodern accounts of popular culture can be characterised by recognition that the process of decoding messages from cultural media is no less important than the initial process of encoding them; there is no 'correct' reading to be uncovered, just as there is no fixed and predictable idealised audience, who will interpret the messages as they were intended to be interpreted. Audiences are plural and fluid, and they create meaning for themselves – perhaps an extension of the process of bricolage mentioned above.

Finally, these postmodern interpretations arguably describe a thoroughly postmodern world, at least in the West. According to Baudrillard (1983), we now live in a society characterised by hyper-reality, a realm where, largely thanks to television, fact and fiction are no longer separate entities, where chains of signification refer to nothing but themselves, and where copies are made without the existence of an original (simulacra). For example, thanks primarily to the crime drama *CSI*, some juries are now asking for forensic evidence to be supplied in trials in order to reach a conviction, *even where it is irrelevant* – a phenomenon now referred to as the 'CSI effect' (Carpenter and Tait 2010). Likewise, Fettes College, one of the most prestigious schools in Scotland, now promotes itself as being like Hogwarts. The shortcomings of postmodern theory, and hence also of postmodern analyses of popular culture, are discussed in Chapter 12.

In summary, the assertion that popular culture is rubbish, and conceptually irrelevant, makes a lot of assumptions, most of which do not hold up to contemporary analysis. First, contending that popular culture is awful is normally premised upon a comparison with the supposed excellence of high culture, or to put it another way, is premised upon the modernist binary: high/good, popular/bad. Second, it is a gross generalisation to categorise all popular culture as worthless; certainly, some of it is formulaic and mindless but, in a similar vein, not all classical music is good, just because it's classical. Finally, the study of popular culture is far from irrelevant; over the past 50 years, cultural studies, and the study of popular culture in particular, has told us a lot about how our society works, and a lot about ourselves.

Myth #2 *Teachers Need to Be Up to Date with Student Cultures*

One of the most important requirements for being a good teacher is to be able to relate to the students, and the only way that can be done is to speak the same cultural language as them. It's no use at all if a student talks about the things that interest

them – their media interests, their musical tastes, their styles of dress, their specific
ways of understanding the world – and the teacher can't contribute to the conversa-
tion, then the game is over before it's even really started.

There is no doubt that an important part of teaching involves the construction of a pedagogical relationship between the teacher and the pupil. Ideally, this relationship includes such features as mutual trust and respect, shared goals, good communication, enjoyment and positivity. The question here is: should it also necessarily involve shared frames of cultural reference? Should it involve teachers keeping up to date with youth cultures?

From Popular Culture to Youth Culture

The arguments in the previous section lead to the conclusion that there is no clear binary between high culture and popular culture, and that while social-class-based patterns of consumption do still exist (Bennett *et al.* 2008), these are not exclusive divisions, with the ruling elites only listening to opera and visiting art galleries, while the common people only watch *Britain's Got Talent* and hang velveteen prints of Elvis on their walls. Just as popular culture is not a discreet category, clearly demarcated from high culture, we can draw similar conclusions about a familiar sub-set of popular culture: that of 'youth culture'. But where did youth culture come from?

The concept of youth has been discussed at length in Chapter 6; however, it would be productive at this point to remind ourselves of a number of arguments about how it came to take its present form. First, there is nothing natural about this category. Like childhood, it came into being as a consequence of quite ordinary and seemingly unrelated social changes. Whereas childhood emerged, in part, as a result of inventions such as the printing press (Postman 1994), youth appeared at the end of a long chain of previous categories of pre-adulthood, such as the child, the juvenile delinquent, the adolescent and the teenager. As noted earlier, according to Cashmore (1984), youth initially developed in the early 1950s, both as a result of the demise of national service, and also as a result of the purchasing power of a newly affluent section of the population – too old to be at school, readily employed and cashed-up, too young and having too much fun to be married.

Second, and running in tandem with the appearance of this new 'stage of life' – and having significant feedback loops into it – was the parallel appearance of a culture to go along with the category. Indeed, perhaps the two are, in some ways, inseparable: it is the category that shapes the culture, which continually re-shapes our understanding of the category. That is, the ability of the young to buy the objects and artefacts that interested them almost immediately spawned the category of youth, as well as a youth market, which in turn formed the foundations of a youth culture: music, fashion, identity.

Finally, it has been suggested that, to go along with this new category, there developed a 'generational consciousness', a consciousness of youth. This contention formed one of the central elements of the CCCS approach to culture discussed in the previous section. The CCCS argued that, from the 1950s onwards, youth as a group started to perceive itself as intrinsically different from the parent generation. So even though they shared the same fundamental material conditions as their parents, they experienced those conditions in a somewhat different manner. The writers of the CCCS suggest that the new consciousness of youth is best understood in relation to the life areas of education, work and leisure, with each of these areas having the tendency to reinforce notions of the relative autonomy of youth as a category.

It is important to note that before this time, young people – people who would later be categorised as youth – shared the same culture as their parents, be that some nebulous version of folk culture, popular culture, or even elite culture. Young people did not dress differently, listen to different music, seek to purchase different material goods, or develop a different habitus. The idea that *of course* young people must have their own culture is a relatively recent invention.

A Closer Look at 'Youth Culture'

The myth driving this section of the chapter is that teachers need to be up to date with where their students are at; that teachers need to be plugged into youth culture if they are going to be effective in their job. It is no longer acceptable just to be able to teach maths well; you have to be able to engage learners on their own terrain, and that terrain is cultural. However, this myth is based upon a number of faulty assumptions.

A MONOLITHIC UNDERSTANDING OF CULTURE

The first premise is that there is a single, monolithic youth culture that teachers need to get to know. Imagining that there is a unitary set of practices, social references, forms of self-shaping, and cultural interests, is to ignore all the different groups, and varying degrees of affiliation to those groups, that exist within a school. Which one is *the* youth culture that teachers are supposed to get to know? There is no global, totalised entity that can be called youth culture, really any more than there is its singular mental equivalent – youth consciousness.

A more postmodern approach to youth involves not only recognising that youth is a plural category from the very beginning, but also that even if one culture were picked to represent all youth cultures – some kind of 'average' youth culture – this culture would not have clearly delineated boundaries that mark it out from all other cultures; neither would it have a fixed membership, that you were either part of, or were not; and nor would membership always mean the same thing to everyone. The idea doesn't really hold up to scrutiny.

BINARY #1: EITHER YOU KNOW YOUTH CULTURE, OR YOU DON'T

This myth is founded on the assumption that either you are up to date with youth culture, or you aren't; either you can function effectively within the knowledge-world of the young, or you can't. Premised upon the (erroneous) validity of the first assumption, this means that good teachers can understand and access youth culture, and bad teachers are excluded from it, and that is part of what makes them bad.

A more convincing argument would be to point out that knowledge doesn't work in this way, and neither does any reasonable assessment of the foundations of good teaching (Evans 2014). All social knowledge is partial, fluid and context-bound, and understanding that some young boys spend a lot of time playing *Call of Duty*, or *World of Warcraft*, on their computers – and can build a culture around this activity – does not mean that teachers have to play the game themselves, or even know how to play it, in order to know what the game is, and what it can mean to those involved. There are always going to be different levels of knowledge of 'youth culture'; this myth simply draws a line in the sand between knowledge and ignorance, and pretends it isn't arbitrary.

BINARY #2: YOUTH CULTURE VS ADULT CULTURE

The main faulty component of this myth is the distinction drawn between youth culture and broader, adult culture. These are presented as separate, autonomous domains, and knowledge of one has no relation to having any knowledge in the other; or more specifically, just because teachers are embedded in the wider popular culture, gives them no insight into the unrelated cultural universe of the young.

However, these are not two entirely autonomous domains. Much of youth culture is drawn from the broader field of popular culture. Indeed, young people watch many of the same television programmes and movies that adults watch. These are hybrid cultures, drawing their component parts, sometimes from the same pool, sometimes from different pools; sometimes extracting the same meanings, sometimes creating their own. Once again, the division is often arbitrary and contingent.

YOUTH CULTURE AND INCLUSIVITY

The final problem with this myth involves the idea that young people unequivocally welcome the presence of adults within their cultural universe. Just because a teacher might know enough about some aspects of a given youth cultural form to warrant insider status, does not mean that the teacher will actually be allowed inside, or should go there even if they were.

According to the CCCS, youth subcultures are constructed, in part, as resistance to the dominant social order (Hall and Jefferson 1976). If we accept this proposition (and it does have its flaws), young people find space for themselves through the cultures they construct. Youths often regard themselves as excluded and powerless within the context of adult cultures – so they make their own. Arguably, allowing access to outsiders defeats the object of having the culture in the first place. Would it really be a 'youth culture' if lots of teachers were tramping around inside it?

A Worked Example: the Goths

A good way to illustrate the arguments outlined above is through a specific youth subculture; an appropriate example is the Goths. Goths have been around as a subculture for over 30 years, and their appearance is instantly recognisable: 'They wear black: black clothes, long back-combed hair, black lipstick, eye make-up and nail varnish. Faces are as pale as possible' (Lees 1988, 7).

The very existence of the Goths rebuts the first faulty assumption of this myth: that there is a single youth culture that teachers need to get to know. Goths are just one of a plethora of youth subcultures, many of which are not even discernable from their physical appearance alone (what do *Call of Duty* players look like, other than the fact most are male?). Furthermore, the Goth subculture has itself been divided into a range of sub-subcultures, such as New Goths and Mini-Goths, a differentiation often based upon issues such as age, various specificities of dress, the length of time a person has been a Goth, and the perceived degree of affiliation to the subculture. So just as there is no single youth culture, there is not even a single Goth subculture. Unitary understandings and explanations of these categories simply don't work.

Likewise, the presumption is that teachers either know all about Goths, or they know nothing. Basic logic dictates that it is perfectly possible to know and recognise Goth-inspired dress codes, and to understand aspects of Goth identity formation and persona, without knowing the domain names for Goth websites, or having to listen to *The Cure, The Sisters of Mercy*, or *Siouxsie and the Banshees*. The binary of knowing/ not knowing breaks down before it even really gets started.

The second binary is the mutually exclusive distinction between adult and youth culture, or in this case, between dominant culture and Goth culture, and once again, the binary breaks down completely. After all, the notion of 'the Gothic' began in wider, adult culture, and only mutated into a youth subculture some 1000 years later. Leaving aside the sixth-century Germanic peoples of antiquity who sacked Rome, the term originated as a disparaging, Renaissance way of describing non-classical architecture (Germann 1972). The Gothic revival of the eighteenth and nineteenth centuries was closely tied to the rise of the Romantic Movement, and extended beyond the architectural into the literary, with the 'Gothic Mood' informing poetry and the new literary form – the novel (Clark 1978). This mood emphasised a number of familiar motifs, such as the macabre, repressed desire, isolated settings, innocent young women, and a man with sinister secrets.

Interestingly, some of our greatest 'high culture' literature is, if not Gothic in its entirety, is certainly informed by the Gothic Mood. Leaving aside Bram Stoker's *Dracula* (1897), and Edgar Allen Poe's *Fall of the House of Usher* (1839) as two obvious examples, other high culture classics might include Emily Bronte's *Wuthering Heights* (1846), Charlotte Bronte's *Jane Eyre* (1847), and Oscar Wilde's *The Picture of Dorian Gray* (1891). The point here is that contemporary Goth culture does not exist as a discrete entity, entirely removed from dominant adult culture; the two draw from the same well. In fact, not only are dominant models of popular culture quick to employ Gothic symbolism on a regular basis (The *Batman* movies – Gotham City anyone?), but so too are our exemplars of high culture.

Finally, there is the issue of the exclusivity of youth subcultures. Would the Goth subculture survive as part of the romantic fashioning of youthful identity, if a number of teachers started dressing all in black, with long black hair, and white pancake make-up – assuming they would still have a job? There wouldn't be a single Goth left in school by the end of the first week.

In summary, every time there is a call for teachers to be more 'down with the culture of the kids', the following questions should arise. Which kids? Which culture? Which parts of which culture? All teachers can do is to try and understand and recognise as many of the broad brush strokes of the cultures they find in their classroom, and manoeuvre their way through and around them as best they can; and within this context, structure the best pedagogic relationships they can.

Myth #3 *Popular Culture Has No Place in the Classroom*

Have we really come to the point where texts that have stood the test of time, such as Shakespeare's Romeo and Juliet or Macbeth, have been replaced in the curriculum by whichever 'text' is currently in fashion? Surely some intrinsic underlying value has to be present in a book before it's worth presenting to our children. Nobody is going to be talking about Twilight in ten years' time, not teenage girls, not cultural studies lecturers, nobody. So why teach about it now?

According to this myth, our schools have all but abandoned the literary classics, and we are now teaching, with a straight face, whatever happens to be the latest pulp novel at the top of the airport shelves; we are as likely to study articles from women's magazines, as we are to study *Macbeth*. The trouble is, this just simply isn't the case. As discussed in Chapter 8, this straw man argument appears primarily designed to whip up public support for a return to the good old days of a 1940s education. Apart from a few, slightly hysterical, claims made by the more conservative end of the political/ educational spectrum, the best evidence suggests that the literary canon is actually as much a part of the curriculum as ever.

Of course, this myth also implies that old literature is good, and that anything new finding a place in the school curriculum must therefore be bad/pulp. Consequently, the literary canon can have the appearance of being 'frozen in time'. As discussed in myth #1, there are surely recent examples of literature that would pass the Leavisite test of quality; it would be a foolhardy traditionalist who considered Salman Rushdie's *Midnight's Children* (1981), or Gabriel García Marquéz's *One Hundred Years of Solitude* (1970) as unworthy of inclusion.

So does this mean there is no debate to be had about popular culture in the classroom? And where does the notion of 'literary worth' fit into this debate? There are still a number of issues to be addressed regarding the link between literary worth and popular culture, and in truth, these have not always been restricted to the opinion pages of the *Daily Express* and the *Daily Telegraph*. In *High Culture, Popular Culture: the Long Debate*, Goodall (1995) suggests that the notion of 'literary worth' is a difficult one, and contends that just as the preoccupation with high culture accelerated the downfall of the traditional study of English, then so too might the refusal to engage with the issue of 'value' prove to be the undoing of cultural studies. That is, by refusing to rule on the worth of various examples of popular culture, by refusing to delineate its boundaries clearly, it is in danger of becoming everything and nothing. As Goodall (1995, 172–3) states:

> A 'Cultural' studies which feels it is able to ignore high art, Culture with a capital C . . . seems to me to be a fatally compromised project. While the notion of a study of texts, unworried and undifferentiated by any notions about quality, in their broad discursive contexts, has much to recommend it, one must point out at the same time, what is lost in the abandonment of the aesthetic dimension in the study of the text.

Goodall cites Eagleton (1983), one of the foremost advocates of the cultural studies position, who rightly notes that part of the problem lies in the fact that traditional literary criticism cannot justify restricting its scope to works of 'value', when it is part of the process by which they are allocated 'value' in the first place – a perfect example of a self-fulfilling prophesy. Eagleton has a point.

All this leads to one of several options when trying to conceptualise the high/ popular culture divide, as it pertains to the curriculum. The first is to retreat into Leavisism; this would certainly make Michael Gove and other conservative educationalists happy. We can pretend that thirty years of postmodernity has never happened, and return to the modernist belief that there is an inherent truth to a text; that literary qualities are timeless and a-contextual; and that such qualities can be objectively assessed, ranked and passed on uncritically to yet another schooling generation.

Second, we can abandon the notion of 'value' altogether. It certainly is complex and, at times, seemingly completely arbitrary. Is it the place of teachers to tell children why one book is good, and another isn't – as if the issue of personal taste doesn't exist – and why one cultural form is good, and another isn't? We were once told Elvis Presley's music wasn't just bad; it was evil. Whatever happened to that? The trouble with this position is that it falls relatively easily to a *reductio ad absurdum* argument: are we really ready to accept that *Hamlet* has no more intrinsic artistic value than some beer commercial – both are 'texts', after all. Is anyone *really* suggesting we go down this path? (That said, it can sometimes be quite instructional to study a good example of a bad example.)

Perhaps a third option is to begin by pointing out that the notion of 'value' is a difficult one. It is always constituted in terms of specific genre; it has currency at particular times and in particular places; it necessarily has its own history as a scale of assessment; and it is contingent upon who is making that assessment and why. Concluding that *Romeo and Juliet* belongs in the English curriculum, and *The Da Vinci Code* doesn't, should perhaps be based upon making these sorts of judgements explicit; perhaps this is how the notion of 'value' can be salvaged. The funny thing is, it sounds very like the way the issue is currently dealt with in schools already.

Three Approaches to Popular Culture in the Classroom

So having concluded that the binary between '*Popular culture is bad; we need the classics*,' and '*The high/popular culture divide is an illusion, so anything goes*,' is itself an illusion, how can we go about managing the relationship between popular culture and the classroom? White and Walker (2008) make three main suggestions.

EDUCATION VIA POPULAR CULTURE

Most people would agree with the contention that education should be interesting and engaging; too many likely remember their own school days as exactly the opposite: boring, repetitious and irrelevant. Using popular culture in the classroom is one way teachers have attempted to make a connection with pupils who might otherwise remain disconnected, not only from the material normally utilised, but also from the entire schooling process. If students are at least listening, then surely they are part of the way to learning.

What may seem to be a no-brainer – using resources that engage with the students – is not without its critics. Needless to say, there are those traditionalists for whom the use of popular culture in the classroom is completely unacceptable, irrespective of its purpose; these opinions have already been addressed in some detail. Then there are also those who regard education as an unwaveringly serious business, and as such, there can be no place for the triviality that comes with popular culture:

> A common sentiment among administrators and other school officials is that schools are for work and not for fun. The idea of barring fun from the school day seems to be

gaining momentum, compelled by the 'north-bound high-stakes testing train'. It is common knowledge that it is easier to get on board that train than it is to stand in front of it . . . (White and Walker 2008, 16–17)

In spite of this, popular culture can be employed to teach everything from geography (Bell and Gropshover 2005) to business (Kneavel 2005). Indeed, the use of science fiction to engage students in the study of science has proved to be particularly successful (Gough 1993; Weaver, Anijar and Daspit 2004). Re-workings of classic texts, but modelled from within popular culture, are also effective within the teaching of English, whether directly, as in Baz Luhrmann's version of *Romeo + Juliet*, or indirectly, such as *Macbeth* via films like Brian De Palma's *Scarface*.

One further criticism raised regarding the use of popular media in the curriculum, involves the possibility of rendering popular culture 'neutral' in the process of knowledge production. That is, by employing popular culture in an uncritical manner, simply to hold student attention, or to make other kinds of unrelated educational points, there runs the risk of reinforcing the belief that such messages have an inherent natural validity, and are therefore unworthy of scrutiny in their own right. This concern is precisely the issue for the second approach to popular culture in the classroom.

POPULAR CULTURE AND SOCIAL DECODING

One of the most widely proffered reasons for addressing popular culture in the classroom relates to concerns over its effects on young people. As such, popular culture is not employed as a way of engaging students with the curriculum; it *is* the curriculum. The life worlds of young people are shaped within the relentless contexts of popular culture – television, film, music, magazines, the internet, fashion – and it is important that they are able to make sense of the messages they receive.

This issue has already been addressed in Chapter 8, on the importance of possessing the skills to decode the media, and the arguments here are essentially the same. The issues of genre, selection, production, language choice and bias are as relevant here as they are when listening to the news. For example, consumer culture (arguably inexorably intertwined with popular culture) largely provides the vocabulary through which young people assemble their identities. That is, by choosing one form of self-representation over another, by buying certain commodities, by reading particular magazines or listening to particular kinds of music, chosen identities are shaped and re-shaped (Miller and Rose 1990, 25). Arguably, it is important for those engaged in this process – 'the artful assembly of a lifestyle put together though the world of goods' – to at least be taught about the rules of the game.

This form of social decoding via popular culture also extends to students acquiring the ability to step outside many of our most familiar social narratives, and to develop viable alternates – not just about others but also about themselves. As Sfeir (2014, 17) states, using popular culture in the classroom can 'facilitate a change of perspective on many complex issues, especially in the area of class, race and gender'.

EDUCATION, POPULAR CULTURE AND COMPLEXITY

This approach to popular culture seeks to address how the texts of popular culture can be interpreted in different ways; how we are positioned and shaped by its influence; and how our subjectivities are organised through complex relations of power. The issue here is not simply to present the skills to decode popular culture; it is about allowing students to participate more effectively in the fluid and reflexive processes of textual analysis, interpretation and, ultimately, enjoyment. This approach to understanding the relationship between education and popular culture is postmodern to its very core.

And it is this approach to the use of popular culture that seems to irritate some traditionalists so much. White and Walker contextualise this irritation by linking it back to an unapologetically modernist understanding of the function of education. This approach believes that schools should restrict their curricula to the basics – the three Rs, classic literature and preparation for work. What constitutes real knowledge is virtually self-evident; there are not multiple readings of texts, there is the correct one, which students will be informed of by the teacher. Defoe's *Robinson Crusoe* can't be read as a metaphor about colonialism; it's simply an adventure story about a brave sailor, and his uncivilised black friend.

Some of those who think that schools should play a more complex and challenging role have suggested that popular culture may have a useful role to play in this process. Furthermore, this more challenging view of education is not simply about reading texts from a wider range of sources, and with greater insight; it is also about expanding the ethical possibilities of schooling. As White and Walker (2008, 26) state:

> By learning to read texts from a variety of viewpoints, students can develop litera-
> cies that value difference, and can use the awareness of difference in creating
> a moral vision that a single perspective can never offer.

In summary, culture is a moveable feast, whatever label is placed upon it: high, popular, youth, folk. None of these is set in stone, and yet, when it comes to choice of material for our schools, it seems that some voices would have us do precisely that. It seems strange to limit ourselves to a choice of texts that no longer necessarily reflect who we now are as a community, or what we are interested in, or what we consider worthy. We do not have to abandon the notion of 'value', just because we may choose to step outside someone's idea of the literary canon. We do not have to fall into a postmodern Neverland, just because we accept that texts may be understood in more than one way.

Conclusion

This entire area, though thoroughly colonised by postmodern thought, still seems to find itself shoehorned into modernist binaries when it comes to wider fields of debate. The list is quite impressive: high vs popular culture; adult culture vs youth culture; popular culture is good vs it's worthless; teachers need to know about youth culture vs no, they don't; finally, popular culture belongs in the classroom vs no, it doesn't.

Every time we see one of these reductionist and homogenising binaries, we should pause and reflect on the complexity of the issues we are dealing with. Part of the problem lies in the fact that the two different sides of these binaries represent competing views about the future of British education. One side represents a traditionalist view of what counts as a good education, the view that what constitutes an appropriate curriculum does not change with the seasons. The other represents the view that this type of education harks back to a romantic myth about our schools that only ever had limited purchase on reality; it also contends that we now live in a complex social and cultural world, and our education system needs to be able to prepare students for it.

Perhaps if we point to the artifice of these binaries for long enough, we can go some way towards removing them from the field of debate between competing models of education; and if so, perhaps we can find a role for popular culture within the classroom that can be valued by everyone.

TECHNOLOGY 10

Some might suggest that information and communication technologies (ICTs) aren't really that important a subject; certainly they don't deserve their own chapter in a book on the sociology and philosophy of education. We don't need to discuss technologies such as tables and chairs, so why the fuss over computers and smart phones – they all just make teaching a bit easier. It will be argued here that the situation is significantly more complex than that.

More often than not, the advent of contemporary information and communication technologies is presented as one of the great success stories of contemporary school-ing, and while it has the potential to be a transformative force within education, the issues are complicated and the outcomes far from certain. The field is often divided into those who grew up with such technologies – digital natives/students – and those who have come to these technologies at a later date – digital immigrants/teachers. This binary articulates a central problem within a power relation where teachers are normally expected to know more than those they teach. Furthermore, such new technologies do not simply represent mechanisms for accessing more information, more quickly, and in more interesting ways. By stepping outside the domain of traditional linear texts, traditional understandings of literacy start to lose their mean-ing. New digital technologies necessitate the adoption of the notion of 'multiliteracies', a plural understanding of literacy that encompasses a range of other modes of contemporary meaning-making – hypertext, audio, video, and so on – modes integral to the digital universe.

> **Myth #1 'Technologies' aren't that important; they don't affect the fundamentals of what it is to be human.** *'Technologies are just 'things we use'. We aren't really any different from Bronze-age people, except we can make phone calls between classes'.* Basic technologies such as the needle and the printing press have shaped us into creatures our ancestors would barely recognise. The early evidence suggests that modern technologies also have the

potential to fundamentally change, not just the most basic of classroom practices, but what we are as human beings.

Myth #2 Digital technology is the answer to all our education problems. *'Computers don't know if you're rich or poor; or male or female; or even a refugee. Inequalities of educational access are a thing of the past. Just log in and learn'.* Digital technology does not guarantee an excellent learning experience; in fact, there are arguments to suggest quite the reverse. Furthermore, such technologies can exacerbate issues of educational inequity, regarding who has access, who has the necessary skills, who actually gets to use them, and who uses them in ways that prove to be educationally and economically productive.

Myth #3 Technology signals the end of teaching. *'We don't really need teachers anymore; we probably don't even need schools. Everything children need to learn is right there on their computer screens'.* Teachers have always dealt with new technologies, and information and communication technologies are ultimately no different. Given the exponential rise in the amount of information available to students, teachers will be required more than ever to guide those students in appreciating the difference between the mere accessing of information, and the shaping of useful knowledge.

Introduction

This book is full of contemporary debates and worries about education: from concerns over decreasing funding for state schools, to the difficulties in teaching for a multicultural society; from questions about the rise of Ritalin use among children, to arguments over teacher competence and responsibility levels; from moral panics over progressive models of education, to how best to manage truancy rates. All too often, mass education is understood as a site of contestation and disquiet, one where the news is almost always bad.

In contrast to all these worrisome educational reports, the domain of 'Education and Technology' has tended to shine like a beacon. Here is an area where the news almost always seems to be good: computers are spreading like wildfire, even in the most impoverished of schools; because children love computers, they are going to start to love the learning process; problems with access to information will become a thing of the past, even in the most remote of Scottish islands; access to knowledge will become more interesting and more structured; the division between work and play will start to disappear ... the good news just keeps on coming. Sure, there is a wide range of concerns about the consequences of computer technology in the domestic realm – excessive Facebooking, internet predators, developing bad posture, pornography, cyber-bullying, violent games – but the use of computers in the school seems to be relatively immune from these types of criticism.

Is it that simple? Have new information and communications technologies (ICTs) heralded a brave new dawn of truly effective education, or is it all rather more complex than that? Certainly, the dominant discourses around technology and education have generally been positive. But does this actually reflect what is going on in our school? Boody (2001, 12–13) sceptically observes:

> Noted in an advertisement in a magazine for teachers was a quote from a principal in whose school a number of computers were installed: 'While I realise [major computer manufacturer in Silicon Valley] sells computers, I believe they really sell learning.' Really? I did not know that learning was available simply for money. I'd like to buy some myself.

Boody goes on to point out that while the desire for schools to 'keep up to date' is most likely laudable, the problem lies in the fact that this becomes translated as 'How do we get the best technology the quickest?', rather than the far more fundamental questions of 'What kind of education do we want for our children, and what are the best ways of producing it?' That is, we are in danger of mistakenly assuming that we have already answered these questions, and the answer is the same – technology.

Technophobes, Digital Immigrants, and Digital Natives

Early concerns over ICTs and education often centred upon the ability of the existing body of teachers to adapt to the new professional landscape. How were teachers in late middle age, many of whom couldn't even type, going to cope with the Internet, with online curriculum packages, and with HTML – indeed, how were they even going to cope with email? After all, nearly one third of the population was deemed to suffer from *Technophobia*: the fear of technology (Brosnan 1998). Such fears were not even limited to the techno-elderly; they encompassed women, ethnic minorities, the remote, in fact seemingly everybody other than young, white males.

These concerns now almost seem quaint. While not suggesting that your average granny spends her evenings writing programming for software packages, many now email, Skype, and surf the net with perfect competence. More significantly, teachers – whatever their age – are now expected to be able to use most of the technology that makes their schools operate on a daily basis, whether that be for administrative, pedagogic, pastoral or social purposes. The expected wave of teacher resignations, or redundancies, never materialised, and teachers now happily use their smart phones along with everyone else who can afford one.

Rather than technophobia then, the focus soon came to fall upon the distinction between those who have grown up with ICTs as a fundamental part of their life world, often referred to as *Digital Natives*, and those who have come to them later in life, who consciously had to 'learn' about them, called *Digital Immigrants* (Prensky 2001, 2011). This binary provided a useful way of articulating the division deemed to exist between students and teachers, and their respective relationships to digital technology.

> ... the single biggest problem facing education today is that our Digital Immigrant instructors, who speak an outdated language (that of the pre-digital age), are struggling to teach a population that speaks an entirely new language. This is obvious to the Digital Natives – school often feels pretty much as if we've brought in a population of heavily accented, unintelligible foreigners to lecture them. They often can't understand what the Immigrants are saying. What does 'dial' a number mean, anyway? (Prensky 2001, 2)

Arguably, this is more significant than simply a 'failure to communicate'. As discussed in Chapter 6, according to Postman (1994), childhood became demarcated from adulthood on the basis of (a lack of) access to knowledge, as determined by knowledge of the written word. Childhood became a time of 'not knowing', particularly regarding issues of sexuality, and adults were those who *did* know. The relationship between teacher and pupil has been founded upon this principal: teachers know, students don't. The issue of students as digital natives versus teachers as digital immigrants has the potential to undercut this principal in the most fundamental of ways.

So what happens now? In order to retain their authority within the teacher/pupil hierarchy, will digital immigrant teachers be continually forced to try to know more than those digital natives who sit in front of them? Remember: teachers know, students don't. In the context of education and ICTs, this sounds rather like a fool's errand, and rather like a misunderstanding of the best use of technology in the classroom. First, good teachers can utilise the skills and capacities of their students without necessarily sacrificing their authority. This is a false binary; teachers don't know everything (nor should they), and those that pretend they do, are probably in for short and disappointing careers.

Second, it has been argued that the 'digital natives/digital immigrants' construct is itself a false binary. Bayne and Ross (2011) suggest that this depiction of the two relationships available to ICTs not only de-privileges the role of the teacher – important within the context of this book – it also sets up, 'not a peaceful co-existence of facing terms, but a violent hierarchy' (Derrida 1981, 41). It is a 'violent hierarchy' because the digital immigrant is necessarily inferior to the digital native, dominated by it, and subordinate to its knowledge. Implicit within this binary are a series of supporting sub-binaries – that is, native/immigrant equals student/teachers, fast/slow, young/old, future/past, playful/serious, and multi-tasking/sequential – binaries which run the risk of inappropriately organising the field of debate about education and technology, before the conversation really even commences.

Multiliteracies

Irrespective of whether the digital immigrant/digital native binary is too much of an oversimplification, it is hard to disagree with the assertion that ICTs are reorganising how we go about accessing information, how we communicate with each other, and how we go about creating meaning. Traditional literacy has always focused solely upon the written word; students have generally been asked to read printed text, and then to write answers detailing their grasp of that text – basic reading comprehension (Cole and Pullen 2010). This is largely a singular, linear, sequential and stable process; meaning is regarded as inherent to the words used; and all students should progress through the text in the same way.

It has been argued that this is no longer the most appropriate way of under-standing literacy. The New London Group (1996) coined the term *Multiliteracies* and, with this, they were pointing to two things. First, that in an era when national and cultural boundaries are breaking down, when we have both 'local diversity and global connectedness', and where English has become the dominant world language, English is fracturing into 'increasingly differentiated Englishes, marked by accent, national origin, subcultural style, and professional or technical communities' (Cope and Kalantzis 2000, 6). The idea of a single, standard version of our language, to which measures of 'literacy' can be attached, has now all but been abandoned.

Second – and central to the subject matter of this chapter – literacy no longer simply refers to the ability to access written texts. 'Multiliteracy' now involves both this initial, textual form of meaning making, as well as a range of other modes, such as the visual, the spatial and the aural. Also, when students access information from web-pages, they are not necessarily reading the words in a traditional fashion, nor are they necessarily making meaning only from the words on the screen; there are sounds, videos, links in and out, hypertext, activities, pop-up boxes, other web pages open, all of which contribute to how meaning is shaped (Burnett 2004b).

Given these variables, and the fact that no two students are likely to engage in this process in exactly the same way, it consequently makes little sense to regard literacy as the acquisition of a single set of skills, neatly bounded and forever useful in its current form. So unless we think we can simply ignore these changes – and pretend that the computer screen is just an ordinary page of a book, except one powered by electricity – then the rise of such technologies requires us to adopt the notion of *multiliteracies* if we are to get the best out of our students, and if we are to equip them properly for the digital age.

Technology and the Formation of 'Us'

With all this discussion of the potential benefits of ICTs for teaching and learning, or of who can use computers effectively and who can't, or of how texts now come in a variety of different forms and the degree to which that actually matters, there is a temptation to think that such new technologies – or *any* technologies for that matter, and not just the classroom varieties – still have very limited relevance to what makes us tick as a species. After all, aren't these are just technical matters, ultimately of no greater collective significance than when televisions were first brought into the classroom, or pocket calculators? Surely the essence of teaching stays the same, and more importantly, surely we stay the same.

Actually, there are convincing historical arguments that suggest we don't stay the same at all. As will be discussed in myth #1, technologies are important, not simply because they help us do things better, faster, or more safely, they have the potential to change the boundaries of the possible, to change how we see each other, and ourselves, in the world, to change how we think and what we value, to fundamentally alter our capacities as human beings. Though very few people would have realised it at the time, the invention of the printing press in the fifteenth century did more than permit the mass production of books. As discussed in Chapter 6, the printing press eventually played an important role in the formation of new categories of person (such as 'the child'), as well as new forms of political organisation, new skills and aptitudes, and even new forms of consciousness. Bearing this in mind, ICTs should probably not be passed off simply as useful practical aids, employed by otherwise stable and unchanging citizenry. ICTs appear to be in the process of making similarly significant changes to *what we are*. Importantly, the classroom is one of the key sites for this transformation.

Technology, Better Teaching, and Educational Equity

In the light of such changes, it has been widely claimed that ICTs have the potential to solve most of our current educational problems. In the realm of 'virtual schools', traditional stumbling blocks to success, such as whether your teacher is any good, what your first language is, how advanced your knowledge is, where you live, how time-rich or time-poor you are, how economically rich or poor you are, how you like to learn, how old you are, all start to melt away in the light of our technological advances (Berman and Tinker 2000).

Myth #2 in this chapter examines this technological fairyland, to see if the predictable structures of access and equity do not apply in the cyber-world. Perhaps not surprisingly, the usual suspects – social class, gender, race/ethnicity, age, geographical location, school type, social authority – all help shape who gets access to ICTs. As long as computers cost money, and some computers are better than others, then there will be differential access to those computers, as with any other educational resource.

But even if computers were free, and everyone was given one upon entering school (which is happening in some schools, though primarily in the private sector, hence they aren't *really* free), this would not guarantee an even take-up across the community. After all, access to a computer does not equal engagement with the possibilities made available via that computer. There remain social, cultural and practical obstacles in the way of computer learning, just as there are in the way of traditional, blackboard learning. There may exist a beautiful, virtual world of limitless learning, but students have to access it from our world, a world with a lot of problems and inequalities; one can't entirely compensate for the other.

Classroom Technology and the 'End of Teaching'

Just because students now have access to limitless information, this does not somehow correlate with limitless knowledge. As will be discussed in myth #3, there is now the belief that teachers are in danger of becoming redundant. Every child with an Internet connection has access to all the best libraries in the world; a virtually limitless storehouse of information, just waiting to be discovered. And while we're ridding ourselves of unnecessary burdens on the taxpayer, do we even need schools anymore? With the rise of 'virtual classrooms', and online interest groups, students can access such groups from anywhere on the planet, and once there, work through structured lessons in the company of other, like-minded students.

It will be contended here that these arguments are not particularly convincing. Schools are more than just buildings, and students get more from them than just information in a classroom. While not denigrating home schooling, education is a 360-degree activity, and the physical environment of the school plays a huge role in contemporary models of education. Likewise, information is not the same as knowledge, and increasingly it will be the task of the teacher to show children the difference. Consequently, if anything, the role of the teacher will likely become more important in the future, not less.

To summarise, the three myths to be dealt with in this chapter are as follows.

> **Myth #1 'Technologies' aren't that important; they don't affect the fundamentals of what it is to be human.**
> **Myth #2 Digital technology is the answer to all our education problems.**
> **Myth #3 Technology signals the end of teaching.**

Myth #1 *'Technologies' Aren't That Important; They Don't Affect the Fundamentals of What it is to Be Human*

Evolution moves so slowly that we're virtually the same creatures we were 50 000 years ago; that is, in spite of all our technologies, inventions, and gadgets, the fundamental essence of what we are, how we think, and how we relate to each other hasn't altered since before the Stone Age. If Fred Flintstone lived in the twenty-first century, once he figured out he didn't have to use his feet to power his own car, he'd fit right in. In the final analysis, in the classroom or anywhere else, technology just isn't that important.

In some ways, Plato is responsible for this argument. As will be discussed in more detail in Chapter 12, Plato believed that the world we all know, and exist within, is merely an illusion, a flawed copy of an alternate, ideal realm. Yes, we may have triangles, and rabbits, and people, and everything else you can possibly think of, but they are just imperfect reflections of the perfect triangle, the perfect rabbit, and the perfect person existing elsewhere. This philosophical approach, generally referred to as Idealism (and not necessarily as philosophically strange as it sounds), had one unintended conceptual consequence: it fixes the present in amber, like a forty-million-year-old insect. Of course rabbits can't change, because the *eide* (the essence) of the 'perfect' rabbit must always stay the same. Likewise with humans; of course humans don't change – we have an essence, and it remains what it has always been. Indeed, it was the vestiges of this Platonic belief-system that eventually ran headlong into the Theory of Evolution in the nineteenth century, constituting one of the main reasons why Darwin's ideas initially struggled for acceptance (Wolpoff and Caspari 1998).

With apologies to Plato, this isn't the case at all. Deeply ingrained though this essentialising viewpoint about humanity often still is, at least at a subliminal level, it is now contradicted by all the best available scientific and historical evidence. Humans do change, both in an evolutionary sense, and in a social/intellectual sense. We're in the process of changing now; physically we're probably not that different, but we certainly bear little resemblance, socially or intellectually, to our medieval forebears, let alone our paleolithic ancestors. The factors underlying these changes are many and complex, but one of the most important can be addressed productively here: the use of technology.

Two issues need to be mentioned here. First, technologies aren't just things that require electricity. When we talk about technology now, we're normally referring to the pointy-end of modern innovation, and according to that logic, something like an iPhone is 'technology', and a toothbrush isn't. The definition of technology here is much broader: 'a human arrangement of technics – tools, machines, instruments, materials, sciences, and personnel – to make possible and serve the attainment of human ends' (Hood 1983, p. 347). A flint was a very early human technology, and the chalkboard is a relatively recent educational one, and neither of them plugged in.

Second, and most importantly, technologies are not just something we use – objects deployed by us to achieve specific goals – which we can put down at the end, and which leave us unchanged. Technologies are actors in the complex processes of shaping ourselves socially, culturally, and historically (Johnson 1998; Latour 1996). For example, knives and forks might be simple bits of metal, but determining how to use them appropriately became one of the pivotal criteria for organising 'civilised' behaviour from the eighteenth century onwards, and remains so today (Elias 2000).

'Technology Evolved Us'

As a way of illustrating how technology has shaped us into what we are today – *and also illustrating why it is so vitally important to understand the power and potential of contemporary technologies within the classroom* – what follows is a very brief discussion of the rise of four important examples of transformative technologies. The intention is to reinforce the final point made above: that technologies do not have an existence independent of ourselves; we develop in combination with them. (On a cautionary note, it is not being suggested here that particular tools directly *cause* the appearance of certain changes. A better approach would be to understand them as a significant part of a range of circumstances that permitted new physical and social attributes to develop. The printing press did not *cause* the invention of childhood, but it set the scene wherein its emergence became possible.)

THE FLINT: MAKING US HUMAN IN THE FIRST PLACE

It is now widely accepted that human evolution has one significant difference to all other living creatures. While we are all at the developmental mercy of selection pressures from others of our kind, other species, food scarcity, climate change, disease and natural disaster, human development has been influenced by one additional factor that no other creature appears subject to: the effects of tool use.

> Many writers have argued that the progressive adaptation and specialization of the hominid pelvis and other skeletal changes are related to the use of tools. It is suggested that once a way of life is established in which survival is increasingly dependent on the use of implements... then selection pressures will operate in favour of those physical and mental features which are an advantage in tool use, such as coordination, stereoscopic vision, hands free from locomotion, and so on. (Hirst and Wooley 1985, 14)

It is very difficult to hold on to a tool while moving on all fours. The first tools could be carried and utilised far more effectively by bipedal animals. Consequently, the more bipedal we became, the more we could use flints (and other technologies), and the more effectively we could compete in an evolutionary sense. This became a circular, self-propelling process: the use of tools, better hunting, more protein, larger brains, better use of tools, and so on. It was the use of early technology – such as the flint – that started us on our current evolutionary track, and it was the use of technology that kept us there.

Taylor (2010) has recently taken this argument one stage further. He suggests that we are not really biological entities at all, in the way that other animals are. Rather, we are animal/technological hybrids, and have been since we first began our evolutionary move away from the other great apes. We did not evolve, and as we got smarter, simply learned to use technology along the way – quite the reverse: 'technology evolved us' (Taylor 2010, 9).

THE NEEDLE: SEEING OFF THE OPPOSITION, EXPANDING OUR BOUNDARIES

We weren't the only upright apes on the block. Although we're not certain of how many others there were (at least three), we know quite a lot about one other version in particular: the Neanderthals. So how come we won the evolutionary marathon, and not them? There is no evidence that we directly killed them off, although there is evidence we interbred with them to some degree (Villa and Roebroeks 2014). But still, however you look at it, we're here, and they aren't.

This is particularly puzzling since evidence suggests that Neanderthals were stronger than us, and more resilient than us; they had mastered the production of fire, and the use of basic, simple tools; also, they could live in cold climates that we could not physically tolerate (Miller 2012). However, according to Gilligan (2007), it could well be that this very ability to tolerate the cold meant they were not under evolutionary pressure to develop technologies specifically for staying warm. Simple clothing was sufficient for the vast majority of their needs, and they could survive most climatic conditions with their single layered, unfitted animal skins.

This was not the case for modern humans. As a consequence, we were pressured to develop more complex forms of clothing – multilayered, close fitting – if we were to survive as a species. This type of clothing requires specific technologies for its production, most importantly, *needles*. By the use of such devices, along with more effective cutting tools, we were able to create far more efficient forms of clothing, clothing than not only allowed us to move beyond the temperate zones in which we had previous lived, into what had been Neanderthal-only territory, but also allowed us to survive extreme spikes in climate. Gilligan argues that the best evidence suggests that it was precisely such spikes in cold during the Upper Pleistocene Epoch that killed off the Neanderthals. In contrast, we survived these climate events due to our technological pre-adaptation, and from there we went on to export our needles, and our portable micro-climates of clothing, over the rest of the globe.

THE PRINTING PRESS: SETTING THE SCENE FOR MODERNITY

Of all the technological innovations acting as a catalyst for social and cultural change, the invention of the printing press is the most frequently used example. As has already been discussed in Chapter 6, from the advent of print onwards, adulthood was no longer a biological inevitability; the full status of adult was now to be granted to those who learned to read, in doing so leaving behind a new category of existence – childhood – reserved for the pre-literate. Furthermore, there soon developed the associated idea that some forms of knowledge were best reserved for adults, children being too innocent to be exposed to them.

Important though they were, these were not the only changes brought about by the printing press. The new ability to print and distribute Bibles meant that it was no longer just priests who could read the word of God. It has been widely argued that it was the greater access to His word that sparked not only the Protestant revolution, but the first calls for universal public schooling, which was rightly seen by Martin Luther as being crucial to creating the levels of public literacy required by his new 'people's' religion (Luke 1989). However, it was not just religious knowledge that was now spreading among the general population, it was all forms of knowledge, and as with religion, these knowledges were to be subject for the first time to public discussion and criticism (Eisenstein 1979). The argument here is that the arrival of the printed word lay behind the formation of a new kind of modern citizen, the type of citizenship we now take for granted – literate, engaged, knowledgeable, curious, and importantly, critical.

There was a wide range of other corollaries, consequences, and outcomes following the spread of printing. According to McLuhan (1962), there occurred the slow diminishing in the importance of the spoken word. The histories of nations and people were now to be clearly and publically fixed in print. Previously, such histories had generally been passed down orally and hence tended towards uncertainty, fluidity and ambiguity, or if written by hand, were only to be found in 'drifting texts and vanishing manuscripts' (Eisenstein 1979, 53). Thus, with the advent of print, we started to exist in a world where the certainties were greater, where 'truths' and 'facts' were more clearly defined, and where knowledge seemed more stable and more objective. All of these were important pre-requisites for the beginning of the Enlightenment and the era of Modernity, beginning some 200 years later.

Interestingly, the changes brought about by the technology of the printing press were not all unequivocally positive. Just as we gained new social, cultural and personal capacities – the dramatic rise in literacy, the objectification of knowledge, the production of a more engaged and critical citizenry – so too did we gradually lose some capacities. For example, by contemporary standards, medieval people were possessed of incredible memories: 'our memories have been impaired by print; we know we need not 'burden our memories' with matter which we can find merely by taking a book from a shelf (Chaytor 1945, 116).

THE MICROPROCESSOR: WHO KNOWS?

The current rate of technological change is truly staggering; it is certainly greater than at any other point in human history. Most of these changes now have, as part of their development or their design, the microprocessor (or its equivalent). The intention here is not to speculate on where such omnipresent technologies might take us in the next few years; there are already enough writers out there suggesting that we are either on the verge of a wonderful new era of human development (Hay 2014), or we are in the process of turning our children's brains to mush (Carr 2011). The point is simply to illustrate that, as with the other technologies discussed in this myth, they are likely to have very significant implications for what it is to be a human.

Actually, it is difficult to know which elements of contemporary technology are likely to have the greatest effects on us. The list of technological candidates is impressive: ICTs, artificial intelligence, robotics, supercomputers, bioengineering, stem-cell research, 3-D printing, genetics, fusion reactors, green technologies, or any combination of the above. All of these on their own have the potential to radically reorganise how we see ourselves, and how we interact with each other. Add to this list all the technologies that can become part of the body, and in doing so, reconstitute us as hybrid beings: artificial hearts, robotic limbs, hearing implants, *in vitro* organs. Surely it is just a matter of time before we decide that Google Glass is cumbersome and we physically implant ICTs in our body – certainly, it's hard to believe we made the evolutionary move to bipedalism, just to have the hands permanently occupied by smart-phoning. And when we do, those beings will be as socially and culturally unrecognisable to us, as we would be to those proto-humans who invented the needle.

So What Has All This Got to Do With Education?

As discussed in Chapter 4, there exists the myth that a classroom is a classroom, irrespective of when and where – that its essential features and practices are not up for negotiation or change. According to this logic, it is always the case that the teacher stands at the front of the class, and the students listen; the teacher has a plan for the lesson, which they deliver to the entire class; the students take tests and are then compared with each other. Chapter 4 debunked this myth by pointing to the rise of new forms of governance, and how these transformed the classroom into a giant machine for regulating the population. However, a second way this way myth can be debunked is by simply examining the role that the introduction of mundane teaching technologies have played in changing the face of education.

Take the blackboard. Prior to its introduction in Scotland at the start of the nineteenth century, teaching was pretty much a one-on-one practice; students had their own slate, and the teacher walked around the room giving individual guidance. By creating a unitary, widely visible system of communication and instruction at the front of the room – the blackboard – teaching was quickly transformed into a far more collective activity, one where the teacher could now structure the learning of everyone simultaneously. Moreover, that teacher could now teach literally hundreds of pupils at the same time, a change fundamental to making mass education even a possibility (Krause 2000). Perhaps most importantly, the blackboard gave rise to the standardisation of public education, in that for the first time, generic lessons could be planned for all teachers to use via a single medium. So important was this new technology, that in 1841 it was considered that 'the inventor or introducer of the system deserves to be ranked among the best contributors to learning and science, if not among the greatest benefactors of mankind' (Tyack and Cuban 1995, 121).

Or the pencil. When this technology was first introduced, it was treated with the same scepticism as many new technologies are today – why would we possibly need a portable writing implement (Baron 2002)? However, it soon proved to be an incredibly transformative device. From scratching clumsily on slates as a way of learning to write, pupils could now develop their handwriting with far more skill and clarity. Furthermore, given that pencils are relatively cheap and easy to mass produce, it meant that *everyone* could now learn to write properly – not just the rich with their quills and inkpots – with all the associated benefits for mass public literacy. The pencil also transformed assessment practices; indeed, it can be argued that without this technology, modern assessment practices could never have emerged, thereby removing the foundational element of our ability to differentiate the population. First, it meant that teachers could now take their pupils' work away for marking, thus structuring far longer and more complex forms of assessment than was possible on a small and heavy slate. Second, the widespread use of the pencil meant that from the 1950s onwards, it became possible, through the use of basic scanning technology, to compare tens of thousands of students' multiple-choice papers, in many ways taking the first steps towards the era of Big Data.

In summary, the point here is simple. There is the temptation to think that new classroom technologies are of only passing significance, much like getting a new textbook, or designing a nicer school uniform – welcome changes, but ultimately unimportant. There is also the temptation to think that they don't change us when we use them, that they are just objects and devices that can be put down again, without effect or implication. As this section has attempted to demonstrate, neither of these assertions is correct. Technologies are not trivial, and we do not exist independently of them – remember, *technologies evolved us*. The modern classroom, and the people in it, exist in a state of technological symbiosis. Consequently, we need to continually reflect on what technology can and can't do *for* us, and *to* us, both as teachers and as citizens.

Myth #2 *Digital Technology Is the Answer to All Our Education Problems*

The digital revolution has drastically improved teaching. Teachers can now access virtually any resource they want, and school lessons are all the better for it. Rubbish teaching will be a thing of the past; so too will be bored schoolchildren. And what's more, education will become more equitable. Traditional models of schooling are almost inevitably unfair; some schools are rich, some schools are poor; some children can afford extra tuition, others can't; some children fit in, others don't. None of this applies to online education. All you need is a computer, and someone to point you in the right direction, and maybe not even that.

Arguably, mass schooling has had a number of false dawns; moments when the clouds appeared to part, and we thought we knew for certain that some existing educational problem was about to be put to rest. There was the advent of Comprehensive Education in the UK, where the elite Grammar schools were abolished, and everyone had to muck in together; equity at last! Except it didn't really work as planned, as wealthy areas often generated successful schools, and poorer areas often didn't, which became self-perpetuating cycles of improvement and decay, respectively. Comprehensive education wasn't *all* bad news by any means, but it wasn't a magic bullet either. Likewise, there was the advent of Ritalin to deal with hyperactivity; no more troublesome children! Except, as discussed in Chapter 6, it now seems we are prepared to drug any child who manifests any kind of difference; and our schools seem the same as they ever were.

Digital education is the latest issue to be greeted with this kind of optimism, in that not only did it promise a revitalisation of stale old teaching practices, but it also held out the promise of finally eradicating some of our most ingrained forms of educational inequality. Improved teaching quality, within the context of improved equity – who wouldn't be enthusiastic about that? So is this the real deal, or is this Ritalin all over again?

What's So Great About Digital Teaching?

The advantages of contemporary teaching practices over their predecessors seem self-evident. A blackboard and some chalk seems pathetically inadequate in comparison with an entire world of information and resourcing available through a networked classroom projector. Teachers can now have access to interactive net resources, high-quality images and videos pertaining to their subject, pre-designed lesson plans, integrated PowerPoint presentations, instant online assessments, activities the teachers and the students can operate synchronously, and anything else that software designers can think up.

It certainly sounds better; perhaps it *is* better. It offers the potential of depth and variety, and it operates across familiar terrain for the students. Given the choice, you would be hard pressed to find a teacher who would prefer the option of only chalk, to the option of everything technology has to offer. The issue here is that teaching with the benefit of ICTs is not *necessarily* better. There is the danger that technology-based teaching becomes an end in itself, and not a means to an end. To put it another way, it is quite easy to mistake a lesson comprised of lots of PowerPoint slides and video resources, for a lesson where important learning takes place; where students are encouraged to think critically, and with organised purpose. Teaching can become deceptively and monotonously easy.

In her book, *Digital Hemlock: Internet Education and the Poisoning of Teaching*, Brabazon (2002, 3) describes a scene familiar to most of us:

Settle down, people. . .

In keeping with our bullet-point culture, I will now dim the lights and attempt to activate my Power-Point presentation. Hopefully the projector will work. As I have not prepared a lecture, I will talk to the slides, filling in the space between the headings with banal comments and self-evident nonsense. You will, however, see some attractively coloured graphs . . .

Everything you need to complete the assignments is found in my Power-Point bullet points. Copying them down accurately will determine the calibre of your grade. . .

Brabazon suggests a number of problems with technology-driven learning. First, expanding on the point above, the ubiquitous nature of software such as PowerPoint can lead to formulaic, homogenised, short-cut teaching. This is not to say that having decided to utilise such a program, undesirable outcomes will inevitably follow, just that the structure of programs like PowerPoint are not neutral; they frame the presentation of knowledge according to certain rules, and within pre-defined boundaries.

Second, she argues that as a generation of students learns to organise their thinking in terms of bullet points, much of the subtlety and beauty of language are being lost. One of the principal ways of learning has always been to actually partici- pate in the activity, and in an era of searchable databases and generic competencies, students no longer develop the skills of writing in the ways they once did. Knowledge is reduced to bite-sized chunks of information, with no necessary logical connection between them.

Third, she suggests that digital technologies, and online learning, are not generally conducive to critical reasoning. Various software packages may well be useful for activities such as drills and simulations, and for navigating oceans of information, but they are not so effective in the stimulation of autonomous thinking. There is still something rather either/or about the digital learning environment, and as she notes: 'If a definitive answer can be given, then the wrong question has been asked' (Brabazon 2002, 192).

Finally, and particularly within the context of the university, she suggests that it would be naïve to think that much of the drive towards augmented teaching technol- ogy was driven by anything other than cost. Generally speaking, with online learning environments, more students can be dealt with, and by far fewer staff. This is not pedagogy; it is economics.

Brabazon's position is not without its own problems, as she admits. There is more than a streak of nostalgic romanticism here, in harking back to the practices of a better era, back to a time when students actually read books, and weren't on Facebook during lectures. There is also something of a binary in operation: Socratic face-to-face education is good, versus online digital education is bad. That may be so, but as a polemic, her argument acts as an effective antidote to utopian arguments that suggest digital technology is the answer to all our educational problems.

The Digital Divide

Even if digital technology was as good as its proponents suggest in strictly practical terms, there is another problem that ought to limit our celebrations. All the various components of the digital universe – the Internet, computer hardware, software, elements both real and virtual – do not blanket the earth evenly, like oxygen, where everyone gets an equal chance to do some breathing. As with every other resource you can think of, some people have ready access, some people have limited access, and some people have no access at all. The question is: who gets what?

There is an important proviso in this short section of the book. The conclusions to be drawn are only as good as the data they are based upon, and even though the majority of those conclusions here are probably fairly predictable, this is a rapidly changing field – more so than any other discussion in this book. Digital technology does appear to be spreading quite quickly, and some of the claims here may date equally quickly. That said, as will be discussed, having access to technology is not the same as knowing how to use it; and knowing how to use it is not the same as using it in ways which benefit education.

ACCESS TO DIGITAL TECHNOLOGY

In its broadest sense, our globe can be subdivided into zones of differing technological access. Not surprisingly, in developed countries 78% of homes have internet access, compared with 31% in developing countries, and less than 20% in Africa. Likewise, mobile broadband penetration levels are at 64% in Europe and 59% in the Americas, compared with only 23% in Asia–Pacific and 19% in Africa (United Nations 2014). In the realm of technology at least, the First World/Third world divide is alive and well.

This divide is not limited to comparisons between nations; it is also relevant *within* specific nations, and the UK mirrors the patterns of most industrialised countries. Chapters 1 to 3 of this book gives a pretty good indicator of what those patterns might look like. After all, why should the inequalities of access to technology be any different to other zones of inequality.

> We had always known that the cross section of race, ethnicity, class, and gender defined the social structure of our society, and our goals were to diminish the ability of these socially constructed boxes to render individuals invisible and excluded. Access to ICTs not only crystallized these endemic problems but also added nuances and complicated our historical views. (Modarres 2011, 5)

Holley and Oliver (2011) take this a stage further and argue that the digital divide actually *intensifies* existing forms of privilege and exclusion. That is, lacking access to ICTs, perhaps due to socio-economic disadvantage, acts to exacerbate that disadvantage; those digitally poor, due to poverty, get poorer. By way of a brief summary, the overwhelming evidence suggests that access to ICTs is restricted in predictable ways according to social class (Livingstone and Helsper 2007; White and Selwyn 2013), gender (Cooper 2003; Hilbert 2011), race/ethnicity (Samaras 2005; Wodajo and Kimmel 2013), age (Milward 2003; Choudrie *et al.* 2013) and remoteness (Curtis 2014).

At this point, it should be mentioned that the notion of a digital divide based solely upon access to digital technology was very much a product of the early days of analysing computer demographics; this is now regarded as something of an over-simplification. As more and more people gained access to computers – for example through schools, Internet cafés, or libraries – this did not translate into individuals from otherwise socially and technologically marginalised groups suddenly gaining educational parity.

Fink and Kenny (2003) wrote one of the main papers discussing the complexity of the digital divide issue. They note that while access to information and communication technology is undoubtedly the starting point for understanding technological equity, there are three other aspects that also have impact. The first is knowing what to do with the technology once you have it; what kind of skills base do those with access actually have? The second is actually using that technology; how often the ICTs are used, and for what purposes? The final issue relates to the impact of using that technology; what kind of returns does the technology give those who use it? While undoubtedly access and use are generally regarded as the most important, all are worth addressing, even if only briefly.

KNOWLEDGE OF DIGITAL TECHNOLOGY

In a utopian world, ensuring all students owned their own computer sounds like the perfect cure for the digital divide; unfortunately, it only addresses part of the problem. As everyone who has ever acquired a computer for their grandparents would know – in the hope of plugging them in to the twenty-first century – a computer is just a large box in the corner of the room unless someone also gives them the skills to make it work. They may now have access to ICTs, but so what?

The research suggests that those who have the skills to use ICTs, use them far more often. The possession of those skills is generally broken down according to the familiar patterns of advantage and disadvantage already discussed. Indeed, the evidence suggests that children whose parents regularly use the Internet at home are almost twice as likely to use the Internet themselves, as compared with children whose parents do not possess those skills. Likewise, children whose parents use the Internet at work are nearly 50% more likely to use the Internet (Cleary, Pierce and Trauth 2006). Since parents with ICT skills are more likely to be white and middle class, white middle-class children are therefore more likely to find themselves on the winning side of the 'knowledge and skills' digital divide.

USE OF DIGITAL TECHNOLOGY

So, hypothetically, if there *was* equal access to ICTs, and an equal range of skills in using those ICTs, then what could possibly be left of the digital divide? Well just because technology *can* be used in particular ways, doesn't mean that it *will*. Modarres (2011) argues that different patterns of ICT usage have unforeseen implications for those who use them. He uses the example of American research by Smith (2010), which finds that African Americans and Hispanics are more likely than the white population to access the Internet on their mobile phones, with whites tending to use networked home computers. As a consequence of this difference, the former are more likely to be restricted to *consuming* information, as opposed to being in a position to *create* it.

> . . .it is much easier to fill out job applications and develop content for a Web site on a computer than on a cell phone. If we have presumably resolved the problem of the digital divide by increasing the number of cell phones among minorities and low-income populations, have we improved critical engagement with the content, including its creation? Or have we elevated the digital divide to the next level of content and differential usage pattern? (Modarres 2011, 6)

As the focus has largely shifted from a concern over equal access, to a focus on widening participation (Goodfellow 2006), the question needs to be asked: just what counts as participation? Clearly, some forms of participation have a far greater payoff in the non-virtual worlds of education, economics, and social advantage than others.

OUTCOMES FROM DIGITAL TECHNOLOGY

Given these different patterns of ICT usage, it is not surprising that the outcomes are also different. Those who have access to ICTs, who have the skills to use them, and who use them in academically and professionally productive ways, will end up with a wide array of significant advantages in terms of outcomes, particularly concerning employment (Bynner *et al.* 2008). Those individuals are more likely to do well at school, more likely to gain entry to university, more likely to get more prestigious, higher paying jobs, and more likely to gain promotion within those jobs. This is the most important consequence of the 'digital divide'.

Even though the notion of the 'digital divide' is a useful construct for trying to understand who gets to benefit from ICT technology, as with many of the topics in this section of the book, there is more than a hint of a false binary here. In the real world, it is not a case of the 'haves' and the 'have-nots', with a clear distinction between what each group does, and does not, have access to or use; rather, there is a sliding scale of advantage and disadvantage. However, in spite of this, the term remains a convenient shorthand way of describing an important social and educational issue.

In summary, information and communication technologies may well have a great deal to offer education. However, they are not the answer to all our problems, and they come with a few problems of their own. They can lead to formulaic teaching, to bullet-point reasoning, and to impoverished writing. They do not offer a solution to existing patterns of educational inequality; currently, the best evidence suggests they tend to simply dovetail into them. Lockard and Pegrum (2006, 1) paint a salutary picture of the current state of affairs.

> The early, halcyon days of electronic education are gone. There is no longer a unifying belief, common during the Internet boom of the early 1990s, that this new medium provides a means for universal educational development. Many who embraced personal computers and the internet, and who devoted their work to creating new forms of electronic education have grown dissatisfied with the trend towards commodification and corporatization, a paucity of critical thought in e-learning, poor quality and inappropriate uses of distance learning, hierarchical organization, and the growing exploitation of teaching labour.

Myth #3 *Technology Signals the End of Teaching*

Do we need teachers anymore? After all, we don't really need schools, when students can just plug in their computer and join a virtual classroom; we could do something more useful with the buildings – bulldoze them for parks, sell them for real estate – and it would certainly stop the problem of children chatting at the back of the class. And with all this information available, who needs teachers to tell children where it is? You don't need a teacher to tell students how to click on the 'Go To Library' button on their computer; they can figure that out for themselves. With digital technology, we can just have online copies of the very best teachers talking about all the various topics on the curriculum. Who needs all those teachers at your local school? They probably aren't as good as that person on the video from America anyway.

Perhaps ICTs aren't the answer to every single equity problem that has ever beset mass education, and perhaps ICTs might lead to disjointed, bullet-point thinking, but we are are still in a far better position than if they didn't exist; or maybe not. Myth #1 suggests that contemporary technology is in the process of improving education out of sight. Whether or not this is the case (most likely, not), this same rosy path to the future is not predicted for our teachers; their professional future is deemed to be bleak.

There are two parts to this miserable bit of soothsaying. The first is that teachers have never had to deal with a potential onslaught on their professional survival such as the one posed by technology. Teaching has always been based around the body of the teacher: their voice, their physical presence, their pure ability to communicate with their students. The suggestion here is that for the first time, technology is interposing itself into that equation.

The second argument is that teachers have always been needed to provide information for the students to learn. Apart from a few books that could be acquired from the school library, it was teachers who brought information into the classroom, and who set it out in ways their students could internalise. That professional function is no longer required. All the information in the world is only a computer screen away, and there are more than enough instructional programs on the Internet to guide students through it. Let us take these two assertions in turn.

There's Nothing New About Technology

Part of the problem here lies in the term 'technology'. Within the context of education, the word now seems to be used almost exclusively to refer to ICTs. It suggests, at very least, a range of objects and devices in the classroom that have to be plugged in. More specifically, it implies some form of connection to computers, to complex software, and to the Internet. Teachers have never had to deal with 'technology' before; what on earth will they do?

This, of course, is the first error in reasoning. 'Technologies' are far broader reaching than just the narrow association with ICTs. As discussed in myth #1, arguably it is the use of technologies that has made us what we are as humans, that has marked us out from other species, and that has allowed us to build our societies and our cultures, and has kept those cultures moving and changing. At their most fundamental level, Rammert (1999) contends that technologies are composed of four elements. The first is the materials from which the technology is made; the second is the specific shape it is formed into; the third is the end for which it is designed; and the fourth is the efficient action that results.

ICTs fit neatly into this model. For example, take a classroom computer. It is made from a complex array of materials; it is moulded, soldered and screwed into an even more complex set of interrelated shapes; it is designed to process data at dizzying speeds; and it results in access to information in ways that were unthinkable before the technology was introduced – there are the four parts of the technology: material, shape, use and efficient action.

But ICTs are not the only things that fit this definition; so do some of our most primitive tools. A spear is largely made from wood; it is shaped to be long and thin, with a point at one end; it is designed to stick into things; and it allows us to kill animals more efficiently, and from a greater distance. As such, technologies are simply another word for tools.

This brings us to the second error in reasoning. Teachers have long dealt with new technologies in the classroom, without either giving up in befuddlement, or facing redundancy; take, for example, the blackboard, discussed earlier in this chapter – reputedly invented by Scottish teacher James Pillans in 1820. Following the four-part model: the original blackboard was made of slate; it was shaped into a large, flat sheet; it was used for writing on with chalk; and in terms of efficiency, it allowed teachers to write information out only once, rather than on the slate of every individual student. The same argument applies to the technology that largely replaced the blackboard – the overhead projector. This device, at its most popular in the 1980s and 1990s, allowed teachers to bring pre-prepared material to the classroom, and to write in a more comfortable, horizontal manner, rather than vertically.

The classroom is full of technologies, and always has been. ICTs are simply the latest tools to be deployed within the teaching space. Teaching has never been about a pure, unmediated relationship between teacher and pupil; technologies have always been in there somewhere, whether they be quills, parchment and canes, or uniforms, class bells and panopticons, or webcams, touchscreens and the Internet. Teachers have generally greeted such changes with guarded optimism. After all, this is a dynamic profession, and teachers adapt.

From Information to Knowledge

Having rejected the assertion that technology is something new, something that teachers have no experience in dealing with as a profession, the second part of the myth asserts that ICTs allow access to such huge amounts of information that teachers are now surplus to requirements. There is all the information that students could ever need, just at the click of a mouse. The argument here will be that this surfeit of information is precisely why we *need* teachers – at least in part – not need to do away with them

We live in a world now containing almost inconceivable amounts of digital information. According to Bohn and Short (2009), American households consumed 3.6 zettabytes of information in 2008 – a zettabyte is a 1 with 21 zeros after it, and that's rather a lot. This does not even include any of the information consumed in the workplace. In a similar vein, the CEO of Google, Eric Schmidt, stated that every two days, we now create as much information as we did from the dawn of civilisation, up until 2003 (Siegler 2010).

In addition to this, students don't just have their school library; they have access to literally thousands of libraries online. They can't just access books on history, maths, and English; they can access books on *anything*. They don't just have access to the voices of peer-reviewed authors; they have access to the voices of anyone and everyone in the blogosphere who wants to start talking – the wise, the weird and the witless.

The point here is that students aren't at school to gain information; they are at school to gain knowledge. This sounds like a matter of semantics, but the difference is an important one, one that teachers play a pivotal role in managing. A useful model for exploring the role teachers play in stepping beyond an information-based focus has been given by Ackoff (1989), and his 'Wisdom Hierarchy', also called the 'DIKUW

Hierarchy'. DIKUW is an acronym referring to Data-Information-Knowledge-Understanding-Wisdom, and the argument here is that you are only likely to get a short distance up this hierarchy without the help of a teacher. Let us take these five concepts in turn.

Data are regarded as raw facts existing in the world, unconceptualised and without organisation. The world is full of an almost infinite amount of data, and these data have no meaning until conceptual schema are applied to them. The room you are sitting in is full of such abstract data – the number of molecules in the air, the length of the walls, the varieties of bacteria on the cover of this book – but they remain abstract until recorded and organised.

Information is regarded as data that has been given meaning; information is organised data. The Internet is full of information; indeed it is *composed* of information – zettabytes and zettabytes of it. Children do not really need teachers to access information. All they have to do is turn on their computers, and information pours out at them.

Knowledge is a more difficult concept to define. It is largely regarded as applied information; it is not just an understanding of 'what', but also of 'how', and while knowledge certainly exists on the Internet, it is often difficult to delineate from mere information.

> Knowledge is a fluid mix of framed experience, values, contextual information, expert insight and grounded intuition that provides an environment and framework for evaluation and incorporating new experiences and information. It originates and is applied in the minds of knowers. (Davenport and Prusack 1998, 5)

Understanding is the ability to take knowledge and to place it in wider contexts. If information is about *what* something is, and knowledge is about *how* that something operates, or came to be, then understanding is about *why*. There is a great deal of information available about the rise of mass education – dates, locations, curricula, instructional techniques – but knowledge requires linking these together to frame how the system came to take its current form, which represents a far more complex form of evaluation. Arguably, understanding is the ability to answer the question of *why* mass schooling developed – an even more complex process still.

Wisdom is the ability to take that understanding and to project into the future. Wisdom involves the moral dimension of assessing what might be the right course of action to take. If we now understand why mass schooling developed in the way it did, wisdom denotes the ability to decide, as a society based upon principals of justice and democracy, where we need to take it next.

Having set out the main elements of the DIKUW hierarchy, we can return to the assertion that in the age of ICTs, tech-savvy children, and online education, we no longer really need teachers. The most obvious reply to this claim is to suggest that if we were to limit our education to the bottom two elements of the hierarchy – the D and the I – then that may well be correct. British students can download as much as they like from the web; facts galore, facts about everything. However, our concept of a good education is based upon significantly higher expectations than this. We expect our students to make it past the D and the I, to the K and the U, and for this they need teachers. In an era of almost limitless web-noise, arguably it will be one of the primary tasks of teachers in the future to help students understand the difference between this noise, useful information, and knowledge; and from there, to eventually mould that knowledge into understanding. As for the W – wisdom – all any of us can do is hope for a little of that.

In summary, for those prophesying the ICT-induced end of teaching as we know it, this is not a new phenomenon. The same claims were made about the advent of television when it first became popularised (Seattle Times 1962). Technologies change, and the circumstances of classroom life change, but if we want to continue working toward a 'wise' citizenry, then we need to accept that students will always learn more with a teacher than without, and learn in more profound and lasting ways.

Conclusion

This chapter has sought to address the rise of new technologies – and in particular, ICTs – within contemporary education. The first myth involves the assertion that technologies are not that important, either to the essence of what we are as humans, or to how we go about educating our children. The best archaeological, historical and anthropological evidence suggests otherwise, and that we grew up as a species in tandem with, and as a function of, a wide range of technologies. These shaped us into what we are now, and they will undoubtedly continue to do so; indeed, there is every reason to believe that technologies such as ICTs have to potential to reorganise, at very least, how we go about the process of educating, and at most, how we see ourselves as people.

Some aspects of contemporary education have already changed as a result. We now appear to be in the era of multiliteracies, and for a schooling system that intends to equip its graduates for life in the twenty-first century, it is no longer sufficient solely to work on the skills required for textual literacy. While the ability to read traditional linear texts is still crucially important, so is developing literacy skills across a diverse range of other forms. That said, the second myth dealt with the assertion that ICTs are now the answer to all our educational problems. This would remain just an interesting, if somewhat erroneous, view on the future of education, if it were not for the fact that such beliefs can have significant policy implications for where we place our priorities, and where we direct our funding. Useful though they are, ICTs do not inevitably equate with teaching excellence, and they are not the answer to all our ingrained problems of educational equity.

The third myth dealt with the belief that ICTs sound the death knell for traditional teaching; who needs teachers when we have instant access to all the wonderful resources of the Internet. This assumption overestimates the value of the Internet – at least without the guidance of someone who understands the difference between information and knowledge – and it underestimates the importance, and the resilience, of teachers. Technologies will come and go; teachers are here to stay.

The final point of this chapter is to note, once again – as with all the topics in this section – that there appears to be an abundance of binaries operating here. We have digital natives versus digital immigrants; we have the digital divide, which implies that you are either inside or outside the world of ICTs; and we have the dichotomous claim that we either will, or won't need teachers in the future. While such binaries can be useful in loosely highlighting specific issues, from that point onwards they tend to have the effect of reducing complex problems to catch-phrases, and removing any subtlety and nuance from our policy solutions.

GLOBALISATION 11

A lot has been written recently about the emergence of a 'global society', one in which economies, cultures and political systems of different nations have started to coalesce. Perhaps unsurprisingly, these commentaries have often taken the form of binary debates – globalisation is all-encompassing vs globalisation is pretty irrelevant; globalisation is the glorious road to the future vs globalisation is the road to hell; globalisation is a fundamentally economic issue vs globalisation is really about cultural homogenisation. Generally speaking, these binaries aren't helpful, and the phenomenon of globalisation deserves a less reductive, more thoughtful, analysis, as it increasingly affects us all, particularly within the sphere of education.

Myth #1 Understanding globalisation is easy; it's simply another word for Americanisation. *'The entire world is dominated by the United States; that's all globalisation is. Every year, we just become more like America'.* Actually, there's a lot more to it than that. While almost all commentators would agree that there have been global shifts in patterns of economic activity, cultural practice and political configuration, other issues, such as the degree to which this has occurred, the processes by which it has happened, what the implications are, and what the future holds – let alone the role that the United States has played in this – are all still highly contested.

Myth #2 We have a British education system here, not any kind of 'globalised' one. *'If we're now living in a globalised world, this news hasn't filtered down to our education system yet. Our schools and universities are still very much British'.* In fact, the evidence suggests that we have become educationally globalised in ways that we probably don't even recognise. For example, our apparent obsession with standardised testing, such as SATs, is something we've picked up from the global educational community. Likewise, our devolved schooling system is part of a broader international neo-liberal agenda, with its emphasis on economic rationalism, deregulation, competition and individual responsibility; see also issues relating to our curriculum, our school retention rates, and our tertiary sector.

Myth #3 'Education for Sustainability' has nothing to do with globalisation; it's a politically inspired waste of time. *'Caring about the environment has absolutely nothing to do with globalisation, and as for 'sustainability education', we don't need either side of politics forcing their ideas into the curriculum'.* Arguably, current concerns over global warming are part of a broader realisation that we all inhabit the same planet, a realisation that also forms a foundational element of globalisation. It is an unfortunate fact that the issue of global warming has become overtly politicised; however, the notion of 'Education for Sustainability' extends beyond this single concern to become a broader 'ethic for living' – one that surely deserves a place, not just within the fabric of contemporary schooling, but within our society in general.

Introduction

When we talk about 'globalisation', the conversation normally contains a number of assumptions, percolating quietly under the surface. After all, most of us probably have a pretty firm idea of what we're talking about when we use the word: we're likely to think it's something fairly new; it's mostly to do with the economy, and maybe our culture (or American culture); and we often have some quite vehement opinions on whether or not we think this is a good thing.

Before we begin addressing any of the specifics of globalisation, it would be useful to take a look at these underpinning suppositions in a little more detail, as they will prepare the ground for the rest of the chapter. First, regarding the idea that globalisation is something new, Robinson (2007) suggests that we have actually had three waves of globalisation as a species; this is the third. The first wave refers to humanity's initial migration out of Africa 125 000 years ago and from there around the world, a process that probably lasted between 5000 and 10 000 years. The second wave involves a mere 500-year timeframe, involving the spread of capitalism and modernity by the imperial maritime European powers from the fifteenth century onwards. The final wave of globalisation – the one we are generally referring to when we currently use the term – is a relatively recent phenomenon, involving 'post-industrialisation, postmodernisation or the restructuring of capitalism', over the past 25–35 years (Robinson 2007, 127).

Second, regarding the presupposition that globalisation is all about the economy, is 'post-industrialisation and the restructuring of capitalism' a reasonable explanation of globalisation? When Robinson expands upon precisely what he thinks globalisation is, he goes on to suggest that there are five sets of phenomena that lie at the heart of the term: the emergence of a globalised economy; transnational cultural patterns and flows; globalised political processes and forms of governance; the rapid movements of people around the globe, forming new identities and communities; and new social hierarchies and forms of inequality. Turner (2013) has a somewhat different take on exactly what globalisation is, suggesting instead four identifiable phenomena. He suggests that it is constituted by the compression of time and space; increased connections between human groups and cultures; increasing levels of trade; and the emergence of various types of global consciousness. Robinson and Turner's somewhat different understandings of globalisation constitute only two of the many possibilities out there; however, Turner rightly states:

> Although there has been much dispute over the definition of globalisation, we need not concern ourselves too deeply over definitional disagreement at this stage. The problem of defining 'money' satisfactorily has not stopped the progress of economics any more than the absence of a wholly coherent notion of 'power' has inconvenienced the development of political science. (Turner 2013, 5)

The third assumption about globalisation normally involves whether or not we think it is a good thing. As with many of the issues covered in Part III of this book, this is often structured as a neat binary: either it's fabulous, or it's awful. Much of the literature is structured around precisely this divide. Friedman (2007) contends that, as a result of globalisation, 'the world is now flat', allowing for individual empowerment and massive reductions in world poverty. Suter (2000) suggests that globalisation holds out the promise of having people work together on common transnational problems, as well as the empowerment of various organisations within civil society for the betterment of humanity as a whole. Furthermore, individual nation-states – with their inherent blinkered regionalism and self-interest – will begin to fade in importance as larger political entities, capable of seeing the big picture, start to take over. Stiglitz (2003) points to the role that globalisation is playing in enabling developing markets to open up far more quickly than would otherwise have been the case; in doing so, he contends that millions of people are far better off. Economic growth is the most important issue here, and globalisation can provide that.

Other writers see the effects of globalisation very differently. Klein, in her influential book *No Logo* (2000), contends that multinational corporations spawned by globalisation have become so large and powerful that they have superseded national governments, and unlike such governments, they are unaccountable to the public. Likewise, Van de Pijl (1998) argues that globalisation simply serves the interests of a transnational business elite – with their willing cadres of experts, consultants, managers and bureaucrats – who use neoliberal ideologies to get richer and richer; in the meantime, very little money trickles down to the poorer citizens of the world at all. Pogge (2003) contends that within the context of a globalised economic system, affluent developed nations have made very little attempt to use their power and influence to make any substantial democratic or egalitarian changes within their Third-World counterparts. Instead they have largely chosen to use existing endemic poverty and corruption to their own advantage.

In a slightly different vein, the book *The World Is Not For Sale* (2001) by two French farmers, Bové and Dufour, offers a scathing critique of the rise of globalised junk food – they once famously dismantled a McDonalds restaurant – based upon the need to protect local communities, farm produce and existing ways of life. Their argument is founded on the assertion that there is much more to life and culture than the relentless pursuit of money, as exemplified by globalised big business.

So Is There Any Agreement on Globalisation at All?

Within debates over globalisation, McDonalds is often held up as the poster-child for the concept. Not only is it a gigantic transnational corporation, it is also a global cultural icon; McDonalds feeds nearly 70 million people every day and employs close to 2 million people; however, it also epitomizes the notion of junk food and has been implicated in the destruction of rainforests; and it is American. Myth #1 examines the assertion that, in the final analysis, globalisation is really just Americanisation. It doesn't matter much where you live in the world, burgers are being eaten, Coke is being drunk, and American films are being watched. Is there really any more to globalisation than that?

Yes, there is. Globalisation is not the same as Americanisation; the field is far more complex. While there is little disagreement that *something* transnational is happening concerning international trade and communication, there is no consensus on the degree to which this might constitute a new phenomenon in its own right. There also tends to be disagreement over the primary driving engine of globalisation. Is this fundamentally an economic trend, or can it better be understood as cultural changes, or even a set of political reconfigurations? There are also debates over whether globalisation can be understood in terms of periodicity, in that perhaps it started as an economic phenomenon but quickly become more complex. Though America, and its multitudinous and powerful corporate entities, is undoubtedly a very significant player within globalisation, the two concepts are far from synonymous.

Education and Globalisation

While the effects of globalisation might be easy to spot in the areas of burger consumption and cola drinking, they are not so obvious within the world's education systems. Certainly a casual glance at our schools and universities doesn't lead to the conclusion that globalisation is running rampant through their corridors. They seem to be structured in pretty much the same way as they always were: similar types of curriculum, same old management structures, exams at the end of every year and the usual suspects doing well, or not. Maybe globalisation has nothing to offer education, and has simply passed it by.

Myth #2 suggests that isn't the case. A closer examination of our education system notes that it has been significantly transformed by the effects of transnational ideologies, policies, markets, expectations and practices. For example, as was discussed in Chapter 7, the SATs did not spring complete and fully formed from the minds of British educators; it is part of a global move towards standardised testing. Similar programmes are now in place all around the world, and students are compared against each other, principally via the Organisation for Economic Co-operation and Development's (OECD) Program of International Student Assessment (PISA). Nations desperately clamour to do well in the rankings, lest they are seen to have a 'failing' education system, both in the eyes of the world and their own voting public, with massive consequences for all concerned

This is by no means the only impact of globalisation on education in the UK. There are also the matters of neo-liberalism and devolution, school retention rates, global qualifications, the global marketisation of universities and issues of curriculum choice. All of these areas lead to the conclusion that, far from being immune from the effects of globalisation, our education system is in the process of being rapidly transformed by it.

Globalisation and the Environment

One area that has been closely linked to globalisation is the rise of the environmentalist movement. While this doesn't necessarily seem to have much to do with transnational flows of economic capital, the emergence of world cultures and identities, or the compression of time and space, it does have a lot to do with an increasing sense of a global consciousness. Arguably, it was as part of this globalisation-driven consciousness that the early environmental movement of the 1960s went from a set of niche concerns to its current status as an international force to be reckoned with.

As a result of this growth in awareness, environmental issues have made their way into curricula around the world, including curricula in the UK. However, it has also become apparent that such inclusions are now often highly politicised; the very presence of 'green' issues in the school is considered by some to be an unwelcome intrusion of politics in a place where it doesn't belong. Rather than accepting this viewpoint, the question can be posed instead: how did something as self-evidently necessary and laudable as 'Education for Sustainability' become a political football, to the extent that it is now at risk of disappearing from the curriculum altogether?

In summary, the three myths addressed in this chapter are as follows.

Myth #1 Understanding globalisation is easy; it's simply another word for Americanisation.

Myth #2 We have a British education system here, not any kind of 'globalised' one.

Myth #3 'Education for Sustainability' has nothing to do with globalisation; it's a politically inspired waste of time.

Myth #1 Understanding Globalisation Is Easy; it's Simply Another Word for Americanisation

There's nothing complex about globalisation; it doesn't need any multilayered body of theory to explain it, and it certainly doesn't need to be discussed in a book about education. It's simple – America dominated the last century and it'll probably dominate this one too. From Budapest and Beijing, to Buenos Aires and Birmingham, the world eats McDonalds, drinks Coca-Cola, listens to American music and watches American films. That's everything you need to know about globalisation right there.

When most people think of multinational corporations, they probably think of McDonalds, or Ford Motors, or ExxonMobil, or Apple; and when they think of the artefacts of global culture, they probably think of baseball hats, or *Avengers* movies, or hip hop music; and when they think of 'the leader of the free world', they are almost certainly thinking of Obama (until 2016). All of these companies/things/people are American, so it is perhaps not surprising then that globalisation is often held to be synonymous with Americanisation. Conversely, none of the above is British. While America has 17 companies in the world's top 50, we only have one – British Petroleum. Even Germany and France have four each (Fortune 2015). And when we think of any of those in charge of the major British political parties, 'leader of the free world' is not a phrase that comes to many people's mind.

Interestingly, as Turner (2013) notes, early globalisation theory in the 1980s also assumed that the path to global cultural standardisation was also the path to Americanisation. Even into the 1990s, there was an assumption that the world was converging towards a single template for industrialised societies, and that template was an American one (Spybey 1996). Schiller (1991) argued that imperialism was alive and well, but it had simply altered its form. America no longer had to send its gunboats overseas to bend the world to its will (although it was not above doing so), it simply had to use its 'soft power' to achieve the same goals. Whereas this certainly involves corporate transnationalism, it also involves the hegemony of American media production, such as the export of American soap operas, the global popularity of Hollywood movies and the building of Euro-Disney.

However, by the start of the new century it had become obvious to almost all commentators in the field that globalisation was actually far more complex, multi-factored and fluid than that; so while confusing Americanisation for globalisation is an understandable mistake, it's still a mistake. There are still undoubtedly some significant connections between the two. Nye (2003) suggests that the United States plays a key role in all elements of contemporary globalisation – indeed globalisation has helped reinforce and distribute American power – however, the question really concerns the nature of that role. Nye uses the metaphor of a wheel, with the United States as the hub; that hub may be the most crucial part of the wheel, with all other elements relying upon it, but the (globalised) wheel is so much greater than just the hub itself. And the wheel isn't going anywhere without the spokes, rim, inner tube and tyre (i.e. the other nations, cultures, transnational political organisations, communication technologies, and so on). Turner (2013) rightly points to the importance of Asia to the fundamental processes of globalisation, specifically noting the impact of Japan upon management systems, automobile manufacture, fashion and film.

The Extent of Globalisation

So far, the evidence suggests that globalisation can't be understood in terms of a reductionist good/bad binary, or bounded by a single satisfactory working definition; it also can't be given a specific national character, or point of origin. Probably the most we can say about it so far is that it is a complex amalgam of transnational networks, flows, practices and transformations. However, this raises a further question: just how important and extensive are these four elements? In answering this question, we run across the second reductionist binary associated with this topic.

Held and McGrew (2003) initially point to two opposing positions regarding the significance and reach of globalisation – the *Hyperglobalist* (it's very big and important) and the *Sceptical* (actually, no it isn't) – before suggesting a compromise position, the *Transformationalist* (it's important, but its effects are uncertain). Each can be compared by contrasting their approaches to what is new about globalisation, what its dominant features are, how it understands the role of the nation-state and what it sees for the future. Let us now take these in turn.

THE HYPERGLOBALIST POSITION

Those who see globalisation from this perspective, whether they think the change is positive or negative, consider that we are entering a new, global age. Approaching the issue primarily from an economic point of view, hyperglobalists point to the development of an integrated global economy, one based upon neo-liberal principles of 'sound economic management'. This is not its only dominant feature; this new civil terrain will involve various forms of global governance, all of which will have the effect of reducing the importance of national boundaries and national governments. The British government will consequently become less important, so too perhaps even the very notion of 'the United Kingdom' itself.

> Since the nation economy is increasingly a site of transnational socio-economic activity, the authority and legitimacy of the nation state are challenged: national governments become increasingly unable either to control what transpires within their own borders or to fulfil by themselves the demands of their own citizens. Moreover, as institutions of global and regional governance acquire a bigger role, the sovereignty and autonomy of the state are further eroded. (Held and McGrew 2003, 4–5)

In the final analysis hyperglobalists predict the end of nation-states (countries), and the rise of a global civilisation. After all, they maintain, there is nothing natural and inevitable about this political unit, which was only brought into being in 1648 by the Treaty of Westphalia. The 'Westphalian System', as it is now known, can go just as easily as it came. Strange (2010), in her article 'The Westfailure system' makes exactly this point, when she says that nation-states have failed us economically, environmentally and socially, and maybe it's time to try something else.

THE SCEPTICAL POSITION

While accepting that some degree of internationalising is taking place, this perspective suggests that the hyperglobalist claims are all overstated. We are not entering a Global Age, rather we are simply reorganising trading blocs based upon new flows of goods and information; indeed according to the sceptical position, the world is now less interdependent than it was in the 1890s. And the global population is not getting somehow uniformly richer as a function of the arrival of a global civil society, far from it. The countries of the north are just getting richer at the expense of those of the south.

It is also argued by the globalisation sceptics that these nation-states – whether from the north or south – are not about to dissolve into some 'global government' any time soon. In fact, in the post-9/11 world, the boundaries of individual countries appear more important, not less; feelings of nationalism have increased, as have levels of xenophobia (Roudometof 2009). Likewise, far from fading away, new smaller countries are still trying to emerge from within older, larger ones—for example, see Scotland and Catalonia.

Ghemawat (2011) calls the hyperglobalist perspective 'Globaloney'. He argues that the world has not turned into one vast transnational market, but rather many small interconnected entities, with only limited degrees of openness to each other. He also refutes the claim that globalisation is inevitably leading to homogenisation, whether that be economic, cultural or political.

THE TRANSFORMATIONALIST POSITION

Held and McGrew propose a third approach, one which navigates between the binary of the hyperglobalist and sceptical positions. This approach still accepts the premise that *something* is happening in terms of global changes to the economic, social and political order, however rather than being either all-encompassing or relatively minor, the transformationalist position contends that the direction of the changes remains uncertain. It is agreed that the world currently has historically unprecedented levels of global interconnectedness, both as a function of increased speed of travel and transport, and because of the rise of modern information communication technologies (ICTs). Held and McGrew refer to this as 'thick' globalisation, where the extensive reach of global networks is matched by their high impact and high velocity (contrasted against, for example, the 'thin' globalisation of the fourteenth-century silk and spice trade between Europe and Asia, where impact and velocity remained low).

The main difference in this position is that, while it does not foresee the demise of the nation-state, neither does it foresee it remaining untouched by globalisation. It considers it very likely that nation-states will be, in ways yet uncertain, restructured and reconstituted. After all:

> The world order can no longer be conceived as purely state-centric or even primarily state governed, as authority has become increasingly diffused among private agencies at the local, national, regional and global levels. Nation-states are no longer the sole centres or the principal forms of governance or authority in the world.' (Held and McGrew 2003, 9)

Bearing these factors in mind, the Transformationalists neither see the world inexorably marching towards a single global civilisation, nor alternatively forming regional trading blocs with increased levels of local nationalism, rather they see the future as uncertain, most likely characterised by both global integration and fragmentation.

Stages of Globalisation Theory

How else then might globalisation be understood? As previously noted, Robinson argues that we are currently in the third wave of human globalisation. Is it possible that this third wave can itself be broken down into some kind of periodicity? While making no claims about globalisation itself, Axford (1995, 2013) suggests that globalisation *theory* has gone through three stages of development – which, of course, may say more about the perceived viability and popularity of particular theoretical approaches at any given moment than it does about any actual transformations within the fabric of globalisation.

The first stage of theoretical development, one closely tied to both the hyperglobalist and the sceptical positions, treats globalisation as an economic phenomenon. These theorists included economists (naturally), as well as world-system theorists, and various classical, Gramscian, and cultural Marxists. The second stage of development moved through to a greater focus on culture, with questions over the formation of various types of identity, both local and transnational, the degree to which local cultures survive, or are transformed or obliterated, and the role played by resistance within cultural formation. The final stage of development relates to the political dimensions of globalisation, more specifically about world governance and the degree of order and disorder existing within the context of late-modernity/postmodernity and changes to the nation-state. None of this really speaks to the possibility of delineating a progressive history of contemporary globalisation itself. Indeed, Rizvi and Lingard (2010, 25) regard this as something of an impossible task:

> Global integration is far from complete and, as we have already noted, clearly benefits some communities and people more than others. This suggests also that global processes are dynamic, constantly changing in the light of new economic and political, as well as technological, developments. It is thus impossible to periodise globalisation because its different forms are spatially and temporally specific.

If any kind of periodisation is theoretically unworkable, how then can we divide such a broad concept as globalisation into more intellectually manageable pieces? Rizvi and Lingard answer this question by proposing a three-fold model, one not requiring its elements to be mutually exclusive, but rather one which describes different aspects of the same phenomenon.

Globalisation as Fact, Ideology and Social Imaginary

Rizvi and Lingard first posit *globalisation as an empirical fact*. They suggest that the observable evidence all points to the world becoming increasingly interconnected and interdependent; people from around the globe can now experience events simultaneously. This is in large part due to technological developments in transport, communications and data processing, which in turn have given rise to global media. Likewise, the rigidity of Fordist production techniques has been superseded by far more flexible transnational organisational strategies equipped for highly differentiated markets, and there has been a concomitant move from manufacturing to service jobs. As global capitalism has become more fragmentary, the giant corporations have increased their power around the world, which is not to follow the hyperglobalist logic that nation-states are becoming redundant, but suggests instead that such states have been transformed into entities that play a crucial role in allowing global capital to flow, and in allowing various levels of economic and social governance to occur simultaneously, including their own.

The second element of the model is to understand *globalisation as an ideology*. Rizvi and Lingard (2010, 31) contend that 'globalisation represents a range of loosely connected ideas designed to describe new forms of political-economic governance based on the extension of market relationships globally.' Governance is no longer to be principally about 'the conduct of conduct' (Gordon 1991, 2) or the well-being of the population (see Chapter 4), it is inexorably instead tied to the ideology of neo-liberalism. According to this reasoning, state intervention would now be wound back, emphasising instead the logics of economic rationalism, competition, efficiency, choice, deregulation and privatisation. Growth would now be seen as more important than issues of equity and social welfare. Interestingly, the success of neo-liberalism as an ideology in relation to globalisation has been its ability to posit itself as the only logical option for the future, an inevitable teleological step towards tomorrow; that is, by making 'global market logic' the only game in town, the ideology of neo-liberalism has largely removed itself from the terms of the debate – a wonderfully effective sleight of hand.

The final element of the model involves *globalisation as a social imaginary*. A social imaginary is a largely implicit shared way of thinking, a common understanding that both makes sense of, and organises, everyday life – as such, it has many similarities with Bourdieu's notion of 'habitus' discussed in Chapter 1. The social imaginary exists in the stories we tell about ourselves, the narratives, ideas, myths and tales that pervade our culture. Within the global context of transnational mass media, cultures around the globe are now bathed in the same pool of images, practices and potential vocabularies of identity formation; consequently there are some ways of seeing, social similarities and cultural themes that occur within a wide variety of international contexts and settings. However, this is by no means the same as the development of some form of 'unitary global consciousness', as the social imaginary is still always shaped simultaneously by both global and local forces. As Rizvi and Linguard note, this is a plural process, and we now inhabit a world of multiple social imaginaries, in spaces that are always contested, both from above and below.

In summary, there is nothing simple, obvious and clear-cut about understanding globalisation. As we have seen, it is the subject of two familiar and recurring binaries – it's really good/it's really bad; it's all-pervasive/it's not that important. We know that America plays a large role in it, but ultimately globalisation is very much more complex than just straightforward Americanisation. Also, it operates on a number of different levels, as a fact, an ideology, and as a social imaginary; and finally, almost everybody wants an intellectual piece of it. As Robinson (2007, 125–6) states:

> All disciplines and specialisations in the academy, it seems, have become implicated in globalisation studies, from ethnic, area and women's studies, to literature, the arts, language and cultural studies, the social sciences, history, law, business administration, and even the natural and applied sciences. The proliferating literature on globalisation reflects the intellectual enormity of the task of researching the breadth, depth and pace of changes underway in human society in the early twenty-first century.

Of course, we should add education to this long list of disciplines with an interest in globalisation. As we will see in myth #2, globalisation is currently transforming education in a number of very important ways.

Myth #2 *We Have a British Education System Here, Not Any Kind of 'Globalised' One*

We have a British education system here. Everything here is ours alone: the structure, the curriculum, the way it's administered. If we're now living in a 'globalised' world, this news hasn't filtered through to our schools and universities. There is no evidence of any of the broader agendas that supposedly characterise international education.

The argument here is that even though the United Kingdom is clearly a significant First-World nation, well in tune with the all events and developments of the twenty-first century, this is not the same as suggesting that we have the shape of its education system dictated to us by the rest of the world; we make our own decisions here, and our schools and universities are organised according to our needs, beliefs and protocols, and of course, our history. However, in reality the issue is not whether we get to organise our own system – obviously we do – but rather whether many of those needs, beliefs and protocols are actually acquired from the broader global community. That is, many of the education systems around the world have started to share similar characteristics, often based around neo-liberal ideologies, and upon closer examination, the United Kingdom appears to be no different (Pusey 1991; Ball 2008).

The question is then: how has globalisation changed British education? This will be answered by addressing a range of different issues, starting with what has been referred to as the 'McDonaldisation' of education, continuing through the practices of devolution and standardisation, ending with changes to school retention rates, as well as curricula.

(1) The McDonaldisation of Education

As discussed in Chapter 4, we have come to expect schools to take a certain form. As exemplars of a disciplinary society, such institutions are now usually based around a panoptic design, where teachers can surveil their students, and those students eventually learn to regulate their own conduct. The working day is broken down into manageable sub-units, as is the curriculum; students often wear uniform, and are individuated to their own desks; and those students are continually assessed, with the results of that assessment used to create banks of normal curves, through which their conduct is managed and regulated.

The point here is that from the nineteenth century onwards, as will be addressed in greater detail in Chapter 14 on postcolonialism, schools the world over adopted this organisational system, as part of the spread of European colonial power. The argument here is that the globalisation of schools has recently taken a further step. In the same way that the organisational logic of the early modern prison and school soon spilled out into wider society (Foucault 1977), in *The McDonaldisation of Society*, Ritzer (2013) contends that the organisational rationalities of the fast-food restaurant – efficiency, calculability, predictability and control – also came to shape the broader social environment and its institutions. This metaphor, and four-part schema, can be used to help explain recent changes to our education system.

EFFICIENCY

Schools have now become hyper-structured institutions. Space on the curriculum and the use of teacher time are now commodities to be spent in the most productive and profitable ways possible. As will be discussed shortly, restricted budgets are one of the driving features of contemporary devolved education systems, and the continual focus on efficiency puts the emphasis upon doing more with less. As most teachers would acknowledge, efficiency can become its own tyranny, and with the culture of standardised testing, time for teachers to expand on points of interests at their discretion is rapidly being lost.

CALCULABILITY

Schooling outcomes are now largely only counted as valid if they can be quantified; the more intangible elements of our education, which were often considered some of the more important parts, are now deemed an unaffordable luxury, or worse, a waste of time. In many ways this is the driving logic of standardised testing: students need to have their capacities measured, so they can be compared against each other; teachers need to be accountable to the people who pay them, and the only way to be certain of their efforts and achievements is by checking their statistics.

PREDICTABILITY

Schools have become far more homogeneous learning environments, in that they have increasingly strict guidelines about what can be taught, how it can be taught, and by whom. Not only have we moved towards a national curriculum, we have rigorous standards and expectations for our teachers; there is far less room for unusual or quirky teachers within the McDonaldised school. As Ritzer (2013, 15) states: 'The workers in McDonaldised systems also behave in predictable ways. They follow corporate rules as well as the dictates of their managers. In many cases, what they do, and even what they say, is highly predictable'. This is all the more pertinent given the recent conservative push for 'Direct Instruction' literacy teaching, where teachers no longer teach in any traditional sense of the word, but rather simply follow preset lesson scripts, with student learning reinforced by rewards (Luke 2014).

CONTROL

The final element of the McDonaldisation of schools concerns the degree of direct command exerted over educational processes. Even though the system has ostensibly become more devolved in recent years, there are still high levels of centralised control exercised when necessary. This includes far more than just disciplinary mechanisms for both pupils and staff, but also for the governance of the school itself. As discussed in Chapter 7, when schools fail to reach required standards on Ofsted testing or the SATs, irrespective of any socio-cultural catchment issues, the school can be in deep trouble. Control doesn't get any more rigorous than that.

The McDonaldisation theory of global contemporary culture, and hence education, is not without its critics (Turner 2006). However, there does seem to be some truth in the observation that we are mass-producing school graduates, with an industrial standardised efficiency and a calculable burger-like predictability that would make a restaurant chain proud.

(2) The University Industry

Aside from the fact that McDonalds now has its own 'Hamburger University' in Illinois, USA, complete with 19 professors and 7500 students in attendance per year, arguments about the McDonaldisation of our education system can be extended to the tertiary sector. All the observations made above about our schools also apply to our universities, with the widespread efficiency-based moves towards online learning offerings, the global university rankings calculated according to publication rates and grant success, the national standardisation of expectations across faculties and the top-down models of university administration and regulation.

In addition to this, the university sector has expanded as universities have simply become businesses. In 1950, fewer than 20 000 students graduated from universities in the United Kingdom; by 2012, that number has increased to nearly 550 000 (Bolton 2012). In one sense, this has had the positive effect of democratising access to tertiary education; although there are still socio-economic issues in play relating to university entry, it is no longer the case that a tertiary education is restricted to the wealthy. However, the increased number of students entering university has resulted in an ongoing process of 'qualification inflation', where at least a Master's Degree is becoming the norm for anyone who wants to get promoted within an organisation. Within the British teaching profession, post-graduate qualifications are becoming a prerequisite for those thinking of moving up to head of department or deputy principal, and professional doctorates are becoming common among those wishing to be heads of school. As Bagnall (2013) rightly notes, 20 years ago just possessing a degree generally guaranteed access to most jobs, whereas now this is often an expectation for just getting an interview.

Given that universities are now globalised businesses, it is useful to note that higher education is worth over £10.7 billion annually to the United Kingdom's economy. British universities are now forced to compete for the lucrative trade in foreign students against other nations' universities in the world academic market-place, indeed the UK has 12.6% of the world's international students, second only to the United States (Universities UK 2014). Following the same logic, British students can now take their degrees online anywhere in the world, wherever they can find a 'product' that suits them.

> The notion of universities as institutions for the collective good has largely been usurped by the need to survive in an increasingly cut-throat marketplace ... (with) workers immersed in the rush of corporate activity, mostly aimed at peddling their institutions' educational wares and maintaining market share. This change has been accompanied by bureaucratic practices and corporate jargon common to other sectors – inputs, outputs, targets, key performance indicators, performance management, unit costs, cost effectiveness, benchmarking, quality assurance, and so on. (Hil 2012, 10)

Arguably, this model of the contemporary university is a direct product of neo-liberal economic ideologies. This is also the case for the next three issues illustrating the globalisation of British education.

(3) Global Devolution

At this point, there is really no need to further explain the ideas underpinning the global ideologies of neo-liberalism; it is enough to restate that they are based upon economic rationalism, deregulation and efficiency. A central pillar of this ideology has been the constant pressure for reductions in the size of government, which is positioned as unnecessary, unwieldy and intrusive. One of the central mechanisms by which this reduction in the size of government has been achieved has been the global movement towards devolution. Devolution of government means the transfer or delegation of power away from the centre to the periphery. Governments have succeeded in redu-cing their sizes by outsourcing many of their previous responsibilities down to local levels, or by privatising them altogether; in fact, in many ways, these two are often almost synonymous – take, for example, the British schooling system.

Throughout the 1990s, the United Kingdom went through a process of devolving their education systems. The 1988 Education Reform Act required local authorities to engage in what was referred to as 'local management of schools' (LMS), whereby much of school expenditure was devolved from the local authority down to the school governing bodies – in large part with the hope that the school would opt out of the system altogether, and become a 'grant-maintained school' (GMS) (Hartley 1997). Even though GM schools no longer exist in this form – having morphed into our current 'Academies' – the overall general effect of this devolution has been to reduce the size of education departments, devolve decision-making down to local levels, introduce single-line budgets for schools, allow schools to be responsible for their own hiring, and allow schools to tailor their curricular offerings to suit their potential 'consumers'. This has also had the effect of turning heads of schools into de-facto CEOs, and turning entire school systems into a loose collection of competitors, with schools now forced to market themselves in order to survive (Meadmore, 1999). The most recent exemplar of this outcome is the annual frenzy over SAT scores and the school performance tables, as discussed in Chapter 7. Almost every school in the country would now also put out glossy brochures designed to attract prospective parents; likewise with websites.

In addition to any of the benefits that the global move towards devolution might have brought our education system – a more responsive curriculum, some cost savings, greater parental choice – these have come at quite a price. Schools in affluent areas have thrived, while poorer schools struggle even more; schools that once readily cooperated as part of a system of mutual benefit are now competitors in a struggle for survival; schools are forced to look anywhere they can for extra sources of funding – corporate sponsorship, increased ascertainment of students for disability funding, chocolate raffles; and single-line budgets mean that within schools, erstwhile colleagues have to battle for funding: '*If you get your bassoon, we don't get our trampoline*'.

(4) International Standardisation

The significant problems with SATs and school performance tables have been discussed at length in Chapter 7. It is important to restate that the United Kingdom did not decide on its own that standardisation was the way forward, and that we should suddenly put in place a nationwide system of high-stakes assessment, just on the off chance it might improve literacy and numeracy. Standardisation is part of a global educational prerogative, both in the sense that (1) countries around the world are now furiously measuring their students on the questionable belief that everything that counts about a good education can be counted, and in the sense that (2) they are now comparing those students against students from everywhere else. International league tables comparing different education systems are now the principal currency of educational success, and bad news from the publication of these tables has the potential to bring down governments. That is, if the United Kingdom doesn't have the world's best education system – according to PISA rankings, which are *surely* beyond reproach – then someone must be to blame. And blaming politicians would make a welcome change from just blaming teachers (although neither is particularly appropriate).

(5) School Retention and the Jobs Market

In the UK, the school leaving age has been 16 since 1972. However, in 2008 the Education and Skills Act increased the age at which young people can end their education – at least in England. Currently, school is now compulsory until the age of

18, unless the student is undergoing education through either an apprenticeship or traineeship, or the student works or volunteers for at least 20 hours per week in part-time education or training (GOV.UK 2015). The most familiar narrative on these figures is that we suddenly realised as a nation that education was important, and that qualifications had become a prerequisite for most employment, whether that was A-levels, apprenticeship certificates, or a university degree. These shifts in British cultural practice appeared to be a largely domestic matter – a set of changes in youth expectations and practices.

Bagnall (2013) paints a somewhat different picture – applicable to all western industrial countries – one far more closely tied to the effects of globalisation. He contends that as a result of the creation of a global marketplace, low-skilled manufacturing jobs moved overseas to places with the cheapest supply of labour. Those jobs that may once have been there for a 16-year-old school leaver are now all-but gone, and they aren't coming back. Staying on at school past the compulsory leaving age has suddenly become much more attractive; furthermore those jobs that remained have far greater numbers of applicants, and as discussed previously, even the lowest level managerial jobs now require a degree to get an interview. So to put this another way, the fact that in 1950 only 7% of 17 year olds were in full-time education in England, as opposed to 76% in 2010 (Bolton 2012) – with all the knock-on effects relating to school size, curriculum design and teacher employment – is, in large part, a direct function of globalisation.

The two final issues illustrating the globalisation of British education concern credentialing and curriculum. Both of these areas are in the process of undergoing noteworthy transformations, and these changes can be tied to wider, transnational issues.

(6) Global Qualifications

In an increasingly globalised educational context, many British schools are now adopting the International Baccalaureate (IB), a global qualification that first started in 1968 in Switzerland and is now available in over 150 countries. The United Kingdom now has the fifth largest number of IB schools.

> The reasons schools gave for offering the IB included its international focus, curriculum choice and ability to cater for an increase in overseas students. It was seen as a magnet for attracting other students. Principals sometimes felt concern about the lowering of standards in the local system and wanted their staff to be involved in an international curriculum. It was favoured for its apparent portability, its service to internationally mobile parents and for its academic excellence. (Bagnall 2013, 288)

Interestingly, all of these points in favour of the IB credential dovetail neatly with the previous assertions about education and globalisation: it makes economic sense for the school, both in terms of attracting students from other countries, but also as an effective way of differentiating themselves from other local competitors in a tight marketplace; it positions the school within a global learning environment; it facilitates international mobility; and it speaks to the social imaginary about global citizenship.

(7) Global Curriculum

Of course, the International Baccalaureate is a curriculum as much as it is a qualification. Globalisation has changed what is taught in schools in a number of different ways; the IB is but one of those. Some subjects have always been on curricula around the globe: maths, science, history, physical activity and second languages (although the specifics of language choice may have changed as English has become the international *lingua franca*). However, other subjects are now making their way onto the curriculum, if not as a direct result of globalisation *per se*, then as a result of the kind of global communitarian consciousness that goes with it. One example is 'Education for Sustainability' and that will be dealt with in greater detail in myth #3.

In summary, the evidence suggests that British education has undergone significant transformations in the face of globalisation; our schooling system does not exist in isolation from the rest of the world, and the forces that have impacted other nations' education systems affect us just as much. However, just because these forces have wide reach and considerable power, does not mean that we should resign ourselves to the inevitability of their consequences, particularly when those consequences may not benefit the majority of us in the community. While neo-liberalism undoubtedly has benefits as well as costs, it is worth remembering that its rules are not fixed in amber, and neither is it the only game in town.

Myth #3 'Education for Sustainability' Has Nothing to Do With Globalisation; it's a Politically Inspired Waste of Time

Caring about whether or not the world is currently heating up has absolutely nothing to do with globalisation; most people have always kept a bit of an eye on how their environment is going. Besides, the jury is still out on that whole global warming thing, so we certainly don't need either side of politics forcing their ideas into the curriculum. 'Education for Sustainability' is just a fad that tells us stuff we already know; the sooner it goes away the better.

At the risk of stating the obvious, this is an important issue and it needs to be addressed clearly and rationally. At present, concerns over the global environment take many forms: deforestation and loss of habitat, pollution and loss of air and water quality; issues of biodiversity; overpopulation and land degradation; nuclear and chemical dangers; overfishing and so on. However, almost everyone would be aware that the most important environmental issue is currently deemed to be global warming and the role that human civilisation plays in it.

The rest of this chapter is going to proceed based upon four basic assumptions: first, 'the environment' is now a globalised concept, problems which will ultimately require global solutions. Second, everyone – irrespective of their political persuasion – thinks that the environment is worth looking after, and this involves teaching our children to do the same. Third, the biggest of these problems, global warming, is almost certainly our fault; 97% of scientists have reached this conclusion (Cook *et al.* 2013) and that number ought to be convincing enough for anyone, it seems, except diehard political partisans, a few nutty conspiracy theorists and people who have a vested interest in claiming otherwise. Finally, this is a *very, very big problem*, which will consequently require the use of every weapon at our disposal, including our education system.

There are three separate elements to this myth. The first is that the environmental movement really has little relation to contemporary globalisation, having much more to do with the hippy movement of the early 1960s. The second is that concerns over the environment – and in particular global warming – are simply a stalking horse for the political left, and should therefore be disregarded. Finally, that 'Education for Sustainability' is simply part of this agenda, serving no useful academic or social purpose whatsoever. We now take these elements in turn.

Globalisation and the Environmental Movement

We have not always been concerned about the environment; for most of human history it has seemed like an endless bounteous resource, put there for us to use as we wished. The first moves towards environmental protection only occurred in the second half of the nineteenth century, with the establishment of wildlife conservation societies, the passing of several clean air acts as a result of growing industrialisation and the formation of national parks in areas of particular national beauty. These remained a relatively niche set of concerns right up until the 1960s, and it was only with the publication of *Silent Spring* (Carson 1962) – a book examining the effects of the widespread use of pesticides (mostly DDT) on birdlife – that the modern environmental movement began to take shape. In combination with the Campaign for Nuclear Disarmament (CND) and a couple of very notable oil spills (the *Torrey Canyon* in 1967 in Cornwall and the *Santa Barbara Channel* spill in 1969), there began to develop the beginnings of a general social awareness of some of the possible consequences of human action on the environment.

Similar to Robinson's (2007) second and third waves of globalisation discussed in the introduction to this chapter, Christoff and Eckersley (2013) outline two 'fuses' leading to global environmental degradation and from there, to the environmental movement. The first – 'the long fuse of modernity' refers to the age of empires and imperial expansion across the world which reached its peak towards the end of the nineteenth century. The second – 'the short fuse of twentieth century globalisation' – has burned much faster and brighter, and arguably with much greater consequences for our environment. With regards to this 'short fuse', Christoff and Eckersley point to the rise of neo-liberal economic philosophies as not only providing the philosophical foundations of globalisation (in agreement with most other commentators in the area), but also as playing an instrumental role in triggering the current ecological crisis. This is for two reasons: first, the primary goal of the neo-liberal state is to increase the efficiency of economic activities and to become more competitive in the global marketplace. Consequently, auxiliary functions of governance, such as welfare and the environment, are often positioned as brakes on this process and are hence sidelined. Second, even if there was a will to do so, given that a fundamental tenet of neo-liberalism is the shrinking of government, and hence a reduction in its capacity to 'interfere', there has consequently been far greater difficulty in passing comprehensive environmental regulation, regulation which may well have stopped the short fuse from burning before we got to our current ecological predicament.

It is this latter context that has given the modern environmental movement its shape and reach. While it was certainly born in the 1960s, and found its first home in the counter-culture of the period, it was the side effects of globalisation and augmented levels of international trade and consumption that spawned the kinds of transnational environmental consciousness that lie at the heart of twenty-first century environmentalism.

Politicising the Environment

In the United States, a recent poll of voters were asked about global warming, and what if anything was causing it (Leiserowitz *et al.* 2014). The results showed that 93% of left-leaning Democrats believe that climate change is occurring, with 75% stating that we are responsible. Conversely, only 28% of right-leaning Republicans think global warming is occurring, with 22% stating we are responsible. The United Kingdom has a similar, although arguably less marked, division between political left and right. Clements (2012) found that, within the British population, climate change scepticism is associated with being male, less well educated, having right-wing ideological beliefs, and supporting the Conservatives. What on earth is going on here?

> It is plausible that some people's voting intentions were influenced by each political party's stance on climate change. An alternative proposition is that, despite low levels of reported trust, people's attitudes towards climate change are based largely on the stance taken at any given time by the political party they intend to vote for. (Leviston and Walker 2011, 14)

Actually, the question 'What on earth is going on here?' requires a more complex answer than this. First, how did scientific truth become a matter of popular opinion?

One of the world's leading science bodies, the American Association for the Advancement of Science (AAAS) recently stated that we are as certain that humans are causing global warming as we are that smoking causes cancer (American Association for the Advancement of Science 2014). Nobody conducts public polls asking about the 'truth' of smoking and lung cancer; we accept the scientific consensus on the issue. Second then, why is this not the case for global warming, and how has it become a party-political issue? The answer to these questions can be found in the contrasting underlying philosophies of (particularly American) conservatism and liberalism, and the deployment of a familiar political strategy used to undercut the policy proposals of the environmental movement.

THE CLASH OF CULTURES

McCright and Dunlap (2011) contend that contemporary conservatism is premised upon a (perfectly laudable and defensible) belief in individual freedom, limited government and the promotion of free markets. These ideals can be directly contrasted with the political left, which champions (an equally laudable and defensible) belief in collective rights, significant provision of social services and targeted market regulation. There are occasions when these ideological differences have only a limited differentiating effect on whether policy initiatives are supported or not, for example concerning national security, the provision of infrastructure, or the functioning of emergency services. However:

> Global environmental problems like climate change pose a stronger challenge
> to conservative's faith in unfettered industrial capitalism as the desired path to
> progress ... more specifically, the possibility of an internationally binding treaty to
> curb greenhouse gas emissions is viewed as a direct threat to sustained economic
> growth, the spread of free markets, the maintenance of national sovereignty and the
> continued abolition of governmental regulation – key goals of conservatives.
> (McCright and Dunlap 2011, 160)

And herein lies the root of the problem. Accepting that the climate is changing and that we are responsible leads to only one of two plausible options: (1) shrug your shoulders, do nothing and say you don't care, or (2) get onboard with other governments around the globe committed to enacting legislation aimed at large-scale global reductions in greenhouse gas emission. The first of these responses is regarded as unacceptable by anybody who wants to be seen as a decent human being; the second however requires a significant expansion of national and international forms of governance and regulation – not a problem for the political left, but regarded as highly ideologically undesirable by both conservatives and big business.

Of course, the choice of doing nothing becomes a viable (desirable) option... but only if the pesky science is wrong and the world isn't actually heating up. And the science *surely* has to be wrong; isn't it just a bit too much of a coincidence that the 'big-government, anti-business, anti-growth' policy changes required to combat global warming effectively are just what the political left has wanted all along? And here, right on time, is a convenient excuse to ram it all through.

THE MANUFACTURE OF UNCERTAINTY

The all-out assault on climate science started in the mid 1990s. While mainstream university science headed quickly towards a consensus of anthropogenic climate change, the conservative movement (supported by Big Oil) has employed its own 'scientific expertise', in the form of a very small number of contrarian scientists, largely publishing in non-peer reviewed journals, to set up a 'debate' between two opposing positions. Now able to recite the constant mantras of *the science isn't settled* and *we should hear from both sides of the debate* – along with the ludicrous *there's a global conspiracy among mainstream scientists* – it has now become ethically possible to do precisely nothing.

For those with an interest in history, this strategy has been employed before. Contrarian scientists have been employed in the past to set up 'debates', and thereby claim that the science isn't settled. They have argued that DDT is safe, that there is no such thing as acid-rain, and that smoking doesn't cause cancer. Interestingly, as Oreskes and Conway observe in the book *Merchants of Doubt* (2010), it is the same handful of 'scientists-for-hire' who have made these arguments on each occasion. In the cases of DDT, acid-rain and smoking, the battle was eventually won in the court of public opinion (where it shouldn't have been fought in the first place). Unfortunately, in the case of global warming, by then it may be too late.

It is appropriate to include a very brief proviso on this section of the chapter. As with this entire book, the intention here hasn't been to take political sides, but rather to point out a particularly unethical, bad-faith political strategy to justify doing nothing. The scientific debate is over; accusing thousands of climate scientists of participating in a global fraud is absurd; important and legitimate debates between left and right are still to be had over how we should move forward. Let's get on with it.

The Value of 'Education for Sustainability'

Given its unquestionable importance, it would seem logical to include some form of environmental education in the school curriculum. Even the most enthusiastic and optimistic neo-liberal would accept that the much increased levels of economic growth brought about by globalisation are likely to put stresses on our natural environment that will require careful assessment and management. However, the seemingly inherent political tension between the forces advocating growth and those advocating environmental protection has meant that any moves to introduce environmental issues into the curriculum has been met with distrust, a distrust only compounded by the intensity of the global warming 'debate'.

The most recent attempt to educate children about the environment takes the form of 'Education for Sustainability' (EfS). According to Davis (2015), EfS traces its roots back to the 1992 Rio Earth Summit, the 2002 World Summit on Sustainable Development, and the 2005 announcement of the United Nations Decade of Education for Sustainable Development (UNESCO 2005). Davis contends that two of the earliest approaches to environmental education – education *about* the environment; and education *through* the environment – appeared to have little impact on behaviour. Consequently, it was a third, more overtly political approach – education *for* the environment – that came to form the framework for EfS.

> EfS is founded on principles of critical inquiry, empowerment, participation, democratic decision making, action taking that supports sustainable living and aims for social change – it is transformative education. As such, there is recognition that education that delivers 'more of the same' is deeply inadequate in terms of contributing to the necessary social transformations required for sustainability. (Davis 2015, 18)

The EfS movement has gained considerable traction around the world with a significant number of countries making this a foundational part of their curriculum, for example Sweden (Arlemalm-Hagser and Engdahl 2015) and South Korea (Ji 2015). However, in the United Kingdom – where it is most frequently referred to as 'Education for Sustainable Development' (ESD), as well as 'Sustainability and Environmental Education' (SEED) – there has been, at best, mixed success.

The area of study started well. In the 1999 National Curriculum Handbook, Key Stages 3 and 4, ESD was positioned under 'Learning Across the National Curriculum', with the statement stressing its significance, given that it 'enables pupils to develop the knowledge, skills, understanding and values to participate in decisions about the way we do things individually and collectively, both locally and globally, that will improve the quality of life now without damaging the planet for the future' (Qualifications and Curriculum Authority 1999, 23). In 2000, ESD was made a requirement in geography, science, design and citizenship; schools were also asked to promote sustainable development on a personal, national and global level. ESD was broken down into seven key concepts: interdependence, citizenship and stewardship, the needs and rights of future generations, diversity, quality of life, sustainable change, uncertainty and precaution, with the QCA producing curriculum documents explaining their contours and relevance. In 2003 the Government's Sustainable Development Education Panel (SDEP) published *Learning to Last*, setting out a comprehensive sustainability strategy covering all aspects of education. From this point, as noted by the charity 'Sustainability and Environmental Education' (Sustainability and Environmental Education 2015), the years 2003–2010 were the most successful for the movement.

However, from this promising start, the push for sustainability in the United Kingdom, particularly in education, appears to have stalled. With the election of the

Conservative government in 2010, 'Education for Sustainability' has largely dropped off the pedagogic radar. Schools are no longer required to integrate sustainability into the curriculum in any comprehensive way. Most of the ESD material has been removed from government websites, and while ESD issues may remain a voluntary element of some parts of the curriculum, such as geography, it has been removed from the politics, economics and social sciences curricula. Given the overt politicisation of the environmental issues around the world, this response should not have come as a surprise.

In spite of these significant setbacks, there remains some momentum behind ESD. There is now a Sustainable Schools Alliance which seeks to continue the foregrounding of environmental and sustainability issues within schools; Scotland has also positioned Learning for Sustainability as an important component of its post-2011 'Curriculum for Excellence'.

In summary, if we accept that protecting our environment is of utmost importance, then we have to educate our future citizens accordingly; and it takes a curriculum to do that. As long as we allow concern for the environment to be characterised as 'ideology' or 'politics' – as appears to be the case with critics of 'Education for Sustainability' – then there's not much hope for any of us.

Conclusion

We are undergoing a period of rapid globalisation, a term that most of us have a visceral understanding of, but which is very difficult to pin down in definitional or conceptual terms. It continues to have some very profound effects upon our educational system, in terms of who goes to school, how long they stay, what they learn when they get there, how they are assessed, and how the school is run. Globalisation continues to have an enormous impact on our environment, but the politicisation of 'environmentalism' has meant that its place in the school curriculum is becoming increasingly marginal.

There are two points that warrant mentioning again. First, reducing arguments over globalisation to a binary of either 'good' or 'bad' is simplistic and unhelpful. Globalisation has brought advantages in economic growth and in the distribution of new political ideas and practices; alternatively, it has allowed unelected multinational corporations to shape government policy, it has put even greater pressure on our environment and it has further exacerbated differences in wealth between rich and poor, creating a 'borderless but deeply asymmetric world' (Ball *et al.* 2010, 523). In terms of education, globalisation has made new links between disparate education systems and has opened up options for study across the world; alternatively, it has triggered a mania for standardised testing, which brings with it problems of its own and has homogenised education to a virtual production line. The issue here is that any evaluation or critique of globalisation needs to be specific in setting the terms of its analysis; just saying it's good or bad doesn't really contribute to the debate at all.

Second, most commentators place the political and economic juggernaut of neo-liberalism at the heart of globalisation. As has been pointed out, part of the success of neo-liberalism is to define contemporary economics, governance and politics within its own terms. The notions of deregulation, efficiency, privatisation, competition and choice are often made to seem like the only vocabulary of practices available to us, and more than that, each of them is individually fixed and immutable. This is not the case. We can proceed as far down this path as we choose, and select the elements we choose. Economic rationalism is not the only option open to us; there are many who would argue that there should be more to education, and to society itself, than turning a profit.

PHILOSOPHY AND MASS EDUCATION

In the previous three parts of this book, the main tools of analysis have been primarily sociological and historical. Addressing issues of class, gender and race has always been the central prerogative of sociology; likewise, the chapters on the relationship between education and various elements of contemporary culture are also largely investigated through sociological reasoning. Alternatively, understanding the scope and impact of social governance, in all its forms, has principally been the result of detailed historical analysis. However, these are not the only options open to us; some of the most useful and far-reaching methods of inquiry belong to the discipline of philosophy.

If the intention is to look at mass education with a fresh pair of eyes, then philosophy can provide the necessary critical tools to do precisely that. As a discipline based upon clear thinking and cogent argument, philosophy is useful not only for the production of thoughtful future citizens, it is also a valuable skill set for anyone interested in studying our education system. Furthermore, mass education is also an ethically complex domain, with important dilemmas continuing over issues such as social inclusion and disability – a fact that the philosophical study of ethics can help us address with greater clarity and fairness. Finally, if we are seeking the 'truth' of mass education, philosophy can help us at least understand what we might mean by that, as well as better understand the relationship between truth and the school curriculum.

Chapter 12 – *Philosophy* – examines the value of this discipline within education. It questions the assertions that we no longer need non-job-producing subjects like philosophy in our school curriculum, the suggestion being that it's too abstract, too esoteric, and no longer relevant to the digital generation. It questions the notion that education is fundamentally self-evident, and by invoking the need for philosophy to study it, we are making it more complicated than it really is. It also examines the ways in which we can shape a personal philosophy of education, and why this is an important component of doing the job properly.

Chapter 13 – *Ethics, Disability and the Law* – investigates the importance of the philosophical study of ethics, and its relation to education. It questions the common view that a good grasp of ethics is irrelevant to being a good teacher, and that mass education is now free of the ethical concerns and dilemmas that may have once characterised it. Focusing on the issue of disability and inclusion, the chapter examines some of the shortcomings of the logic of 'the greatest good for the greatest number', particularly as related to minority groups within education.

Chapter 14 – *Truth and Postcolonialism* – addresses the relationship between the notion of truth and our school curriculum. It questions the belief that truth is the purest and most fundamental of all logical forms, a state that exists independently of human thought and action; and that the curriculum is full of nothing but unequivocal, universal truths – truths that would hold up to scrutiny irrespective of the social and cultural circumstances of the school in which they are presented. The chapter then goes on to examine postcolonial theory, using this to help contextualise aspects of the form and content of current school curricula, both in the United Kingdom and elsewhere.

In many ways, Chapters 13 and 14 are designed to act as case studies to illustrate the potential of philosophy, both as a discipline in general, and more specifically, as it relates to the particular ambitions of this book. Ethics and epistemology – the study of truth, or more specifically, of knowledge – are two of the most important branches of philosophy, and here they are applied to issues of inclusion and the postcolonial curriculum respectively. By the end, the intention is to demonstrate the utility of philosophy for making greater sense of mass schooling; it is also to show that these two important philosophical sub-disciplines can shed much light upon some of the unspoken assumptions that underpin our understandings of the 'normal' pupil, and upon the educational legacy of our status as a former colonial power.

PHILOSOPHY 12

This chapter makes the case for the importance of philosophy, as a discipline in its own right, as a subject area vital to the better understanding of education, and as a set of self-reflective practices that can make us better teachers. Philosophy is largely concerned with those areas of study and speculation beyond the reach of empirical analysis, addressing problems about how we construct knowledge, how we produce a just society, and how we determine 'right' from 'wrong'. Its central research methodology is simply to think with clarity. The significance of this discipline has not been limited to answering abstract questions about the human condition; philosophy has been instrumental both in making us into rational and reflexive citizens, and also in framing the ideas behind our entire system of mass schooling.

Myth #1 Philosophy has no place in the twenty-first-century curriculum. *'We don't have the space in the curriculum to teach philosophy. School children need to study subjects that will actually get them a job'.* The study of philosophy brings with it many benefits within mass schooling, benefits that extend far beyond the directly instrumental: the ability to think clearly and logically, an overall improvement in academic performance, and a greater sensitivity to social and ethical issues, not to mention the capacity to address essential questions about the human condition.

Myth #2 'Education' is self-evident; we don't need philosophy to explain it. *'We all know what education is. There isn't really any disagreement, or any confounding complexity – those with knowledge, pass it on to those without'.* Actually, there's a lot of disagreement over what education is, and how it ought to work in practice. By better understanding how philosophical approaches like Idealism, Realism, Romanticism, Pragmatism, Marxism, and Postmodernism continue to shape our education system, we can better grasp the range of educational possibilities, as well as fashion our own teaching philosophies.

Myth #3 Teachers don't need a 'personal philosophy of education'.
'Bricklayers don't need anything as pretentious as a 'personal philosophy' to build a solid wall, and neither do teachers; teachers just need to do their job'. Arguably, the most effective of contemporary teachers engage in a continual process of reflection regarding their professional practice and, in doing so, fashion a personal philosophy of education. This philosophy is likely to include the prioritising of particular theories of teaching and learning, the meshing of their teaching practices with their own individual strengths and weaknesses, understanding the relationship between the educational and the political in specific ways, and reflecting upon, and often choosing sides within, a range of debates within the philosophy of education.

Introduction
What is Philosophy?

Some subjects are easy to comprehend – not necessarily their subject matter, but certainly what they are about. Medicine is a good example. All the anatomy, bio-chemistry and physiology might be difficult, but the central idea is pretty straightfor-ward: medicine is about making sick people better. The same applies to music. Nobody would pretend that playing the piano is simple, but we all know what music is. Philosophy isn't quite so obliging.

Partially as a result of some of the difficulties associated with defining philosophy, almost every book on the subject starts with its etymology: the word philosophy comes from the Ancient Greek, and it means 'love of wisdom'. However, 'wisdom' is something of a broad field, and this bit of information doesn't really help delineate what philosophers should, and should not, be wise about. In truth, early philosophers didn't really care.

> For Plato and Aristotle there was no fumbling doubt about what they were profes-sionally entitled to do, or the proper limits of philosophical inquiry. They were looking for answers to every conceivable question that could be raised, they were seeking to explain and understand the world in all its aspects. (Barrow 1975, 15)

However, as the empirical sciences have grown, and marked out specific areas of knowledge for themselves, philosophy has tended towards addressing the more abstract and general questions of life; questions about ethics, knowledge, reason and existence. This is not to say that philosophy has no role to play in other disciplines, far from it. It is an ill-equipped scientist who does not have a firm grounding in the philosophy of science, and many forms of knowledge are underpinned by a set of philosophical principles that give their discipline shape and rigour – medicine, for example.

But Western philosophy is not primarily about learning a body of knowledge, although there are texts within every field of philosophy that aspiring philosophers need to be acquainted with. Rather, first and foremost, philosophy is about learning how to reason clearly or, as Popper (1959, 15–16) puts it, 'stating one's problems clearly and of examining its various proposed solutions critically'. Emmet (1991) rightly concludes that while the empirical sciences are about 'going and seeing', philosophy is about 'sitting and thinking'. After all, as Hobbes states, 'Leisure is the mother of philosophy'. Perfect for university study then.

Importantly, philosophy isn't just about pointless speculation on ultimately irrelevant topics. Historically, it has had enormous impact on how we understand ourselves, and how we organise our world. For example, it was the philosopher Descartes' realisation, 'I think, therefore I am' – *Cogito Ergo Sum* – that acted as one of the central triggers for the Enlightenment, in that it showed that the future of human knowledge belonged to *reason*, and not to superstition or blind tradition. Likewise, it was the ideas of political philosophers like Locke that laid the foundations of modern systems of social and political rights, given voice through the French and American revolutions. Finally, as discussed in Chapter 4, it was, in large part, the utilitarian ideas of Bentham and Mill that formed the regulatory framework for the disciplinary society we now all take for granted. These are just a few of the many, many examples of how philosophy has shaped, and continues to shape, how we think and what we do.

However, if the point of philosophy can be summed up at all, it is with the most famous of quotes from the most famous of all philosophers – Socrates, as given voice through Plato (1989, 38a): 'The unexamined life is not worth living'. Unfortunately, if you see no merit in this contention, you might as well just skip to the next chapter.

A Brief History

Philosophy didn't just appear in the world, complete and fully formed; it has been through various stages, and organised itself in different ways, throughout the past 2500 years. The briefest of summaries of these stages might include the following: it all began, in Europe at least, with the *Classical Philosophy* of Ancient Greece, and it has rightly been said that Plato wrestled with most of the philosophical problems we still wrestle with today. After Rome fell, and took philosophy down with it, the next 1000 years of arcane religiously doctrinal *Scholastic Philosophy* produced next to nothing that lasted, and it was only with the rise of Descartes' *Rationalism* – the belief that reason is the root of all knowledge – that the discipline came back to life. This was soon challenged by British *Empiricism*, which claimed instead that the root of all knowledge is experience. Both these approaches were shown to have shortcomings, and after an early attempt by Rousseau's *Romanticism* (which valued emotion over reason), it was Kant who made the most successful, though blindingly complex, effort at finding common ground between the two sides. From there, some of the ideas of Plato had a rebirth through Hegel's *German Idealism*, but philosophy eventually settled into a kind of loosely based theoretical tribalism. German philosophers stuck with their idealism; Americans plumped for *Pragmatism*, the assertion that all ideas must be founded upon how useful they are; the English focused upon *Analytic Philosophy*, with its concern over the truth and falsity of particular statements; and the French based their philosophy – in the forms of *Phenomenology* and *Existentialism* – around the issue of subjective experience. Finally, add some political philosophy through *Marxism*, and a little *Neo-Romanticism*, with the ideas of Kierkegaard and Nietzsche, and there you have it: the world's most oversimplified history of philosophy.

This is perhaps not that useful in itself, but it is a good list of places to start for those who are interested – and these are only the Western philosophies. There are other forms of knowledge, ones that don't necessarily have Ancient Greece in their ancestry. Equally valid and long-lived forms of philosophy have emerged from China, India and the Middle East. However, these ideas never became part of the Western canon, and hence missed out on the global diaspora of Classicism that came with European Colonialism.

Importantly, philosophy isn't just a set of generalised speculations about life, it has always clustered into different areas of concern, some of which won't be dealt with here (such as justice and free will), and others that will (such as ethics and truth). The philosophy of education is one of the oldest, and most important, of all these areas. Socrates is important as a philosopher, not only because he had something important to say about education – 'Education is the kindling of the flame, not the filling of the vessel' – but also because he founded an entire technique of teaching: the *Socratic Method*. This approach, still widely used, particularly at university level, involves asking a rolling set of questions that lead the respondent to reassess the strengths and weaknesses of their position, and hence to consider the possibility of adopting another.

In general terms, though, why is philosophy so important? Yes, it has an interesting history; yes, it has brought about some important social, intellectual and political changes; and yes, it deals with some important areas but, on a more specific basis, why still do philosophy? The question forms the basis for myth #1 of this chapter.

The Importance of Philosophy

As discussed in the introduction to this section, even though philosophy has often struggled to find space within the twenty-first-century teacher-education syllabus – mostly due to short-term pressures favouring curriculum knowledge and instruction guidance subjects – few doubt its long-term intellectual value. As a general subject, philosophy has a lot to offer. It provides the tools for addressing some of the most important issues of life; fundamental questions of free will, truth and existence have still found their most convincing answers within this discipline. In addition, it provides the training to think with clarity and precision, to weight evidence fairly and appropriately, and to construct valid arguments, as well as to recognise those that are not. It also provides the solid intellectual foundation for a range of other knowledges. In the final analysis, science, medicine, law – and education – all have philosophies that bind their discipline together.

Philosophy is particularly important to education. It has long been realised that education is a complex business; there have been 2500 years' worth of disputes about exactly what it is, and how it ought to work. Philosophy succeeds in organising how these complexities might be understood, and in doing so, also gives us a better grasp of what kind of educational choices we have, both as an individual teacher, and as a society. Philosophy has a lot to offer in the context of the school. It is not only adults that benefit from reflecting upon life; children also ask questions that philosophy is best equipped to answer. Young children can also learn the basics of critical reasoning and organised thinking, with all the spin-off benefits that this brings, not only to their other studies, but also to their social interactions.

Approaches to the Philosophy of Education

While no two philosophers would be likely to agree on precisely what content needs to be taught for a philosophy of education course, they would all agree that the course needs to be taught, in contrast to the belief that 'education' speaks for itself, as in myth #2. This content could equally well involve education's links to other philosophy sub-disciplines, such as social justice or knowledge production; it could involve the works of famous writers in the field, anyone from Aristotle to Montessori; or it could be based around fundamental approaches to the philosophy of education – the 'isms' – of which there are many.

It is this latter model that will be adopted here. Arguably, the six approaches chosen cover the greatest range of philosophical ideas, historically, conceptually and in terms of influence on the field. That said, of those philosophers who agree with this overall strategy, many will still disagree with the list of specific approaches chosen, in this case Idealism, Realism, Romanticism, Pragmatism, Marxism and Postmodernism. After all, remember the first law of philosophy: *for every philosopher, there is an equal and opposite philosopher.* (Second law: *they're both wrong.*)

Developing a Personal Philosophy of Education

Most significantly, perhaps, and certainly for those contemplating a career in teaching, the academic discipline of philosophy plays a large role in allowing us to develop a personal philosophy of education. After all, if education is to be more than simple instruction, more than a simple run-through of the contents of the textbook from start to finish, it requires significant reflection by all of us about precisely what kind of teachers we want to be. It will be argued here that the discipline of philosophy allows us to develop a firm foundation for our choice of teaching strategies, it allows us to figure out exactly what it is we're doing when we teach, and why we're doing it, and it allows us to think our way through many of the other complexities of the profession, clearly, logically and effectively. In short, it can be the difference between merely acceptable teaching and teaching excellence.

To summarise, the three myths to be dealt with in this chapter are as follows.

Myth #1 Philosophy has no place in the twenty-first-century curriculum.
Myth #2 'Education' is self-evident; we don't need philosophy to explain it.
Myth #3 Teachers don't need a 'personal philosophy of education'.

Myth #1 *Philosophy Has No Place in the Twenty-First-Century Curriculum*

We don't have the luxury of adding a waffly subject like philosophy to our already crowded curriculum. School children need practical subjects that result in quantifiable outcomes. They need subjects that feed directly into the requirements of the employment market. Student teachers don't need philosophy either; they need instruction on how to get kids through exams, and how to keep classrooms quiet.

In some circles, philosophy is depicted as the best exemplar of a pointless education: impractical, self-indulgent, inconclusive, unproductive and ultimately futile. It is suggested that we live in an era of severe financial pressure on our public institutions, and everything has to pay its way. There can be no passengers, either in terms of staffing or subject choices, and while we'd love everyone to be able to spend leisurely hours doing art, music and philosophy, the state requires more of our schools than that. It requires the specific training of future workers.

This section of Chapter 12 will present a coherent counter argument to this instrumentalist position. It will suggest that just because the benefits of philosophy are often less tangible than the ability to do double-entry book-keeping, they are no less real; in fact, philosophy is far broader in its reach, both in the practical sense of producing students who can reason clearly and effectively, but also because it has the potential to help us address some of the more important issues in life.

Why Do Philosophy?

TO ANSWER IMPORTANT QUESTIONS

Many questions can be answered simply by assessing the evidence. What kind of cell is that? Look through the microscope. Who murdered the Vicar? Test the knife for fingerprints. How long does it take to boil an egg? Just boil some eggs and find out. Unfortunately, not all questions come with a ready blueprint as to how they should be answered, let alone convenient forms of verification. This is where philosophy comes in.

Hospers (1997) argues that after we have taken the empirically testable questions off the table – that it, questions that can be directly confirmed or falsified – what remains is the domain of philosophy; and that philosophy is the *study of justification* and the *analysis of concepts*. It is the study of justification in that it is concerned about how we justify the many assertions we make. For example, Descartes asked the question: *'If you say that something really happened, how do you know you did not simply dream it?'*. Hume asked the question: *'You say we have free will, but how do you know?'*. He also asked: *'If you say something is "wrong", where do you look for that "wrongness"?'*. In each case, the philosophers are asking for people to explain and justify the claims they make.

In addition to the study of justification, philosophy is also the analysis of concepts. As Hospers (1997, 5) states: 'We speak of justice, but what is justice? We describe things as beautiful, but what is beauty? We speak of before and after, but what is time? We describe things as real, but what is reality?'. These are some of the most important questions we can ask ourselves, particularly 'What is reality?', undoubtedly one of the most important questions in the history of philosophy. There is no microscope to peer through to draw definitive conclusions to these questions, no fingerprints to take. There is simply the possibility of 'sitting and thinking' until we arrive at viable answers. Some of those answers have been discussed since the time of Socrates, and we benefit from both the answers we have arrived at, and from the discussion itself.

TO THINK MORE CLEARLY

We benefit from the discussion because philosophy sharpens our thinking; it looks for *clarity*. Within philosophy, it is not enough to bluff your way along, using dodgy premises, within badly reasoned arguments, which then get passed off as truth. Actually, that also happens in philosophy, but you're more likely to get caught. Here are two examples:

> *Lots of young boys have ADHD now, and hate sitting still.*
> *Joe hates sitting still.*
> *So, Joe must have ADHD.*

At first glance, this argument seems perfectly valid – indeed, this argument currently gets used in British classrooms every day of the year. However, it is an example of a *logical fallacy* called 'Affirming the Consequent'. (If A then B; B, therefore A.) Just because Joe hates sitting still, does not logically mean he has ADHD, irrespective of the previous causal link between young boys with ADHD, and hating sitting still (let's given him Ritalin anyway, just to be on the safe side).

ADHD is fertile ground for logical fallacies. There is a fallacy called 'Petitio Principii'. (Why A? Because of B. Why B? Because of A.) This is otherwise known as 'Circular Reasoning' – which covers the underlying logic of ADHD perfectly.

> How do you know a child has Attention Deficit Disorder (ADHD)? Because he's impulsive and out of his seat. Why is he impulsive and out of his seat? Because he has ADHD. (Weist *et al.* 1999, 121)

Importantly, studying philosophy doesn't only enable you to spot logical fallacies, although this is a useful skill to acquire. In a far more general sense, it also fosters the ability to think critically. Rather than accepting every truth-claim that we hear, like a sponge mopping up water, a solid grounding in philosophical thinking enables us to sort out the valid from the invalid, strong arguments from weak, and the plausible and the reasonable from the misleading. Philosophy equips us to distinguish between knowledge, and drivel masquerading as knowledge.

TO PROVIDE A SOLID FOUNDATION FOR OTHER AREAS

Philosophy does not sit out on its own as a discrete discipline, calling out good advice from the sidelines. It has become a foundational component of many other disciplines. Science is probably the best, and most far-reaching, example here. Very few tertiary institutions would have science faculties that did not also offer units in the philosophy of science for its students. Science is in the business of making truth claims – the universe is expanding, the globe is warming, biodiversity is decreasing, and so on – and all good scientists understand that finding 'truth' is a far more complex business than simply having the equations add up (see Chapter 14, myth #1).

All of these concerns have been shaped and bounded within the philosophy of science, and this hasn't even touched upon the topic of research ethics, upon how to decide what studies should, and should not, be done, and how they should be carried out. Deciding *whether* we should do embryonic stem cell research is an ethical issue, not a scientific one. Consequently, it is a question best addressed by someone with an expertise in ethics, not in cellular biology; it is a question best addressed by a philosopher. Of course, as we shall now see, philosophy also underpins the entire discipline of education.

Why Study Philosophy of Education?

TO GAIN A BETTER UNDERSTANDING OF OUR EDUCATION SYSTEM

Education is neither a simple nor a straightforward concept. It has varied across time, and between cultures. For example, in Ancient Athens children received a broadly based education – including music, literature and gymnastics – with the intention of producing 'rounded' citizens. Only a few hundred kilometres away in Ancient Sparta, education existed solely as a preparation for war; learning was written into the contours of the body, and the fighting skills it came to possess, all shaped within a pedagogy of brutality and death. Perhaps fortunately, we have adopted a model of schooling far closer to the Athenian system. . . with the possible exception of a couple of well-known rugby schools.

The point here is that all education systems are based upon underlying sets of beliefs, assumptions and practices – whether we realise it or not (and often we're so close to our own schooling systems, we don't recognise that they could be organised otherwise). These sets of beliefs are called *Educational Philosophies*, and some of our most important will be addressed in myth #2 of this chapter. Clearly those that underpinned the education systems of Athens and Sparta were very different. Of course, unlike education, some disciplines don't require a philosophy at all; valuable though it is, you'd be hard pressed to discern any philosophy underpinning electrical engineering.

Two issues are of note here. The first is that systems of education have underlying philosophies for a very simple reason: education is incredibly important to us; Socrates and Plato fretted over how best to educate the young, and nothing much has changed. Second, the best way to understand these educational philosophies is through the discipline of philosophy. There are two different uses of the word 'philosophy' here, but hopefully the thrust of the argument is clear: if you want to understand our education system, the discipline of philosophy is a good place to start.

TO GAIN A BETTER UNDERSTANDING OF OUR CHOICES AS A SOCIETY

There is a close relationship between the kind of schools a society sets up – or more specifically, the kind of educational philosophy that underpins those schools – and the kind of society that its citizens are trying to produce. The Spartans didn't put their children through 14 years of relentlessly violent schooling, where they were turned into fearsome warriors, because they were a pacifist society who liked nothing better than a little bit of poetry. They educated their children that way because their society was a war machine.

However, not all the philosophies underpinning schooling systems are quite so obvious, instrumental and easy to read as those of Sparta, and the discipline of philosophy not only enables us to understand the kinds of ideas and approaches that currently animate our schools, but also to plan for the kind of schools we'd *like* to have. After all, should education be about personal development? Should it be about preparing future citizens for their social role? Should it be about learning a central core of timeless knowledge? Should it simply be about learning how to think? Should it be about producing citizens with a commitment to a just society? Each of these approaches has their strengths and weaknesses, and philosophy helps us determine what they are.

TO DEVELOP A PERSONAL PHILOSOPHY

Philosophy is not just about acquiring a better understanding of the various possible approaches to education, or about which of these society ought to adopt, it is about organising a satisfactory personal relationship with the role of teacher. Arguably, this process has a number of interrelated components. For instance, good teaching involves developing a personal philosophy of classroom practice – what teachers should actually do in their professional lives, and why. This includes not only acquiring the self-awareness to know what their own strengths and weaknesses are, and organising their teaching accordingly, it also involves deciding upon a personal philosophy of instruction, whether this has its origins within the Socratic dialogues of Ancient Greece, Dewey's learning facilitation, or even Skinner's stimulus–response.

Teachers also need to reach personal conclusions regarding what they think education – and more specifically, mass schooling – is all about. Do we agree with Rousseau that education should be about the full development of the human spirit, or are we more persuaded by the arguments of contemporary critical theorists, who suggest that schools are simply mechanisms for replicating and legitimating the existing social order: the clever (wealthy) stay on the top, the stupid (poor) stay on the bottom? Philosophy can help us to figure out where we stand, and it can also help us to take a position on important educational questions relating to right and wrong, knowledge and epistemology, and freedom and constraint. All of these issues will be dealt with in greater detail in myth #3 of this chapter.

Why Teach Philosophy to Children?

FOR THE SAME REASONS AS FOR ADULTS

Children do not occupy an entirely separate conceptual space to adults, and if the case can be made that adults benefit from the study of philosophy, then the same arguments surely apply to children. If adults can use philosophical reasoning to address some of life's more intangible questions, then why can't children? If adults can learn to reason more effectively, and hence think more clearly and critically, then why can't children? And the sooner the better.

In spite of the apparent value of philosophy to both life and learning, it has struggled to find a regular place in the contemporary curriculum, finding only a scattered presence within some, mostly primary, schools, and often in a variety of different forms such as via Philosophy for Children (P4C), and through the Philosophy foundation. It is also available as a specific A-level, and has a limited part to play within the Religious Studies GCSE – both of which are clearly elective in nature. The case for a more general inclusion of philosophy in school curricula is well made by Bini *et al.* (2009). They rightly note the following.

> Almost every country in the world includes philosophy in its curriculum. Philosophy is recommended for inclusion in national curricula by the UN – and, in particular, by UNESCO – because of its importance in creating the conditions for a free and democratic society, and because of the role it plays in developing the general capabilities of citizens. (Bini *et al.* 2009, Part 3)

More specifically, they conclude that philosophy in schools brings both academic and social benefits. The following points summarise some of their arguments.

FOR ACADEMIC BENEFITS

While philosophy can contribute positively to most general educational capacities, the evidence suggests that there are specific benefits that accrue from philosophical study in schools. As previously mentioned, the cluster of important mental activities that might be called *thinking skills* – developing, analysing and criticising arguments; problem solving; decision making; critical reasoning – are engendered by philosophy inquiry. Similarly, *creativity* is also significantly enhanced by philosophical studies. After all, the ability to be creative is fundamentally tied to intellectual flexibility, to the capacity to generate new ideas and new ways of seeing, and to the ability to be open-minded and adaptable. Importantly, the improvement in these two general capabilities is not just of a passing, theoretical interest. Research has shown that such improvements produce the most direct of educational benefits: better all-around academic performance (Topping and Trickey 2007).

FOR SOCIAL BENEFITS

One domain of philosophy is ethics, and it is important that students as well as teachers learn the ability to justify their ethical decisions, as will be discussed in Chapter 13. In the long term, citizens who are more able to think deeply about ethical issues are more likely to create a just society; after all, a complex problem often requires a complex solution, not a simple, unreflected knee-jerk response. In addition to fostering ethical behaviour, the study of philosophy in the form of 'communities of inquiry' also enhances teamwork and social competence. Debating issues, listening to opposing arguments and responding reasonably, agreeing upon conclusions and new lines of discussion, all add to students' social skills and coop-erative abilities. Finally, philosophy has a significant role to play in civics and citizen-ship, in that it helps to set out possible parameters of a 'good' society, as philosophy has tried to do since the time of Socrates. As is rightly noted, philosophy does not simply teach what 'democracy' is, or where it came from; by studying concepts such as justice, freedom, truth and rights, philosophy actually teaches students to *be* democratic (Bini *et al.* 2009, Part 2). Improving social capacities in these areas not only leads to better students, it also leads to a better society.

In summary, the reasons for studying philosophy are compelling. It is a subject that allows us to address some of life's more difficult questions, and to address them with clarity and perception. It allows educators to draw more informed conclusions about what mass schooling is, and about what kind of teacher we want to be. Finally, given the opportunity, it can be of great benefit to students: intellectually, academically and socially. All in all then, it's pretty useful.

Myth #2 *'Education' Is Self-Evident; We Don't Need Philosophy to Explain it*

> *Some things don't need any deep explanation, and education is one of them. It's all pretty simple: young people don't know very much, and if we want them to grow up to be useful, then someone has to teach them – someone who knows more than they do. You don't need a 'philosophical perspective'. You just need a classroom, a teacher, and a curriculum.*

This myth is fairly easy to debunk. If education was as straightforward as is implied here, we most certainly wouldn't have spent 2500 years arguing about it, and it would be a six-week certificate course, and not a four-year university degree. As it turns out, education has been one of the great topics of philosophical debate, one that has allowed the main theoretical approaches to do intellectual battle with each other.

Addressing 'the Content' of Philosophy

At this stage, it might appear as if philosophy is mostly about learning to think clearly, and then using that clarity to address a range of somewhat abstract questions, questions that the empirical sciences are largely unable to answer. While these are certainly an important part of the discipline, it tells only part of the story. There must also be something to think about – a body of knowledge, a range of 'stuff' to know. After all, it is surely important to gain knowledge of the arguments that have already been employed and assessed by previous thinkers, or we'll spend our time continually re-inventing the philosophical wheel.

There are a number of ways that this task could be managed when specifically addressing the philosophy of education. First, this could be approached by examining education through a series of topics – education and justice, education and language, education and governance, education and knowledge. In some ways, this entire book is structured in this manner; however, it works less well when trying to understand, in the broadest possible terms, what 'education' is.

A second approach could be to address some of the most influential texts within educational philosophy – *The Nicomachean Ethics* (Aristotle 1980), *Some Thoughts Concerning Education* (Locke 1970), *Education as Initiation* (Peters 1964), *Culture and Anarchy* (Arnold 1963), *Deschooling Society* (Illich 1973); philosophers could argue over this list for years. However, the central purpose of unpacking each of these texts would be to try to understand the different ideas supporting each. Why not just go directly to those ideas and divide the field up accordingly?

The third approach does precisely that, and it is the strategy adopted here. This section of the chapter addresses a series of approaches to the philosophy of education, approaches that largely define the history of the ways in which education has been conceptualised. This is neither a definitive list of important approaches, nor is it a list that all philosophers would agree upon, by any means. However, it is a good enough place to start.

Each of the six philosophical approaches discussed here – Idealism, Realism, Romanticism, Pragmatism, Marxism, and Postmodernism – will be approached in the same, four-part way: what the central ideas of the position are; how those ideas have been applied to education; how those ideas affect education today; and the ways in which those ideas have been criticised.

Idealism

Idealism represents the first great Western philosophical system. It operates from the premise that, in the final analysis, reality is mental rather than physical (Winch and Gingell 2008). These ideas have their origins in the writings of Plato, who contended that life is primarily about the search for truth. However, given that truth is perfect and unchanging, it cannot lie in the material world, which is imperfect and ephemeral. Consequently, there must be another realm of existence – the ideal realm – of which our world is but an imperfect copy. Plato famously uses the *Allegory of the Cave* to make his point. He described prisoners chained in a dark cave, staring at shadows cast on a wall. The prisoners took the shadows to be reality, when in fact reality was being played out behind them, and it was only when a prisoner managed to escape their chains and turn around, that they realised the truth.

Plato regarded education as a way of escaping our chains, of casting off the illusions of our material world, the 'false reality' of our cave, and slowly learning to access the realm of ideas, the realm of truth. In *The Republic*, Plato even envisaged an education system that would produce an ideal, three-tier society (Plato 1974). The society would consist of wise rulers, Guardians, schooled in philosophy; Auxiliaries, who protected the state; and Artisans, who produce the goods required for daily life. Education then, should be tailored to the tasks required of each citizen – an early version of streaming – with the brightest and the best given the intellectual skills to 'escape their chains', grasp the eternal truths present in the realm of ideas, and hence govern within justice.

Along with its influence on many later philosophers, such as Berkley, Kant and Hegel, the central legacy of idealism within modern education is the argument that the primary focus should be upon those things of lasting value; the great truths that animate our existence; the fundamental intellectual disciplines upon which all our knowledge is founded. According to this logic, schools should not be about the provision of mere skills, technical abilities that come and go. Such competences give no insights into truth, and they add nothing to our development as worthwhile and self-realised citizens. Schooling for the workplace is no schooling at all.

Idealism has been subject to a number of criticisms (Ozmon and Craver 2009). It has certainly struggled to find a place within an education system so heavily geared towards social and economic utility. Indeed, Idealism could almost act as a metaphor for philosophy's wider struggle for inclusion in the contemporary curriculum. *Does it help with double-entry bookkeeping? No? Then no thanks.* However, Idealism's problems are as much theoretical as they are practical. In addition to the criticism that idealists have produced absolutely no evidence of the existence of a parallel ideal realm, it is also seen as an inherently conservative philosophical approach, in that it continually refers to 'timeless' and 'unchanging' ideals. More importantly perhaps, it has also been criticised as elitist; after all, arguably this kind of education is only relevant to future 'wise rulers'. Is it really relevant to someone who just wants to learn how to fix motors?

Realism

Standing in fairly stark contrast to Plato's Idealism, is the realism of his most famous pupil, Aristotle. Rather than regarding reality as being constituted within the world of ideas, Aristotle contended that we actually inhabit a material order of reality, one comprised of physical objects, and one that we can come to know and construct knowledge about (Harrison-Barbet 2001). To put it more simply, there isn't some special other place; this world is all we have, it exists independently of our thoughts; there is a physical reality we can come to understand.

Part of Aristotle's greatness lies in the ways that he translated his observations of our 'real' physical world into categories of knowledge, categories we now take for granted, and which are still an integral part of our curriculum. As a reflection of the realist belief in a logical and orderly universe, the realist curriculum has emphasised the practical study of the physical world, with a particular focus on mathematics and the various natural sciences. Furthermore, this information is to be transmitted from teacher to pupil in systematic and standardised way. There is little room within this model for the Socratic method of teaching, relying as it does upon dialogue and mutual intellectual exploration. Rather, the realist teacher is required to know the content of each of the various subject areas, and to be able to pass that information on to students.

Arguably, the repeated calls for the 'three Rs' are part of the realist imperative within modern education; education has to be practical and useful to be deemed valid. By extension, the recent drive to vocational education can probably be traced to the same logic, although this is by no means what Aristotle had in mind.

> Aristotle was particularly derogatory about using education for any extrinsic or instrumental purposes and it is here that some of his aristocratic prejudices come out most clearly. Vocational education was fit only for the lower classes, for the Greek citizen it was the idea of education as making you a fuller and more cultured person that counted. (Hobson 2001, 18–19)

Realism has had its fair share of critics. While initially standing in opposition to Idealism, those disagreeing with this position also came from the ranks of Romanticism, and then latterly Postmodernism. The most obvious criticism of Realism is that it has spawned a model of schooling that is too instrumental, and too focused upon ephemeral skills associated with the perceived needs of the employment market at any given moment, to the exclusion of more important and long-lasting types of knowledge. Also, postmodernists in particular have criticised Realism for its belief that objective truth is out there, just waiting to be uncovered; the contrary position being that all knowledge is ultimately socially constructed. This debate will be discussed at length in Chapter 14.

Romanticism

With its emphasis on reason and objectivity, the Enlightenment project of the eighteenth century was not without its critics. Leaving aside those who resented the rise of modern civil and political rights, a disparate group of artists, writers and thinkers also bemoaned what they saw as the destructive and homogenising effects of the growing obsession with reason. These 'Romantics' stressed the importance of emotion, creativity, and intuition to the human spirit, rather than the soulless predictability of the new scientific model. Romanticism valued subjectivity over objectivity, expression over analysis, and nature over society.

The first of the great romantics was Rousseau, who was instrumental in shaping the 'childhood as innocence' model discussed in Chapter 6. One of his most important books was *Emile*, and in this text he pointed to the corrupting influence of society: 'Everything is good as it comes from the hands of the Maker of the world but degenerates once it gets into the hands of man' (Rousseau 1956, 1). Rousseau's revolutionary idea was that children were to be best served not by learning through oppressive and relentless regimentation, but by encouraging the full development of their natural, untainted spirit.

These ideas have been incredibly influential. In one part, they were instrumental in the development of the free schooling movement, such as *Summerhill* (Neill 1962). Such schools abandoned traditional notions of discipline and curriculum, and instead allowed children to follow their own intellectual paths. Far more significantly, Rousseau's ideas were pivotal to the rise of *Progressivism* in education, a 'child-centred' model of learning, one that dominated the first half of the twentieth century (Darling and Nordenbo 2003), and one that could equally well have been given a section to itself.

Criticisms of Educational Romanticism are numerous. For example, given the greater contemporary understanding of the social construction of childhood, upon what is Rousseau's model of the natural, innocent child based, other than an historical fiction? Also, in an era that increasingly expects measurable outcomes from the schooling process, romantically inspired Progressive education, where children are allowed to explore for exploration's sake, has – rightly or wrongly – come to be viewed as an unsupportable luxury.

Pragmatism

Pragmatism is generally regarded as an American philosophy, and is normally associated with the late-nineteenth-century work of James, and follows the logic that theorising is a pointless activity, in and of itself. The only relevance that theorising can have is when it is converted into the solution of concrete intellectual problems. A philosopher must ask: what is the practical worth of a particular idea? If the answer is 'nothing whatsoever', then the issue should be of no philosophical interest.

In relation to education, the main pragmatic philosopher is Dewey, probably the most influential of all twentieth-century writers in the field. His wide-ranging ideas are difficult to summarise, but – in contrast to Plato's Idealism – he built his theories on the pragmatic belief that ideas are only of value in terms of their consequences for human existence. Many of Dewey's educational ideas were centred upon the notion of growth, and the belief that education is not simply preparation for life, but is part of life. Consequently, when deciding on the subject matter of education, student interests should be regarded as more important than a simple calculus of future social needs. Students must be shaped as active participants in their own education, in contrast to dominant, authoritarian models of teaching.

Just as Rousseau influenced Progressivism, so too did Dewey, although in a different way. Winch and Gingell (2008, 167–8) note the following.

> The Rousseau variant emphasises the importance of the individual in constructing his own cognitive world, while the Dewey variant stresses the role of the group in doing so. The former strand appeals to the work of Piaget while the latter appeals to

the social constructivism that is (questionably) associated with the work of the psychologist Vygotsky. These tensions have practical effects on pedagogic strategies. While Rousseauian progressives emphasise individual learning at a pace chosen by the learner, Deweyans stress group and project work.

Criticisms of pragmatic approaches to education have largely centred upon the shortcomings of Progressivism, an approach Dewey himself found fault with (e.g. classroom 'freedom' for its own sake). It has also been suggested that for Dewey's educational vision to be realised, the almost utopian skill and knowledge sets required of teachers exceed the reach of our current education system, particularly given the ongoing unwillingness of Western governments to fund education to the levels that would be required (Ozmon and Craver 2009).

Marxism

As has been discussed in Chapter 1, Marxism has been highly influential within educational theory. In the final analysis, this philosophical approach is premised upon significant concerns over social and economic inequality. Marxism splits the social world into two opposing halves – those who have power, and those upon whom power is exercised – and it is this essential division that underlies all social structures, practices and forms of organisation. While Marxism eventually morphed into Critical Theory, a more subtle explanation of how society works, both are still principally concerned with issues of inequality.

Education is deemed by Marxists/Critical Theorists to play a crucial role in the ongoing success of the class system. Students aren't just educated; they are educated for particular social roles and outcomes, outcomes that are predetermined by social class. The system might look like a meritocracy, but this is an illusion: most of us end up in exactly the same social place as our parents. As such, schools aren't really about education; they are about social reproduction. That is, in practical terms, education isn't a vehicle for structural change, or personal social mobility. Schools are about subtly legitimating the contention that while you were given the opportunity to move up, you chose not to take it, or lacked the capacity to do so.

The effects of Marxism/Critical Theory can still be felt within contemporary education. Although a variety of philosophical approaches retain a commitment to social equity, it is generally Critical Theory that keeps this concern front and centre. Other writers influenced by Marxism also remain a potent voice within educational theory. For example, Freire (1970), in *Pedagogy of the Oppressed*, examines the way in which the lack of adequate education – and in particular, lack of basic literacy skills – has been used as a mechanism of social and political disempowerment for poor people. Although he was writing largely about South America, his arguments have wider application and significance.

In the past couple of decades, Marxist/Critical Theoretical approaches have been subject to considerable criticism. Indeed, much of Part II of this book can be seen in this light. Two central problems can be pointed to here. The first is that this approach necessarily regards the exercise of power as coercive; indeed the whole of our society and culture is regarded as a complex by-product of the rich exercising their power over the poor. Theoretical approaches based upon governance downplay the coercive aspects of power, focusing instead upon its productive potential. The second problem is that Marxism/Critical Theory is something of a Master Discourse, an explanatory model that tries to explain absolutely everything within a single framework. Postmodernism in particular has criticised this tendency as being reductionist; that is, it contends that the real world is far more complex than the one described by Marxism.

Postmodernism

Towards the end of the eighteenth century, the Enlightenment, with its emphasis on human reason, had given birth to the era of *Modernity*. For the next 200 years, society was underpinned by the logic of Modernism – truth, progress, objectivity – perhaps best exemplified by the rise of the scientific method. However, from the 1980s onwards, there was a growing belief that the Enlightenment project had failed in its goals, and that perhaps it was all rather more complicated than this. The resulting postmodern approach questioned the validity of singular, grand-narrative explanations of the world, the assumption that society was inevitably getting better, and the belief that socially neutral knowledge was possible (Lyotard 1984a).

With regards to education, Postmodernism shares many of Critical Theory's concerns over equity, but rejects the possibility of a single explanatory model, or even the possibility of agreement over what 'equity' might look like.

> No longer, for example, can the call: 'a free and equal education for all' provide a universal rallying point. Instead, we have a collection of quite separate and isolated groups often with conflicting or even mutually exclusive beliefs and goals . . . feminists, homosexuals, environmentalist, neo-Nazis, Christian and Islamic fundamentalists . . . It is very hard to mount a modernist universal call for justice and truth when so many cannot agree over what these things are or indeed over whether they exist at all.
> (O'Farrell 1999, 13–14)

If Postmodernism has manifested itself within contemporary education at all, it is by a fragmenting of some of the traditional certainties within the schooling system. There is no longer deemed to be a belief in a single, ideal curriculum, as with the old notion of the great liberal education, where the education of the best was the best education. Likewise, there has been a rejection of unitary models of truth and value; previously marginalised voices have started to be heard in subjects like history, literature and social science. Also, there are now multiple pathways through education, rather than just a linear filtering system that simply pushed the unworthy out at regular intervals.

Although the most recent of the philosophical approaches, Postmodernism has not been immune from significant criticism. Postmodernism's refusal to give singular, simple explanations has been used against it, in that it is often characterised as overly complex, muddled and incoherent. Furthermore, following on from Critical Theory as it did, Postmodernism has been accused of being apolitical, and lacking commitment to social and educational change. The argument here is that by refusing to stand for a particular version of freedom and equity, it is in danger of not standing for anything at all.

In summary, the six approaches addressed here – Idealism, Realism, Romanticism, Pragmatism, Marxism and Postmodernism – are just some of the philosophies that continue to give shape to our understanding of education. There are others that could have legitimately claimed a place here. In addition to approaches such as Progressivism and Existentialism, there are a number of philosophies that deal explicitly with issues of gender, cultural diversity and indigeneity, as well as a wealth of non-Western philosophies that are often overlooked by Western universities (as will be discussed in Chapter 14). Needless to say, it is in the nature of the beast that some philosophers will be irritated by the absences here, let alone the depictions of those that have been included. Unfortunately, there is no 'perfect' selection.

Let us return to the myth that began this section: we don't need philosophy to explain education. Rather than regarding mass schooling as some kind of self-evident, finished product, philosophy enables us to trace many of the ideas that have animated education over the past 2500 years. This begins with the initial idealist proposition that education should be directed towards uncovering the great truths that underwrite existence, to the subsequent realist emphasis of the more practical aspects of learning, manifest today in the calls for the three Rs. The eighteenth century gave birth to romantic notions of childhood innocence, and naturalistic ideas of education, which themselves formed part of later pragmatic approaches, with the positing of children as active participants in their own learning. By the twentieth century, more critical theories of mass schooling focused on the role of education in the reproduction of social inequality, concerns echoed by postmodern philosophers, but without any of the simple causal frameworks, or one-line solutions.

All of these philosophies – old and new – continue to play a role in shaping contemporary education: in shaping curriculum documents and informing classroom practice, in stimulation debates about policy and direction, and in providing the substance for irate editorials in our newspapers. By grasping how these philosophies work, and by understanding their strengths and weaknesses, we are all the more equipped to participate in this crucial process.

Myth #3 *Teachers Don't Need a 'Personal Philosophy of Education'*

Most jobs don't feel the need to assert the necessity for any kind of underlying philosophy. Most simply have specific goals and requirements; if you meet those, you've done your job, and if you don't, you haven't. In the final analysis, teaching is the same; if the students learn, you've done your job... all this talk of philosophy is just there to make the profession sound more profound than it actually is.

In truth, the vast majority of experienced teachers understand that being good at what they do involves continually reflecting upon all elements of their professional life, and that the end point of this ongoing process of reflection is the development of a personal philosophy of education. Those teachers understand that their profession requires far more than a robotic transmission of curricula, far more than a series of piecemeal strategies and practices, all cobbled together to make the classroom slightly more interesting, and the information sink in slightly quicker. Successful teaching requires a coherent underpinning logic, a comprehensive, rigorous, profound, and stable conceptual and practical foundation. As Grasha (1996, 92) states:

> Developing a teaching style is not about selecting particular methods from a bag of teaching tricks. Our teaching styles, like scholarship, should be based upon a conceptual base that forms our philosophy of teaching. This philosophy of teaching acts like a roadmap and helps guide our thoughts, behaviours, the selection of instructional techniques, and our general outlook on who we are and what we want to become as teachers. *Without an explicit philosophy of teaching, our teaching styles are hollow.*

Developing a Personal Philosophy of Education

... ISN'T ONLY ABOUT PHILOSOPHY

The term 'personal philosophy of education' can be something of a misnomer. In this instance, the word 'philosophy' covers far more ground than that relating solely and specifically to the academic discipline of philosophy. As has been discussed in previous chapters, contemporary teaching is a complex, multidisciplinary profession, and teachers are now required to master the application of a range of different knowledges within their daily classroom life. For example, teachers are expected to have grasped a number of theories of teaching and learning, anything from the Operant Conditioning of Skinner (1938) through to the Social Constructivism of Vigotski (1978), and then have drawn conclusions about the utility of such ideas to their own professional practice. Likewise, teachers will have reasoned opinions about the ethics and the effectiveness of different approaches to classroom management, from the laissez-faire 'Freeschooling' of Neill (1962), to the Assertive Discipline of Canter and Canter (1992). Teachers will also develop specific ideas about how to best shape their school-based identity and its relationship to students, from the charismatic, total involvement of Kohl (1967), to the detached, cautious professionalism of Woodhouse and Woodhouse (2012).

All of these knowledges and practices – and the ensuing decisions made about their validity, effectiveness and personal applicability – even though they are not explicitly connected to the discipline of philosophy, still form part of a teacher's personal philosophy of education. That said, it should also be pointed out that neither are they entirely disconnected from philosophy either. All of them, to varying degrees, are based upon different philosophical foundations, whether it be, for example, Romanticism in the case of Neill (as discussed in myth #2 of this chapter), or Pragmatism for Kohl, and the lessons to be learned from his approach to teaching disadvantaged youth in Harlem, New York.

PUTTING 'PERSONALITY' INTO A PERSONAL PHILOSOPHY

Differing approaches to teaching are also shaped by more personal issues than simply whether a given individual is more convinced by the philosophy of Rousseau than that of Dewey. Arguably, the personality, character and capacities of each teacher have an important role to play in shaping an educational philosophy. Teachers become experts at playing to their own strengths, and developing a professional philosophy that can incorporate these strengths seamlessly and efficiently. Some people become great teachers because they have extraordinary personal empathy, and they can translate that empathy into welcoming, nurturing and pastoral learning environments (what Apps (1991), in his famous typology of teaching styles, called 'a gardener'). Other effective teachers possess immense energy and enthusiasm, and they can infuse that enthusiasm into their pupils. Others still structure enjoyable and productive classroom cultures that employ humour and laughter as their fundamental currency.

In each case, a professional philosophy is likely to develop, at least in part, based upon pre-existing zones of comfort and confidence for each individual teacher. This is not to say, for example, that only teachers who are funny, and comfortable in the use of humour, can develop a teaching philosophy with laughter as a cornerstone, but the evidence suggests that such teachers are likely to find the process far more straightforward, and less vulnerable to catastrophic miscalculation, than those for whom humour is something of a foreign land (Booth-Butterfield and Booth-Butterfield, 1991; Wanzer *et al.* 2010).

While these first two factors shaping a personal philosophy of education don't necessarily have anything directly to do with the academic discipline of philosophy itself, the remaining three do. First, philosophical choices are made regarding preferred approaches to teaching practices; second, philosophical conclusions are drawn about what we think we are accomplishing when we teach, which in turn can affect how we manage our professional responsibilities; and finally, philosophy has a significant role to play in reaching wider conclusions about aspects of mass schooling and the role it plays in contemporary society. We will now take these in turn.

A PERSONAL PHILOSOPHY OF INSTRUCTION

There is no single, perfect way to teach. Successful educators are always very sensitive to the pedagogic contexts in which they find themselves, often varying their approaches according to audience, subject matter, ability level, location, class size and even time of day. While bearing this flexibility in mind, most teachers also tend to have preferred methods for their tuition, methods which work well for them, and which they can justify, both professionally and philosophically. Many of these methods have long and successful histories, and are now axiomatic in the way we educate. They can extend, for example, from the participatory, dialogic philosophies of the Socratic Method and Dewey's Educational Facilitation, through to the more didactic, authoritarian approach of the Aristotelian Lecture.

The ancient Greek philosopher Socrates famously declared, 'All I know is that I know nothing', and proceeded to (falsely) demonstrate this when engaged in philosophical discussion, by asking a series of seemingly naïve questions. Rather than simply stating 'the truth' to his students, he would lead them into logical self-contradiction – much like leaving a trail of breadcrumbs to the edge of a cliff – thereby persuading those students to teach themselves, to change their *own* minds. In a somewhat similar vein, Dewey (1916) contends that students should not be passive spectators to their own education, but rather that knowledge can only be gained by active effort on their behalf. The principal role of teachers should therefore be to *facilitate* learning, by 'moving education from a delivery of static knowledge to a dialogical relationship where knowledge is co-created' (Gregory 2006, 99). Arguably, such methodologies – teaching through questioning, and latterly through facilitation – can form an effective methodological scaffolding for a contemporary philosophy of instruction, for those who wish to employ them. However, they are far from the only valid choices.

At the other end of the participatory continuum is 'the lecture' – still the practical bedrock of contemporary education, both at school, and most definitely at university. Having its origins in the teaching practices of Aristotle, it is based in the fundamental premise that given the vast amounts of knowledge in the world (even in Ancient Greece), some people know more about it than others. While 'Socratic' conversations might have their uses, they also have significant limitations, particularly where, by definition, one side of that conversation hasn't got much of a clue as to what they're talking about. Obviously, the *'Talk from the front, I know stuff, and you don't'* approach to teaching has some inherent flaws (Griffin 2006); however, it can also be a perfectly appropriate philosophy when done well. Some people *do* know a lot more than you on particular subjects – surely it would be bizarrely arrogant and anti-intellectual to think otherwise. Most university students at some point will sit through a lecture where they are not in dialogue with the person behind the podium, and yet an engaging, thoughtful speaker makes the subject matter come alive, where two hours just fly past, and where they leave the lecture theatre buzzing with ideas and new knowledge. This is an example of where a particular philosophy of educational instruction works perfectly, given both its delivery and its context. Unfortunately, most university students have also sat through lectures where, after only 10 minutes, they wanted to stab themselves in the eye with a pencil.

Obviously, these are by no means the only options to choose from when shaping a personal philosophy of teaching practice; however, they are three of the most familiar, and the most popular. Importantly, in addition to making decisions about how to actually teach, a personal philosophy of instruction may well also include making decisions on how the learning spaces should be organised, which might emphasise support and pastoral care, or hierarchy and structure, or fun and enjoyment. It might also include how to use curricula material, whether as the sole source of classroom study, or a general framework for learning, or just a set of vaguely useful suggestions. Finally, it might also include making decisions about the primary goal of that instruction, which could be directed towards generalised learning, or an enjoyment of the subject, or just the passing of exams. This final set of concerns is of particular importance.

THE POLITICS OF A PERSONAL PHILOSOPHY OF TEACHING

As discussed in myth #2 of this chapter, education has been conceptualised in a number of different ways. However, the six theories dealt with there are of greater significance than simply offering some generalised abstract framework for understanding what education 'does'; they also offer a vocabulary of ways in which teachers can explain – to themselves – what it is that they actually do. In accomplishing this task, these theories can help teachers form a personal macro-philosophy of education, and thereby chart their way through their careers in a way that sits comfortably with their beliefs. Some examples might be useful here.

It could be that we find ourselves agreeing with Plato, that the important parts of schooling are those that teach us the deepest forms of knowledge. As a consequence of this, perhaps we are prepared to spend less of our time 'teaching for the test', and instead focus our educational practices more upon the great underlying ideas, the timeless truths of the human condition, even if the people hiring at local businesses think they are a waste of time. Alternatively, we might think that Aristotle's ideas have more to offer – or at least, the modern, instrumentalist version of them – and believe that education's first responsibility is to be practical and useful. Perhaps 'teaching for the test' is less intellectually defensible, but still worth doing anyway. After all, the students who pass that test are more likely to get a job, contribute to society, do useful things; perhaps this ought to be a teacher's first responsibility. Finally, perhaps we have a sneaking suspicion that Marx is right, and that mass schooling is simply a clever device for legitimately funnelling working-class kids into working-class jobs. If so, maybe we should spend part of our career, or even all our career, working in the type of school where we can help some of those kids change their stars. As can be seen from these three brief examples, whether we realise it or not, teaching is necessarily a 'political' act. Philosophy helps us to figure out where we stand.

OTHER ELEMENTS OF PHILOSOPHY

Teachers with a sophisticated professional philosophy are also likely to have taken philosophical positions on educational issues emerging from fields beyond the specifically educational, such as ethics and epistemology. For example, when teachers are faced with an ethical dilemma, what kind of framework do they use for solving that dilemma? Do they do what they know a 'good' person would do? Do they follow the rulebook, even if it means the majority of students will suffer as a consequence? The answers to questions like these can be found within the field of normative ethics, dealt with at length in Chapter 13. Also, when we look at the content of the curriculum, do we regard it to be the truth? Is what we teach in our history lessons *really* what happened, or is it just the viewpoint of the powerful, and the victorious? Answers to questions like these can be found within the field of (postcolonial) epistemology, dealt with at length in Chapter 14. Good teachers have well-reasoned opinions about such important issues, and those opinions form yet a further part of their personal philosophy of education.

In conclusion, being good at teaching involves continually reflecting upon all elements of one's professional life. The end-point of this ongoing process of reflection is the development of a personal philosophy of education. Importantly, and conversely, a personal philosophy of education is not *just* an end-point, rather it can act as a guide to the choices made within in a career, not simply be the nominal outcome *of* those choices. As Grasha (1996) stated at the start of this myth, successful teaching is not about having the biggest bag of pedagogic tricks; it is about developing a philosophical roadmap that can guide us through the complexities of what is arguably the most challenging of all the professions.

Conclusion

If we are to make sense of mass schooling, the central purpose of this book, then a solid understanding of philosophy is just as important as a good grasp of history and social science. The study of philosophy offers us a lot. It provides us with the intellectual tools to answer some of the most important questions of life; furthermore, it allows us to address those questions in a clear and organised way. This clarity of thought is not then limited in its usefulness to the realm of esoteric inquiry. Such acquired skills spill over into daily life, and into the reasoned thinking required by all other intellectual disciplines, including education.

Philosophy also helps us plan for our educational future. Our system of mass schooling has, hidden within its fabric, significant traces of many of the various philosophies that have dominated education at different times, in different places, and for different reasons. This is of interest, not only for abstract, historical reasons, but also because understanding how these philosophies work, and which parts of them are still relevant to us, allows us to explore the possibilities of what schooling could be, and to work towards constructing a system based upon solid and viable conceptual foundations.

Finally, here are two final assertions regarding the relation of philosophy to mass schooling: first, philosophy has a lot to offer in the education of children, and more space should be found for it in the curriculum. Second, teaching is a profession that requires significant reflection, and philosophy helps teachers to do that more systematically, and more productively, than any other discipline.

ETHICS, DISABILITY AND THE LAW

13

This chapter address one of the most important areas of philosophy – ethics – and uses it to examine aspects of the role of the law within education. Of all the areas of philosophy, more has probably been written about ethics, and over a longer period, than any other. In addition, all cultures are structured around a fundamental ethical system: the law. However, irrespective of their importance, both subjects are currently notable for their lowly status within the teacher education curriculum.

Myth #1 Understanding ethics doesn't help you to be a good teacher.
'Knowing about ethics isn't a crucial part of being a good teacher. Teachers are there to teach a curriculum, not engage in complex ethical decision-making'.
Teaching is an ethically challenging profession. By having a solid grasp of the strengths and weaknesses of different ethical approaches – such as virtue ethics, consequentialism, and Kantian ethics – teachers are more able to make informed moral choices, and hence contribute to a more just schooling system. This is particularly important when it comes to issues such as disability and inclusion.

Myth #2 Unlike ethics, the law is a straightforward system of right and wrong; everyone agrees what it is, and what it does. *'The law is the clear expression of our most important rules. There is no serious dispute over its purpose, or its objectivity'.* On the contrary, our system of law is complex, multilayered and highly contested. There is only limited agreement on how the law can be conceptualised, from being an extension of 'natural' rights and wrongs, to simply a political tool for the wealthy. Arguably, and somewhat ironically, right and wrong have only a limited relationship with the law.

Myth #3 We have an ethical education system; it does not discriminate. *'We've come a long way from the days when racial and sexual* *discrimination were part of the system – discrimination is a thing of the past, particularly in schools'*. While it's true that we have laws to protect a wide range of categories of individuals from discrimination – and this is a good thing – these laws are far from perfect. Schools are still the site of more subtle forms of discrimination, especially regarding disability. Just because we have laws against discrimination doesn't mean they will apply to you; even if they apply to you, you still may not be protected. Welcome to the law.

Introduction

Having set out in Chapter 12 what philosophy is, what it can accomplish, and some of the main approaches that have been adopted within the discipline, this chapter will examine one particular area of philosophy – ethics – and then use it as a way of unpacking a second important area within contemporary education: the law. As will be seen in this chapter, these two sets of knowledge are both important in their own right, but are also closely and crucially related and, at times, intermeshed. Certainly, both of these are vital to the modern school, and it would be a foolhardy teacher indeed who regarded these topics as unrelated to their professional conduct or responsibilities. However, both appear to have a limited place within teacher-education curricula, and the vast majority of teachers would be hard pressed to explain the main elements of a philosophy of ethics, or demonstrate a working knowledge of those parts of the law that affect what they do every single day.

It is probably fair to say that people generally mean three different things when they talk about ethics. The first usage is synonymous with the term morals; the second is a set of principles, most often derived from moral values; the third is a body of academic knowledge, something you study at university. Interestingly, the vast majority of university study into ethics now concerns what is referred to as *Meta-Ethics*: 'questions *about* morality, not *of* morality' (Cooper 1998, 3). To put it another way, whereas the philosophy of ethics has always been devoted to finding the best way to live a 'good' life, in recent years academic focus has fallen upon the nature of moral claims themselves. Just what is a moral claim? Are there objective moral facts? And why do we bother being moral at all?

Ethics and Teaching

Important though these questions are, they won't necessarily help us decide how we ought to act; how we can be ethical teachers. However, the other dominant type of ethics – *normative ethics* – may do just that. For most of its long history as a discipline, ethics has sought the means to determine right from wrong, with both validity and consistency. Myth #1 addresses the assertion that the relationship between teaching and ethics is a straightforward one, and one that needn't be worried about too much. Arguably, this is incorrect for two vital reasons. First, ethics itself is not a straightforward matter, in that it is not simple to define what we mean when we say something is wrong (i.e. is that just someone's opinion, or is it more than that?), and there is significant philosophical disagreement about how to structure any overarching framework for ethical conduct. There are a number of different 'normative' ethical systems that attempt to give consistent answers about how we should act, and what kind of people we should be, and each guides our conduct as teachers in different ways.

Second, teaching is inherently an ethically complex discipline. Any profession that deals with the allocation of resources and the distribution of life-chances, with the conduct of children and the organisation of punishment, with the valorisation of some identities and the marginalising of others, with normality and difference, with deciding whose history gets taught and whose culture gets to count, with deciding who deserves a second chance and who doesn't – and all on a daily basis – needs to be acutely aware of the mechanics of ethical decision-making.

Ethics and the Law

The link between these two areas is a fairly obvious one. It is often held that the law is simply right and wrong, set out in a legislative form; that our most important ethical principles are distilled into codified social rules, rules reinforced by social obedience and organised punishment. After all, surely we all know what the law is, and approximately how it works; there's no great mystery to the law. Myth #2 addresses these assertions.

First, our Common Law legal system is only one of several possibilities; other cultures and nations organise their mechanisms for the buttressing of right and wrong quite differently. We have an intricate mix of statute and judge-made law, a hierarchy of courts, and a wide range of different legal areas. All of these impact directly on how the law operates, and more specifically, how schools work and how teachers are required to do their job.

Second, there is considerable disagreement over exactly what the law is. Is it simply natural laws of right and wrong applied to humans? Or is it the mechanism by which those with power get to tell us what we can do and what we can't, based upon their own self-interest; for example, which acts deserve significant punishment (robbery), and which generally do not (tax avoidance) and, where punishment is to be applied, what that punishment should be.

Discrimination

One significant area of law that ties directly to ethics is that of discrimination. The question of whether it is right to treat someone differently on the basis of a given attribute is one that is of particular importance within education. Given that twenty-first-century schools are awash with laws, rules, regulations, policy documents, ethical guidelines and codes of conduct, myth #3 suggests that it is inconceivable they could be the site of anything as morally reprehensible as discrimination.

The evidence actually paints a far more complex picture of discrimination under British law. Though primarily concerning the Equality Act 2010, there also exists a wide range of other pertinent legislation, covering a range of different, although sometimes overlapping, areas. The Equality Act deals with both direct and indirect discrimination, harassment and victimisation. We will now define these terms.

Direct discrimination involves overtly directly denying rights to someone based upon some given attribute – 'No you can't go to school there; you're in a wheelchair'.

Indirect discrimination (which may, or may not be, inadvertent) involves denying rights to someone by setting up a prerequisite condition with which they can't comply – 'Of course you can go to school there; as long as you can get your wheelchair up the stairs'.

Harassment involves unpleasant or bullying behaviour which creates an untenable environment – 'Let's keep chaining that kid's wheelchair to the stair, until she gets the message'.

Victimisation occurs when a person is treated unfavourably because of something they have done in relation to the act – 'Because I made a fuss about having my wheelchair chained to the stairs, teachers are now failing me in my subjects'.

However, there is more to the legislation that this, as there also appear to be mechanisms within those very same laws – special measures (loopholes) – that effectively permit discrimination to continue as before. As is often the case, the devil is in the detail or, more specifically, in the exemptions.

To summarise, the three myths to be dealt with in this chapter are as follows.

Myth #1 Understanding ethics doesn't help you to be a good teacher.
Myth #2 Unlike ethics, the law is a straightforward system of right and wrong; everyone agrees what it is, and what it does.
Myth #3 We have an ethical education system; it does not discriminate.

Myth #1 *Understanding Ethics Doesn't Help You to Be a Good Teacher*

Complex ethical decision-making isn't a necessary part of being a good teacher – after all, we're not philosophers. You just need to do your job, keep your head down, and stay away from anything controversial. We're not being asked whether or not we should have euthanasia, or the death penalty, or whether our troops should go to war. We are simply being asked to teach a curriculum.

Even educators with the most simplistic understanding of their own discipline would have trouble accepting this myth at face value. Teachers are acutely aware not only of the difficult ethical questions raised by our education system, but also of the complexity of the ethical choices they are asked to make personally. For example, our system of education raises a number of familiar macro-ethical questions: is it appropriate that we allow parents who can afford it to buy a better education than those that can't? Should we have 'Special Schools' for children with physical or intellectual differences, or should those children be in mainstream classes? On a more individual level, moral questions might include: should I spend part of my career teaching in a low SES school, and thereby contribute directly to educating less economically fortunate children? To what extent will I allow my own understandings of appropriately gendered conduct impinge upon my teaching? There are hundreds of questions, just like these, that teachers continually need to address. For the most part, we all bumble through the process as best we can, often without anything but the haziest of convictions that we're doing the right – ethical – thing. The point here is that it is possible to equip educators to better understand the strengths and weaknesses of the various ethical choices made. This is the substance of normative ethics.

Normative Ethics

Normative ethics seeks to provide codes of conduct, or action guides, through which any given moral choice may be assessed and directed. Three dominant normative positions will be addressed here: virtue ethics, consequentialist ethics and deontological ethics.

VIRTUE ETHICS

According to virtue ethics, in order to find 'goodness', the first place to look should be at a person's character. It is good character that best reflects and organises what we regard to be desirable, and this desirability is normally reflected in the virtues they possess, such as courage, temperance, wisdom and justice. These four are often regarded as the 'cardinal' moral virtues, however this list may also include generosity, benevolence, constancy and industry, although these are by no means fixed or agreed upon (Tannsjo 2002). The logic of virtue ethics is straightforward: if you have a moral dilemma, the correct course of action lies in what you know a good person would do.

Virtue ethics has its origins in the writings of Aristotle in the fourth century BC, principally in the *Nicomachean Ethics* (Aristotle 1980). In this text, he argues that 'the good' is the inherently worthwhile end point for all actions, and that by working towards this, we are able to achieve happiness. This approach differs from its rivals – consequentialism and deontological ethics – in a number of significant ways, the most important way being the kind of ethical questions that need to be asked. Rather than inquiring 'What is the best way to live?', virtue ethics asks 'What kind of person should I be?' This is because the kind of person you are (e.g. a virtuous person) determines how your actions are to be interpreted (i.e. good). This reverses the logic of the other approaches that assess the nature of the person based upon a prior assessment of the specific action (e.g. stealing is wrong. . . you stole. . . *ergo*, you are bad).

Virtue ethics is generally regarded as the weakest of the three approaches. First, there is no necessary agreement as to which virtues should be considered important in the formation of a virtuous person. MacIntyre (1998) notes that virtues are relative to time and place, and that identifying core virtues can be a difficult proposition. Second, there appears to be circularity in parts of the reasoning. If a virtuous person does an act, the act is therefore good. But how do we determine that a person is virtuous? Mostly because of their good acts. Finally, if a good act is one done by a virtuous person, does this mean virtuous people are incapable of bad acts, and that bad people are incapable of good acts? Or, if both good and bad people do the same acts, are the acts to be interpreted differently?

CONSEQUENTIALIST ETHICS

Consequentialism holds that moral evaluation between different courses of action should be made on the basis of a comparison of the consequences of those actions: that is, the action that brings about the best outcome is the right thing to do. The most important consequentialist position is *utilitarianism*. Harman (1977, 152) defines utilitarianism as, 'the theory that you ought always to act so as to maximise social utility, where "social utility" is simply another name for the general welfare'. The idea of utilitarianism was first developed in the eighteenth century by the British empiricist Hume, before being made fully explicit by Bentham (1988), and later in a more qualified way by Mill (1957). This theory has at its core the belief that an action is right if it is useful for increasing overall happiness; conversely an action is wrong if it decreases overall happiness.

Suppose you are confronted with a choice between two possible options. Utilitarians would argue that the correct decision is one which, when considering all relevant factors, produces the larger balance of good over bad, pleasure over pain. In this manner, according to utilitarianism, you are freed from all ethical decision-making, other than the ability to sum up the relevant components of the equation and thereby reach a conclusion. This strict form of utilitarianism – championed by Smart (1973) – is called 'act-utilitarianism'. A somewhat more sophisticated version of the theory is called 'rule-utilitarianism'. This latter approach stresses all the main points associated with act utilitarianism, but proposes that choices are more often made on the basis of rules rather than by addressing individual consequences of specific actions. In this manner, the principle of utility is maintained, but not at the level of single judgements.

Both forms of utilitarianism have also been subject to significant criticism. Williams (1972, 1973) presents three main flaws within its logic. First, he argues that its fundamental axis – happiness – is problematic, suggesting that it is only viable if it is in some way a generalisable, cumulative concept, which it does not appear to be (the 'preference satisfaction' arguments of Arrow (1978) aside). After all, a happy life may include a wide variety of moral values, all of which have little or nothing in common. The second problem is the issue of negative responsibility. Williams uses the example of having to execute one innocent person to save twenty, an unproblematic act within utilitarian thinking. He concludes that allowing a bad deed, in order to prevent a worse one, is symptomatic of utilitarians' inability to address issues such as social justice, individual fairness or personal integrity. His last criticism concerns the presumption that good can be simply defined in terms of the happiness of the greatest number. As Williams (1985, 86) states: 'If racist prejudice is directed towards a small minority by a majority that gets enough satisfaction from it, it could begin to be touch and go whether racism might not be justified'.

DEONTOLOGICAL ETHICS

Deontological ethics, otherwise called duty ethics or Kantian ethics, provides a coherent alternative to the utilitarian position. Supporters of this position argue that the consequences of an action should not enter into any judgement of whether that action is to be deemed right or wrong. Rightness or wrongness is inherent within the very nature of the act, and it should not matter what happens afterwards. Deontological ethics are almost always discussed in terms of the ideas of Kant, developed in the late eighteenth century. Kant's moral theories are complex and far-reaching, but three significant components are dealt with here.

The first addresses the centrality of the notion of duty. Kant believed that the pivotal element of morality is *motive*, and that acting in a particular manner simply because of a concern for the consequences is not to act morally. An act is only moral when an agent realises that they have a duty to act in a particular way even to their own detriment. Therefore, what happens after an act is done – crucial to the utilitarian position – is completely irrelevant.

The second element of Kant's moral theory is his most well known. Kant sought to identify a moral absolute against which all actions could be measured, stating: 'act only in accordance with that maxim through which you can at the same time will that it become a universal law' (Kant 1998, 31). This is the famous *'Categorical Imperative'*. It is immoral for someone to lie because, by lying, they are asserting that it is acceptable for everyone to lie. As this is clearly unacceptable, we must therefore always tell the truth. After all, if we didn't follow this rule, the notion of telling the truth would become incoherent.

The final notable component of Kant's moral theory is sometimes referred to as the *'Practical Imperative'*. The operative principle here is that nobody should ever be thought of simply as a means to an end, rather they should always be regarded as ends in themselves. As an almost direct rebuttal of utilitarianism, this imperative precludes the possibility overriding the rights of the one in the name of the many. The point here appears to be that fundamental issues of equity and fairness cannot be traded away for some other 'greater' good.

Two main criticisms have been raised about deontological ethics. First, if you are asked to make choices on the basis of your duties, what happens when those duties are in conflict? Ethical decisions often involve more than one moral variable. If you promise to keep a secret, but are then asked to tell the truth about some matter contained in that secret, there are conflicting moral duties here, in terms of keeping a promise, and in terms of not lying. Second, Kant did not believe in making exceptions to his moral rules. After all, such rules would be fairly pointless if, every time the circumstances proved difficult, it was possible to make an exception. Consequently, Kant would not accept that it was ever morally acceptable to lie, even if it meant preventing a much greater wrong. Certainly, there is little room in Kant's universe for sympathy or compassion.

At this point, having outlined the main elements of the three great systems of normative ethics, we can apply them to a given ethical problem to see how they stand up to closer scrutiny.

The Case of *XXXXX vs The Learning Trust*

In 2012, an 11-year-old boy (referred to as XXXXX in the Tribunal documents) with Special Educational Needs (SEN) was refused access to a school; the boy had mild cerebral palsy. The school argued that the boy's presence would compromise the education of other children or, more specifically, that the child's admission 'would be incompatible with the efficient education of other pupils at the academy' (Harris and Vasagar 2012). The boy's mother failed to see the logic in this assertion, stating:

> In what way can you possibly say (he) is going to interfere with the other children's education? He's top of the year in all his subjects, he's got GCSE Maths A* already, he's won the pan-Hackney debating challenge two years running, he's a prefect and a reading mentor at his school.

The dispute went to the Special Educational Needs and Disability Tribunal, which rejected the boy's claim. The boy's family then appealed to a higher tribunal, which sent the case back to the lower tribunal, which eventually found in the boy's favour. This case became the subject of a great deal of discussion, not only among those involved in inclusive education, but also among mainstream classroom teachers, school administrators, lawyers and the general public. The legal aspects of the case, as they relate to anti-discrimination law, will be discussed at length in myth #3; however, the case also raises a number of specifically ethical issues about teaching, which will be addressed here.

Some of the ethical issues raised are quite familiar. For instance, there is an ongoing dispute between those who question whether a mainstream education is the best choice for those children with disabilities, even those as mild as XXXXX's, and those who claim that such children have a perfect right to a place in the normal classroom, and that other children, far from being disadvantaged, will learn vital life skills of flexibility, compassion, cooperation and respect for difference. The issue of exactly whom a teacher ought to be reasonably expected to teach also caused a great deal of discussion and concern. This concern most frequently revolved around the question, 'What are the ethical responsibilities of a teacher, as related to disability?' Unfortunately, this is a question that does not lend itself to an easy answer.

Normative Ethics and the Attempted Exclusion of XXXXX

The intention now is to use the three normative positions to gain a better purchase on the decision by the school to seek XXXXX's exclusion from the classroom. The intention here is neither to applaud nor to castigate those involved; they are simply being employed here as exemplars of a broader debate.

EMPLOYING VIRTUE ETHICS

This approach produces some ambiguous results. If the teachers and administrators at the school are good people, and there is no reason to believe that they are not, then denying XXXXX access to the school was the right thing to do. It is possible that the decision reflected the presence of some of the 'cardinal' virtues of courage (in the face of a difficult decision), wisdom (for realising the decision needed to be made) and justice (in their concerns for the welfare of the other children). However, it could equally well reflect the absence of some of these virtues. It may well have been the lack of courage and sense of justice, as well as a lack of benevolence and industry, that resulted in XXXXX being told to go elsewhere. Only those involved can know for sure, which admirably demonstrates one of the great weaknesses in virtue ethics: are these good acts by good people, or bad acts by bad people? Maybe they are neither.

EMPLOYING CONSEQUENTIALIST ETHICS

It is fairly clear that the central rationale behind the decision to refuse admission to the school was largely based upon utilitarian reasoning. Under these circumstances, a utilitarian calculation was clearly made – the 'good' for disabled boy weighed against the 'good' for the many – and the maximum good (at least for the school) was deemed to lie with refusing the boy entry, although against his wishes and those of his mother. The family's lawyer makes the utilitarian nature of this calculation perfectly clear.

> When you get a school saying it's full, that's not the end of it. The child or his parents should be able to say: does our disadvantage outweigh the disadvantage to the other children? There's a balancing act that has to be struck.

This neat piece of mathematics demonstrates some of the flaws within utilitarianism. First, there appears to be little regard for issues of social justice and minority rights; if the majority feel that they will benefit from refusing the boy admission, then his normal right to enrol in the school is irrelevant. As previously mentioned, if the harmony of the classroom is likely to be disrupted because of the arrival of someone with different colour skin, this logic may well support refusing them admission to the school as well. Second, the calculations involved in utilitarianism are necessarily incomplete. When does the calculating stop? After all, any perceived initial benefits of not having the boy in the class (a more 'efficient education of the other pupils') may need to be balanced against the acquisition of undesirable long-term beliefs that most difficulties can be solved by exclusion, that basic compassion is unnecessary, and that those with differences do not belong with the rest of us. It is not surprising that utilitarianism has struggled in the face of these criticisms.

EMPLOYING DEONTOLOGICAL ETHICS

It seems fairly unequivocal that Kant would regard the decision to refuse a boy admission to a school simply because he had cerebral palsy to be a wrong act. The fact that the school was concerned about the *consequences* of the boy's inclusion in the school meant therefore that they were justified in excluding him is irrelevant within Kant's ethical universe. XXXXX is being treated as a means to an end – the 'better' welfare of others – thereby contravening the practical imperative. Also, unless we have as a general rule that it is acceptable to discriminate against disabled children, the categorical imperative suggests that discrimination against him was wrong. This does appear to be a somewhat simplistic, harsh and inflexible model of ethical analysis.

COMPROMISE POSITIONS

While not exempt from criticism itself, the theoretical adaptation of Kant by Ross (1930) offers one possible route out of this impasse. He points to seven *prima facie* duties – fidelity, reparation, gratitude, justice, beneficence, self-improvement and non-maleficence – which must be adhered to before any other issues, such as consequences, can be taken into consideration. Using the example of XXXXX, the *prima facie* duties of justice, beneficence and non-maleficence probably apply to the teachers under these circumstances, in that they had a duty to prevent the improper distribution of good and bad, to help improve the conditions of others and to prevent (emotional) injury. The school would then have to demonstrate that other serious reasons had caused them to resile from these duties, most likely by noting their duties to other children. Whether this argument is accepted would then be a matter of interpretation of the facts.

It is not only deontologists who have sought to find some common ground. Brandt (1978) argues that utilitarian conclusions need not be binding upon an individual; rather they may simply be used as a guide for action. Ross would consider this proposal to be acceptable only if utilitarian concerns were to be lightly overlaid on a solid deontological foundation, rather than the other way around. Arguably, this approach would probably be one of the most palatable within the discipline, given that most moral philosophers are now deontologists (Olen 1983).

In summary, it would appear that schools and teachers are required to deal with ethical issues of great complexity. Understanding why being 'a good person' might not be enough to act as a foundation for an entire system of moral decision-making, why the utilitarian notion of 'the greater good' might not be the answer to everything, and why the Kantian imperative to 'act as if it were to become a universal law' might struggle with issues of compassion, would allow teachers to weigh their choices with greater confidence, and help produce a more just education system.

Myth #2 *Unlike Ethics, the Law Is a Straightforward System of Right and Wrong; Everyone Agrees What it Is, and What it Does*

The law is our ultimate set of rules – clear, direct and unequivocal. If you follow the rules, you're fine; if you don't, those rules come with an equally clear set of punishments. Importantly though, the law is more than just rules, everyone knows the law represents the best of our culture's morality, translated into legislative form.

When we talk about breaking the law, we are generally taught to conceptualise this in a similar way as breaking school rules, or breaking one of the Ten Commandments, in that the law is depicted as a clear list of things not to do. The law sets out our rights and obligations, delineates what we can do from what we can't, gives us certainty in our interactions and agreements, provides a mechanism for addressing wrongs and prescribes appropriate punishments for those who fail to behave as they should. It's all very straightforward.

Unfortunately, it's a lot more complicated than that. First, the law is not a single and neatly bounded set of rules. It is a complex, continually evolving mixture of statute and common law, shaped by government, yet assembled according to judicial precedence across a hierarchy of courts, divided into different branches and types. Furthermore, as we will see, there is no real agreement on precisely what 'the law' is, or what it does.

The Basics

In stating that we do not have a legal system defined by given sets of rules and collections of codes, does not mean that such a system does not exist; the majority of the world's legal systems follow precisely this model – referred to as the *Civil Law* system – that initially developed from Roman Law. With the exception of those countries following Islamic (Sharia) Law, the main alternative is referred to as the *Common Law* system, so called because from the early Middle Ages there developed a system of laws that became 'common' to all the people of England, in contrast to the local rules that governed the customs in various different areas.

The modern legal system in the UK is organised despite its complexities. It is composed of the laws made by Parliament, by the common law and in equity. Most law emerges through legal cases, and is organised according to the doctrine of precedent. The various courts are set up in a hierarchy, with lower courts having to follow the legal precedents set by the higher courts. Courts ascend from Magistrates Courts, County Courts and various tribunals, through Crown Courts and the High Court, to the Court of Appeal and, finally, to the Supreme Court. All of these bodies have a role in the production, modification and implementation of our laws, including those that affect mass education.

The law is also not composed of one enormous area of regulation; it is broken up into different fields and domains. These include the law of contract, equity, tort, property, public law, administrative law, constitutional law, family law, international law and criminal law. Each of these is apt to impact directly upon the way schools are organised and operated. The most commonly alluded to division within the law is probably between criminal law and the law of torts, that is between those wrongs that have historically been deemed sufficiently important to be punished by the State – such as murder and theft – and those wrongs that are left up to the individual to pursue – such as negligence and trespass.

The intention here is not to advocate the 'simple' Civil Law system over our Common Law – far from it. Common Law countries are justifiably proud of their legal systems, and while these systems have many advantages over their Civil Law equivalents (such as flexibility, consistency and expediency), simplicity is not always one of them. Rather, the intention is to note that the mass school, and its inhabitants, are subject to an incredibly wide variety of laws, both in terms of statute and precedent, from a range of disparate legal areas, spawning an equally wide range of policies, rules and guidelines, supported by a myriad of interventions, disciplinary procedures, professional penalties and criminal sanctions. There is absolutely nothing simple and straightforward about our law.

So What Is the Law?

While not underestimating the importance of discipline and governance within contemporary education, as discussed in Chapter 4, we can see here that the mass school is also organised within complex networks of legislation that provide a generalised framework for organising the functioning of the institution. However, the question remains: just what is the law?

> How does the law differ from and how is it related to orders backed by threats? How does legal obligation differ from, and how is it related to, moral obligation? What are rules and to what extent is law an affair of rules? To dispel doubt and perplexity on these three issues has been the chief aim of most speculation about the 'nature' of law. (Hart 1961, 13)

Although the answer to the question has produced a wide range of answers, arguably the four most important of these will be addressed here: natural law, legal positivism, critical legal studies and postmodern jurisprudence. It will be argued that each of these answers leads to a different understanding of the role of law within education.

NATURAL LAW

This understanding of the substance of law has a very long tradition. Cicero located the source of law within nature when he said 'True law is right reason in agreement with nature; it is of universal application, unchanging and everlasting' (Cicero 1995, Book 3, Ch. 22). This idea was later taken up by religious scholars, such as St Thomas Aquinas, who contended that human laws should always be measured against the absolute values given to us by God, deduced through our understanding of the natural world.

The connection between schooling and law is also founded within nature. Following Plato, the law is employed to organise an education system best able to shape a society based around the most important of all natural forms: 'the good'. As such, morality is placed front and centre, and the role of legislation is to make manifest the laws we need to produce the schools we 'ought' to have.

Natural law has been heavily criticised, most frequently from the viewpoint that it is based upon nothing more than metaphysical speculation, given that no one is capable of determining what the empirical substance of natural law actually is. The most damning criticism of natural law was set out by Bentham, the utilitarian, who regarded the entire position as 'nonsense on stilts', contending that claims to some transcendental point of origin render the project empty of real substance.

LEGAL POSITIVISM

This approach to law is not based upon an understanding of the law as 'positive', but rather refers to the law as 'posited', or written. That is, this model supports the belief that the law is a set of judicial norms established by the State, one that excludes any appeal to a higher transcendental authority, such as nature. The founder of legal positivism, Austin (2000), summed up the positivist critique of natural law when he stated 'the existence of law is one thing: its merit or demerit is another'.

A legal positivist understanding of schooling and the law would not seek to go beyond the text of the law concerned. Removing 'ought' from the equation suggests that debates over, for example, the relative ease by which schools can sidestep Anti-Discrimination Legislation, as in the case of *XXXXX vs The Learning Trust* discussed in myth #1, have no useful correlate within positivist jurisprudence. The law is the law, and the rest should be debated elsewhere.

Needless to say, legal positivism has garnered a significant amount of criticism, not least because it largely regards as irrelevant the purpose behind legislation. Just as it developed out of dissatisfaction with the metaphysics of natural law, so too did legal positivism itself trigger new conceptual models, ones emphasising the social and political context within which laws are made. The first of these was *legal realism*, but this paradigm eventually evolved into critical legal studies.

CRITICAL LEGAL STUDIES

Closely tied to Critical Theory, as discussed in Chapter 1, critical legal studies emphasises the relations of power underpinning the law. Indeed, far from being a reflection of some idealised natural order, or a neutral collection of rules and procedures, the law in real life is deemed to be partial, fluid, inconsistent, often inequitable, and inevitably political. The law is not the ultimate objective arbiter of disputes; it is an object to be fought over by the powerful, who then use it in their own interests. Hutchinson and Monahan (1984, 206) note that: 'law is simply politics dressed up in a different garb; it neither operates in a historical vacuum nor does it exist independently of ideological struggles in society'.

As critical legal studies understands the law primarily through the lens of social and political domination, the law as it specifically relates to schools is no different. It regards the law as providing primary support for an education system committed to social reproduction. Children are compelled to go to school, thereby ensuring a plentiful and docile workforce; the law sets up different schools for different classes, as well as for the normal and for the disabled. The law was even used to ensure that married women were forced to leave the teaching profession altogether.

The criticisms of this position mirror those pertaining to Critical Theory outlined in Chapter 1; most significantly, that this is a reductionist and homogenising understanding of the law, one which has struggled to maintain its intellectual authority in the face of its postmodern successors.

POSTMODERN JURISPRUDENCE

Although critical legal studies dealt a severe blow to legal positivism, the *coup de grâce* came in the form of postmodern jurisprudence, an intellectual movement that eventually killed off critical legal studies as well, or at least, forced its mutation into new, and more specific, forms of criticism. One important point raised by postmodern jurisprudence involves the notion of legal objectivity. The notion of 'the reasonable man' occupies a central place within Western canons of law, and this pervasive legal fiction constitutes the abstract rational actor who forms the core of legal objectivity. However, many recent writers have noted that this 'reasonable man', supposedly the rational subject of the enlightenment, is actually a pseudonym for a white, upper-middle-class, educated, Western male. Such writers, whether discussing gender (Bottomley 1996), cultural difference (West-Newman 2001), or the effects of postcolonialism (Lenta 2004), all contend that such an assumption marginalises all other voices and experiences within the legal system. A postmodern understanding of the law presupposes no such singular objective position, no singular truth that animates the system, and no single knowledge base that deserves pre-eminence over all others.

Viewed through this lens, education law moves a long way from the positivist depiction of a neutral, disembodied set of rules and regulations that merely give the structure an effective framework. Such an approach regards the laws involved as a moveable pastiche of sometimes contradictory imperatives and rationalities, one that both lacks a singular set of animating principles, and fails to cohere within a singular logic. When freed of notions of false objectivity, such as that evidenced within the common law 'reasonable man' fiction, this approach has a far easier time explaining the French ban on headscarfs in schools, or laws that prevent equal access for girls to specific school sports – subjects upon which critical legal studies would also have much to say, though for different reasons.

In summary, teachers inhabit a complex legal environment. Not only is modern schooling cross-cut by a complex web of statutes, case law, regulations and policies, but also the system from which this law emerges is inherently complex. Indeed, there is even only limited agreement on what the law actually is, and certainly we can't just point to it and say 'Here is the ultimate neutral umpire. You have a difficult problem within education? Stop worrying and let the law sort it out'. If only it were that simple.

Myth #3 *We Have an Ethical Education System; it Does Not Discriminate*

We've come a long way from the era when black people weren't allowed in schools, women weren't allowed in university, and disabled people were made to go to their own 'special' places. Everyone has to be treated the same now – we've even got laws to make sure this happens. Discrimination is pretty much a thing of the past, most certainly in schools.

This myth is partly correct. We *have* come a long way since the era when it was perfectly acceptable – ethically and legally – to discriminate on the basis of any one of a wide range of characteristics, from religion to disability, from race to sexuality. That said, it was not that long ago when female teachers had to resign from their positions if they decided to marry, a policy that never applied to men; or to put it another way, social concerns over discrimination are, for the most part, relatively new. Importantly however, the problem of discrimination has not gone away, and the solutions we have put in place appear far from perfect.

Discrimination and the Law

The issue of discrimination has been dealt with at length in Chapter 3. It has been defined as *the process whereby members of particular groups are denied equal treatment, based solely upon their membership of that group.* Issues of overt and covert discrimination, as well as individual, institutional and cultural discrimination have also been discussed. The focus here will fall specifically upon attempts by the law to address the problem of discrimination. It should be noted from the outset that this is not intended in any way as a functional analysis of the legislation; that task belongs elsewhere.

Anti-discrimination legislation has been enacted within a wide range of legal instruments. Up until fairly recently, the field was relatively crowded with The Equal Pay Act 1970, the Racial Relations Act 1976, the Sex Discrimination Act 1986, the Disability Discrimination Act 1995, the Pensions Act 1995, the Employment Equality (Religion or Belief) Regulations 2002, the Civil Partnership Act 2004 and so on – nine in all, and nearly one hundred sets of regulations. All of these have been replaced by a single piece of legislation: the Equality Act 2010, with the intention of simplification and consolidation, and of removing inconsistencies and anomalies (Department for Education 2014b).

Like most anti-discrimination legislation, the Equality Act 2010 is relatively simple in its operation. What follows below is an outline of the central operating sections of the act, followed by a speculatively worked example – the case of *XXXXX vs The Learning Trust.*

Elements of the legislation

The provisions in the acts do not cover every aspect of life; that is not all forms of selection, amount to discrimination. There may be many moments when we may feel we have been discriminated against that would not rise to the necessary standard to be covered by the legislation. For example, you (who happen to be a Mormon) may once have been left on the bench for an entire game by the coach (who happens to be an atheist) of your local Under-10 football team – on the sole grounds that you were complete rubbish. This may have been cruel, but the question here is: have you been discriminated against, as understood and addressed by the relevant legislation?

ACTIVITY

The first criterion to be satisfied is that the nature of the activity said to be discriminatory is covered by the legislation; not all activities are included. General areas covered include employment, the provision of goods and services, health care, housing, transport, public bodies and, of course, education. The primary thrust of the legislation is to cover public life, and while all aspects of schooling are protected by the various acts, it is less likely to be deemed applicable the further away a complaint gets from issues such as education and employment. Sporting clubs should still be covered by the legislation, and hence your footballing grievance.

PROTECTED CHARACTERISTICS

The second criterion to be satisfied involves the grounds upon which the discrimination occurred. Section 4 of the Act lists nine protected characteristics: age, disability, gender reassignment, marriage and civil partnerships, pregnancy and maternity, race, religion or belief, sex and sexual orientation. In order to bring an action under this legislation, the discrimination must involve one of these grounds.

As 'lack of football ability' is not a functioning attribute in the legislation upon which discrimination might occur, unfortunately then, with regards to the match you spent on the sidelines, you have no remedy under anti-discrimination law. However, if you had been left on the sidelines because of your religion, one of the attributes on the list, you may have had a case. The situation is more complicated with regard to physical disability, more on which shortly.

TYPE OF DISCRIMINATION

The third criterion to be satisfied is that discrimination of one of four types must have occurred: direct discrimination, indirect discrimination, harassment or victimisation. Let us take these in turn.

1) <u>Direct discrimination</u> (Section 13). This is where a person is treated less favourably on the basis of a particular attribute. This is the more straightforward or obvious type of discrimination: you can't have the job because you are disabled, or because you are black, or because you are a woman, or because you are gay. These are all protected characteristics, as is 'because you're a Mormon'.

Interestingly, in cases of direct discrimination, the motive for discrimination is irrelevant. So, with your local Under-10 soccer game, if the coach put you on the bench because he dislikes Mormons, he would obviously have discriminated against you; but in addition to this, if the coach put you on the bench, not because he dislikes Mormons but because the coach was worried that you would be jeered by some Mormon-hating spectators, that coach would nonetheless have still discriminated against you.

(2) <u>Indirect discrimination</u> (Section 19). This occurs where a person is unreasonably required to comply with a particular requirement, and because they are unable to do so to the same degree as most other people, they are treated less favourably. The prohibition against indirect discrimination is designed to capture the effect of a particular requirement. As Butler and Mathews note:

> Indirect discrimination arises where policies or practices which may appear fair in form and intention are discriminatory in impact and outcome. Accordingly policies or practices are judged by their effect rather than the employer's intention or motivation. (Butler and Mathews 2007, 183)

An important thing to bear in mind is that, generally, in cases of indirect discrimination the requirement imposed must be unreasonable. Back to the hypothetical football game: as noted above, if the coach left you on the bench because he doesn't like Mormons, this would be direct discrimination. If the coach leaves you on the bench because you won't join with the rest of the team in having Gatorade at half-time, because it might contain caffeine – which many Mormons won't drink – this may well amount to indirect discrimination. So even though the coach states that your omission has nothing to do with your religion, and that it's solely about the Gatorade, under anti-discrimination legislation, this amounts to the same thing.

A more plausible example of indirect discrimination involves the case of Kingston & Richmond Health Authority v. Kaur (1981). A Sikh women, who wished to train as a nurse was accepted into a two-year training course. Following the tenets of her religion, she wished to wear trousers; however, she was told she had to wear a uniform skirt. Ms Kaur agreed, but asked to wear trousers underneath; this was refused. Ms Kaur's complaint was upheld as an example of indirect discrimination. The intention may not have been to discriminate again Ms Kaur; however, given that Sikh women are not able to comply with the 'skirt' requirement to the same extent as non-Sikhs, and that the requirement wasn't actually that crucial to doing the job properly, this amounted to discrimination.

(3) <u>Harassment</u> (Section 26). This involves engaging in unwanted conduct related to one of the protected characteristics; this conduct must have the effect of creating an intimidating, hostile, degrading, humiliating or offensive environment. Back to our football example: if the coach encouraged an environment where your life was made a misery because you are utter rubbish at the game, then you have no remedy under the Equality Act, as this is not a form of harassment protected by the legislation – in fact, this sounds pretty much like most junior football teams. However, if the coach encouraged an environment where you are teased for being a Mormon, the Equality Act 2010 would likely have afforded you some protection.

(4) <u>Victimisation</u> (Section 27). This involves treating someone unfavourably because of something that has been done in relation to the act. If the coach made your life a misery because your mother had objected to the fact that he and the rest of the team constantly tried to humiliate you about being a Mormon, that would be conduct that contravened the Equality Act.

EXCEPTIONS

The fourth element of the legislation covers various circumstances in which the law may not apply. In Schedule 11 of the Act, certain schools and circumstances are exempt from the normal intent of the legislation. For example, single-sex schools are able to refuse applications from students of the opposite sex. Also, religious schools can discriminate on the basis of their stated faith, both in relation to admissions and to benefits, facilities and services; however, they can't refuse admission to a student of another faith if the school has unfilled places.

While the intention of the Act is still not 'loophole-free', it is no longer acceptable simply to assert that the school is unable to accept given students because of the difficulties this might cause them; and this is particularly the case with regard to disability. Schools are now required to make 'reasonable adjustments' in order to accommodate disabled people, encompassing school provisions and practices, auxillary aids and services and physical features. Of course, it doesn't necessarily work quite this way.

An Example of Disability Discrimination

It would probably be useful now briefly to work through an example of the discrimination process specifically as it relates to education, and what better case to choose than *XXXXX vs The Learning Trust*, as discussed in myth #1. First, this can be discussed as a hypothetical example of what would most likely have happened had this been a straightforward case taken to a tribunal (which it wasn't). Second, there will be a discussion of what actually happened.

XXXXX VS THE LEARNING TRUST . . . HYPOTHETICALLY

Since the boy's mother was unhappy with the decision to refuse admission to the school, she could seek a remedy through the anti-discrimination legislation. Working quickly through the Equality Act 2010:

Activity

Education is an activity covered by this Statute. More specifically, under Part 6, Chapter 1: Schools, Section 85(1)(a): 'The responsible body of the school to which this section applies must not discriminate against a person in the arrangements it makes for deciding who is offered admission as a pupil'.

Protected Characteristics

'Disability' is one of the nine characteristics covered by the statute under Section 4 of the *Act*.

Discrimination

XXXXX was denied admission to the school based upon his physical disability. As such, he was treated less favourably than an ordinary child would be treated under the same circumstances. This is an example of direct discrimination, and contravenes Section 13(1) of the Act. So far, so good.

Exceptions

None of the exceptions set out in Schedule 11 of the Equality Act 2010 apply. This is not a girl's school; neither is it a faith school, a faith to which XXXXX does not belong.

In summary then, *prima facie*, XXXXX would have a remedy under the Equality Act 2010 against The Learning Trust for discrimination. The Trust acted illegally in denying the boy admission to the school on account of his disability. Interestingly however, the analysis would probably not stop there. Under the Education Act 1996 schools have certain responsibilities towards disabled children. In a child's statement of Special Educational Needs, an appropriate school is named which then obligates that school to provide an education. The school is deemed to be appropriate 'unless is it incompatible with the provision of efficient education for other children' (Section 316 (3)). Sound familiar? This is precisely the language used by the school to deny admission. It seems the exceptions loopholes no longer even have to be in the *Act* itself to be effective in countering the intended effects of the legislation.

XXXXX VS THE LEARNING TRUST . . . WHAT ACTUALLY HAPPENED

The school refused admission to the boy, based upon the difficulties he would cause to the school. The boy's mother took the case to the First-tier Special

Educational Needs and Disability Tribunal, which refused to hear the case. The tribunal's argument was that the Academy in question was not bound by the Equality Act 2010. Cooper *et al.* (2015, 199) argue that the consequences of this are as follows.

> Academies are positioned as an 'equal opportunity' provider, through the admittance of SEN statemented pupils. However, the Academies Act 2010 situates such institutions as independent schools, absolving them of the legal right to accommodate pupils statemented as SEN. This implies that Academies are not legally obliged to be named on a statement as a provider of education, justifying its position through weak notions of 'incompatibility'.

The mother appealed this decision to an upper tribunal, and that tribunal held that it *was* within the purview of the first tribunal to hear the case; the first tribunal then found in favour of XXXXX. Whether or not the boy was finally admitted to the school is unknown; schools rarely give up easily under these circumstances, and mechanisms for enforcing such laws are notoriously weak.

This form of discrimination is very far from unusual. At the time of the XXXXX case, eight others were under consideration within the same relatively small jurisdiction. In the neo-liberal market place of schools, each school now competes against all the others for the best students, the highest grades, the best place on the league tables and the highest profile. While admitting new students each year is always something of a lottery, some children are seen as being likely to be an almost certain 'plus' in this ongoing competition – the smart, the affluent, the athletic and those with social and cultural capital. Others are regarded as likely to be a more of 'burden' to the school, and SEN kids pretty much sit at the top of that list – with judgements often clearly made about their admission without even meeting the child involved. After all, logically which school wouldn't want a pupil who could top all their classes and get an GCSE A* at maths aged just 11... unless they were disabled.

Importantly, as a way of demonstrating the breadth of possible discrimination in schools against SEN children, the Equality Act 2010 by no means limits its affects to school admissions. Section 85(2) also covers discrimination in the way education is provided for pupils, the way it affords access to facilities and services, and the way it decides who gets excluded and who doesn't. This last area is particularly relevant. The statistics suggest that pupils with a statement of Special Educational Needs are nearly seven times more likely to be permanently excluded from school than those children without; they are also nine times more likely to receive a fixed period exclusion (Department for Education 2012c). As Parkes (2012, 125) notes:

> With indirect discrimination now extending to disability discrimination under the Equality Act, the question of whether exclusions are a proportionate means of

achieving a legitimate aim becomes even more pertinent given the number of exclusions which involve SEN pupils... The aim of exclusions may be to punish pupils and to manage poor behaviour as well as protect the environment of the pupil population in general. Many of those involved, however... seriously question the effectiveness of the exclusions system in meeting its aims.

A report by the charity Contact a Family (2013) has found that children with a disability, special needs or additional needs are routinely illegally excluded from school, in that the correct procedures are not followed, and that the underlying causes of the behaviour are not taken into account in assessing breaches of codes of conduct. Almost a quarter of the children in the study were illegally excluded every week. In terms of both ethics and the law, this appears to be a clear example of discrimination.

In summary, discrimination is still with us, and will likely remain. We have enacted laws to address the problem. These laws address many different forms of discrimination, across most areas of public life, and they address different forms of discrimination, in that discrimination does not always have to be intentional to be covered by the legislation. However, the law also contains a number of exceptions, both within the legislation and elsewhere. Getting the law to do what it was intended to do is not always easy. Furthermore, it seems that 'the law' and 'justice' often have a very uneasy relationship.

Conclusion

A greater understanding of the discipline of ethics helps us make clearer ethical decisions in daily life, or at least, it provides us with the tools to recognise what kind of moral reasoning we are employing, and what the shortcomings of that reasoning are likely to be. This is particularly the case with simplistic consequentialist reasoning, a logic which often seems to punish those least able to protect themselves, such as the disabled. In addition, education is an ethically complex domain, both in terms of how we choose to structure our schools, and also in terms of the ethical choices teachers make as they try and do their jobs as best they can – often under very challenging circumstances.

As well as ethics, a greater understanding of the law is also useful for teachers, and not only as it applies to disability. The law represents our broadest understanding of right and wrong made manifest in statutory form; also, all aspects of education, and teachers' professional lives, are now subject to legal scrutiny. Butler and Mathews (2007) state the following.

> The legal environment in which schools operate and teachers work is increasingly intrusive. There are more statutes, more cases, more regulations, more departmental policies. The law is more complex and compliance is more difficult. Breaches are more serious, more heavily penalised and noisily publicised.

So, just as teachers need to understand the strengths and weaknesses of the various ethical positions they take, they also need to know their many rights and obligations under our most visible and important of ethical systems – the law. These rights and obligations are neither self-evident nor timeless; instead they are organised within given social and historical contexts, and according to specific relations of authority.

TRUTH AND POST-COLONIALISM 14

This chapter argues that the issue of 'truth' has played a foundational role, not only within the discipline of philosophy, but also within many different aspects of our culture. However, there seems to be little agreement on what it really is, and while some philosophers contend that truth is a meaningless concept – a linguistic mirage – most would argue there's *something* of importance there, but what is it?

Even if we struggle to determine the real nature of truth – as we did with the real nature of right and wrong, in Chapter 13 – at least we structure our culture, our knowledges, and our school curricula around stuff we know to be unequivocally true... or do we? Arguably, many of the assumptions we make do not stand up to close scrutiny, even within a domain as supposedly 'objective' as the school curriculum. Worldviews are often presented as 'truth' that actually remain open to dispute and contestation, worldviews that suit particular groups and that subtly act to reinforce given social, political and national interests.

Myth #1 'Truth' is the most straightforward thing there is. *'Truth is simple. Certain things about the world are "facts". If we report them accurately, we are telling the truth; if we don't, we aren't. That's all there is to it'.* Actually, no it isn't. Philosophers have been debating the notion of truth for over 2500 years, debates that have resulted in very different approaches to this issue, most frequently divided into *realist* and *anti-realist* models. These models in turn generate different kinds of truth tests, which can be applied to given problems and statements. All in all, ascertaining what is true, and what is not – in the curriculum, or elsewhere – remains a complex and contested process.

Myth #2 The knowledge in our school curriculum is both true and culturally neutral. *'There is nothing untrue or biased about our school curriculum. You could teach it anywhere in the world and it would be appropriate'.* The evidence suggests that, like all countries, the United Kingdom employs school curricula that tell a particular set of stories, which we, as a nation, like to regard as the truth, stories which deal with our history, with our role in the world as a colonial power, with what literature we deem to be of cultural value and even what science we regard to be true, or useful. Many of these stories are self-serving, to say the least.

Myth #3 We haven't tried to colonise anyone for more than a century, so postcolonial theory has nothing relevant to tell us about 'truth', the world or ourselves. *'The fact that we were once a colonial power is an irrelevance today. Everybody's got over all that Empire stuff now; no-one in India or New Zealand is affected by it anymore, and neither are we'.* Just because the British Empire has now become a set of independent countries does not mean that they do not still carry a considerable legacy from their colonial past, a legacy which determines whose voices are heard in the production of truth, which ideas are listened to, who becomes 'the other', how new hybrid identities are formed, and how cultural and social boundaries are drawn. Even in the UK, we continue to play out our colonial past in the shape of continued contestations over truth, and in our multi-ethnic make-up in the twenty-first century.

Introduction

So far, this final section of the book has presented an overview of philosophy, and given an explanation of why it is of such immense value to educators (Chapter 12), and it has also addressed one specific area of philosophy – ethics – and briefly applied this to the field of disability and the law, also of significant value to educators (Chapter 13). This final chapter of Part IV will unpack arguably one of the most important areas of concern within the discipline of philosophy: the notion of truth. It will then employ any conclusions reached to better understand the claims made by those writers and researchers interested in the legacy of colonialism, both around the world and in the United Kingdom itself. These 'postcolonial' thinkers rightly contend that the concept of truth, and the knowledges that spring from it, are far more complex than they may initially appear.

Of all the areas of philosophy, the search for truth is often deemed to be the most important. There is probably no other word in the English language that carries with it as much symbolic and romantic baggage. Henkin (1966, 1) states: 'The word "truth", as well as such words as "beauty" and "justice", refer to concepts so broad, and so deeply stirring to the human spirit, that some have set them as the aim of life'. Indeed, truth has not only been described as providing the principal foundation of the aforementioned beauty (Keats 1951) and justice (Disraeli 1851), but also virtue

(Holyoake 1902), knowledge (Russell 1983), subjectivity (Kierkegaard 2001) and even human nature itself (Bacon 1985). Indeed, answering the question, 'What is truth?' has been described not only as the central purpose of philosophy (Foucault 2000), it has even been described as its *sole* purpose (Bierce 1995).

So What Is 'Truth'?

In spite of the apparent importance of truth to most of our conceptual frameworks, there is actually considerable disagreement about exactly what it is. After all, the nature of things like 'facts' – from which models of truth are assembled – seem to be given to us with cultural assumptions already built into them. As Lin Yutang, a Chinese writer, observes:

> Western philosophers have always gone on the assumption that fact is something cut and dried, precise, immobile, very convenient, and ready for examination. The Chinese deny this. The Chinese believe that a fact is something crawling and alive, a little furry and cool to the touch, that crawls down the back of your neck. (Lin Yutang, cited in Christian 1981, 62)

Recent research involving undergraduate education students reveals a similar lack of agreement as to exactly what the concept of 'truth' entails, most specifically that most of us appear to think that there are no 'right' and 'wrong' answers, in philosophy or in life, thus anything can be true (Tait *et al.* 2012). In contrast to this position, most philosophers would argue that truth is far more elusive than that, if it exists at all. Some philosophers – called *deflationary* theorists – contend that the whole problem of truth is nothing more than a 'linguistic muddle' (Ramsay 1927). When the statement is made, 'It is true that this book is made of paper', a deflationary theorist such as Frege (1977) would argue that its content is identical with the statement 'This book is made of paper' and therefore ascribing the property of truth adds nothing at all. That is, truth stands for nothing within a sentence, other than purposes of assertion or negation, and is hence not a genuine concept (Ayer 1935). As Horwich (1990, 5) notes about truth: 'No wonder that its "underlying nature" has so stubbornly resisted philosophical elaboration; for there simply is no such thing'.

Perhaps not surprisingly, this approach leaves most philosophers feeling rather unhappy – i.e. that truth is simply a linguistic illusion – and they have consequently come up with a number of other approaches. The common-sense *realist* approach to truth, as exemplified by myth #1, often depicts truth as the most straightforward thing there is: the direct correspondence between a particular statement, and the reality it depicts. However, there are also convincing *anti-realist* alternatives to this model (such as *pragmatic theory* and *coherence theory*) which suggest instead that truth is far from being objective, unchanging, universal and self-evident, and as we shall see, the implications of this position are very far-reaching indeed.

Truth and the Curriculum

If we accept that truth is never fixed or absolute, and there are good reasons why we should, then this leaves truth, and the knowledges shaped from it, in a far more precarious position than might previously have been the case. After all, it is often comforting to think that all the things we have been told are true: science is unequivocally true, what we are taught on the school curriculum is unequivocally true, what we have been told about our culture and its place in the world is also unequivocally true. Unfortunately, the evidence suggests that this just isn't the case. 'Truth' is more complex than that, and while the opposite of a truth isn't necessarily a lie, it is most certainly a falsehood.

Most philosophers would argue that, in a perfect world, all our academic disciplines would be founded upon a more solid understanding of the limits of their own truth claims, and we would better realise the degree to which such disciplines are, in very important ways, the products of their own intellectual histories. As discussed in Chapter 3, the science of 'race' was based upon the (spurious) historical belief that white people are somehow intrinsically different from, and better than, black people – and yet this was taught in schools as 'truth' for nearly 200 years. And so, far from teaching timeless, indisputable, culturally neutral truths, our schools bear the ready imprint of our imperial past, and our political present, in terms of the knowledges we learn and the truths they tell – very often truths which airbrush that past, and subtly predetermine who is most likely to prosper in our future.

Examples are not hard to find. This book has already discussed recent political disputes over precisely what constitutes worthwhile literature, and how 'English' that curriculum should be (Chapter 9); it has also discussed the political disputes over the science curriculum and the 'truth' of global warming, and whether this knowledge belongs in the school (Chapter 11). Similar political debates can be seen evidenced within the 'Citizenship' programmes of study for the national curriculum. Of course, the clearest demonstration of the inherently problematic and flexible nature of truth involves our history curriculum, which presents versions of history that, while 'true' in London and Leeds, are unlikely to be regarded as such in Dublin, New Delhi, Sydney or Buenos Aires.

Postcolonialism

As an attempt to explain the ways in which various countries have dealt with their histories as European colonies, a body of theory has developed that investigates the social, cultural and educational legacy of colonialism, examining the many often-unspoken truths, world views, and forms of knowledge bequeathed to those who remained in the colonies, both as colonisers and colonised. Postcolonial theory addresses issues such as forces shaping identities within colonial environments, the ways in which some groups are co-opted and romanticised while others are excluded and their voices silenced, the ways in which cultural mimicry occurs as well as cultural rejection, and even the manner that social theory itself is used to marginalise the ideas of the colonised. Postcolonial theory talks to the many social, cultural, political, governmental and educational traits that still clearly mark out many nations' colonial heritage. Often this heritage is welcomed by some within those countries, and resented and challenged by others. Indeed, constructing viable identities in the face of the residual Britishness (or whatever the particular colonial power happens to be) is precisely the focus of a great deal of postcolonial theory.

Importantly, postcolonial theory doesn't just speak to issues and truths that have currency somewhere 'over there' – thousands of miles away from us here in the UK. Arguably, these tools are useful to us as part of explaining the complexities of identity formation, cultural adaptation and social inclusion within a multi-ethnic society such as we currently inhabit. Many of those former colonial citizens did not stay 'over there'; they came here, and now form an important part of the social and cultural fabric of this nation. And more than that, it is also possible to explain some of the complexities of England's relationship with Ireland, Scotland and Wales through this set of theoretical lenses. After all, for more than 1000 years, it certainly appears than England and Scotland have often struggled to organise their truths in the same way.

To summarise then, these are the three myths to be dealt with in this chapter.

Myth #1 'Truth' is the most straightforward thing there is.
Myth #2 The knowledge in our school curriculum is both true and culturally neutral.
Myth #3 We haven't tried to colonise anyone for more than a century, so postcolonial theory has nothing relevant to tell us about 'truth', the world or ourselves.

Myth #1 'Truth' Is the Most Straightforward Thing There Is

> Truth is simple. We go to school to learn the truth... the truth about numbers, the truth about history, the truth about biology; we set up our legal system so we can protect the truth... who is in the right, who is in the wrong, how we can ensure justice for all; we even invented an entire system of knowledge acquisition – science – for impartially uncovering the truth of the universe. The truth may try to hide, but after you strip away all the rubbish, all the camouflage, and all the mystery, there it is.

The common sense understanding of truth is that it exists independently of us. After all, surely the truth doesn't change just because we want it to, or because we approach the problem from a different angle, or because someone else has conducted the tests, or because we elect a new government. What is there to debate? Actually, as we shall see, the notion of 'truth' is not a simple matter at all.

Differing Approaches to Truth

Philosophers have struggled over the notion of truth since the ancient debate between Socrates and Protagoras, and this argument is yet to be resolved. Socrates, as given voice by Plato, believed in the existence of absolute standards, standards having a reality independent of human action or perception. This is not to say that feelings, attitudes, biases and preconceptions are irrelevant in the process of constructing truth; however, once these are stripped away – i.e. by the kind of critical reasoning espoused by Socrates himself – then it would be possible to know the truth (Plato 1956). This understanding of truth is most frequently labelled as a *realist* approach. James (1917, 233) summarises this view by pointing to its reliance upon the notion of a 'world complete in itself, to which thought comes as a passive mirror'. It certainly constitutes the most familiar and widely used understanding of the relationship between ourselves and the world in which we live, and as will be discussed in greater detail shortly, the vast majority of science also appears to be based upon this logic. This is not, however, the only version of truth available to us.

In addition to *realism*, there also exists an *anti-realist* approach that can boast an equally long history and a formidable theoretical foundation. Lined up against Socrates in Ancient Greece was a group of itinerant teachers called Sophists, the most eminent of whom was Protagoras, who famously stated that 'Man is the measure of all things' (Plato 1974, 160). Sophists believed that finding absolute and unequivocal truth was impossible, and hence man had to learn to live, and construct knowledge, in its absence. In more modern times, this position is most clearly articulated by Nietzsche (1954, 46), who asks: 'What then is truth? A mobile army of metaphors, metonyms, and anthropomorphisms – in short, a sum of human relations...'. His point here is that truths are formed, shaped and deployed within social contexts. The truth is not 'out there', waiting to be discovered, but is rather something that is brought into existence by force of the human will (Nietzsche 1967).

Nietzsche's approach to truth forms a crucial component in the work of many subsequent thinkers, specifically in relation to the exercise of power. Like Nietzsche, Foucault also proposes that truth is something that cannot exist in absolute terms, contending instead that there is a variety of truths, constructed within definite contexts as the product of specific legitimated knowledges. Therefore, because truth is actually the product of legitimated knowledges, as those knowledges change, then so too will truth (Foucault 1980, 131). Different societies produce different *regimes of truth*, and the production of these regimes is internal to the exercise of power.

These two generalised positions outlined above – the realist and anti-realist – while representing the primary philosophical subdivision over the issue of truth, by no means provide a comprehensive analysis of the field. The two approaches spawn a number of other, more specific, theories concerning the nature of truth. That is, the realist approach is most frequently understood in terms of *correspondence theory*, and the anti-realist approach in terms of *pragmatic theory* and *coherence theory*.

Realism and Truth

In the book *Truth in Context*, Lynch (1998) describes realism about truth as being based upon how the world is, not upon what we think about that world. Thus, it should make no difference as to who conducts an investigation into the nature of the world, the truth will always be the same, regardless of how different the researchers may be, or how diverse their backgrounds. The statements made by those researchers are true when they correspond to the external reality; that is, something is true if it corresponds to the facts. This is called correspondence theory.

CORRESPONDENCE THEORY

The first formulation of what later became correspondence theory is normally attributed to Aristotle, who stated 'A statement is true if, as it signifies, so it is'. Aristotle is thereby comparing what is said about reality, with reality itself, and if there is a match, the statement can be said to be true. If the statement is: 'This book has 1000 pages', this statement can be compared with the final number at the bottom of the last page. Is it 1000? Nowhere near actually, and so the statement is not true. Simple.

The central appeal of correspondence theory is its self-evidence, in that it seems to support a basic human perception as to the nature of truth. Furthermore, since it rules out human interpretive agency from the process, it objectively delineates the true from the false, thereby further adding to its apparent clarity and utility. For those who take up this position, it becomes possible to argue that once the direct link to 'reality' is removed from the truth equation – as with anti-realism – then it becomes possible that anything might be true (a contention which will be discussed in greater detail later).

However, the fact that the rigour and validity of correspondence theory appear to be self-evident, does not necessarily make it so. One criticism of the theory is that, having stripped away the rhetoric of 'obviousness' from this model, there appears to be little in the way of conceptual foundation. Horwich (1990, 1) makes precisely this point when he states: 'The common-sense notion that truth is a kind of "correspondence with the facts" has never been worked out to anyone's satisfaction. Even its advocates would concede that it remains little more than a vague, guiding intuition'. A second criticism concerns the problem of gaining knowledge about a mind-independent reality from our own sense data. As Christian (1981, 193–4) notes, correspondence theory:

compares a concept with a set of sensations – the sensations we use when we go about inferring what exists in the real world. Therefore, we are checking a subjective concept with a subjective set of sensations. If they match to some tolerable degree, then we call the concept true; if they don't, we call it false. This is not really a happy condition to live with, but given our present knowledge of the cognitive processes, the predicament seems inescapable... we can never be certain of anything.

That said, correspondence theory is still the dominant paradigm, perhaps not within the discipline of philosophy, but certainly in terms of common usage, and also within almost the vast majority of scientific discourse. However, the mechanisms by which science has attempted to come to terms with the notion of truth, have resulted in the unearthing of a number of equally obstinate and seemingly intractable philosophical problems.

SCIENCE AND TRUTH

The scientific method was first outlined in 1620 by Bacon in his book *Novum Organum* (Bacon 1952). His theory is premised upon the belief that the general aim of science is to push back the boundary between what is known and what is not known. This process is begun by scientists, who observe and record many examples of an event during the course of an experiment, thereby adding to the stock of knowledge around a particular subject. Eventually, as each scientist adds information to the totality, general rules emerge. Theories are then advanced that explain the existing pattern of events and can be used to predict future happenings of the same event, and by combining these theories, global laws are constructed. Thus, a limited number of experimental results become extrapolated into 'laws of nature'. The central principle here, that of 'induction', suggests that assumptions can be made about all members of a class from examining a few members of the class.

Unfortunately, inductive reasoning has a major flaw, first pointed out by Hume in 1737 in his *Treatise of Human Nature* (Hume 1969). He argued that assumptions cannot be made about all members of a class from examining a few members of that class. No matter how many times a specific 'cause A' is followed by 'effect B', it does not logically follow that A will *always* cause B. As Russell (1983) notes,

> The man who has fed a chicken every day throughout its life at last wrings its neck instead, showing that more refined views as to the uniformity of nature would have been useful to the chicken.

Popper (1963) argues that the consequences of this observation for science and truth are severe: it becomes impossible to prove anything as true, no matter how many times an event occurs. Therefore, science should give up its quest for truth by attempting to prove a phenomenon to be true, and scientists should rather try to falsify existing theories, thereby creating new theories that would, in their own turn, be disproved. Advancement in science is thereby not by proving something to be true, but being unable to prove it false.

According to this logic, truth no longer belongs in the realist domain. Rather, truth is necessarily transient, being surpassed in time by new truths, ones that can account for both the new data, as well as the information that spawned previous theories.

Anti-Realism and Truth

In contrast to the realist position on truth – based upon the belief that there exist indisputable facts about a singular reality – the anti-realist position argues that facts themselves necessarily reflect particular points of view. The central animating assumption is that it is impossible to describe any fact in the absence of a conceptual framework. Lynch (1998, 23) characterises this position as being founded upon the postulation that, 'There is no scheme-neutral way of making a report about the world. It would be a mistake to search for the scheme that tells it like it "really" is – there is no such thing.' Putnam (1981) argues that in the absence of a 'God's Eye' point of view, which many would argue is the unspoken prerequisite of realism, all that can remain are various interpretations of how the world is. Reality does not come 'ready made and complete' as realists would have us believe, but rather is shaped by our own interpretations of it.

It should be pointed out here that accepting anti-realist accounts of truth does not necessitate a slide into *radical relativism*, where truth becomes so nebulous that it can be found anywhere. Admitting that the truth is intimately associated with experience is not the same as suggesting that, as a consequence, all truths are equally valid. As Putnam (1981, 54) wryly observes,

> If anyone believed that, and if they were foolish enough to pick a conceptual scheme that told them they could fly, and act upon it by jumping out the window, they would, if they were lucky enough to survive, see the weakness of the latter view at once.

Anti-realist approaches to truth generally come in two distinct forms: pragmatic theory and coherence theory.

PRAGMATIC THEORY

Pragmatism is normally associated with the work of James (1911), and follows the logic that theorising – whether about truth, or anything else for that matter – is a pointless activity in and of itself. The only relevance that theorising can have is when it is converted into the solution of concrete intellectual problems. A philosopher must ask, what is the practical worth of any particular claim? That is, what difference would it make if a set of claims were believed to be either true or false? If the answer is 'none whatsoever', then the issue should be of no philosophical interest. If an explanation can be translated into a verifiable and predictable outcome – an observable effect – then that explanation is true, if not, then the explanation is either false, or irrelevant, or both.

> Pragmatism asks its usual question. 'Grant an idea or a belief to be true,' it says, 'what concrete difference will its being true make to anyone's actual life? ... What, in short, is the truth's cash-value in experimental terms?' The moment pragmatism asks this question, it sees the answer: *True ideas are those that we can assimilate, validate, corroborate and verify*. False ideas are those we cannot ... The truth of an idea is not a stagnant property inherent in it. Truth *happens* to an idea. It *becomes* true, is *made* true by events. (James 1975, ix)

Thus, James rejects the realist notion that truth is a property independent of human intentionality. Pragmatic theory avoids the requirement for a 'God's Eye' view for a final and complete understanding of truth. Rather, a statement is deemed true because it works as an explanation, not because it corresponds to an abstracted objective reality.

COHERENCE THEORY

This theory evolved as an attempt to sidestep some of the problems of correspondence theory. Since we can never know whether a statement corresponds to external reality, all that can be said is that the statement coheres with a given set of already accepted beliefs. Generally, things we believe to be true form part of a huge, interrelated matrix. The truth of a statement is therefore assessed by how well it fits into that matrix – if it dovetails well with the ideas in the matrix, it is regarded as true; if not, it is regarded as false. For example, we readily accept the truth of the statement that 'dogs can't fly', because it coheres easily with everything we already know about dogs, birds, paws, wings and gravity.

Of course, the questions arise of 'What counts as coherence?' and 'Under what conditions?'. The clearest answers to these questions are given by Putnam (1981), who argues that within an anti-realist understanding of truth, the coherence of any given truth-claim should be assessed by an 'ideally rational enquirer', which suggests that valid truths cannot be created by the deranged, the deluded or the drunk, just because they really admire dogs. That is, the alleged coherence of any given truth-claims to a wider matrix of truths must still withstand significant scrutiny.

However, in stating that there are no external truths, no absolute facts that exist independent of human experience, it is equally false to identify truth with rational acceptability; the two are not synonymous. Putnam uses the example of the historically changing shape of the earth, pointing out that the earth has not actually changed from being flat to being a sphere over the past 500 years, only accepted truths have changed. Therefore, what remains is an understanding that 'truth is an idealisation of rational acceptability', a rational acceptability which is both tensed and relative (Putnam 1981, 51).

Anti-realist theories of truth, such as pragmatic theory and coherence theory, are not without their critics. For example, it has been argued that they are both unable to account for the possibility of there being a discrepancy between what we *believe* to be true, and what actually *is* true (Horwich 1990: 9). After all, simply believing something to be true, does not necessarily make it so. However, both anti-realist theories would regard this as an invalid criticism; pragmatism, because if it works as an explanation, what's the difference anyway; and coherence, because of the role of the ideally rational inquirer.

Truth Tests

Importantly, these three theories are not simply abstract categories of interpretation; all are actually useful, in that they translate directly into truth tests. A truth test is a device for checking particular statements and assessing whether they are true or false. As will be shown, any statement making a fact-claim can have its veracity checked against one, or all, of the three tests. Indeed, when the truth of a particular claim or statement is being assessed, normally more than one truth test is applied.

THE CORRESPONDENCE TRUTH TEST

This simply involves comparing a mental concept with an actual event, which can be done in a number of direct ways, such as by listening, by looking, by feeling, and so on. For example, if the statement is 'It's a sunny day', this can easily be checked by walking outside and looking: if the sun is shining, if it is warm, and if there are not many clouds in the sky, then the statement will probably be accepted as true – although correspondence is always a matter of degree, and the more clouds there are in the sky, the less the correspondence, and the less likely the statement is to be categorised as true. Importantly, all forms of direct comparison between statement and event would come under this truth test.

THE PRAGMATIC TRUTH TEST

This involves testing whether a statement is true by checking if it works in a practical sense. This test of truth often involves the establishment of a working hypothesis by a process of elimination. For example, if a person's arms are pink and painful at the end of each day during summer, by a process of elimination, any number of possible causes can probably be ruled out – allergies, abrasion, dermatological issues, paint – especially if long sleeves and/or sun-block seem to solve the problem. That is, it is true that the pink and painful arms are actually sunburn because this works as an explanation.

THE COHERENCE TRUTH TEST

This involves comparing a mental concept against a set of concepts that are already taken as true. Once again, this can be done in a number of ways. For example, if the statement is 'January is generally a cold month', then the process of determining the truth of the statement would begin by comparing it with any number of other sets of knowledges within a generalised matrix of accepted truths. These might include personal memories about January, meteorological inputs relating to temperatures, geographical knowledge about the hemispheres, even cultural data about what kinds of events happen in January. If the information in these sets of knowledges is taken to be true, and if the statement coheres with those knowledges, then the statement is deemed to be true.

It would be useful at this stage to work through an example taken specifically from education. Given Chapter 5 of this book deals with the governance of subjectivity and the rise of behaviour disorders, the issue of ADHD is probably the best place to start.

ADHD and Truth

Attention Deficit Hyperactivity Disorder (ADHD), which is primarily a theory concerning the misbehaviour of children, has yet to reach the status of 'established truth', in spite of what some of its more optimistic advocates may claim. Debates over the disorder continue, not only within the pages of learned journals, but also in the popular media, where various treatments and protocols of diagnosis are discussed, alongside the arguments of those who refuse to recognise the disorder at all. So, if truth is such a simple concept, perhaps we can use the three truth tests to determine, once and for all, whether the claim 'ADHD is an objective disorder that exists in nature' is true or false.

TRUTH: ADHD EXISTS IN NATURE

First, employing the correspondence test to check the truth of ADHD presents a number of difficulties. ADHD is not a physical object that can be held up for scrutiny and compared to the subjective concept of the disorder. Rather it is an amalgam of various types of data – statistical, observational, behavioural, pharmacological, experiential, educational – which have been assembled to the point where their combined presence is deemed to correspond to the existence of an objective disorder. All in all then, the correspondence truth test isn't much help.

The pragmatic truth test is rather more useful. As has been discussed, the principal question regarding ADHD would normally be: 'Does this truth *work*?'. Given that ADHD was originally formulated around the educational needs of a particular kind of at-risk student, there is little doubt that it aims to make a concrete contribution to the educational and emotional well-being of a specific category of child. Similarly, since the truth of ADHD is determined by whether the category works, it can be argued that the disorder provides a straightforward *workable* explanation as to why otherwise seemingly healthy and normal children are incapable of behaving well in class.

Finally, a coherence test of truth would also appear to work in ADHD's favour. The notion of ADHD meshes easily with any number of other sets of accepted beliefs within the truth matrix. For example, ADHD is based upon the premise that some kind of minor brain dysfunction results in unwelcome social behaviour, behaviour which had previously been categorised simply as naughtiness and inattentiveness. This reappraisal coheres readily with a wide range of other accepted truths concerning the relationship between specific mental problems and undesirable forms of conduct. Also, ADHD involves the belief that, by uncovering more and more mental disorders, science is finally discovering the real workings of the human mind. ADHD thereby fits snugly into this understanding of the psychological sciences, and coheres with (and adds to) the validity of all the other new disorders.

It's decided then: 'ADHD is an objective disorder that exists in nature' is a true statement, since it appears to pass two of the three truth tests... except for one tiny problem: a completely contradictory statement, 'ADHD is simply a by-product of the governance of subjectivity' also passes two of the three truth tests.

TRUTH: ADHD IS A SOCIAL CREATION

Like the first statement, this second statement is also not particularly amenable to the correspondence truth test; social governance can no more be held up, examined, and compared to a mental concept, like a piece of brain tissue, than can ADHD.

The pragmatic truth test yields better results. A governmental understanding of ADHD works as an explanation of why there are so many new behaviour disorders, and why previously untapped areas of human conduct are now being pathologised; that is, *it allows for more effective normalisation*. This understanding of ADHD also works to explain why such disorders are discovered almost exclusively in areas where they pose a threat to effective social and educational management.

Likewise for the coherence truth test: a governmental understanding of ADHD coheres neatly with a truth matrix comprised of accepted historical theories and interpretations. It also dovetails into the widely accepted proposition that social governance is becoming more and more densely layered, as reflected in the fact that the number of accepted behaviour disorders continues to increase exponentially.

So what happens now? Both sides of the debate can make some solid claims to truth. Is ADHD a fact, 'cut and dried, precise, immobile, very convenient, and ready for examination', or is it something 'crawling and alive, a little furry... '? It would appear that 'truth' is not a simple matter. Some – realists – regard it as objectively ascertainable; it is 'out there' waiting to be uncovered. Others – anti-realists – regard it as inexorably tied to human conceptual frameworks, and that 'there are no eternal facts, as there are no absolute truths' (Nietzsche 1997, 12). If philosophical debate were a football match, then the anti-realists would currently be winning handsomely. That said, weigh the arguments and take your pick.

Myth #2 *The Knowledge In Our School Curriculum Is Both True and Culturally Neutral*

We teach the truth in our schools. This isn't Nazi Germany, where the curriculum was used to indoctrinate children with utter falsehoods, such as that there is a race called the 'Aryans' who are somehow better than everyone else, and that the only reason the Germans lost World War I was because of the Jews. It's not like that in twenty-first-century Britain; our curriculum is made up of undeniable truths. You could teach our curriculum anywhere and it would still be regarded as true.

The argument here is that our curriculum is about knowledge, not ideology. It's not as if our schools were set up to deliberately peddle a particular world-view, whether that involves justifying Britain's place in the world, or somehow propping up the interests of the powerful. Surely we are beholden to no-one and our school curricula will reflect this fact; schools here in the UK deal in teaching children the 'truth'. Likewise, no-one in India or Australia could care less about our world-view anymore; their schools now march to the beat of their own drums.

While this all sounds nice, unfortunately it's a lot more complicated. School curricula, wherever they are from, reflect the historical and cultural contexts in which they are assembled; that is, school curricula have a past, as well as a present, and the knowledges presented there – the 'truths' to be taught to children – reflect this fact. And arguably this is the case whether we are looking at those places to which we exported our education system, all the outposts of the British Empire – Canada, India, New Zealand, Australia, Kenya, Burma, Rhodesia, and so on – or whether we are looking at our own education system, here in the UK. Let us now take these two sites in turn.

Education and the Colonies

Hickling-Hudson, Matthews and Woods (2004) note that education systems, such as those in the countries listed above, still tend to be full of colonial assumptions, knowledges and customs. As the great colonial powers spread out around the globe, they took with them specifically Western systems of education, and although the schools they established were often mere shadows of the institutions back in Great Britain (or Spain or Holland or Portugal), the logic was the same, their internal structures were the same, their world-view was the same, and the truths they taught were the same. Poddar (1997, 62) makes the point that this did not occur by accident.

> ... western secular education was seen by the British establishment as the most convenient and effective means to establish 'the foundation for a stability that "even a political revolution will not destroy and upon which after many ages may rest a vast superstructure"'. (From an 1826 *Asiatic Journal*, cited in Viswanathan 1989, 117)

Two particular elements of the colonial school are of particular importance here, both in terms of how education continues to operate in the postcolonial era, as well as addressing the implication for colonised peoples. The first is the structure of the institution itself, and the second is the curriculum.

THE MASS SCHOOL

As was discussed at length in Chapter 4, the great institutions of the nineteenth century all developed according to the same logic (see Foucault 1977). Whether they were prisons, factories, hospitals, asylums or schools, all were structured around the minute subdivision of space and time, around continual surveillance, around hierarchical observation, around the examination, around uniforms; they were structured around *discipline*. Schools based upon these principles became not only the norm for European education, but also came to be regarded as the only viable model for schooling. It is hardly surprising, then, that when colonial administrators sought to put in place all the necessary elements of effective governance in the far-flung corners of Empire, they knew exactly what the schools ought to look like; i.e., there was a 'proper' way for this to be done.

The implications here are significant, both in terms of the enforcement of European frames of reference, and the marginalisation of Indigenous peoples. Three familiar aspects of the mass school, almost chosen at random, can illustrate how this occurs so easily.

The Subdivision of Time

We often think that there is something self-evident about time, that in keeping with the logic of the correspondence theory of truth, it exists independently of our perception of it. If this is correct, it is only so at a very simplistic level. Many cultures understand time, and measure its passing, in completely different ways. Certainly, very few other than ourselves have chopped it up into tiny, manageable pieces that subdivide each day into 'specific places you have to be at any given moment'. By imposing this regimen upon the structure of the school, native peoples generally not only found schooling strange, they often struggled to meet this disciplinary requirement, a requirement that had no meaning or purpose within their cultural frames of reference. The outcome of this was both the gradual marginalisation of other, non-disciplinary ways of understanding time – other truths about how time should be conceptualized – but also the development of potent stereotypes about Indigenous peoples being 'unreliable' and 'lazy'.

The Uniform

The notion that everyone should dress the same, and in a particularly Western style, within the mass school also runs contrary to the practices of many cultures. Furthermore, as is the case within non-colonial education settings, the unwillingness or financial inability to wear the uniform appropriately is often translated as resistance to the education system in total. So when the issue is actually one of cultural mismatch, or simply of poverty, pupils failing to meet the uniform requirements often have this conduct translated as 'lack of respect' – with all the associated implications this has for their chances of success within the school.

The Examination

This important legacy of the colonial system continues to have very specific roles to play within the education system – and beyond. Not only does it reinforce the Western notion that knowledge can be divided up into discrete little boxes, each of which can be measured, assessed and normalised independently, it also acts as an 'objective' tool through which the 'fair race' of the education system is run, and students from colonised communities are generally found wanting.

THE CURRICULUM

In addition to the structure of the school, some important observations can be made about the curricula. It is probably easiest to take a specific national example here. In Australia, the curriculum has remained recognisably British until relatively recently: British history, British sports, British literature. However, as the nation has grown in stature and confidence, and as migrants have arrived from a far greater variety of places and cultures, significant efforts have been made to de-colonialise the materials used in schools. The question is: how successful has this process been, and do they now have a genuinely postcolonial curriculum, or is it as British as it's ever been?

In the area of teaching literature, various writers have pointed to the problems associated with the ongoing dominance of the European and American literary canon within Australia. Not only does this perpetuate the logic of Eurocentrism, now so out of place within postcolonial contexts, it also actively disengages many young Australian students, who fail to recognise themselves, or their experiences, within any of the texts they are asked to read (Bean 2004). Similar observations have also been made about the teaching of art (Crouch, Chan and Kaye 2004) and music (Hickling-Husdon 2000).

If there has been one curriculum area wherein the struggle between the old and the new has been writ large in Australia, between colonial and postcolonial viewpoints, it is in the teaching of history. In what has been dubbed 'The History Wars', within the past decade defenders of more traditional 'white male ' histories of the colonisation of Australia, have responded critically to various attempts to give curriculum space to other perspectives, other truths, in this process – Indigenous truths, non-Anglo migrants' truths, women's truths—not all of them pretty (Parkes 2007). This is particularly the case with regards to Indigenous histories of Australia that do not tend to understand the founding of Australia in terms of heroic discovery, exploration and national coming-of-age; unsurprisingly, their histories largely focus instead upon dispossession, subjugation and attempted genocide.

So who gets to write history then? Within postcolonial frames of reference, the obvious conclusion is that there's no singular truth to be told about the founding of Australia, and that many other voices also have the right to be heard when it comes to telling the story of its past. However, bearing all these criticisms in mind, there is no suggestion here that a 'good curriculum' is therefore one somehow entirely purged of Western influences and truths:

> A postcolonial perspective does not seek to turn the tables and suppress the important legacies of European or 'Western' learning in order to promote Indigenous perspectives ... A postcolonial curriculum is a hybrid one, engaging with the elements of non-Western learning and experience which colonialism so determinedly cast aside. (Hickling-Hudson and Ahlquist 2004, 43)

Consequently, this does not mean that the West should therefore take all its 'truths', and its education system, and just go away. While some colonial truths can certainly be seen to be fallacious, self-serving, and ultimately repressive (e.g. we brought British 'civilisation' to the world, and the world should be grateful for it), it is also important to note that other Western truths have proved invaluable to the cultures into which they were introduced – the notion of universal human rights providing a particularly vivid example.

Truth and the UK Curriculum

The evidence suggests that we exported a culturally loaded education system to our Empire, one whose forms of organisation, social practices, truths and aesthetics supported our own interests and worldview, and so because we deemed cricket, Chaucer and herringbone uniforms to constitute the very fabric of a good education, it was *obviously* only natural that people in India would too. The issue now is: to what extent do our own school curricula stand up to close scrutiny. Are our curricula chock-a-block with indisputable truths, or are the knowledges therein just as open to question and challenge as those in Australia that told the Aborigines how lucky they were to have the British there?

There are a number of curriculum areas and issues that speak to this question. Two have already been addressed in this book, and they relate directly to the way in which our curriculum comes to be shaped by political forces that extend far beyond simple questions of knowledge and objectivity. The first concerns the teaching of literature. In Chapter 9, there was a discussion of the ongoing debate over precisely what literature should be used in the GCSE English curriculum, with the assertion by Michael Gove (2010) that British literature is 'the best in the world' and that this should dominate the discipline. Lined up against this position is a range of more left-leaning voices which suggest that a prerequisite for writing classic and timeless literature is not a British passport. And while the issue of objective 'truth' is not applicable in determining the 'value' of literature – if such a thing even exists – certainly the notion 'cultural neutrality' is, as set out in the title of this myth. Clearly, our English curriculum falls well short of this goal.

The second concerns teaching about the environment and climate change. In Chapter 11 it was noted that the push for Sustainability Education had stalled with the election of the Conservative government in 2010. Schools are no longer required to integrate sustainability into the curriculum in any organised or comprehensive way, and most of the ESD material has been removed from government websites. Given the current importance of climate issues to global welfare, and in particular concerns over global warming, it seems unusual that learning the 'facts' of one of the greatest ever threats to humanity, according to the globe's scientific community, is not a compulsory topic in our schools – unusual, that is, until we remind ourselves that school curricula are essentially political documents, and global warming, in particular, is very much a party political issue.

A further example of the political shaping of the UK curriculum concerns the issue of Citizenship within the National Curriculum. Citizenship is intended as a subject that educates about democracy, law and the justice system, human rights, key elements of the constitution, and how to participate in civic life as an informed member of the community. The issue, however, becomes one of interpreting how citizenship should actually be understood and enacted by members of that community. Jerome and Bhargave (2013) suggest that it is possible to paint a picture of the ideal citizen that emphasises individualism and the acquisition of civic skills, or one that foregrounds political engagement/critique and community welfare. These are very different visions of civil society, and they note that the most recent version of the Citizenship curriculum 'marks a return to older models of Tory citizenship, marked by minimalist, individualistic and voluntaristic conceptions of the citizen, and thus represent a neo-liberal perspective in place of New Labour's communitarian–civic republican conceptions' (Jerome and Bhargave 2013, 1).

So far, when discussing curriculum areas such as English literature, climate change and Citizenship, the issues are less about 'truth/falsity' and more about matters of emphasis and omission. The teaching of history also involves questions of weighting and perspective; however, we are also getting much closer to the realm of the just-plain-not-true.

There are a number of possible examples of this. Teaching about Britain's role as a colonial power is probably a good place to start. Recent research suggests that four out of ten Britons regard colonialism as a good thing, with only one in five taking the opposing view (Owen 2016). The central point here is that a largely romanticised version of the Empire has always been taught in schools, one that generally justified our conduct in terms of 'bringing civilisation' to native peoples. Owen cites several British history professors who have a very different opinion:

> The basis of empire is that you rule other people, you deny them independence, you exploit their labour and resources. (Jackson, cited in Owen 2016)

> (There is) a collective amnesia about the levels of violence, exploitation and racism involved in many aspects of imperialism, not to mention the various atrocities and catastrophes that were perpetrated, caused or exacerbated by British colonial politics or actions. (Major, cited in Owen 2016)

> An unwillingness to engage with the 'warts and all' of imperial history makes Britain particularly blind to how governments and the people of other countries view British society. (Branch, citied in Owen 2016)

As Ahmed (2016) notes, if Britons are proud of colonialism, 'clearly they need some lessons about the reality of the British Empire'. Obviously, up to this point, those lessons have never included any information about the thriving British slave trade, Boer concentration camps, the Amritsar Massacre, or the Bengal famine, to name but a very few. If you have never heard much about these historical events, you surely have to ask your history teacher, why not? Significantly, the current government asked the conservative historian Niall Ferguson to write school history curricula, a historian who states: 'I am fundamentally in favour of empire. Indeed, I believe the empire is more necessary in the 21st century than ever before' (Ferguson 2004, 24).

Perhaps an even more vivid example of the likely shortcomings of our school history curriculum has always involved teaching about Oliver Cromwell. His role in the English Civil War has long been a staple of British school history curricula – the New Model Army, the battle of Naseby, the execution of Charles 1, the Rump Parliament – but little or nothing was normally mentioned about his terrible treatment of the Irish. For those curious about this topic, perhaps a more useful reference might be an Irish school history textbook. In particular, look up the slaughter of the population of the town of Drogheda.

All of this this leads back to addressing myth #2 directly: our curriculum is both true and culturally neutral. Is the knowledge in our curriculum true? From what has gone before in this chapter, it can be seen that this is a complex question. What exactly do we mean by 'true'? If we mean *objectively* true in some realist sense, most philosophers would find this difficult to accept. If we mean 'true' in a more anti-realist sense – that we create various truths, and some of those are in our curriculum – then this sounds significantly more plausible, although still questionable. Is the knowledge in our curriculum culturally neutral? The briefest of glances at our history curriculum, as well as the ideas of the postcolonial theorists to be discussed in the next section – Fanon, Said, Guha, Connell, Bhabha – along with work from a wide variety of educational writers, would suggest that it is not.

It is important to point out here that there is no suggestion that the United Kingdom is somehow alone in its politicised curriculum, or its rather selective view of history. Other nations make the same kind of choices, for the same kinds of reasons. It is unlikely that the Belgian curricula focus extensively of their nation's appalling conduct in the Congo, or the French in Algeria. That said, approaching the past with truth and honesty is surely the first step to making sure such conduct remains firmly in the past.

Myth #3 *We Haven't Tried to 'Colonise' Anyone for More Than a Century, so Postcolonial Theory Has Nothing Relevant to Tell Us About 'Truth', the World or Ourselves*

Nobody cares about our 'colonies' anymore; it's just not relevant to modern-day Britain. Probably the only time we ever think about 'the Empire' is during the Commonwealth Games. Given this fact, we certainly don't need to know about the intellectual tools used to understand 'postcolonial' issues. Who cares about ideas such as 'hybridity', 'othering' and 'subaltern'. The Empire is long gone… culturally and politically; let's talk about something that actually matters.

While this all sounds superficially plausible, there are strong arguments to suggest that the situation is considerably more complex, and this is the case for both them and us. For example, simply stating that our old colonies are free of any significant British legacy doesn't necessarily make it so. While these nations may no longer sing 'God Save the Queen', have pounds as their currency, or appeal to the United Kingdom's Privy Council to settle legal disputes, they are often still playing out remnants of the cultural hand we first dealt them hundreds of years ago. As was argued in myth #2, their education systems can be a perfect example of this, with the evidence indicating that, at their core, there often still beats a Eurocentric heart, and whether they realise it or not, the systems of knowledge and representation they valorise, and the truths they accept, have many of their origins there.

We are also not free of the legacy of our colonial past. As previously mentioned, we are now a multi-ethnic society – in large part because citizens from our former colonies in India, Pakistan, Bangladesh, Jamaica, Barbados, Kenya, Nigeria, Australia, New Zealand, Fiji and Samoa, to name but a few, have returned to the motherland to make it their home. How these people adapt and manage their identities to fit into broader British society, along with the knowledges and truths they bring and the worldviews they inhabit, are just as interesting and complex a set of questions as those that relate to the identities, truths and world-views formed in the countries they left behind.

It has been argued that these very complexities have necessitated the development of a very specific set of intellectual tools for understanding the postcolonial world. These tools will be addressed shortly, but first it is probably necessary to contextualise colonialism itself a little more thoroughly.

Colonialism and Postcolonialism

For over 500 years, a number of European countries – primarily Great Britain, France, Spain, Portugal, Germany and Holland – extended their influence across the globe. Wave after wave of exploration across the Americas, Africa and Asia ultimately resulted in the foundation of global empires, empires largely built upon the resources they took from the lands they encountered. This was not a one-way process. Though the minerals, spices, timber and even the inhabitants, were shipped away by the Europeans, they left small versions of their homelands behind: hybrid adaptations of Spain in Central and South America, of France in North Africa, Holland in South Africa, and of Great Britain in North America, India and Australasia.

These colonies were not just collections of towns and ports, clustered under the flag of a distant power. They introduced new languages, entirely different political and education systems, alternative forms of conduct, other ways of understanding the world – altogether new truths – as well as imported social, cultural and epistemological hierarchies. This last point had particular significance for the lives of the colonised. As McLeod (2000, 19) states:

> Under colonialism, a colonised people are made subservient to ways of regarding the world which reflect and support colonialist values. A particular value-system is taught as the best, truest world-view. The cultural values of the colonised peoples are deemed as lacking in value, or even as being 'uncivilised', from which they must be rescued. To be blunt, the British Empire did not rule by military and physical force alone. It endured by getting *both colonising and colonised people* to see their world and themselves in a particular way, internalising the language of Empire as representing the natural, true order of life.

It is not as if when the British set out to build the Empire that the various Indigenous cultures they encountered were understood as being of equal value, such that a 50–50 hybrid culture might somehow emerge; far from it. The beliefs and practices of the colonisers were assumed to be infinitely superior, with the locals 'obviously' needing to be rescued from their cultural inferiority. Many would argue that even after hundreds of years – particularly in countries like Australia – very little has changed.

Of course, European colonisation has not continued unchecked. First, there is really nothing left to colonise, no land left unclaimed or unconquered – even the

Antarctic has been divided up like a giant cake – but if there were, the economic and ideological world superpower is now the USA, and the smart money would be on them to be the first to stake a claim (McDonalds everyone?). More importantly for our purposes, since the 1950s, there has been a reversal of the colonising process. The world over, nations initially formed as colonies have gained independence from their colonial masters, either by negotiated political settlement, or by bloody struggle. However, this is far from the end of the matter.

Postcolonial Theory

It is not as if, upon gaining independence, the former colonies suddenly and magically returned to their original state. Each postcolonial country has to deal with its own set of colonial legacies, and not just political and economic, but in terms of shaping viable identities, both at the scale of nationhood *and* of individual citizenship, former coloniser and former colonist. This is not an easy task, as the recent history of Australia amply demonstrates. The body of work that has attempted to address these difficulties is called *postcolonial theory*. It covers a wide range of areas, and the work of a plethora of writers. Five in particular will be dealt with here, specifically addressing how their work speaks to the notion of truth.

FANON: POSTCOLONIAL IDENTITIES

Fanon was a highly educated psychiatrist from Martinique, who struggled against the French colonisation of North Africa. Though most famous for his book on revolutionary decolonisation, *The Wretched of the Earth* (Fanon 1961), he also wrote *Black Skin, White Masks* (Fanon 1952). In this text he discusses how those with black skin always come to be defined as 'other' within colonial settings. This process of definition is not limited to whites – those who might consider themselves 'true' representatives of a national identity – but actually manages to co-opt blacks into the same reasoning. As such, those with black skin come to regard themselves as somehow 'less' than their white counterparts, never a colonial *subject*, but rather always an *object;* different and outside.

Once again, the British colonisation of Australia provides a useful example of this argument. Bearing in mind the logic set out in Chapter 3 about white race privilege, it is unlikely that when a white Australian person looks in the mirror that the colour of their skin plays any role in how they understand themselves. They are not a 'white Australian'; they are simply Australian. This cannot generally be said for the Indigenous. After 200 years of colonisation, Aborigines fully understand that they are necessarily 'the other', marked out not only by the colour of their skin, and their physical appearance, but also by elements of their hybrid identity, always excluding them for being 'true' Australians – an irony that needs no further comment.

SAID: MISREPRESENTING 'THE OTHER'

One of the most influential texts within postcolonial theory is *Orientalism* (Said 1995). In this book, he discusses how 'the truth' of the Middle East – the Orient, as it was referred to in the late nineteenth and early twentieth centuries – was constructed with only limited reference to its subject matter. That is, western experts ('Orientalists') came to shape our understanding of the Arab/Islamic world, not as a direct, objective reflection of the culture they were describing, but rather as an amalgam of the romanticised preconceptions, stereotypical prejudices, oversimplifications and ethnocentrisms that they brought with them in the first place.

> The Orient and Islam have a kind of extrareal, phenomenologically reduced status that puts them out of reach of everyone except the Western expert. From the beginning of Western speculation about the Orient, the one thing the Orient could not do was to represent itself. Evidence of the Orient was credible only after it had passed through and been made firm by the refining fire of the Orientalist's work (Said 1995, 283).

To put it another way, the truth of the Arab world only became *the truth* when it was authored by someone from the West, and importantly, this truth was necessarily a function of the colonial relationships of power from which it emerged: i.e. Arabs aren't like us; they are lazy, strange, exotic, dangerous; they are 'the other'. Once again, arguably very little has changed.

GUHA: THE SUBALTERN

Guha is one of the most important writers within the field of *Subaltern Studies*, a sub-branch of postcolonial theory. The term 'subaltern' refers to those of lower social status, those whose voice is not generally heard when it comes to the production of truth. While representations of nation and identity are generally shaped by the colonisers and not the colonised (the subaltern: after all, do we really think that local world views carry the same weight and truth value as those associated with the West?), this is not to say that similar divisions don't also exist within the colonised themselves; between those whose voice is heard, and those who are silenced.

A good example of this silencing can be seen in Guha's essay 'On some aspect of the historiography of Colonial India' (Guha 1988) in which he notes that the written history of the decolonisation of India has privileged the voices of the native elite, wherein they placed themselves, virtually alone, at the intellectual and political forefront of the struggle against British rule. Largely absent from these same histories are the activities and efforts of the many subaltern groups – those castes who generally lack the power to make themselves heard – and consequently, their efforts, and their truths, will ultimately vanish from the record.

CONNELL: EUROCENTRIC THEORY

While there may be a temptation to think that while everything is slanted in favour of the West, in favour of the colonial powers that shaped the world in their own image, then at least the intellectual tools by which we conduct our analysis – the theories behind it all – are neutral in their application, and hence the truths produced by our Social Sciences are founded upon solid ground. This would be a mistake.

In *Southern Theory*, Connell (2007) points to a number of ways that the social theories of the colonisers subtly marginalise the ideas of the colonised. There is the assumption of intellectual universality, for example in that the philosophy taught in Western universities remains valid across all cultural and intellectual contexts, whereas 'African philosophy' is a niche subject, with an equally niche application. Likewise, there is a self-replicating process of selective exclusion, wherein Western ideas provide virtually all the content for books such as this, to the exclusion of equally valid work that simply made the mistake of being written by someone of non-European origin; unfortunately it's true… check the reference list at the back. Finally, she points to a 'grand erasure' of previous subaltern ideas and experiences from our analysis, as if our theories, and the worlds they describe, had sprung from nowhere, pure and fully formed. As such, our truths become written on the spaces created by the erasure of other truths. Connell (2007, 47) states that just as modern Australia was built on the myth of *Terra Nullius* – land belonging to nobody – so too are many of its ideas:

> *Terra nullius*, the coloniser's dream, is a sinister proposition for social science. It is invoked every time we try to theorise the formation of social institutions and systems from scratch, in a blank space. Whenever we see the words 'building block' in a treatise of social theory, we should be asking who used to occupy the land.

BHABHA: AMBIVALENCE, MIMICRY, HYBRIDITY

It would be pretty depressing to think that the effects of colonialism can simply be summed up by a long list of the ways in which native peoples and ideas have been subordinated to the will of the colonisers. While Indigenous peoples have undoubtedly been 'othered' by European colonisation, and their cultures given subaltern status, those peoples have equally sought to make space for themselves, on their own terms, within their new social environment. It is not as if British culture has cleanly and unproblematically been stamped onto the existing inhabitants of various countries, producing in the process lots of perfect little copies of people from the home counties of England. Instead, the colonised negotiate this process in a number of different ways.

Bhabha (1984, 1994) uses three important conceptual tools to better understand how those who 'used to occupy the land', to use Connell's phrase, manage the imposition of a new culture upon their own; the first is *ambivalence*. According to this proposition, far from simply internalising the new culture in a straightforward way, the colonised often oscillate between an accepting of the new order, and all it represents, and a rejection of it; there is both complicity with that culture, and a resistance to it. As such, there is never the comfortable certainly of obedience and submission from the subordinated peoples. Their relationship will always remain, at best, one of both attraction and repulsion (Ashcroft, Griffiths and Tiffin 2013).

Second, when the colonisers attempt to produce colonial citizens in their own image, perfect reproductions of themselves, all they tend to achieve instead is a form of *mimicry*. The point Bhabha is making is not that, oh well. . . near enough is good enough, but rather that it's a very fine line between mimicry and mockery, and that with mockery comes a certain menace. As Bhabha (1984, 129) states, 'mimicry, articulates those disturbances of cultural, racial, and historical difference that menace the narcissistic demand of colonial authority'. Arguably, the adoption of certain aspects of Western culture by the locals has always had its tongue firmly in its cheek.

The final theoretical device in Bhabha's postcolonial toolkit is the notion of *hybridity*. Rather than there being a wholesale adoption of various colonial identities by the colonised – arguably one of the central cultural intentions of the colonising process – or conversely, a total rejection of them, there is often a third option/space available. New identities are shaped which incorporate both the old and the new, and which offer both a form of cultural exchange, as well as the opportunity for subtle forms of social resistance. For example, there are forms of hybrid subcultural identity adopted by Indigenous Australian youth which, while incorporating stylistic themes common within the wider youth community, also involve elements of more traditional Indigenous cultures.

In summary then, in terms of a theoretical way forward for postcolonial studies – particularly regarding the issue of identity formation – the concept of hybridity has a lot to offer. As McLeod (2000, 219) states:

> The concept of hybridity has proved very important. . . as a way of thinking beyond exclusionary, fixed, binary notions of identity based upon ideas of rootedness and cultural, racial and national purity. Hybrid identities are never total and complete, like orderly pathways built from crazy-paving. Instead, they remain perpetually in motion, pursuing errant and unpredictable routes, open to change and reinscription.

Postcolonial Theory and the United Kingdom

While the concept of postcolonialism is usually used to explain the ongoing cultural, economic, linguistic and educational authority of the mother country over ostensibly decolonised nations, it can also refer to the broader effects of that colonisation, both within that mother country and globally. As previously mentioned, some of the outcomes of Britain's colonial history can be seen on our streets every day – people of different colours and backgrounds, with inter-cultural fusions of dress and social practice, speaking anything from Jamaican patois to broad cockney. Importantly, the conceptual tools which are used to interrogate the effects of colonialism in India and New Zealand can be used to good effect right here at home.

People from once-colonised countries have been coming to Britain in significant numbers from the 1950s onwards, in our case, specifically recruited to cope with labour shortages in areas such as transportation and health (McLeod 2000). These people have often formed diasporic communities – communities which, to some degree, still acknowledge an 'old country' – throughout the United Kingdom, whether those communities are Asian, African or Caribbean. The conceptual tools provided by postcolonial thinkers are just as applicable to these identities, experiences, cultural formations and power relations. These would undoubtedly include some basic conceptual argument around Fanon and Said's notions of 'othering', but more specifically it would be likely to involve Bhabha's arguments about hybridity.

Hybridity is particularly relevant here for a number of reasons. First, diasporic communities tend not to hold on to their old cultural identities endlessly in some pure and unchanged form – perfect little islands of Barbados, for example, in the middle of Norwich or Aberdeen. They are affected by the broader, dominant cultures in which they have become partially immersed; as such new spaces are opened up as a form of cultural exchange. While this is never an entirely equal exchange, given the likely power differentials between the communities, it is still an exchange – and cultural hybridity is borne from that.

Second, this process does not occur in any kind of uniform way; there are significant generational, classed and gendered differences here. For example, those born to migrant peoples – second- and third-generation Britons – are likely to have strong allegiances and adherences to the cultural mainstream, yet still retain a sense of belonging to a diasporic community, and the kinds of hybrid identities formed in such spaces will reflect this complexity. As was discussed in Chapter 3, Hall (1992, 433) points out that there remains no single 'black' subject position upon which essentialised identities can be founded; there is no common black experience, just a diversity of 'subjective positions, social experiences and cultural identities which comprise the category "black"'. Consequently, there is never simply one version of a hybrid culture – 'Barbados meets Britain' – they are often local, piecemeal, fragmented and fluid.

Finally, it has been argued that a full understanding of hybridity, specifically regarding black identities in the United Kingdom, requires extending the analysis beyond the shores of both the 'old country' and the new. In *Black Atlantic*, Gilroy (1993), contends that there is a transnational element to black identities – spanning Africa, the Caribbean, the USA and Britain – which mitigates against any simple or essentialised understanding of black settler cultures in Britain. He puts forward 'the suggestion that cultural historians could take the Atlantic as one single, complex unit of analysis in their discussions of the modern world and use it to produce an explicitly transnational and intercultural perspective' (Gilroy 1993, 15).

In addition to postcolonial theory providing the conceptual tools for analysing settler cultures in the United Kingdom, it has also been argued that such theories are useful in addressing the national relationships within the United Kingdom itself, i.e. between England and Northern Ireland, and England and Scotland. Lehner (2005) notes that it is very easy to argue that England colonised Ireland and Scotland in much the same way that the United Kingdom later came to colonise other countries around the world. As such, the conceptual tools of postcolonialism – in particular, the notion of 'the subaltern', in that it speaks to the cultural and political hegemony held by the English over the Irish and the Scottish – are perfectly applicable in this context. She also notes that this might be regarded in some quarter as a just a bit rich, citing Ashcroft *et al.* (2003, 31–2):

> While it is possible to argue that these societies were the first victims of English expansion, their subsequent complicity in the British imperial enterprise makes it difficult for colonised peoples outside Britain to accept their identity as post-colonial.

Conclusion

This chapter has sought to demonstrate that 'truth' is not a simple issue; it has provided the substance for philosophical debate for 2500 years and, to be honest, we are still arguing about many of the same things now. Does truth exist independently of human thought and action, as suggested by the realists? Or is truth simply a function of the social contexts within which it is formulated, as suggested by the anti-realists? These questions are important because, emerging from the wealth of truths we discover/accept, comes human knowledge, in all its forms – and surely, this is what schools are all about. If Protagoras is right, and if 'Man is the measure of all things', does this mean that knowledge about the universe, and ultimately about ourselves, can never be built upon completely solid ground? Most contemporary philosophers would say, 'Probably not'.

This chapter has also sought to demonstrate that many of the truths we take for granted are very much the product of the social, political and historical contexts from which they emerge. This is the case, irrespective of whether it relates to who we think we are, how we understand our nation's role in the world, how we understand other peoples and cultures, or whose voices get to be heard. Importantly, the evidence suggests that our schools play an important role in replicating and reinforcing often-questionable 'truths' about who writes the best books, what kind of citizen we ought to be, and what kind of country we live in. That is, there are many models for understanding the world, and we are often only presented with one.

Finally, while the three chapters comprising Part IV of this book have set out to demonstrate the vital importance of the discipline of philosophy in gaining better understanding of mass schooling, it is also important to note, particularly regarding the substance of this chapter, that all knowledge appears to be context-bound, and philosophy is no exception.

One of the most robust and suspect theoretical moves of Western philosophy is to assume historical, temporal and spatial synchronicity – that indeed we might live in a 'universal' world where singular theoretical constructs and textual conceits might have generalisable explanatory and practical power. Yet the answers obviously depend upon where, to whom, by whom, when, with which available discourses and in which material conditions (Luke 2004, 251).

CONCLUSION:
THE CENTRAL AIMS
OF THIS BOOK

This book set out with some very specific goals in mind, even if it has not necessarily achieved them all. The first is to address the issue of mass education in ways that have something to offer a range of different readers. This book is not aimed specifically at undergraduates, anymore than it is at practising teachers, or university academics. Each chapter has been organised with a progressive layering of complexity and density, such that readers with differing levels of knowledge and expertise should still be able to get something out of it. This has not been written as a textbook, with bite-sized pieces tailor-made for tutorial digestion. The book was put together for a range of reasons: it is a summary of the current state of play within contemporary theories of education; it is a resource book for those interesting in assessing the weight of different conceptual approaches to mass schooling; it is an analysis of various issues within modern society, as they relate to education; it is a (relatively) gentle critique of reductionist analyses of our schooling institutions and their outcomes; and it is a call for us not to forget the value of philosophy within the broader play of the social sciences.

Second, the intention has been to use a language that is as inclusive as possible. This has not been done with the intention, in any way, of dumbing down the content – far from it. Simple language, carefully used, can still convey all the nuances required from a text dealing with complex ideas. The goal was simply to write a book in a more conversational manner – in part because it is often more enjoyable to read, but also because it's certainly more enjoyable to write. This style has also not been adopted as a veiled criticism of books that maintain a rigorously academic voice throughout; both styles have their place. However, if a book is intended for a broad audience, it surely needs to be written in a broadly accessible manner.

Third, the book has been written with the intention of addressing a wide range of issues and ideas as they relate to mass schooling, without descending into some sort of a scattergun approach, one giving five pages to every unit in the education faculty curriculum. It should be possible for anyone who wants to know more about the social, cultural and philosophical underpinnings of contemporary schooling to go to a book like this and find most of what they are looking for. This book covers the central axes of social inequality, in class, gender and race. It covers the rise of mass schooling as a disciplinary institution, including the governance of subjective experience, the regulation of various categories of pre-adulthood and the growth of Big Data. It examines various cultural influences on the field of education, from the news media, through popular cultural forms, to the rise of digital technologies and the effects of globalisation. Finally, it addresses the influence of philosophical thought upon education, as well as issues of ethics and morality, and the truth claims we make. As such, most of the main debates and topics within the contemporary sociology of education are covered here.

Finally, this text was written deliberately in a single voice. While there are many advantages in co-authoring books – workload, shared expertise, a greater communal safety net for errors, misstatements, and misjudgements – the overall coherence of a book is not generally one of them. After all, conceptual disputes with oneself are not common, although succumbing to theoretical fence-sitting is (on second thoughts, perhaps conceptual disputes with oneself *are* common; perhaps that is the primary function of a book like this. . . to engender such disputes). Likewise, edited collections can be uneven, contradictory, and prone to containing large chunks of irrelevance. Hopefully, *Schooling and Society* has none of these shortcomings.

The Intended Approach of This Book

This book also sets out with a very specific approach in mind. First, by utilising the idea of 'common myths', the intention has been to ground the book in some of the concrete, mundane ideas that appear to exist within public discourses about education, and then start working out from there. This is a very different proposition to the usual approach of outlining the parameters of a given theory, and then applying that theory to a range of different issues. In keeping with the general aim of accessibility, a criterion fundamental to this book, this seemed like a logical way to go.

Second, by grounding the book in the world of public discourse – i.e. starting with familiar meritocratic claims and questions, such as 'It's all up to the individual, isn't it?', rather than theoretical ones, such as 'Cultural capital is often misread as "ability"' – this book not only continues the theme of accessibility, it can also more readily act as an antidote to the multitude of simplistic discourses and aphorisms about education that those with knowledge in the area hear almost every day, generally coming from those without.

The third noteworthy aspect of the approach taken by this book is that it does not set out to champion a particular theoretical framework for the study of mass education. While Part I of this book does find significant shortcomings with traditional modernist approaches to the study of class, gender and race, it does not then seek to position its postmodern successor as the answer to all our theoretical problems. Neither does it suggest that governmental approaches to the study of mass schooling somehow trump everything that has gone before. Likewise, the final part on philosophy is not put there as a trans-disciplinary solution to the problem of theory, suggesting that in the final analysis, philosophy outdoes sociology. It would be a strange book indeed that ends with a chapter on the intangible nature of truth, and then claim to know the 'truth' of social theory. All theories have their strengths and weaknesses – some weaknesses more terminal than others – and understanding those theories, and what they say about mass schooling, isn't really a quest for the 'right' answer.

Lastly, the four parts are not simply organised according to subject matter, whether this be the three main axes of social inequality in Part 1, or various manifestations of contemporary culture in Part 3. They are also organised according to a specific conceptual logic, a logic where each is built upon the reasoning of the last – or at least acts as a counterpoint to it – and each contributes to an effective lexicon of approaches for better understanding mass schooling. This book is not just a list of topics, with some associated guidelines for how to best address each one. Upon finishing the book, readers should have a sound grasp of how various theoretical positions work, how they relate to each other, and a knowledge of some the domains in which those ideas can be applied.

Finally

Some concluding observations: first, while the dominant, modernist models of educational analysis have some demonstrable shortcomings, elements of these approaches still retain conceptual and practical utility. The suggestion here has not been to throw out the notions of class, gender, and race altogether as no longer possessing any theoretical viability or merit. For whatever those terms now mean, when employed with a solid grasp of their limitations and weaknesses, they can still tell us a lot about how we are shaped as citizens, how our education system works, and who is most likely to win the race of life.

Second, a theoretical framework based around social governance, either alone or in tandem with aspects of the above, can offer an effective new lens through which to understand education. By regarding power as fundamentally productive rather than coercive, the mass school can be seen, not as a giant engine for the replication of social inequalities, but rather as a crucial component of an otherwise piecemeal set of processes aimed at regulating the conduct and capacities of the population. That is, the mass school wasn't established with the intention of keeping the working classes in their place, or making sure women stayed in the kitchen (although it may have had a role to play in their occurring), rather it provided an efficient mechanism through which the population could be normalised.

Third, perhaps more than ever, the mass school needs to be understood as located within a complex mosaic of cultural practices, forces and innovations. This mosaic doesn't exist as an external distraction to formal learning, or as something that should, or should not, be incorporated into classroom practice. Education is not a separate domain, one that sought to remain somehow pure and unaffected by the distractions of culture. To paraphrase Dewey, we do not educate *for* life; education *is* life, and culture, in all its forms, is the context within which that life is shaped.

Finally, the working life of educators – whether in schools or universities – has become dauntingly complex, with the relentless focus on standards and testing, pressure to ensure equitable outcomes, managerialist working environments, ever-growing professional responsibilities and expectations, increasingly heterogeneous classrooms, and fairly relentless media criticism, to name only a few of the issues. The job requires continual self-reflection, a commitment to life-long learning, and an ongoing dedication to the profession to remain viable at all. Making sense of it all is not an easy task. Hopefully this book can help a little.

REFERENCES

Ackoff, R. 1989. From data to wisdom. *Journal of Applied Systems Analysis* 16: 3–9.

Adoniou, M. 2013. Losts for words: why the best literacy aproaches are not reaching the classroom. *The Conversation. http://theconversation.com/lost-for-words-why-the-best-literacy-approaches-are-not-reaching-the-classroom-19561* (last accessed 30/1/16).

Adorno, T. and M. Hormheimer. 1979. *Dialectic of Enlightenment*. London: Verso.

Ahmed, J. 2016. So Brits are proud of colonialism? Clearly they need some lessons about the reality of the British Empire. *The Independent*, 22 January.

Althusser, L. 1971. *Lenin and Philosophy, and Other Essays*. London: New Left Books.

American Association for the Advancement of Science. 2014. *What we know*. http://whatweknow.aaas.org/ (last accessed 15/3/15).

American Psychiatric Association (APA). 2013. *The Diagnostic and Statistical Manual of Mental Disorders*, 5th edn. Washington DC.

Amory, E. 2003. Migrants blamed for diseases. *Daily Mail*.

Anderson, M. 2003. Whitewashing race: a critical perspective on whiteness. In *White Out: the Continuing Significance of Racism*, eds. A. W. Doane and E. Bonilla-Silva, **xii**, 328. New York: Routledge.

Apple, M. 1982. *Education and Power*. Boston: ARK.

Apple, M. W. 1979. *Ideology and Curriculum. Routledge Education Books*. London, Boston: Routledge & K. Paul.

Apps, J. 1991. *Mastering the Teaching of Adults*. Malabar, FL: Krieger.

Aries, P. 1962. *Centuries of Childhood*. Harmondsworth: Penguin.

Aristotle. 1980. *Nicomachean Ethics*. Oxford: Oxford University Press.

Arlemalm-Hagser, E. and I. Engdahl. 2015. Caring for oneself, others and the environment: education for sustainability in Swediah preschools. In *Young Children and the Environment: Early Education for Sustainability*, 2nd edn, ed. J. Davis. Melbourne: Cambridge University Press.

Arnold, M. 1963. *Culture and Anarchy*. Cambridge: Cambridge University Press.

Arrow, K. 1978. *Social Choice and Individual Values*. New Haven: Yale University Press.

Ashcroft, B., G. Griffiths and H. Tiffin. 2013. *Postcolonial Studies: the Key Concepts*. Oxford: Routledge.

Atkins, D. 1996. A learning process. *The Courier Mail*, 23 January.

Au, W. 2009. *Unequal By Design: High-Stakes Testing and the Standardisation of Inequality*. New York: Routledge.

Austin, J. 2000. *The Province of Jurisprudence Determined. 1832*. New York: Prometheus.

Australian Government. 2014. *Review of the Australian Curriculum: Final Report*, Canberra: Australian Government Department of Education.

Australian Literacy Educators Association (ALEA). 2013. *Submission to the Senate Committee on Education and Employment Inquiry in The Effectiveness of the Nation Assessment Program – Literacy and Numeracy (NAPLAN)*, 13 June.

Axford, B. 1995. *The Global System: Economics, Politics, Culture*. Cambridge: Polity Press.

Axford, B. 2013. *Theories of Globalisation*. Cambridge: Polity Press.

Ayer, A. 1935. The criterion of truth. *Analysis* 3.

Bacon, F. 1952. The New Organon (Novum Organon). 1620. In *Great Books of the Western World: Volume 30, the Works of Francis Bacon*, ed. R. Hutchins. Chicago: Encyclopaedia Britannica, Inc.

Bacon, F. 1985. *On Truth. The Essays. 1601*. Harmondsworth: Penguin.

Bagnall, N. 2010. *Education Without Borders: Forty Years of the International Baccalaureate, 1970–2010*. Berlin: VDM Publishing House.

Bagnall, N. 2013. Globalisation. In *Education, Change and Society*, 3rd edn, eds. R. Connell, A. Welch, M. Vickers *et al.* Melbourne: Oxford University Press.

Ball, S. 2008. *The Education Debate*. London: Verso Press.

Ball, S. 2012. *Foucault, Power, and Education*. London: Routledge.

Ball, S., A. Dworkin and M. Vryinides. 2010. Globalisation and education: introduction. *Current Sociology* 58(4): 523–9.

Balz, D. 2013. How the Obama campaign won the race for voter data. *The Washington Post*, 28 July.

Banton, M. 1998. *Racial Theories*, 2nd edn. Cambridge, New York: Cambridge University Press.

Baron, D. 2002. From pencils to pixels: the stages of literacy technology. In *Writing Material*, eds. E. Tribble and A. Trubek. London: Longman.

Barrow, R. 1975. *Moral Philosophy for Education*. London: George, Allen and Unwin.

Barthes, R. 1972. *Mythologies*. London: Paladin.

Baudrillard, J. 1983. *Simulations*. New York: Semiotext(e).

Baudrillard, J. 1993. *Symbolic Exchange and Death*. London: Sage.

Bayne, S. and S. Ross. 2011. 'Digital native' and 'digital immigrant' discourses: a critique. In *Digital Difference: Perspectives on Online Learning*, eds. R. Land and S. Bayne. Rotterdam: Sense.

Bazalgette, C. (ed.) 2010. *Teaching Media in Primary School*. London: Sage.

Bean, T. 2004. The role of multiculural literature as a counter-force to the literary canon. In *Disrupting Preconceptions: Postcolonialism and Education*, eds. A. Hickling-Hudson, J. Matthews and A. Woods. Flaxton: Post-Pressed.

Beauvoir, S., de. 1960. *The Second Sex*. London: Landsborough Publications.

Beaver, M. 2011. Church studied ways to 'cure' homosexuality. *Contra Costa Times*, 20 March.

BECTA. 2008. *How do boys and girls differ in their use of ICT? http://dera.ioe.ac.uk/8318/1/gender_ict_briefing.pdf* (last accessed 30/1/16).

Bell, T. and M. Gropshover. 2005. Pop goes the geographer: synergies between geography and popular culture. In *Popular Culture Studies Across the Curriculum*, ed. R. Browne. Jefferson: McFarland and Co.

Bennett, T., M. Savage, E. Silva, A. Warde, M. Gayo-Cal and D. Wright. 2008. *Culture, Class, Distinction*. London: Routledge.

Benthem, J. 1988. *An Introduction to the Principals of Morals and Legislation (1781)*. New York: Prometheus Books.

Berger, P. 1963. *Invitation to Sociology: a Humanist Perspective*. Garden City, NY: Doubleday.

Berman, S. and R. Tinker. 2000. The world's the limit in the virtual high school. In *Technology and Learning*, ed. R. Pea. San Francisco: Jossey-Bass.

Bernstein, B. 1990. *Class, Codes and Control*. London: Routledge.

Better Education. 2014. http://bettereducation.com.au/SchoolRanking.aspx (last accessed 30/1/16).

Bhabha, H. 1984. Of mimicry and man, the ambivalence of colonial discourse. *October* **28**: 125–33.

Bhabha, H. 1994. *The Location of Culture*. London: Routledge.

Biddle, N. and N. Priest. 2014. Experiences and effects of racism in school: the quantitative evidence. *Presentation to the Australian Institute of Family Studies*, 9 April, Melbourne.

Bierce, A. 1995. *The Devil's Dictionary. 1911*. London: Penguin.

Bini, M., G. Burgh, P. Cam *et al.* 2009. The case for inclusion of philosophy in the National Curriculum. *Paper submitted to the Australian Curriculum, Assesment and Reporting Authority*.

Birbalsingh, K. 2011. Trendy teachers cheat the poor and lay the groundwork for riots. *The Australian*, September 23.

Bishop, K. and D. Wahlsten. 1997. Sex differences in the human corpus callosum: myth or reality. *Neuroscience Biobehavioural Review* 21(5): 581–601.

Blackmore, J., L. Hardcastle, E. Bamblett and J. Owens. 2003. *Effective use of information and communication technology (ICT) to enhance learning for disadvantaged school students*: Deakin Centre for Education and Change; Institute of Disability Studies, Deakin University and Institute of Koorie Eduction, Deakin University.

Bloom, A. 1987. *The Closing of the American Mind*. New York: Simon and Schuster.

Board of Studies, New South Wales. 2008. *Working with Aboriginal communities: a guide to community consultation and protocols*, Government of New South Wales.

Bohn, R. and J. Short. 2009. *How Much Information? Report on American Consumers*. Global Information Industry Centre, University of California, San Diego.

Bolt, A. 2011. Refugee blunder costing us billions. *The Courier Mail*, 8 May.

Bolton, P. 2012. *Education: Historical Statistics*. London: House of Commons Library.

Boody, R. 2001. On the relationship of education and technology. In *Education and Technology: Critical and Reflective Practices*, ed. R. Muffoletto. Cresskill, NJ: Hampton Press.

Booth-Butterfield, S, and M. Booth-Butterfield. (1991). The communication of humor in everyday life: individual differences in the use of humorous messages. *Southern Communication Journal* 56: 205–17.

Bottomley, A. 1996. *Feminist Perspectives on the Foundational Subjects of Law*. London: Cavendish.

Bourdieu, P. 1986. The forms of capital. In *Handbook of Theory and Research for the Sociology of Education*, ed. J. G. Richardson, 241–58. New York: Greenwood Press.

Bourdieu, P. and J. C. Passeron. 1990. *Reproduction in Education, Society and Culture*, 2nd edn, *Theory, Culture & Society*. London: Sage.

Bové, J. and F. Dufour. 2001. *The World Is Not For Sale*. London: Verso.

Bowcott, O. 2015. UK–US surveillance regime was unlawful 'for seven years'. *Guardian*, 6 February.

Bowles, S. and H. Gintis. 1976. *Schooling in Capitalist America: Educational Reform and the Contradictions of Economic Life*. New York: Basic Books.

Boyd-Barrett, O. and T. Rantenen. 2010. New agencies. In *The Media: an Introduction*, eds. D. Albertazzi and P. Cobley, 233–45. London: Pearson.

Brabazon, T. 2002. *Digital Hemlock: Internet Education and the Poisoning of Teaching*. Sydney: Unversity of New South Wales Press.

Brandt, R. 1978. Towards a credible form of utilitarianism. In *Contemporary Utilitarianism*, ed. M. Bayles. Massachusetts: Anchor.

Branston, G. and R. Stafford. 2006. *The Media Student's Book*, 4th edn. Abingdon, Oxon: Routledge.

Bristol City Council. 2010. *Asylum seekers and refugees: FAQs, myths and the facts* (2nd edn) https://www.bristol.gov.uk/documents/20182/33107/Asylum%20se ekers%20and%20refugees%20mythbusting%20booklet.pdf/ac35ad35-9e3e-4 ae5-9b74-0b7ffcb0c58f (last accessed 30/1/16).

British Red Cross. 2015. Refugees and asylum seekers: getting the story straight in 2015. http://www.redcross.org.uk/~/media/BritishRedCross/Documents/Wh at%20we%20do/Refugee%20support/UKS_RefugeeWeek_MYTHBUSTE R_15_WEB.pdf

Brogan, B. 2005. Asylum: you're right to worry. *Daily Mail*, 7 February.

Bronte, C. 1847. *Jane Eyre*. London: Smith, Elder, and Co.

Bronte, E. 1846. *Wuthering Heights*. London: Thomas Cautley Newby.

Brosnan, M. 1998. *Technophobia: the Psychological Impact of Information Technology*. London: Routledge.

Brown, D. 2003. *The Da Vinci Code*. New York: Doubleday.

Brown, L. and I. Jones. 2013. Encounters with racism and the international student experience. *Studies in Higher Education* 38(7): 1004–19.

Bryson, L. 1990. Challenges to male hegemony in sport. In *Sport, Men and the Gender Order: Critical Feminist Perspectives*, eds. M. Messner and D. Sabo, 173–184. Champaign: Human Kinetics.

Bucholtz, M. 2002. Youth and cultural practice. *Annual Review of Anthropology* 31: 525–552.

Buckingham, D. 2014. Selling youth: the paradoxical empowermant of the young consumer. In *Youth Cultures in the Age of Global Media*, eds. D. Buckingham, S. Bragg and M. Kehily. Basingstoke: Palgrave MacMillan.

Buckingham, J. 2014. The key to improving literacy is effective instruction. In *Why Jaydon Can't Read: a Forum on Fixing Literacy*, eds. J. Buckingham, J. Ferrari and T. Alegounarias. The Centre for Independent Studies.

Burchell, G. 1993. Liberal government and techniques of the self. *Economy and Society* 22(3): 267–83.

Burke, P. 1996. *Popular Culture in Early Modern Europe*, 2nd edn. London: Temple Smith.

Burnett, B. 2004a. How does 'othering' constitute cultural discrimination? In *New Questions For Contemporary Teachers: Taking a Socio-Cultural Approach To Education*, eds. B. Burnett, D. Meadmore and G. Tait, 101–12. Frenchs Forest, NSW: Pearson Education.

Burnett, B. 2004b. Technophobes or technophiles. In *New Questions for Contemporary Teachers: Taking a Socio-Cultural Approach to Education*, eds. B. Burnett, D. Meadmore and G. Tait. Frenchs Forest, NSW: Pearson Education.

Burton, G. 2002. *More Than Meets the Eye*, 3rd edn. London: Arnold.

Butler, D. and B. Mathews. 2007. *Schools and the Law*. Annandale, NSW: Federation.

Butler, G. 1995. Teacher in tears over girl. *Courier Mail*, 14 December.

Butler, J. 2002. Asylum seekers' summer fun with your £1M. *Daily Mail*, 24 July.

Bynner, J., S. Reder, S. Parsons and C. Strawn. 2008. The digital divide: computer use, basic skills and employment. *National Research and Development Centre for Adult Literacy and Numeracy*.

Campbell, C. 2010. Class and competition. In *Education, Change and Society*, eds. R. Connell, C. Campbell, M. Vickers *et al.*, 93–129. South Melbourne, Vic.: Oxford University Press.

Canter, L. and M. Canter. 1992. *Assertive Discipline*. London: Lee Canter Associates.

Carpenter, B. and M. Ball. 2012. *Justice in Society*. Annandale, NSW: Federation Press.

Carpenter, B. and G. Tait. 2010. The autopsy imperative: medicine, law, and the coronial system. *Journal of Medical Humanities* 31(3): 205–21.

Carpenter, V. and D. Lee. 2010. Teacher education and the hidden curriculum of heteronormativity. *Curriculum Matters* 6: 99–114.

Carr, N. 2011. *The Shallows: What the Internet is Doing to Our Brains*. London: Atlantic Books.

Carson, R. 1962. *Silent Spring*. Boston: Houghton Mifflin.

Cashmore, E. 1984. *No Future: Youth and Society*. London: Heinemann.

Castel, R. 1991. From dangerousness to risk. In *The Foucault Effect: Studies in Governmentality*, eds. G. Burchell, C. Gordon and P. Miller. London: Harvester/Wheatsheaf.

Central Intelligence Agency. 2015. World factbook. https://www.cia.gov/library/publi cations/the-world-factbook/rankorder/2172rank. html (last accessed 15/3/15).

Ceplak, M. 2013. Heteronormativity: school, ideology and politics. *Journal of Pedagogy* 4(2): 162–87.

Chambers Student. 2015. http://www.chambersstudent.com/where-to-start/newslet ter/2014-gender-in-the-law-survey (last accessed 31/1/16).

Chaytor, H. 1945. *From Script to Print*. Cambridge: Cambridge University Press.

Chilcott, T. and J. Tin. 2010. Queensland OP school grades breakdown busts gender myth. *The Courier Mail*, 31 May.

Children, Schools and Families Committee. 2008. *Testing and Assessment*. HC 169–1.

Choudrie, J., G. Ghinea and V. Songonuga. 2013. Silver surfers, e-government and the digital divide: an exploratory study of UK local authority websites and older citizens. *Interacting with Computers* 25(6): 417–42.

Christian, J. 1981. *Philosophy: an Introduction to the Art of Wondering*. New York: Holt, Rinehart and Winston.

Christoff, P. and R. Eckersley. 2013. *Globalisation and the Environment*. Lanham: Rowman and Littlefield.

Cicero. 1995. *De Re Publica: Selections*, ed. J. Zetzel. Cambridge: Cambridge University Press.

Clark, K. 1978. *The Gothic Revival*. London: John Murray.

Cleary, P., G. Pierce and E. Trauth. 2006. Closing the digital divide: understanding racial, ethnic, social class, gender and geographic disparities in Internet use among school age children in the United States. *Universal Access in the Information Society* 4(4):354–73.

Clements, B. 2012. Exploring public opinion on the issue of climate change in Britain. *British Politics* 7(2): 183–202.

Cline, T. and S. Baldwin. 2004. *Selective Mutism in Children*, 2nd edn. London: Whurr.

Cohen, D. 2006. Critiques of the 'ADHD' enterprise. In *Critical New Perspectives on ADHD*, eds. G. Lloyd, J. Stead and D. Cohen. London: Routledge.

Cohen, S. 1980. *Folk Devils and Moral Panics: the Creation of the Mods and the Rockers*, 2nd edn. Oxford: Robertson.

Cole, R. and D. Pullen. 2010. Introduction to multiliteracies in motion. In *Multiliteracies in Motion: Current Theory and Practice*, eds. R. Cole and D. Pullen. New York: Routledge.

Colic-Peisker, V. and F. Tilbury. 2007. *Refugees and Employment: the Effects of Visible Difference on Discrimination*. Centre for Social and Community Research, Murdoch University.

Collins, S. 2008. *The Hunger Games*. New York: Scholastic.

Comber, B. 2012. Mandated literacy assessment and reorganisation of teachers' work: federal policy, local effect. *Critical Studies in Education* 53(2): 119–36.

Connell, R. 1977. *Ruling Class, Ruling Culture: Studies of Conflict, Power and Hegemony in Australian Life*. Cambridge: Cambridge University Press.

Connell, R. 2005. *Masculinities*, 2nd edn. Berkeley, CA: University of California Press.

Connell, R. 2007. *Southern Theory*. Malden, MA: Polity Press.

Connell, R., D. Ashenden, S. Kessler and G. Dowsett. 1982. *Making the Difference: Schools, Families and Social Division*. Sydney, London, Boston: Allen & Unwin.

Connell, R. and J. Messerschmidt. 2005. Hegemonic masculinity: rethinking the concept. *Gender Society* 19: 829.

Contact a Family. 2013. *Falling Through the Net: Illegal Exclusions, the Experiences of Families With Disabled Children in England and Wales*. London: Contact a Family http://www.cafamily.org.uk/media/639982/falling_through_the_net_-_illegal_exclusions_report_2013_web.pdf (last accessed 31/1/16).

Cook, J., D. Nuccitelli, S. Green *et al.* 2013. Quantifying the consensus on anthropogenic global warming in the scientific literature. *Environmental Research Letters* 8 http://iopscience.iop.org/1748-9326/8/2/024024/pdf/1748-9326_8_2_024024.pdf (last accessed 15/3/15).

Cooper, D. 1998. *Ethics: the Classic Readings*. Oxford: Blackwell.

Cooper, J. 2003. *Gender and Computers: Understanding the Digital Divide*. Mahwah, NJ: Lawrence Erlbaum Associates.

Cooper, J. 2006. The digital divide: the special case of gender. *Journal of Computer Assisted Learning* 22: 320–34.

Cooper, C., S. Gormally, and G. Hughes. 2015. *Socially Just, Radical Alternatives for Education and Youth Work Practice: Re-imagining Ways of Working With Young People*. Basingstoke: Palgrave MacMillan.

Cope, B. and M. Kalantzis. 2000. Introduction: multiliteracies: the beginnings of an idea. In *Multiliteracies: Literacy Learning and the Design of Social Futures*, eds. B. Cope and M. Kalantzis. London: Routledge.

Coppola, A. 2015. Forget the manifesto: big data will win future elections. *Guardian*, 6 May.

Cornelius-White, J. 2007. Learner-centred teacher-student relationships are effective: a meta-analysis. *Review of Educational Research* 77(1): 113–43.

Coster, W. 2007. Social constructions of childhood. In *Childhood and Youth Studies*, ed. P. Zwozdiak-Myers. Exeter: Learning Matters.

Coughlan, S. 2015. Migrants do not lower school results. *BBC*, 17 November. http://www.bbc.com/news/education-34833547.

Counihan, T. 1982. Minding the family: Donzelot and his critics. *Local Consumption* 2–3 August: 19–48.

Courier Mail. 1996. Editorial, August 10.

Courier Mail. 2001. Typhoid found in refugee centres, 23 June.

Craig, T and M. Ludloff. 2011. *Privacy and Big Data*. Sebastopol, CA: O'Reilly Media.

Credit Suisse. 2014. *Global wealth report*. Research Institute, Zurich, Switzerland.

Crenshaw, K. 1991. Mapping the margins: intersectionality, identity politics, and violence against women of colour. *Stanford Law Review* 43(6): 1241–99.

Crikey. 2009. When it comes to asylum seekers, Australia is no Malta. 19 October.

Crouch, C., D. Chan and N. Kaye. 2004. Transforming visual culture: postcolonial theory and the ethically reflexive student. In *Disrupting Preconceptions: Postcolonialism and Education*, eds. A. Hickling-Hudson, J. Matthews and A. Woods. Flaxton: Post Pressed.

Crozier, G. 2014. How fair is Britain? Addressing 'race' and education inequalities – towards a socially just education system in the twenty-first century. In *Educational Inequalities: Differences and Diversity in Schools and Higher Education*, eds. K. Bhopal and U. Maylor. London: Routledge.

Curtis, S. 2014. UK broadband speeds climb as digital divide narrows. *Telegraph*, 3 October.

Daily Express. 2012. Education system 'failing' pupils. 19 November.

Daily Express. 2015. Mass migration is a threat to our children's education. 26 September.

Daily Mail. 2005. Asylum seekers sent to more affluent areas. 23 December.

Daily Mail. 2011. The traditional way to a sound education. 13 January.

Daily Mail. 2012. White working-class boys are consigned to education scrapheap, Ofsted warns. 15 June.

Daily Telegraph. 2014. Yes, its official, men are from Mars and women are from Venus, and here's the science to prove it. 14 September.

Daily Telegraph. 2015. We must stop indoctrinating boys in feminist ideology. 20 July.

Darling, J. and S. Nordenbo. 2003. Progressivism. In *The Blackwell Guide to the Philosophy of Education*, eds. N. Blake, P. Smeyers, R. Smith and P. Standish. Oxford: Blackwell.

Davenport, T. and L. Prusack. 1998. *Working Knowledge: How Organisations Manage What They Know*. Boston: Harvard Business School Press.

Davis, J. 2015. What is early childhood education for sustainability and why does it matter? In *Young Children and the Environment: Early Education for Sustainability*, 2nd edn, ed. J. Davis. Melbourne: Cambridge University Press.

Delgado, R. 2014. Beyond Moneyball: how big data is changing baseball. *Sporttechie November 11*.

Department for Education. 2011. *Statistical First Release. National Curriculum Assessments at Key Stage 1 in England 2011*. London: UK Government.

Department for Education. 2012a. *Statistical First Release. National Curriculum Assessments at Key Stage 2 in England 2011/12*. London: UK Government.

Department for Education. 2012b. *Statistical First Release. GCSE and Equivalent Attainment by Pupil Characteristics in England 2010/11*. London: UK Government.

Department for Education. 2012c. *A Profile of Pupil Exclusion in England*. Educational Standards Analysis and Research Division. London: UK Government.

Department for Education. 2013a. *English Literature: GCSE Subject Content and Assessment Objectives*. London: UK Government.

Department for Education. 2013b. *Statistical First Release. School Workforce in England: November 2012*. London: UK Government.

Department for Education. 2013c. *Statistical First Release. GCSE and Equivalent Attainment by Pupil Characteristics in England 2011/12*. London: UK Government.

Department for Education. 2014a. *Statistical First Release. Destinations of Key Stage 4 and Key Stage 5 Students, 2011/12*. London: UK Government.

Department for Education. 2014b. *The Equality Act 2010 and Schools: Departmental Advice for School Leaders, School Staff, Governing Bodies and Local Authorities*. London: UK Government.

Department for Education. 2015. *Statistical First Release. School Workforce in England: November 2014*. London: UK Government.

Derrida, J. 1981. *Positions*. Chicago: University of Chicago Press.

Deuchar, R. and K. Bhopal. 2013. 'We're still human beings, we're not aliens': promoting citizenship rights and cultural diversity of Traveller children in schools: Scottish and English perspectives. *British Educational Research Journal* 39(4): 733–50.

Devine, M. 2009. The crazy politics of learning to read. *Sydney Morning Herald*. 21 March.

Devine, M. 2013. Kids who read don't light fires. *Sunday Telegraph*, 26 October.

Dewey, J. 1916. *Education and Democracy*. New York: The Free Press.

Disraeli, B. 1851. *February 11*. House of Commons.

Doane, W. 2003. Rethinking whiteness studies. In *White Out: the Continuing Significance of Racism*, eds. A. W. Doane and E. Bonilla-Silva, **xii**, 328. New York: Routledge.

Doherty, S. 2011. Sickly immigrants add £1bn to NHS bill. *Daily Mail*, 14 May.

D'Onofrio, L. and K. Munk. 2004. *Understanding the Stranger: Final Report*. London: ICAR.

Donzelot, J. 1979. *The Policing of Families*. New York: Pantheon Books.

Dooley, K. 2004. How and why did literacy become so prominent? In *New Questions for Contemporary Teachers*, eds. B. Burnett, D. Meadmore and G. Tait, 55–70. Frenches Forest, NSW: Pearson.

Dulfer, N., J. Polesel and S. Rice. 2012. *The Experience of Education: The Impacts of High Stakes Testing on School Students and their Families (An Educator's Perspective)*. Sydney: Whitlam Institute.

Dunn, K., N. Klocker and T. Salabay. 2007. Contemporary racism and Islamophobia: radicalising religion. *Ethnicities* 7(14): 564–89.

Durkheim, E. 1964. *The Division of Labor in Society*. New York, London: Free Press Collier Macmillan.

Eagleton, T. 1983. *Literary Theory: an Introduction*. Oxford: Blackwell.

Ehrenreich, J., L. Santucci and C. Weiner. 2008. Separation anxiety disorder in youth: phenomenology, assessment, and treatment. *Psicol Conductual* 16(3): 389–412.

Eisenstein, E. 1979. *The Printing Press as an Agent of Change*. Cambridge: Cambridge University Press.

Elder, B. 2003. *Blood on the Wattle: Massacres and Maltreatment of Aboriginal Australians since 1788*, 3rd edn. Frenchs Forest, NSW: New Holland.

Elias, N. 2000 (1939). *The Civilizing Process*. Hoboken, NJ: Wiley-Blackwell.

Ellicott, C. and S. Wright. 2015. The 'swarm' on our streets. *Daily Mail*, 31 July.

Emmet, E. 1991. *Learning to Philosophise*. London: Penguin

Equality Act (2010). Available at: http://www.legislation.gov.uk/ukpga/2010/15/con tents (last accessed 30/1/16).

Equality Challenge Unit. 2012. *Equality in Higher Education Statistical Report 2012*. London: Equity Challenge Unit

Evans, D. 2014. Do you need to get down with the kids? *New Teachers*. http://ne wteachers.tes.co.uk/content/do-you-need-get-down-kids (last accessed 30/ 1/ 16).

Ewald, F. 1991. Insurance and risk. In *The Foucault Effect: Studies in Governmentality*, eds. G. Burchell, C. Gordon and P. Miller. London: Harvester/Wheatsheaf.

Ewing, R. 2014. Phonics: its place in the literacy story. *Australian Literacy Educators' Association*. http://www.alea.edu.au/documents/item/943

Exley, B. 2010. A dog of a QCAT: collateral effects of mandated English assessment in the Torres Strait. *Australian Journal of Indigenous Education* 39: 1–10.

Faludi, S. 1992. *Backlash: the Undeclared War Against Women*. London: Chatto and Windus.

Fanon, F. 1952. *Black Skin, White Masks*, trans. C. Markmann 1967. New York: Grove Press.

Fanon, F. 1961. *The Wretched of the Earth*, trans. C. Farrington 1963. New York: Grove Weidenfeld.

Fausto-Sterling, A. 2000. *Sexing the Body*. New York: Basic Books.

Feinleib, D. 2013. *Big Data Demystified: How Big Data is Changing the Way We Live, Love and Learn*. San Francisco: The Big Data Group.

Ferraro, J. 2014. Observations on the 'reading wars'. In *Why Jaydon Can't Read: a Forum on Fixing Literacy*, J. Buckinghom, J. Ferrari and T. Alegounarias. The Centre for Independent Studies.

Finch, L. 1993. *The Classing Gaze: Sexuality, Class, and Surveillance*. Sydney: Allen and Unwin.

Fine, C. 2010. *Delusions of Gender: How Our Minds, Society and Neurosexism Create Difference*. New York: Norton.

Fink, C. and J. Kenny. 2003. W(h)ither the digital divide? *The Journal of Policy, Regulation and Strategy for Telecommunications* 5(6):15–24.

Finot, J. 1913. *Problems of the Sexes*. New York: The Knickerbocker Press.

Fleck, L. 1979. *Genesis and Development of Scientific Fact*. Chicago: University of Chicago Press.

Flood, A. 2013. Academics chastised for bad grammar in letter attacking Michael Gove. *Guardian*, 4 May.

Fortune 500 (Global). 2015. http://fortune.com/global500/ (last accessed 15/3/15).

Foster, L. 1981. *Australian Education: a Sociological Perspective*. Prentice Hall: Sydney.

Foster, V., M. S. Kimmel and C. Skelton. 2001. What about the boys?: an overview of the debates. In *What About The Boys?: Issues Of Masculinity In Schools*, eds. W. Martino and B. Meyenn, **xiv**, 242. Buckingham, England; Philadelphia: Open University Press.

Foucault, M. 1965. *Madness and Civilisation*. London: Tavistock.

Foucault, M. 1973. *The Birth of the Clinic: an Archaeology of Medical Perception*. London: Tavistock.

Foucault, M. 1976a. *Mental Illness and Psychology*. New York: Harper Collins.

Foucault, M. 1976b. *The History of Sexuality: an Introduction*. Harmondsworth: Penguin.

Foucault, M. 1977. *Discipline and Punish: the Birth of the Prison*. London: Penguin.

Foucault, M. 1980. Truth and power. In *Selected Interviews and Other Writings 1972–1977 by Michel Foucault*, ed. C. Gordon. Brighton: Harvester Press.

Foucault, M. 1984. The politics of health in the eighteenth century. In *The Foucault Reader*, ed. P. Rabinow, 273–90. London: Penguin.

Foucault, M. 1987. *The History of Sexuality: the Uses of Pleasure*, Vol. **2**. Harmondsworth: Penguin.

Foucault, M. 1991. Governmentality. In *The Foucault Effect: Studies in Governmentality*, eds. G. Burchell, C. Gordon and P. Miller. London: Harvester Wheatsheaf.

Foucault, M. 2000. Questions of method. In *Power*, ed. J. Faubion. New York: New Press.

Frawley, T. 2005. Gender bias in the classroom: current controversies and implications for teachers. *Childhood Education* 81(4): 221–7.

Frege, G. 1977. *Logical Investigations. 1918*. Oxford: Blackwell.

Freire, P. 1970. *Pedagogy of the Oppressed*. New York: Seabury Press.

Freud, S. 2005. *Three Contributions to the Sexual Theory*. Montana: Kessinger.

Friedan, B. 1963. *The Feminine Mystique*. London: Gollancz.

Friedman, T. 2007. *The World is Flat: a Brief History of the 21st Century*. New York: Picador.

Fuller. 1958. Positivism and fidelity to the law – a response to Professor Hart. *Harvard Law Review* **71**: 630–657.

Gabbay, J. 1982. Asthma attacked? Tactics for the reconstruction of a disease concept. In *The Problem of Medical Knowledge: Examining the Social Construction of Medicine*, eds. P. Wright and A. Treacher. Edinburgh: Edinburgh University Press.

Geay, C., S. McNally and S. Telhaj. 2012. Non-native speakers of English in the classroom: what are the effects on pupil performance? *Centre for the Economics of Education Discussion Paper No. 137*, March.

Gee, J., G. Hull and C. Lankshear. 1996. *The New Work Order: Behind the Language of the New Capitalism*. Sydney: Allen Unwin.

Germann, G. 1972. *Gothic Revival in Europe and Britain: Sources, Influences, and Ideas*. London: Lund Humphries.

Ghemawat, P. 2011. *World 3.0: Global Prosperity and How to Achieve It*. Boston: Harvard Business Review Press.

Gibb, N. 2014. Punishing traditional teaching has to stop. *Telegraph*, 12 May.

Giddens, A. 1990. *The Consequences of Modernity*. Cambridge: Polity Press.

Giddens, A. 1991. *Modernity and Self Identity: Self and Society in the Late Modern Age*. Cambridge: Polity Press.

Gilbert, R. and P. Gilbert. 1998. *Masculinity Goes to School*. St Leonards, NSW: Allen & Unwin.

Gill, M. 2014. The Michael Gove Twitterstorm is ridiculous. And of course Of Mice and Men is boring. *Telegraph*, 27 May.

Gillborn, D. 2008. *Racism and Education: Coincidence or Conspiracy*. London: Routledge.

Gilligan, I. 2007. Neanderthal extinction and modern human behaviour: the role of climate change and clothing. *World Archaeology* 39(4): 499–514.

Gilroy, P. 1993. *Black Atlantic: Modernity and Double Consciousness*. London: Verso.

Giroux, H. A. and D. E. Purpel. 1983. *The Hidden Curriculum and Moral Education: Deception or Discovery?* Berkeley, CA: McCutchan Pub. Corp.

Goodall, P. 1995. *High Culture, Popular Culture: the Long Debate*. St Leonards: Allen and Unwin.

Goode, E. and N. Ben-Yehuda. 2009. *Moral Panics: the Social Construction of Deviance*, 2nd edn. Chichester, UK: Wiley-Blackwell.

Goodfellow, R. 2006. From 'equal access' to 'widening participation': the discourse of equity in the age of e-learning. In *Brave New Classrooms: Democratic Education and the Internet*, eds. J. Lockard and M. Pegrum. New York: Peter Lang.

Goodwin, S. and K. Huppatz. 2010. *The Good Mother: Contemporary Motherhoods in Australia*. Sydney: University of Sydney Press.

Gordon, C. 1991. Governmental rationality: an introduction. In *The Foucault Effect: Studies in Governmentality*, eds. C. Gordon and P. Miller, 1–52. London: Harvester Wheatsheaf.

Gordon, J. 2015. Christian school tells gay students to get back in the closet or get out. *Daily Mail*, 8 February.

Gore, J. 1998. Disciplining bodies: on the continuity of power relations in pedagogy. In *Foucault's Challenge: Discourse, Knowledge, and Power in Education*, eds. T. Popkewitz and M. Brennan, 231–51. London: Falmer Press.

Gorman, C. 1992. Sizing up the sexes. *Time* 139: 42–52.

Gough, N. 1993. *Laboratories in Fiction: Science Education and Popular Media*. Geelong: Deakin University Press.

Gould, S. J. 1996. *The Mismeasure of Man*, revised and expanded edition. New York: Norton.

GOV.UK. 2015. School Leaving Age. https://www.gov.uk/know-when-you-can-leave-school (last accessed 31/1/16).

Gove, M. 2010. *All pupils will learn our island story*. Speech to the Conservative Party Conference, 5 October.

Gove, M. 2013a. I refuse to surrender to the Marxist teachers hell-bent on destroying our schools. *Daily Mail*, 24 March.

Gove, M. 2013b. *What does it mean to be an educated person?* Speech at Brighton College, 9 May.

GO8. 2014. International students in higher education and their role in the Australian economy. https://go8.edu.au/publication/international-students-higher-education-and-their-role-australian-economy (last accessed 15/3/15).

Gramsci, A. 1971. *Selections From the Prison Notebooks of Antonio Gramsci*, trans. Q. Hoare and G. Nowell Smith. London: Lawrence and Wishart.

Gras-Velazquez, A., A. Joyce and M. Debry. 2009. *Women and ICT: Why Are Girls Still Not Attracted To ICT Studies And Careers?* Brussels: European Schoolnet.

Grasha, A. 1996. *Teaching With Style: a Practical Guide to Enhancing Learning by Understanding Teaching and Learning Styles*. San Bernadino: Alliance.

Green, D. 2012. *Teens, TV and Tunes: the Manufacturing of American Adolescent Culture*. NC: McFarland.

Gregory, J. 2006. Facilitation and facilitator style. In *The Theory and Practice of Teaching*, 4th edn, ed. P. Jarvis. Oxford: Routledge, 98–113.

Griffin, C. 2006. Didacticism: lectures and lecturing. In *The Theory and Practice of Teaching*, 4th edn, ed. P. Jarvis. Oxford: Routledge, 28–38.

Gross, M. 2010. So why can't they read? *Centre For Policy Studies*. Surrey: Centre for Policy.

Guha, R. 1988. On some aspects of the historiography of colonial India. In *Selected Subaltern Studies*, eds. R. Guha and G. Spivak. Oxford: Oxford University Press.

Gyngell, K. 2012. Now is the time to break forever the stranglehold of the teaching unions over British education. *Daily Mail*, 12 May.

Gyngell, K. 2012. Our schools need tough guys teaching teenage boys, not feminised men changing infants' nappies. *Daily Mail*, 18 July.

Hacking, I. 1982. Bio-power and the avalanche of printed numbers. *Humanities and Society* 5: 279–95.

Hacking, I. 1986. Making up people. In *Reconstructing Individualism: Autonomy, Individuality and the Self in Western Thought*, ed. T. Heller. California: Stanford University Press.

Hall, G. 1904. *Adolescence: its Psychology, and its Relation to Physiology, Anthropology, Sociology, Sex Crimes, Religion and Education*, 2 vols. New York: Appleton and Co.

Hall, S. and T. Jefferson (eds.) 1976. *Resistance Through Rituals*. London: Hutchinson.

Hall, S. 1992. New ethnicities. In *Race, Culture and Difference*, eds. J. Donald and A. Rattansi. London: Sage.

Hanson, F. 2014. *Technology and Cultural Tectonics: Shifting Values and Meanings*. New York: Palgrave Macmillan.

Harding, L., P. Otermann and N. Watt. 2015. Refugees welcome? How UK and Germany compare on migration. *Guardian*, 3 September.

Harman, G. 1977. *The Nature of Morality*. New York: Oxford University Press.

Harris, J. and J. Vasagar. (2012). Academies' refusal to admit pupils with special needs prompts legal battles. *Guardian*, 24 May.

Harrison-Barbet, A. 2001. *Mastering Philosophy*, 2nd edn. New York: Palgrave.

Hart, A. 1991. *Understanding the Media: a Practical Guide*. London: Routledge.

Hart, D. 2000. Discipline in schools. In *Routledge International Encyclopedia Of Women: Global Women's Issues and Knowledge, Volume 1 Ability – Education: Globalization*, eds. C. Kramarae and D. Spender, 394–6. London: Routledge.

Hart, H. 1961. *The Concept of Law*. Oxford: Oxford University Press.

Hart, V., S. Whatman, V. Sharma-Brymer, J. McLaughlin and M. Dreise. 2011. *Exploring the experiences of embedding Indigenous knowledge and perspectives on teaching practicum through interpretive phenomenology*. Paper presented at the Researching Across Boundaries – Australian Association for Research in Education Conference, Hobart, Tasmania. 27 November–1 December.

Hartcher, P. 2009. At last, we have a real leader – pity that it's not Rudd. *Sydney Morning Herald*, 29 October.

Hartley, D. 1997. *Re-Schooling Society*. London: Routledge Falmer.

Hastings, M. 2010. Ideologues of illiteracy: the terrible damage wrought on our schools by Left-leaning educationalists. *Daily Mail*, 20 July.

Hay, M. 2014. The new technologies that will change human civilization as we know it. *Vitamodularis*. http://www.vitamodularis.org/articles/new_technologies_ that_will_change_civilization_as_we_know_it.shtml (last accessed 30/1/16).

Headley, B., D. Warren and M. Wooden. 2008. *The structure and distribution of household wealth in Australia: cohort differences and retirement issues*: Melbourne Institute of Applied Economic and Social Research.

Hebdige, D. 1979. *Subculture: the Meaning of Style*. London: Methuen.

Hebdige, D. 1988. *Hiding in the Light*. London: Routledge.

Held, D. and A. McGrew. 2003. The great globalization debate: an introduction. In *The Global Transformations Reader: an Introduction to the Globalization Debate*, 2nd edn, eds. D. Held and A McGrew. Cambridge: Polity Press.

Henkin, L. 1966. Truth and probability: the voice of America forum series. *Philosophy of Science* 4(1).

Henry, J. 2009. A day in the life of an ordinary school: drugs, violence and intimidation. *Telegraph*, 4 January.

Henry, M. 2000. It's all up to the individual... isn't it? Meritocratic practices. In *Practising Education: Social and Cultural Perspectives*, eds. D. Meadmore, B. Burnett and G. Tait, 47–58. Frenchs Forest, NSW: Prentice Hall-Sprint Print.

Henry, M., J. Knight, R. Lingard and S. Taylor. 1988. *Understanding Schooling: an Introduction to the Sociology of Australian Education*. London: Routledge.

Herman, E. and N. Chomsky. 1994. *Manufacturing Consent: the Political Economy of the Mass Media*. London: Vintage.

Heywood, C. 2001. *A History of Childhood*. Cambridge: Blackwell.

Hickling-Hudson, A. 2000. Postcolonialism, hybridity and transferability: the contribution of Pamela O'Gorman to music education in the Caribbean. *Caribbean Journal of Education* 22(1 & 2): 36–55.

Hickling-Hudson, A. and R. Ahlquist. 2004. The challenge to deculturisation: discourses of ethnicity in the schooling of Indigenous children in Australia and the USA. In *Disrupting Preconceptions: Postcolonialism and Education*, eds. A. Hickling-Hudson, J. Matthews and A. Woods. Flaxton: Post Pressed.

Hickling-Hudson, A., J. Matthews and A. Woods (eds.) 2004. *Disrupting Preconceptions: Postcolonialism and Education*. Flaxton: Post Pressed.

Hil, R. 2012. *Whackademia*. Sydney: University of New South Wales Press.

Hilbert, M. 2011. Digital gender divide or technologicaly empowered women in developing countries? A typical case of lies, damned lies, and statistics. *Women's Studies International Forum* 34(6): 479–89.

Hilton, A. 2013. The malignant left-wing pathology of educational academics. *Daily Mail*, 21 March.

Hine, J. and B. Williams. 2007. *Youth Crime and Offending, DfES Youth Strategy Review*. Youth Affairs Unit, De Montford University.

Hirst, P. and P. Wooley. 1985. *Social Relations and Human Attributes*. London: Tavistock.

Hitchens, P. 2015a. Did Jesus really say 'blessed are the queue-jumping knifemen?' *Daily Mail*. 16 August.

Hitchens, P. 2015b. British education is a con – or haven't you learned that yet. *Daily Mail*. 23 August.

Hobbes, R. 2007. *Reading the Media: Media Literacy in High School English*. New York: Teachers College Press.

Hobbes, T. 1994. *Leviathon (1651)*, ed. E. Curley. Hacket Publishing.

Hobson, P. 2001. Aristotle. In *Fifty Major Thinkers on Education: from Confucius to Dewey*, ed. J. Palmer. New York: Routledge.

Hochschild, J. and V. Weaver. 2007. *Remaking America: Democracy and Public Policy in an Age of Inequality*. New York: Russell Sage Foundation.

Hoffman, J. 2009. Can a boy wear a skirt to school? *The New York Times*.

Holley, D. and M. Oliver. 2011. Negotiating the digital divide: narratives from the have and the have-nots. In *Digital Difference: Perspectives on Online Learning*, eds. R. Land and S. Bayne. Rotterdam: Sense.

Hollingshead, A. and F. Redlich. 1958. *Social Class and Mental Illness: a Community Study*. New York: Wiley.

Holmes, J. 2010. Today Tonight: refugeees from journalistic decency. *The Drum*. http://www.abc.net.au/news/2011-10-27/holmes-shaming-today-tonight/3 603986 (last accessed 30/1/16).

Holyoake, G. 1902. *Sixty Years of an Agitator's Life*. London: Unwin.

Hood, W. 1983. The Aristotelian versus the Hegelian approach to the problem of technology. In *Philosophy and Technology: Readings in the Philosophical Problems of Technology*, eds. C. Mitcham and R. Mackey, New York: Free Press, 347–63.

Hope, K. 2015. FTSE 100 firms appoint more women to their boards. *BBC*, 25 March.

Hopkins, S. 2002. *Girl Heroes: the New Force in Popular Culture*. Annandale, N.S.W.: Pluto Press.

Horne, D. 1968. *The Lucky Country: Australia in the Sixties*, 2nd revised edn. Harmondsworth, England: Penguin.

Horwich, P. 1990. *Truth*. Oxford: Oxford University Press.

Hospers, J. 1997. *An Introduction to Philosophical Analysis*, 4th edn. London: Routledge.

Hume, D. 1969. *A Treatise on Human Nature. 1739–1740*. London: Penguin.

Hunter, I. 1993. Culture, bureaucracy and the history of popular education. In *Child and Citizen: Genealogies of Schooing and Subjectivity*, eds. D. Meredyth and D. Tyler, 11–34. Brisbane: Institute for Cultural Policy Studies, Griffith University.

Hunter, I. 1994. *Rethinking the School: Subjectivity, Bureaucracy, Criticism*. St Leonards, NSW: Allen and Unwin.

Hurley, P. and R. Eme. 2004. *ADHD and the Criminal Justice System: Spinning Out of Control*. LLC: Booksurge.

Hutchings, M. 2015. *Exam Factories? The Impact of Accountability Measures on Children and Young People*. London: National Union of Teachers.

Hutchinson, A. and P. Monahan. 1984. Law, politics, and the critical legal scholars: the unfolding dramas of American legal thought. *Stanford Law Review* 36: 199–245.

Hyde, J., S. Lindberg, M. Linn, A. Ellis and C. Williams. 2008. Gender similarities characterize math performance. *Science* 321(5888): 494–5.

Illich, I. 1973. *Deschooling Society*. Harmondsworth: Penguin Education.

Independent Schools Council. 2015. *Annual Census Snapshot*. http://www.isc.co.uk/media/2661/isc_census_2015_final.pdf (last accessed 30/1/16).

Jackson, J. P. and N. M. Weidman. 2004. *Race, Racism, and Science: Social Impact and Interaction. Science and Society*. Santa Barbara, CA: ABC-CLIO.

James, W. 1911. *Remarks at the peace banquet. Lecture 12*. In *Memories and Studies*. New York: Longman Green and Co.

James, W. 1917. *Selected Papers on Philosophy*. London: Dent and Sons.

James, W. 1975. *The Meaning of Truth. 1911*. Cambridge: Harvard University Press.

Jarvis, P. 2006. Teaching styles and teaching methods. In *The Theory and Practice of Teaching*, 4th edn, ed. P. Jarvis. Oxford: Routledge, 73–89.

Jefferson, S. 1976. Cultural Responses of the Teds. In *Resistance Through Rituals*, eds. S. Hall and T. Jefferson. London: Hutchinson.

Jenks, C. 1998. Racial bias in testing. In *The Black–White Score Test Core Gap,* eds. C. Jenks and M. Phillips. Washington: Brookings Institution Press.

Jerome, L. and M. Bhargava. 2013. Citizenship (3rd edition): ideology and citizenship in the National Curriculum for England, paper presented to UK TE Network for Education Sustainable Development/Global Citizenship Sixth Annual Conference, *'Changing Times: changing knowledge and Pedagogy for ESD/GC'* Southbank University, 11 July.

Ji, O. 2015. Education for sustainable development in early childhood in Korea. In *Young Children and the Environment: Early Education for Sustainability*, 2nd edn, ed. J. Davis. Melbourne: Cambridge University Press.

Johnson, J. 1988. Mixing humans with non-humans: sociology of a door closer. *Social Problems* 35, 298–310.

Johnston, R., T. Gabbett and D. Jenkins. 2014. Applied sport science of rugby league, *Sports Medicine* 44: 1087–100.

Johst, H. 1933. *Schlageter*. Munich: Langen-Muller.

Joint Council for Qualifications. 2015. *A, AS and AES results*, http://www.jcq.org.uk/examination-results/a-levels/a-as-and-aea-results-summer-2015 (last accessed 31/1/16).

Joint Council for Qualifications. 2015. *GCSE Results*, http://www.jcq.org.uk/examination-results/gcses/gcse-and-entry-level-certificate-results-summer-2015 (last accessed 31/1/ 16).

Jones, K. and K. Williamson. 1979. The birth of the schoolroom. *Ideology and Consciousness* 6, 59–110.

Joyce, J. 1922. *Ulysses*. Paris: Shakespeare and Company.

Kant, I. 1979. *The Conflict of the Faculties*, ed. M. J. Gregor. New York: Abaris Books.

Kant, I. 1998. *Groundwork of the Metaphysics of Morals*. Cambridge: Cambridge University Press.

Kay-Shuttleworth, J. (ed.) 1973. *The Moral and Physical Condition of the Working Class of Manchester in 1832. Four Periods of Public Education*. Sussex: Harvester Press.

Keats, J. 1951. Ode on a Grecian urn. In *The Complete Poetry and Selected Prose of John Keats*, ed. H. Briggs. New York: Modern Library.

Kemp v Minister for Education. [1991] EOC 92–340.

Kendall, F. 2006. *Understanding White Privilege: Creating Pathways To Authentic Relationships Across Race. The Teaching/Learning Social Justice Series*. New York: Routledge.

Kennedy, M. 2014. To Kill a Mockingbird and Of Mice and Men axed as Gove order more Brit lit. *Guardian*, 26 May.

Kierkegaard, S. 2001. Philosophical fragments. In *The Kierkegaard Reader*, eds. J. Chamberlain and J. Ree. Malden, MA: Blackwell.

Killik & Co. 2014. *Killik Private Education Index: A Cebr Report – July 2014*. London: Centre for Economic and Business Research.

Kimmel, M. 1994. Masculinity as homophobia: fear, shame and silence in the construction of gender identity. In *Research on Men and Masculinities*, eds. H. Brod and M. Kaufman. Thousand Oaks, CA: Sage.

Kingston & Richmond Area Health Authority v. Kaur. (1981). IRLR 337, [1981] ICR 631.

Kirk, D. 1993. *The Body, Schooling and Culture*. Geelong: Deakin Uiversity.

Klein, N. 2000. *No Logo: Taking Aim at the Brand Bullies*. Canada: Knopf.

Kneavel, A. 2005. Popular culture in a business curriculum. In *Popular Culture Studies Across the Curriculum*, ed. R. Browne. Jefferson: McFarland and Co.

Knowles, E. and H. Evans. 2012. *PISA 2009: How Does The Social Attainment Gap In England Compare With Countries Internationally?* Department for Education.

Kohl, H. 1967. *36 Children*. Harmondsworth: Penguin.

Kolakowski, N. 2013. Big data and the end of secrecy. *Business Intelligence*. 10 June.

Kolb, J. and J. Kolb. 2013. *The Big Data Revolution: the World is Changing. Are You Ready?* Chicago: Applied Data Labs.

Kostanski, L. 2009. Toponymic books and the representation of Indigenous identities. In *Aboriginal Placenames Old and New*, eds. F. Hodges and H. Koch, 175–186. Canberra: Aboriginal Studies Press.

Krause, S. 2000. 'Among the greatest benefactors of mankind': what the success of chalkboards tells us about the future of computers in the classroom. *The Journal of the Midwest Modern Language Association* 33(2): 6–16.

Kuhn, R. 2010. Newspapers. In *The Media: an Introduction*, eds. D. Albertazzi and P. Cobley. London: Pearson.

Kuper, S. 2013. Keep you eye on the stats. *Le Monde Diplomatique*. http://mondedi plo.com/2013/07/15foot (last accessed 15/3/15).

L v Minister for Education. 1996. QADT 2.

Ladwig, J. 1996. *Academic Distinctions: Theory and Methodology in the Sociology of School Knowledge*. New York: Routledge.

Lampert, J. 2012. Decoming a socially just teacher: walking the walk. In *Introductory Indigenous Studies in Education*. 2nd edn, eds. J. Phillips and J. Lampert, 81–97. Frenchs Forest, NSW: Pearson Education.

Lane, D. 1990. *The Impossible Child*. Stoke-on-Trent: Trentham Books.

Latour, B. 1996. *Aramis, or the Love of Technology*. Cambridge, MA: Harvard University Press.

Law Society. 2012. Entry trends. http://www.lawsociety.org.uk/law-careers/becom ing-a-solicitor/entry-trends/ (last accessed 31/1/16).

Leavis, F. and D. Thompson. 1977. *Culture and Environment*. Westport: Greenwood Press.

Leavis, F. R. 1930. *Mass Civilisation and Minority Culture*. Folcroft: [s.n.].

Lee, D. and H. Newby. 1983. *The Problem of Sociology*. London: Hutchinson.

Lees, C. 1988. Youth tribes of Australia. *The Bulletin* June 14: 7–13.

Lehner, S. (2005). Towards a subaltern aesthetics: reassessing postcolonial criticism for contemporary Northern Irish and Scottish literatures. James Kelman and Robert McLiam Wilson's rewriting of national paradigms. *eSharp*, **5**.

Leiserowitz, A., E. Mailbach, C. Roser-Renouf, G. Feinberg and S. Rosenthal. 2014. *Politics and Global Warming, Spring 2014, Yale University and George Mason University*. New Haven, CT: Yale Project on Climate Change and Communication.

LeMoyne, T. and J. Davis. 2011. Debunking common sense and the taken for granted: a pedagogic strategy for teaching social problems, *Teaching Sociology* 39(1): 103–10.

Lenta, P. 2004. The Tikoloshe and the reasonable man: transgressing South African legal fictions. *Law and Literature* 16(3): 353–79.

Leviston, Z and I. Walker. 2011. *Baseline Survey of Australia Attitudes to Climate Change: Preliminary Report*. CSIRO.

Levy, A. 2010. Swans killed and fish vanish as 'migrants pillage river for food'. *Daily Mail*, 24 March.

Levy, A. and L. Brown. 2015. Asylum bid by Libyans in sex rampage. *Daily Mail*, 30 September.

Lingard, B. 2010. Policy borrowing, policy learning: testing times in Australian school-ing. *Critical Studies in Education* 51(2): 129–47.

Livingstone, S. and E. Helsper. 2007. Gradations in digital inclusion: children, young people and the digital divide. *New Media and Society* 9(4): 671–96.

Local Government Act 1988. Available at: http://www.legislation.gov.uk/ukpga/1988/9/contents (last accessed 30/1/16).

Lockard, J. and M. Pegrum. 2006. From counterdiscourses to counterpedagogies: an introduction. In *Brave New Classrooms: Democratic Education and the Internet*, eds. J. Lockard and M. Pegrum. New York: Peter Lang.

Locke, J. 1970. *Some Thoughts Concerning Education*. Menston: Scolar Press.

Loeber, R., D. Pardini, D. Homish *et al.* 2005. The prediction of violence and homicide in young men. *Journal of Consulting and Clinical Psychology* 73(6): 1074–88.

Logan, K. 2012. Foucault, the modern mother, and maternal power: notes toward a genealogy of the mother. In *Foucault, the Family and Politics*, eds. R. Duschinsky and L. Rocha. London: Palgrave Macmillan.

Lopes, V. and A. Albano. 2013. Pediatric social phobia. In *Pediatric Anxiety Disorders: a Clinical Guide*, eds. R. Vasa and A. Roy. New York: Springer.

Louden, W., M. Rohl, C. Barratt Pugh *et al.* 2005. *In Teachers' Hands: Effective Literacy Teaching Practices In The Early Years Of Schooling*. Canberra: Department of Education, Science and Training.

Ludowyke, J. 2010. Bursting the MySchool bubble. Professional Educator 9(2): 16–19.

Luke, A. 2004. On postcolonial education and beyond: an afterword. In *Disrupting Preconceptions: Postcolonialism and Education*, eds. A. Hickling-Hudson, J. Matthews and A. Woods. Flaxton: Post Pressed.

Luke, A. 2014. Direct instruction is not a solution for Australian schools. *EduResearch Matters*. http://www.aare.edu.au/blog/?p=439 (last accessed 15/3/15).

Luke, C. 1989. *Pedagogy, Printing and Protestantism: the Discourse on Childhood*. Albany: State University of New York.

Lumby, C., H. Caple and K. Greenwood. 2010. *Towards a Level Playing Field: Sport and Gender in Australian Media*. Australian Sport Commission: University of New South Wales Journalism and Media Research Centre, and Media Monitors.

Lynch, M. 1998. *Truth in Context: an Essay on Truth and Objectivity*. Cambridge: Bradford.

Lyon, D. 2014. Surveillance, Snowden, and big data: capacities, consequences, critique. *Big Data and Society*, July–December, 1–13.

Lyotard, J. 1984a. *The Post-Modern Condition: a Report On Knowledge*, trans. G. Bennington and B. Massumi. Manchester: Manchester University Press.

Lyotard, J. 1984b. *The Postmodern Condition: a Report on Knowledge*. Manchester: Manchester University Press.

Macdougall, N. 2008. Getting to know you: the journey from African refugee to African-Australian. Unpublished PhD Thesis, Murdoch University, Melbourne.

MacIntyre, A. 1998. The nature of virtues. In *Ethics: the Big Questions*, ed. J. Sterba. Oxford: Blackwell.

Mail on Sunday. 2005. Asylum seekers given votes to get loans, 1 May.

Mallinson, A. 2012. As thousands of servicemen are made redundant, how many will be turned away from homeless shelters that are packed full of immigrants? *Daily Mail*, 25 June.

Mares, P. 2002. Reporting Australia's asylum seeker 'crisis'. In *Regional Seminar on Media and Ethnic Conflicts,* Makati City, Philippines, 22–24 May.

Marquez, G. 1970. *One Hundred Years of Solitude*. New York: Harper Collins.

Martino, W. 2000. The boys at the back: chalenging masculinities and homophobia in the English classroom. *English in Australia* 127–**128**: 35–50.

Mauss, M. 1973. Techniques of the body. *Economy and Society* **2**(1): 70–87.

Mauss, M. 1985. A category of human mind: the notion of the person; the notion of the self. In *The Category of Person: Anthropology, Philosophy, History*, eds. M. Carrithers, S. Collins and S. Lukes, 4–12. Cambridge: Cambridge University Press.

Mayer-Schonberger, V. and K. Cukier. 2013. *Big Data: a Revolution That Will Transform How We Live, Work and Think*. London: Murray.

Mayer-Schonberger, V. and K. Cukier. 2014. *Learning With Big Data: the Future of Education*. Boston: Eamon Dolan.

Maynes, M. 1985. *Schooling in Western Europe: a Social History*. Albany: State University of New York.

McArthur, G. and S. McMahon. 2011. It's Official! Boys lose in the battle of the sexes at school. *Herald Sun*, 30 April.

McCabe, J., E. Fairchild, L. Grauerholtz, B. Pescosolido and D. Tope. 2011. Gender in twentieth-century children's books: patterns of disparity in titles and central characters. *Gender and Society* 25(2):197–226.

McCallum, D. 1993. Problem children and familial relations. In *Child and Citizen: Genealogies of Schooling and Subjectivity*, eds. D. Meredyth and D. Tyler. Griffith University: Institute for Cultural Policy Studies.

McCright, A. and R. Dunlap. 2011. The politicization of climate change and polarization in the American public's views of global warming. *The Sociological Quarterly* 52: 155–94.

McGraw, B. 2014. *Statement from the Chairman, ACARA*. 11 September. http://www.acara.edu.au/news_media/acara_news/acara_news_2014_09.html (last accessed 15/3/15).

McIntosh, P. 1997. White privilege and male privilege: a personal account of coming to see correspondences through work in women's studies. In *Critical White Studies: Looking Behind the Mirror*, eds. R. Delgado and J. Stefancic. Philadelphia: Temple University Press.

McIvor, J. 2015. Scottish education: the return of standardised testing? *BBC*, 1 September. http://www.bbc.com/news/uk-scotland-34108172

McKenzie, P., J. Kos, M. Walker and J. Hong. 2008. *Staff in Australia's Schools 2007*. Department of Education, Employment and Workplace Relations.

McKenzie, P., P. Weldon, G. Rowley, M. Murphy and J. McMillan. 2014. *Staff in Australia's Schools 2013: Main Report on the Survey*. AGDE: Commonwealth of Australia.

McLeod, F. 2008. Glass ceiling still firmly in place. *The Australian*, 27 June.

McLeod, J. 2000. *Beginning Postcolonialism*. Manchester: Mnchester University Press.

McLuhan, M. 1962. *The Gutenberg Galaxy*. New York: Routledge.

McLuhan, M. and Q. Fiore. 1967. *War and Peace in the Global Village*. New York: Bantam.

McRobbie, A. 1982. Jackie: an ideology of adolescent femininity. In *Popular Culture: Past and Present*, eds. B. Waites, T. Bennet and G. Martin. London: Croom Helm and Open Uiversity Press.

Meadmore, D. 1998. Re-thinking the ADD/ADHD epidemic. *Perspectives on Educational Leadership* 8 (4):1–2.

Meadmore, D. 2004. The rise and rise of testing: how does this shape identity? In *New Questions for Contemporary Teachers: Taking a Socio-Cultural Approach to Education*, eds. B. Burnett, D. Meadmore and G. Tait, 25–38. Frenchs Forest, NSW: Pearson Education.

Meadmore, P. 1999. Education at what price? In *Understanding Education: Contexts and Agendas for the New Millennium*, eds. D. Meadmore, B. Burnett and P. O'Brien. Frenchs Forest, NSW: Prentice Hall.

Meyer, A. 2007. The moral rhetoric of childhood. *Childhood* 14(1): 85–104.

Mickelburough, P. 2011. Enough illegals to populate a city: 60,000 – and most of them are Brits and Americans. *The Courier Mail*, 21 November.

Migration Observatory at the University of Oxford. 2015. UK public opinion towards immigration: overall attitudes and levels of concern.

Mill, J. S. 1957. *Utilitarianism (1861)*. New York: Bobbs-Merrill.

Miller, B. 2012. *Cultural Anthropology*, 7th edn. Cambridge, MA: Pearson.

Miller, K. 2010. The walk that drives men wild. In *Cosmoplitan*.

Miller, P. and N. Rose. 1990. Governing economic life. *Economy and Society* 19(1): 1–31.

Miller, T. 2008. 'Don't know much about history': a critical examination of moral panics over student ignorance. In *Moral Panics Over Contemporary Children and Youth*, ed. C. Krinsky. Aldershot: Ashgate.

Milward. 2003. The 'grey digital divide': perception, exclusion and barriers of access to the internet for older people. *First Monday* 8(7). http://firstmon day.org/htbin/cgiwrap/bin/ojs/index.php/fm/rt/printerFriendly/1066/986 (last accessed 30/1/16).

Modarres, A. 2011. Beyond the digital divide. *National Civic Review* 100(3): 4–7.

Montagu, A. 1974. *Man's Most Dangerous Myth: the Fallacy of Race*, 5th edn. New York: Oxford University Press.

Mosedale, S. 1978. Science corrupted: Victorian biologists consider 'the woman question'. *Journal of the History of Biology* 11(1): 1–55.

Mullis, I., M. Martin, P. Foy and A. Arora 2012. *TIMSS 2011 interntional results in mathematics*. Chestnut Hill, MA: TIMSS & PIRLS International Study Centre, Boston College.

National Center for Education Statistics. 2009. *Digest of Education Statistics*. US Department of Education.

Needham, J. 2013. *Distruptive Possibilities: How Big Data Changes Everything*. Sebastopol, CA: O'Reilly Media.

Neill, A. 1962. *Summerhill: a Radical Approach to Education*. London: Gollancz.

New London Group. 1996. A pedagogy of multiliteracies: designing social futures. *Harvard Educational Review* 66(1): 60–92.

New South Wales State Government. 1977. Anti-Discrimination Act.

Newsworks. 2015. *Daily Mail – Readership Data*. http://www.newsworks.org.uk/Daily-Mail (last accessed 30/1/16).

Nicholl, F. 2004. 'Are you calling me a racist?': teaching critical whiteness theory in indigenous sovereignty. *Borderlands eJournal*. 3(2).

Nicholson, L. 1994. Interpreting gender. *Signs* 20: 79–105.

Nietzsche, F. 1954. On truth and lie in an extra-moral sense. 1873. In *The Portable Nietzsche*, ed. W. Kaufmann. New York: Viking.

Nietzsche, F. 1967 (1911). *The Will to Power*. New York: Random House.

Nietzsche, F. 1997 (1878). *Human, All Too Human*. Stanford: Stanford University Press.

Nietzsche, F. 2007 (1891). *Thus Spoke Zarathustra*. New York: Barnes and Noble.

NILS Report. 2005. *National Indigenous languages report*: Australian Institute of Aboriginal and Torres Strait Islander Studies.

Nishimuta, Y. 2008. The interpretation of racial encounters: Japanese students in Britain. *Journal of Ethnic and Migration Studies* 34(1): 133–50.

Nye, J. 2003. Globalisation and American power. In *The Global Transformations Reader: an Introduction to the Globalization Debate*, 2nd edn, eds. D. Held and A. McGrew. Cambridge: Polity Press.

O'Brien, G. 2013. *Framing the Moron: the Social Construction of Feeble-Mindedness in the American Eugenic Era*. Manchester: Manchester University Press.

O'Brien, P. and N. Osbaldiston. 2010. ePortfolios and preservice teachers: governing at a distance through non-human actors. In *Interaction in Communication Technologies and Virtual Learning Environments: Human Factors*, ed. A. Ragusa, 170–92. New York: Informntion Science References.

OECD. 2012. Programme for International Student Assessment – United Kingdom. http://www.oecd.org/pisa/keyfindings/PISA-2012-results-UK.pdf (last accessed 31/1/16).

Office for National Statistics. 2010. *Social Trends No. 40*. London: Office for National Statistics.

Office for National Statistics. 2015. Wealth in Great Britain Wave 4, 2012 to 2014. London: Office for National Statistics.

Office for the Children's Commissioner (OCC). 2012. *Raising the Attainment of Minority Ethnic Pupils: Schools and LEA Responses*. London: HMSO.

O'Farrell, C. 1999. Postmodernism for the uninitiated. In *Understanding Education: Contexts and Agendas for the New Millennium*, eds. D. Meadmore, B. Burnett and P. O'Brien. Sydney: Prentice Hall.

O'Farrell, C. 2005. *Michel Foucault*. London: Sage.

Olen, J. 1983. *Persons and Their World: an Introduction to Philosophy*. New York: McGraw-Hill.

Olive, S. 2013. Shakespeare in the English National Curriculum. *Alluvium* 2(1). http://dx.doi.org/10.7766/alluvium.v2.1.01.

Olive, S. 2015. *Shakespeare Under the Coalition: an End to Shakespeare For All? Occasional Paper*, King's College London.

Oreskes, N. and M. Conway. 2010. *Merchants of Doubt*. London: Bloomsbury.

Oxfam Australia. 2014. *Still the lucky country? The growing gap between rich and poor is a gaping hole in the G20 agenda*. https://www.oxfam.org.au/wp-content/uploads/2014/06/2014-66-g20-report_fa_web-2.pdf (last accessed 30/01/15).

Owen, J. 2016. British Empire: students should be taught colonialism 'not all good', say historians. *The Independent*, 23 January.

Owen, M. 2012. Radio 'king' slammed over boatpeople tirade. *The Australian*, 8 June.

Ozmon, H. and S. Craver. 2009. *Philosophical Foundations of Education*, 9th edn. Columbus: Pearson.

Packer, C., D. Geh, O. Gouldren, *et al.* 2014. No lasting legacy: no change in reporting of women's sport in the British print media with the London 2012 Olympic and Paralympics, *Journal of Public Health*. http://jpubhealth.oxfordjournals.org/content/early/2014/03/11/pubmed.fdu018.full.pdf+html (last accessed 30/1/16).

Palmen, R. 2011. Girls, boys and ICT in the UK: an empirical review and competing policy agendas, *International Journal of Gender, Science and Technology* 3(2): 407–23.

Pandya, A. 2012. The National Association of Head Teachers has undertaken an evil conspiracy to create an illiterate Britain. *Daily Mail*, 9 May.

Parkes, B. 2012. Exclusion of pupils from school in the UK. *The Equal Rights Review* 8: 113–29.

Parkes, R. 2007. Reading history curriculum as postcolonial text: toward a curricular response to the history wars in Australia and beyond. *Curriculum Inquiry* 37 (4): 383–400.

Parnell, S. 2012. Visitors sending our health bills sky-rocketing. *The Australian*, 9 November.

Parsons, T. 1965. *The Social System*. Glencoe: The Free Press.

Partington, G. 2001. When two worlds meet: ethnicity and education in Australia. In *Sociology of education: possibilities and practices*, ed. J. Allen, 183–210. Southbank, Vic.: Social Science Press.

Patterson, A. 2008. Teaching literature in Australia: examining and reviewing senior English. *Changing English: Studies in Culture and Education* 15(3): 311–22.

Patton, G. 2012. Top graduates to get £25,000 to teach in tough schools. *The Telegraph*, 14 June.

Pearson, J. 1983. *Hooligan: a History of Respectable Fears*. London: Macmillan.

Pearson, J. 2014. Left-wing thinking still prevails in schools. *Telegraph*, 11 January.

Pease, A. and B. Pease. 1999. *Why Men Don't Listen and Women Can't Read Maps*. Buderim: Pease Training International.

Pells, R. 2014. 'More women judges will improve the law': Britain's only female Supreme Court judge calls for more diversity. *The Independent*, 27 July.

Peters, R. S. 1964. *Education as initiation: an Inaugural Lecture Delivered at the University of London Institute of Education, 9 December, 1963*. London: Published for the University of London Institute of Education by Evans Bros.

Phillips, J. 2005. Indigenous knowledge: making space in the Australian centre. In *Introductory Indigenous studies in education*, eds. J. Phillips and J. Lampert, Frenchs Forest, NSW: Pearson Education, 11–26.

Plato. 1956. *Protagoras and Meno*. Harmondsworth: Penguin.

Plato. 1974. *The Republic*. Harmondsworth: Penguin.

Plato. 1989. Plato's Apology. In *Bryn Mawr Greek Commentaries*, ed. G. Rose. Bryn Mawr, PA.: Thomas Library, Bryn Mawr College.

Poddar, P. 1997. Buttered scones at 4 pm on Sundays: configuring English in colonial India. In *Teaching Post-Colonialism and Post-Colonial Literatures*, eds. A. Collett, L. Jensen and A. Rutherford. Aarhus: Aarhus University Press.

Poe, E. 1839. The fall of the house of Usher. *Burton's Gentleman's Magazine*, September.

Pogge, T. 2003. Priorities of global justice. In *The Global Transformations Reader: an Introduction to the Globalization Debate*, 2nd edn, eds. D. Held and A McGrew. Cambridge: Polity Press.

Polesel, J., N. Dulfer and M. Turnbull. 2012. *The experience of education: the impact of high stakes testing on school students and their families (Literature Review)*. Sydney: Whitlam Institute.

Poplin, D. 1978. *Social Problems*. Glenview: Scott, Foresman and Co.

Popper, K. 1959. *The Logic of Scientific Discovery*. London: Hutchinson.

Popper, K. 1963. *Conjectures and Refutations: the Growth of Scientific Knowledge*. London: Routledge and Kegan Paul.

Postman, N. 1994. *The Disappearance of Childhood*, 2nd edn. London: WH Allen.

Poteat, V., E. Mereish, C. DiGiovanni and J. Scheer. 2013. Homophobic bullying. In *Bullying: Experiences and Discourses of Sexuality and Gender*, eds. I. Rivers and D. Neil. Hoboken: Taylor and Francis.

Prensky, M. 2001. Digital natives/digital immigrants. *On the Horizon* 9(5): 1–6.

Prensky, M. 2011. Digital wisdom and homo sapiens digital. In *Deconstructing Digital Natives*, ed. M. Thomas. New York: Routledge.

Preston, B. 2013. *The Social Make-Up of Schools: Family Income, Religion, Indigenous Status, and Family Type in Government, Catholic, and Other Non-Government Schools*. Melbourne: Australian Education Union.

Prior, D. and A. Paris. 2005. Preventing children's involvement in crime and anti-social behaviour: a literature review. *A Paper Produced for the National Evaluation of the Children's Fund*. Institute of Applied Social Sciences: University of Birmingham.

Proust, M. 1927. *Remembrance of Things Past*. Paris: Grasset and Gallimard.

Prout, A. 2005. *The Future of Childhood: Towards the Interdisciplinary Study of Children*. London: RoutledgeFalmer.

Pusey, M. 1991. *Economic Rationalism in Canberra: a Nation-Building State Changes its Mind*. Cambridge: Cambridge University Press.

Putnam, H. 1981. *Reason, Truth and History*. Cambridge: Cambridge University Press.

Qualifications and Curriculum Authority (QCA) and the Department for Education and Skills. 1999. *The National Curriculum: Handbook for Secondary Teachers in England*.

Queensland Studies Authority (QSA). 2009. *Student assessment regimes: getting the balance right for Australia* (Draft Discussion Paper), https://www.qcaa.qld.edu.au/downloads/publications/qsa_paper_assess_balance_aust.pdf (last accessed 15/1/15).

Rammert, W. 1999. Relations that constitute technology and media that make a difference: towards a social pragmatic theory of technicization. *Techne: Journal of the Society for Philosophy and Technology* 4(3). http://scholar.lib.vt.edu/ejournals/SPT/v4_n3pdf/RAMMERT.PDF.

Ramsay, F. 1927. Fact and propositions. *Proceedings of the Aristotelian Society* 7 (Supplementary): 153–70.

Rankin, J. 2015. Female bosses are working for free as gender pay gap persists. *The Guardian*, 25 August.

Refugee Council of Australia. 2009. Asking the media to correct mistakes. http://www.refugeecouncil.org.au/archive_rcoa/current/mediablunders.html

Refugee Council of Australia. 2014. Myths about refugees and asylum seekers. http://www.refugeecouncil.org.au/f/myth-long.php

Refugee Council UK. 2015. The truth about asylum. https://www.refugeecouncil.org.uk/ (last accessed 30/1/16).

Reid, S. 2015. From clean-cut students to poster boys for terror. *Daily Mail*, 7 September.

Reiger, K. 1985. *The Disenchantment of the Home: Modernising the Australian Family 1880–1940*. Melbourne: Oxford University Press.

Reissman, L. 1973. *Social stratification*. In *Sociology: an Introduction*, 2nd edn, ed. N. Smelser. New York: Wiley.

Rhamie, J. 2014. Black academic success: what's changed? In *Educational Inequalities: Differences and Diversity in Schools and Higher Education,* eds. K. Bhopal and U. Maylor. London: Routledge.

Rist, R. 2000. Student social class and teacher expectations: the self-fulfilling prophecy. *Harvard Education Review* 70(3): 257–301.

Ritzer, G. 2013. *The McDonaldisation of Society*. Thousand Oaks, CA: Sage.

Rizvi, F. and B. Lingard. 2010. *Globalising Education Policy*. Oxon: Routledge.

Roberts, I. 2007. Adolescence. In *Childhood and Youth Studies*, ed. P. Zwozdiak-Myers. Exeter: Learningmatters.

Roberts, L. 2010. Boys failed by education system says Eton headmaster. *Telegraph*, 19 January.

Robinson, A., B. Shore and D. Enersen. 2007. *Best Practice in Gifted Education: an Evidence-Based Guide*. Waco: Prufrock Press

Robinson, K. 1992. Class-room discipline: power, resistance and gender. A look at teacher perspectives. *Gender and Education* 4(3): 273–87.

Robinson, W. 2006. Teacher training in England and Wales: past, present and future perspectives. *Education Research and Perspectives* 33(2): 19–36.

Robinson, W. 2007. Theories of globalisation. In *The Blackwell Companion of Globalisation*, ed. G. Ritzer. Oxford: Blackwell.

Rock, L. 2007. The 'good mother' vs. the 'other mother'. *Journal of the Association for Research on Mothering* 9(1): 20–28.

Rose, N. 1985. *The Psychological Complex: Psychology, Politics and Society in England 1869–1939*. London: Routledge and Kegan Paul.

Rose, N. 1988. Calculable minds and manageable individuals. *History of the Human Sciences* 1(2): 179–99.

Rose, N. 1990. *Governing the Soul: the Shaping of the Private Self*. London: Routledge.

Rose, N. 1993. Government, authority and expertise in advanced liberalism. *Economy and Society* 22(3): 283–99.

Rose, N. and P. Miller. 1992. Political power beyond the state; problematics of government. *British Journal of Sociology* 43 (2):173–205.

Rosenberg, P. 2004. Colorblindness in teacher education. In *Off White: Readings On Power, Privilege, and Resistance*, eds. M. Fine, L. Weis, L. Powell Pruit and A. Burns, x, 453. New York: Routledge.

Rosenbush, S. 2014. The morning download: how German soccer team scored with big data. *The Wall Street Journal*, 14 February.

Ross, W. 1930. *The Right and the Good*. Oxford: Clarendon Press.

Roudometof, V. 2009. Nationalism and transnationalism. In *The Sage Handbook of European Studies*, ed. C. Rumford. London: Sage.

Rousseau, J. 1956. *The Emile of Jean Jacques Rousseau, 1762*, trans. W. Boyd. New York: Heinnemann.

Rousseau, J. 1991. *Emile: or, on Education*, ed. A. Bloom. Harmondsworth: Penguin.

Rudd, K. and J. Gillard. 2008. *Quality Education: the Case for a Revolution in our Schools*. Canberra: Commonwealth of Australia.

Rushdie, S. 1981. *Midnight's Children*. London: Vintage.

Russell, B. 1983. *The Problems of Philosophy. 1912*. Oxford: Oxford University Press.

Russell, G., L. Rodgers, O. Ukoummunne and T. Ford. 2014. Prevalence of parent-reported ASD and ADHD in the UK: findings from the millennium cohort study. *Journal of Autism and Development Disorders* 44: 31–40.

Ryan, K. and J. Cooper. 2010. *Those Who Can, Teach*. Boston: Wadsworth.

Sadker, D. 2000. Gender equity: still knocking at the classroom door. *Equity and Excellence in Education* 56(7): 22–7.

Sadker, D. 2002. An educator's primer on the gender wars. *Phi Delta Kappan* 84(3): 235–41.

Said, E. W. 1979. *Orientalism*, 1st edn. New York: Vintage Books.

Said, E. 1995. *Orientalism*, 2nd edn. London: Penguin.

Samaras, K. 2005. Indigenous Australians and the 'digital divide'. *Libri* 55:84–95.

Sawyer, W. 2006. Just add 'progressivism' and stir: How we cook up literacy crises in Australia. In *Only Connect: English Teaching, Schooling and Community*, eds. B. Doecke, M. Howie and W. Sawyer, pp. 236–262. South Australia: Wakefield Press.

Santoro, N., J. Reid and L. Simpson. 2011. Teaching Indigenous children: listening to a learning from Indigenous teachers. *Australian Journal of Teacher Education* 36(10): 65–76.

Savage, M., F. Devine, N. Cunningham *et al.* 2013. A new model for social class: findings from the BBC's Great British class survey experiment. *Sociology* 47(2): 219–50.

Scherer, M. 2012. How Obama's data crunchers helped him win. *CNN*. http://edition.cnn.com/2012/11/07/tech/web/obama-campaign-tech-team/ (last accessed 15/1/15).

Schiller, H. 1979. Trans-national media and national development. In *National sovereignty and international communication*, eds. K. Nordenstreng and H. Schiller, 21–32. Norwood: Ablex.

Schiller, H. 1991. Not yet the post-imperialist era. *Critical Studies in Mass Communication* 8(1): 13–28.

Schirato, T., A. Buettner, T. Jutel and G. Stahl. 2010. *Understanding Media Studies*. Melbourne: Oxford University Press.

Scola, N. 2013. Obama, the 'big data' president. *The Washington Post*, 14 June.

Seattle Times. 1962. Seattle World's Fair souvenir edition: space age frontiers. http://seattletimes.nwsource.com/html/worldsfairsouveniredition/2017454924_all_152_pages_from_souvenir_section_in_pdfs.html (last accessed 30/1/16).

Sechrist, F. 1920. *Education and the General Welfare: a Texbook of School Law, Hygiene and Management*. Michigan: Macmillan.

Senate Education, Employment and Workplace Relations Committee. 2014. The effectiveness of the National Assessment Program – Literacy and Numeracy (NAPLAN). Canberra: Commonwealth of Australia.

Sexual Dscrimination Act 1975. Available at: http://www.legislation.gov.uk/ukpga/ 1975/65 (last accessed 30/1/16).

Sfeir, G. 2014. Critical pedagogy through popular culture. *Education Matters* 2(2): 15–25.

Share, J. 2002. *Media Literacy is Elementary: Teaching Youth to Critically Read and Create Media.* New York: Peter Lang.

Sheridan, G. 2014. Christopher Pyne's noble quest for academic rigour. *The Australian*, 11 October.

Sherriff, L. 2015. A graduate had her job offer revoked because the company 'does not accept' braided hair, *Huffington Post*. http://www.huffingtonpost.co.uk/2015/ 11/26/a-graduate-job-offer-revoked-because-the-company-does-not-accept-b raided-hair_n_8654426.html26 November (last accessed 31/1/16).

Shipman, T and J. Doyle. 2013. 4,000 foreign murderers and rapists we can't throw out. *Daily Mail*, 3 January.

Show Racism the Red Card. 2015. Perception vs reality: young people's perceptions of society lead to concerns about the potential development of prejudice, http:// www.srtrc.org/news/news-and-events?news=5778 (last accessed 30/1/16).

Siegler, M. 2010. Eric Schmidt: every 2 days we create as much information as we did up to 2003. *Techcrunch*. http://techcrunch.com/2010/08/04/schmidt-data/ (last accessed 30/1/16).

Skinner, B. 1938. *The Behaviour of Organisms: an Experimental Analysis.* New York: Appleton-Century-Crofts.

Skipp, A., A. Vignoles, D. Jesson, *et al.* 2013. Poor grammar: entry into grammar schools disadvantaged pupils in England. http://www.suttontrust.com/resea rcharchive/poor-grammar-entry-grammar-schools-disadvantaged-pupils-england/

Slack, J. 2013. True toll of mass migration on UK life. *Daily Mail*, 4 July.

Slee, R. 2011. *The Irregular School: Exclusion, Schooling, and Inclusive Education*, 1st edn, *Foundations and Futures Of Education*. London, New York: Routledge.

Smart, J. 1973. Outline of a system of utilitarian ethics. In *Utilitarianism: For and Against*, eds. J. Smart and B. Williams. Cambridge: Cambridge University Press.

Smith, A. 2010. *Mobile Access 2010*. Washington, DC: Pew Research Centre.

Smith, B. 1989. *Discipline: From the Classroom to the Community, Occasional Paper*: Griffith University.

Smith, S. 2014. The teacher (and English graduate) who admits: I'm illiterate. *The Daily Mail*, 10 September.

Snyder, I. 2008. *The Literacy Wars: Why Teaching Children To Read and Write Is a Battleground In Australia.* NSW: Allen and Unwin.

Social Mobility and Child Poverty Commission (SMCPC). 2014. *Elitist Britain*, https://www.gov.uk/government/uploads/system/uploads/attachment_data/file/347915/Elitist_Britain_-_Final.pdf (last accessed 31/1/16).

Sosin, D. and M. Sosin. 1996. *Attention Deficit Disorder*. Highett: Hawker Brownlow.

Spender, D. 1982. *Invisible Women: the Schooling Scandal*. London: Writers and Readers Publishing Cooperative Society Ltd.

Spybey, A. (1996). *Globalisation and World Society*. Cambridge: Polity Press.

Squires, P. and D. Stephen. 2005. *Rougher Justice: Anti-Social Behaviour and Young People*. Cullompton: Willan Publishing.

Stack, M and D. Kelly. 2006. Popular media, education, and resistance. *Canadian Journal of Education* 29(1): 5–26.

Stevens, P. and G. Crozier. 2014. England. In *The Palgrave Handbook of Race and Ethnic Inequalities in Education*, eds. P. Stevens and A. Dworkin. London: Palgrave Macmillan.

Stewart, W. 2015. Are schools altering result – to make them look worse? *Times Educational Supplement*, 6 March.

Stiglitz, J. 2003. The promise of global institutions. In *The Global Transformations Reader: an Introduction to the Globalization Debate*, 2nd edn, eds. D. Held and A. McGrew. Cambridge: Polity Press.

Stockman, J. 2013. Big Data's big deal: the power of pattern in collective human behaviour. *The Boston Globe*, 18 June.

Stoker, B. 1897. *Dracula*. London: Archibald Constable and Co.

Storey, J. 2003. *Inventing Popular Culture*. Oxford: Blackwell.

Storey, J. 2006. *Cultural Theory and Popular Culture: an Introduction*, 4th edn. Harlow: Pearson.

Stow, D. 1850. *The Training System of Education*. Glasgow: Blackie and Sons.

Strange, S. 2010. The Westfailure system. In *Readings in Globalisation: Key Concepts and Major Debates*, eds. G. Ritzer and Z. Atalay. Chichester: Wiley.

Strauss, V. 2014. 11 problems created by the standardised testing obsession. *The Washington Post*, 22 April.

Suter, K. 2000. *In Defense of Globalization*. Sydney: University of New South Wales Press.

Sustainabilty and Environmental Education (SEEd). 2015. *Sustainable schools policy*. http://se-ed.co.uk/edu/sustainable-schools/policy/ (last accessed 31/1/16).

Sutherland, G. 1984. *Ability, Merit and Measurement: Mental Testing and English Education 1880–1940*. Oxford: Oxford University Press.

Sutton Trust, 2010. *Private school pupils 55 times more likely to go to Oxbridge than poor students*, http://www.suttontrust.com/newsarchive/private-school-pupils-55-times-likely-go-oxbridge-poor-students/ (last accesed 31/1/2016).

Sydney Morning Herald. 2009. Rudd slams Tuckey's 'terrorist' asylum seeker comments, 22 October.

Sydney Morning Herald. 2014. No country for young men: notions of gender must evolve, 3 January.

Symes, C. and N. Preston. 1997. *Schools and Classrooms: a Cultural Studies Analysis of Education*. Melbourne: Longman-Cheshire.

Synott, J. and C. Symes. 1995. The genealogy of the school; an iconography of badges and mottoes. *British Journal of Sociology of Education* 16(2): 139–52.

Szasz, T. 1961. *The Myth of Mental Illness: Foundations of a Theory of Personal Conduct*. New York: Harper Row.

Szasz, T. 1973. *The Manufacture of Madness: a Comparative Study of the Inquisition and the Mental Health Movement*. London: Grenada.

Tait, G. 1993. 'Anorexia nervosa': asceticism, differentiation, government. *Australian and New Zealand Journal of Sociology* 29 2): 194–208.

Tait, G. 1999. Rethinking youth cultures: the case of the 'Gothics'. *Social Alternatives* 18(2): 15–21.

Tait, G. 2003. 'The seven things all men love in bed: young women's magazines and the governance of femininity. In *Youth Cultures: Texts, Images and Identities*, eds. K. Mallan and S. Pearce. Westport, CT: Praeger Publishers.

Tait, G. 2006. Setting limits to teacher responsibility. *ACHPER Matters* 1: 3–6.

Tait, G. 2010. *Philosophy, Behaviour Disorders, and the School*. Rotterdam: Sense.

Tait, G., C. Davey Chesters, C. O'Farrell, *et al.* 2012. Are there any wrong answers in teaching philosophy? Ethics, epistemology, and the philosophy in schools program. *Teaching Philosophy* 35(3): 367–82.

Talburt, S. and N. Lesko. 2012. A history of the present of youth studies. In *Keywords in Youth Studies: Tracing Affects, Movements, Knowledges*, eds. S. Talburt and N. Lesko. New York: Routledge.

Talkwar, D. 2012. More than 87,000 racist incidents recorded in schools, *BBC*. http://www.bbc.com/news/education-18155255 (last accessed 31/1/16).

Tannsjo, T. 2002. *Understanding Ethics: an Introduction to Moral Theory*. Edinburgh: Edinburgh University Press.

Taylor, M and H. Muir. 2014. Racism on the rise in Britain. *The Guardian*, 28 May.

Taylor, S. 2004. Gender equity and education: what are the issues now? In *New Questions For Contemporary Teachers: Taking a Socio-Cultural Approach To Education*, eds. B. Burnett, D. Meadmore and G. Tait, 87–100. Frenchs Forest, NSW: Pearson Education.

Taylor, T. 2010. *The Artificial Ape: How Technology Changed the Course of Human Evolution*. New York: Palgrave Macmillan.

The Equality Trust. 2016. How has inequality changed. https://www.equalitytrust.org.uk/how-has-inequality-changed (1/1/2016).

The Poverty Site. 2015. *School exclusions*. http://www.poverty.org.uk/27/index.shtml (last accessed 31/1/16).

Thompson, G. 2013. NAPLAN, MySchool and accountability: teacher perceptions of the effects of testing. *The International Education Journal: Comparative Perspectives* 12(2): 62–84.

Thompson, G. and I. Cook. 2013. The logic of good teaching in an audit culture: a Deleuzian analysis. *Educational Philosophy and Theory* 45(3): 243–58.

Thompson, G. and I. Cook. 2014. Manipulating the data: teaching and NAPLAN in the control society. *Discourse* 35(1): 129–42.

Thompson, G. and A. Harbaugh. 2013. A preliminary analysis of teacher perceptions of the effects of NAPLAN on pedagogy and curriculum. *Australian Educational Researcher* 40: 299–314.

Times. 2015. Thousands of violent primary school children barred. 31 July.

Today Tonight. 2011. Welcome to Australia. *Channel Seven*, 10 October.

Tolstoy, L. 1886. *War and Peace*. New York: William S. Gottsberger.

Tomlinson, S. 1982. *A Sociology of Special Education*. London: Routledge and Kegan Paul.

Tomlinson, S. 2008. *Race and Education: Policy and Politics in Britain*. Maidenhead: Open University Press.

Topping, K. and S. Maloney. 2005. *The RoutledgeFalmer Reader in Inclusive Education*. Oxford: RoutledgeFalmer.

Topping, K. and S. Trickey. 2007. Collaborative philosophical inquiry for school-children: cognitive gains at 2-year follow-up. *British Journal of Educational Psychology* 77: 787–96.

Turner, B. 2006. McDonaldisation: the major criticisms. In *McDonaldisation: the Reader*, ed. G. Ritzer, Thousand Oaks, CA: Pine Force Press.

Turner, B. 2013. Theories of globalisation. In *The Routledge International Handbook of Globalisation Studies*. Hoboken: Taylor and Francis.

Turner, S., D. Beidel and R. Townsley. 1992. Social Phobia: a comparison of specific and generalised subtypes and avoidant personality disorder. *Journal of Abnormal Pychology* 102: 326–331.

Tweedie, N. 2015. 'Lock your doors. Your holiday hotel's full of asylum seekers'. *Daily Mail*, 15 August.

Tyack, D. and Cuban L. 1995. *Tinkering Toward Utopia: a Century of Public School Reform*. Cambridge: Harvard University Press.

Tyler, D. 1993. Making better children. In *Child and Citizen: Genealogies of Schooling and Subjectivity*, eds. D. Meredyth and D. Tyler, 35–60. Brisbane: Institute for Cultural Policy Studies, Griffith Univerity.

Tyler, E. 1871. *Primitive Culture*. London: J Murray.

Uditsky, B. 1993. From integration to inclusion: the Canadian experience. In *Is There a Desk With My Name on it? The Politics of Integration*, ed. R. Slee, **ix**, 268. London: Falmer Press.

UNESCO. 2005. *United Nations Decade of Education for Sustainable Development*, Executive Board Report by the Director General on the United Nations Decade of Education for Sustainable Development. Paris: UNESCO.

United Nations Human Rights Commission. 2012. *Global Trends*. http://unhcr.org/g lobaltrendsjune2013/UNHCR%20GLOBAL%20TRENDS%202012_V08_web.p df (last accessed 30/1/16).

United Nations: International Telecommunication Union. 2014. *Press release:* 2014 *ITU figures*. http://www.itu.int/net/pressoffice/press_releases/2014/23.aspx# .VHM4nFesUXg (last accessed 15/3/15)

United Nations. 1948. *Universal Declaration of Human Rights*.

United Nations. 1951. *Convention relating to the Status of Refugees*.

United Nations. 1965. *International Convention on the Elimination of all Forms of Racism*.

United Nations. 1967. *Protocol relating to the Status of Refugees*.

Univerities UK. 2014. *The Funding Environment for Universities 2014*. London: Universities UK.

US Census Bureau. 2013. *Poverty: 2013 highlights*. https://www.census.gov/hhes/ www/poverty/about/overview/index.html (last accessed 15/3/15)

Valencia, R. 1997. *The Evolution of Deficit Thinking: Educational Thought and Practice*. London: Falmer.

Van de Pijl, K. 1998. *Transnational Classes and International Relations*. London: Routledge.

Van Onselen, A. (2011). Gender gap in the judiciary is still way too wide. *The Australian*, 8 July.

Verger, J 2003. Teachers. In *Universities in the Middle Ages, Vol. 1*, ed. H. Ridder-Symoens, 144–168. Cambridge: Cambridge University Press.

Viana, A., D. Beidel and B. Rabian. 2009. Selective mutism: a review and integration of the last 15 years. *Clinical Psychology Review* 29(1): 57–67.

Vickers, M. 2010. Gender. In *Education, Change and Society*, eds. R. Connell, C. Campbell, M. Vickers *et al.*, 205–34. South Melbourne, Vic.: Oxford University Press.

Victorian State Government. 1995. *Equal Opportunity Act*.

Vigotski, L. 1978. *Mind in Society*. Cambridge, MA: Harvard University Press.

Villa, P. and W. Roebroeks. 2014. Neanderthal demise: an archaeological analysis of the modern human superiority complex. *PLoS ONE* 9(4): e96424.

Viswanathan, G. 1989. *The Masks of Conquest: Literary Study and British Rules in India*. London: Faber and Faber.

Vladeck, S. 2014. Big data before and after Snowden. *Journal of National Security Law and Policy* 7(333): 333–9.

Vonow, B. 2015. Churchie student told it was school's strong preference that he brings 'young lady' to formal. *The Courier Mail*, 6 March.

Wallace, J., S. Goodkind, C. Wallace and J. Bachman. 2008. Racial, ethnic, and gender differences in school discipline among U.S. high school students: 1991–2005. *Negro Educational Review* 59(1–2): 47–62.

Walker, K. 2011. Foreign workers get 3 in 4 new jobs. *Daily Mail*, 13 July.

Wanzer, M., A. Bainbridge-Frymier and J. Irwin. (2010). An explanation of the relationship between instructor humor and student learning: instructional humor processing theory. *Communication Education* 59(1): 1–18.

Weaver, J. A. 2009. *Popular Culture*. New York: Peter Lang.

Weaver, J. A., K. Anijar and T. Daspit (eds.) 2004. *Science Fiction Curriculum, Cyborg Teachers, and Youth Cultures*. New York: Peter Lang.

Weber, M. 2012 (1947). *The Theory of Social and Economic Organisation*. New York: Free Press.

Wedge, M. 2015. *A Disease Called Childhood*. New York: Penguin.

Weeks, J. 1981. *Sex, Politics, and Society: the Regulation of Sexuality Since 1880*. London: Longman.

Weist, M., O. Acosta, N. Tashman, L. Nabom and K. Albus. 1999. Changing paradigms in child and adolescent psychiatry: towards expanded school mental health. *American Society for Adolescent Psychiatry* 24:119–131.

Welch, A. 2010. Cultural difference and identity. In *Education, Change and Society*, 2nd edn, eds. R. Connell, C. Campbell, M. Vickers, *et al*. South Melbourne, Vic.: Oxford University Press.

Welch, M. and L. Schuster. 2005. Detention of asylum seekers in the UK and the USA. *Punishment and Society* 7(4): 397–417.

West-Newman, C. 2001. Reading hate speech from the bottom in Aotearoa. *Waikato Law Review* 9.

Wheater, R., R. Ager, B. Burge and J. Sizmur. 2013. *Achievement of 15-year-olds in England: PISA 2012 National Report*. National Foundation for Education Research, Department of Education.

Whelan, A. and R. Slater. 2012. Refugee who raped a girl, 12, wins battle to stay in the UK. *Daily Mail*, 15 July.

White, C. and T. Walker. 2008. *Tooning In: Essays on Popular Culture and Education*. Plymouth: Rowman and Littlefield.

White, P. and N. Selwyn. 2013. Moving on-line? An analysis of patterns of adult internet use in the UK, 2002–2010. *Information, Communication and Society* 16(1): 1–27.

Wickham, G. 1993. Citizenship, Governance and the Consumption of Sport. Paper presented at the Australian Sociological Association Conference at MacQuarrie University, December, Sydney.

Wilde, O. 1891. *The Picture of Dorian Gray*. London: Ward, Lock.

Wilkes, D. 2002. Patients lose GP surgury to asylum seekers. *Daily Mail*, 5 September.

Wilkins, C. and Wood, P. 2009. Initial teacher education in the panopticon. *Journal of Education for Teaching: International Research and Pedagogy* 35(3): 283–97.

Williams, B. 1972. *Morality: an Introduction*. New York: Harper and Row.

Williams, B. 1973. A critique of utilitarianism. In *Utilitarianism: For and Against*, eds. J. Smart and B. Williams. Cambridge: Cambridge University Press.

Williams, B. 1985. *Ethics and the Limits of Philosophy*. London: Fontana.

Williams, R. 1981. *Culture*. London: Fontana.

Winch, C. and J. Gingell. 2008. *Philosophy of Education: the Key Concepts*, 2nd edn. London: Routledge.

Wilson, D., S. Burgess and A. Briggs. 2005. The Dynamics of School Attainment of England's Ethnic Minorities. Bristol: University of Bristol-CMPO.

Wittgenstein, L. 1952. *Philosophical Investigations*, eds. G. Anscombe and R. Rhees. Oxford: Blackwell.

Wodajo, T. and J. Kimmel. 2013. Explaining changes in the racial digital divide in the United States from 1997 to 2007. *Economics of Innovation and New Technology* 22(5): 483–518.

Wolf, N. 1991. *The Beauty Myth: How Images Of Beauty Are Used Against Women*. New York: Morrow.

Wollstonecraft, M. 1792. *A Vindication of the Rights of Woman: with Strictures on Political and Moral Subjects (1967)*. Norton Library; N373. New York: Norton.

Wolpoff, M. and R. Caspari. 1998. *Race and Human Evolution: a Fatal Attraction*. Boulder, CO: Westview.

Woodhouse, F. and M. Woodhouse. 2012. Professionalism, the professional duties of teachers and legal requirements. In *Training to Teach: a Guide for Teachers*, 2nd edn, ed. N. Denby. London: Sage.

Wright, P. and A. Treacher. 1982. *The Problem of Medical Knowledge: Examining the Social Construction of Medicine*. Edinburgh: Edinburgh University Press.

Yeskel, F. and J. Ladd. 2005. Class? In America? *SOA Watch*. http://www.soaw.org/resources/anti-opp-resources/109-class/623 (last accessed 15/3/15).

Young, M. 1958. *The Rise of the Meritocracy: 1879–2033: an Essay on Education and Equality*. London: Penguin.

INDEX